The Road to
Pearl Harbor: 1941

The Road to
Pearl Harbor: 1941

RICHARD COLLIER

BONANZA BOOKS
NEW YORK

FOR PAT
my wife
with love

This 1984 edition is published by Bonanza Books,
distributed by Crown Publishers, Inc. by arrangement with
Charles Scribner's Sons.
Manufactured in the United States of America

Library of Congress Cataloging in Publication Data
Collier, Richard, 1924-
The road to Pearl Harbor—1924-
Bibliography: p.
Includes index.
1. World War, 1939-1945.   2. World War, 1939-1945 —
Diplomatic history.   3. Pearl Harbor (Hawaii), Attack on,
1941.   I. Title.
D755.3.C64   1984   940.53   84-11162

ISBN: 0-517-448599
h g f e d c b a

CONTENTS

ILLUSTRATIONS

Between pages 118 *and* 119

10 (a) General Guderian on the Russian Front
    (b) Marshal Timoshenko
    (c) General Zhukov

11 (a) Russian peasants fleeing before the German advance on Moscow
    (b) General Dovator's cavalry units on their way to defend Moscow

12 (a) Russian Front: a German tank rumbles over a slit trench with Russians cowering underneath
    (b) Red Army men dislodging Germans from a village

13 (a) General Douglas MacArthur
    (b) American and Philippine troops surrender to the Japanese at Bataan

14 (a) The crematoria at Buchenwald concentration camp
    (b) Lager Nordhausen camp

15 (a) U.S.S. *California* sinking after the Japanese attack on Pearl Harbor
    (b) The wreckage at the Naval Air Station, Pearl Harbor

16   British troops marching along the road to Cyrene with the ancient town behind them

The Road to
Pearl Harbor: 1941

1

"Thy People Shall Be My People"

1 January–12 March, 1941

IN GLASGOW, SCOTLAND, a bitter wind was driving across the River Clyde. By 9 p.m. on Friday, 17 January, snow was drifting from the mountains by Ben Lomond, a white noiseless cloud blanketing tenements and shipyards, but it brought no added warmth. At nightfall the thermometer had showed 24 degrees Fahrenheit and still falling. On Sauchiehall Street, the city's main artery, a few latecomers huddled in the tram shelters, stamping their feet, small foggy haloes of breath trapped by the nipping air.

In Room 21, on the first floor of the four-star North British Hotel, a select private dinner party was drawing to a close. It was now that the host, the Secretary of State designate for Scotland, Tom Johnston, turned to his guest of honour, Prime Minister Winston Churchill. Would President Franklin D. Roosevelt's emissary, who had just returned with the Premier from inspecting the Home Fleet at Scapa Flow, the naval base in the Orkney Islands used by the Fleet in both world wars, care to address the company? All eyes now focused on Harry Lloyd Hopkins, Roosevelt's lanky unkempt personal adviser, as he rose to his feet.

It was an historic moment. His voice barely pitched above a whisper, Hopkins seemed to direct his words to Churchill alone. "I suppose you want to know," he began, "what I am going to say to President Roosevelt on my return. Well, I'm going to quote you one verse from that Book of Books in the truth of which Mr Johnston's mother and my own Scottish mother was brought up. 'Whither thou goest, I will go; and where thou lodgest I will lodge; thy people shall be my people, and thy God my God'." Then, his voice cracking, Hopkins added three words that formed no part of the Book of Ruth: "Even to the end."

"The words seemed like a rope thrown to a drowning man," Churchill's personal physician, Sir Charles Wilson (later Lord Moran) always remembered, but they seemed even more to Churchill. There, in the warm cathedral silence of Room 21, the Premier had broken down and was weeping unashamedly.

*

1

On this 502nd day of World War Two, Churchill had cause for emotion. Only the frail presence of Harry Hopkins, symbolising Roosevelt's determination to provide Britain and her allies with "all aid short of war", stood between the nation and defeat by Hitler's Germany. The beleaguered defiance of the British following the Dunkirk evacuation of 1940 now seemed an echo from the past. Ahead loomed a grimmer reality: the months when Adolf Hitler's Directive No 23 – "to concentrate every means of waging war by sea and air on enemy supplies" – began to bite deep.

Within six weeks, 104 ships – 400,000 tons of merchant shipping – would be lost, a rate of attrition totalling seven million tons a year, more than three times the building capacity of the shipyards. The sole solution was one of make-do-and-mend: 40,000 men were to be released from the armed forces to clear a huge backlog of 800,000 tons of shipping awaiting repair. The Luftwaffe response was a blitz on ports like Plymouth and Liverpool, destroying thousands more tons of supplies.

By now Hitler seemed omnipotent. For six months his troops had manned the ramparts unchallenged from the North Cape to the Pyrenees, and his recent message to the *Wehrmacht* only underlined their invincibility: "Armed as never before we stand at the door of the New Year." Already it seemed an old war: since June, 1940, London had been playing host to six governments in exile.* The Maginot Line, that 1940 symbol of France's play-safe strategy was fast being dismantled: 8,000 of its stoves had gone to heat Berlin's air-raid shelters, its 50,000 tons of steel plate were bound for the smelting furnaces of the Ruhr. Many of its heavy guns now faced the English Channel coastline.

But the threat of a German landing – Hitler's much-vaunted "Operation Sea Lion" – which had haunted the British for seven months was fast receding. "Invasion has, for the present, been given a back seat," the Minister of Aircraft Production, Lord Beaverbrook, wrote to his old friend, Sir Samuel Hoare, the British Ambassador in Spain, "The possibility of strangulation by blockade holds the stage." Thus for 48 million Britons, the buff-coloured ration book had become a way of life, and a symbol of the poorest diet the nation had ever known. "The danger is worse than in the last war," the Minister of Food, Lord Woolton, had asserted as early as New Year's Day, which at once prompted a measured rebuke from Churchill – "I am afraid that your statement will be much used by enemy propaganda and it might even encourage the Germans. . . ."

Every housewife, reduced to four ounces of bacon a week, two ounces of butter and two ounces of tea was now a combatant on what Woolton had dubbed "The Kitchen Front", concocting such strange stomach-stretchers as Woolton Pie (mainly vegetables and potatoes), Lentil Roast

* France, Holland, Belgium, Norway, Poland and Czechoslovakia.

and Carrot Tart, glazed with lemon jelly. The meat ration, 1s 2d worth a week, bought only three quarters of a pound of stewing beef or two small chops; one egg per fortnight was the most that one could hope for. Onions had become as rare as oranges, lemons and bananas; even before Hopkins returned to Washington, a one and a half pound onion fetched £4 3s 4d in a raffle. In one London suburb, a rumour of apples saw a mile-long queue forming at 6 a.m.

In an era when bureaucracy seemed rampant, Britain had become a land of slogans; not for twenty-three years had its people been so exhorted and cajoled. The streets were loud with hoardings and posters: "Don't Be A Food Hog" – "Careless Talk Costs Lives" – "Make Do and Mend". "Dig for Victory" was in itself an illustration of the change the land had undergone; seventeen million acres were now under cultivation and even the Tower of London's famous moat was given over to cabbages.

It all added up to a slow battle of attrition, a drab progression of milkless, eggless, and meatless days, a far cry from the heady euphoria of the Battle of Britain and the London blitz. Waning British morale was now of such concern to the War Cabinet that 10,000 bureaucrats were compiling reports based on surveys of 200,000 letters that were intercepted each month. Any man in the street would have confirmed their findings free of charge: few saw the war ending in a year, fewer still saw how it could end at all.

No comfort could be derived from occupied Europe; under Hitler's hegemony, the people had retreated into themselves. Food was a mild obsession with almost every nation, and not surprisingly; in Paris, a turnip was a meal for a gourmet and many Belgians and Dutchmen had lost up to fifteen pounds in weight. Gold was still jealously hoarded, as a hedge against harder times yet; the value of a *napoléon d'or* had now increased seven-fold. Day and night, the streets were shrouded in brooding silence; ninety percent of private cars were off the road and a second-hand bicycle, priced at 2,500 francs, was precious enough to be kept under lock and key. Among the young, Nazis and anti-Nazis alike found common ground: a bitter contempt for the bourgeois past.

Cut off in their island fortress, the British, by degrees, were succumbing to an insidious apathy. The 300 scrutators of the Mass Observation Organisation, who reported on current topics to the Ministry of Information, noted that four people out of ten no longer followed the war news at all. Absenteeism had doubled in many war factories, while in others a three-hour stint was an average working day. Although legend would hail this as a halcyon period of industrial relations, 1,077,000 working days would be lost through stoppages before the year was out.

Factory workers were failing to clock on, many busmen refused to drive in air raids, dockers were staging a go-slow and coalmen were reluctant to deliver coal. The reasons were not hard to find; in their innermost hearts the British sensed that this was a war they might survive but could never win, without the aid of the world's two most unlikely participants: the United States and Soviet Russia.

"All I can say," summed up one xenophobic Briton, "is the world would be all right with no foreigners."

Thus in the weeks to come Harry Hopkins was to become both the staunch friend and the inspirational driving force of which the war-weary British so sorely stood in need.

*

At first glance, Hopkins was an unlikely ally for the robust Churchill. At 51, he was a man living on borrowed time, a gaunt lean mid-Westerner, his face haggard and sallow, in rumpled loosely hanging clothes. "His lips," noted Sir Charles Wilson clinically, "were blanched, as if he had been bleeding internally"' – as in the past he had. Only narrowly had Hopkins survived an operation for stomach cancer, and even now, plagued by a chronic liver deficiency and pernicious anaemia, he was kept alive by a twice-monthly blood transfusion.

A harness-maker's son from Sioux City, Iowa, and a one-time social worker, Hopkins had first won Roosevelt's trust as an energetic Secretary of Commerce. Later, on a symbolic date – 10 May, 1940, when Hitler struck at Belgium and Holland – he had moved into the White House as a guest and stayed thereafter. Working mostly in a disreputable old bathrobe from a bedroom that had once been Abraham Lincoln's study, his aura, as one man recalled it, was one of "quick cigarettes, thinning hair, brief sarcasms, fraying suits of clothes."

His mission, coinciding with Roosevelt's unprecedented election to a third term of office, was to interpret Churchill's thinking to the President. As what one diplomat termed "the fairy godfather of Lend-Lease" – Roosevelt's December, 1940 decision to supply Britain with munitions for free, to be paid for in kind when the war was over – Hopkins himself saw his role as "a catalyst between two prima-donnas", the emotional rhetorical Churchill and the often devious, frequently ruthless, Roosevelt, who nevertheless had one bond in common: a hatred of Nazi-ism.

It was a hatred that Hopkins shared to the hilt, above all other pre-occupations. Often tactless and irreverent, he had scant patience with Churchill's flights of oratory, as the Premier was to discover during the first week-end they spent together. "After the war, we must make a good life for the cottagers," Churchill promised Hopkins, the onetime social worker, over brandy and cigars, and was startled when Hopkins responded violently, "I dont give a damn about your cottagers – we're only interested in seeing that goddam sonofabitch gets licked." But Churchill took it in good part; from that time on, impressed by Hopkins' incisive brain, he dubbed him "Lord Root-of-the-Matter".

From the day of his arrival, 9 January, Hopkins' purpose was to find out what made the British tick, and he set to work with a will. "They must prove that they are doing their best before we go all out for them," he told the American Military Attaché, General Raymond E. Lee, and to this end, in thirty-one days, he talked to 300 men and women. "Am seeing everything from bombs to President's cousins," he cabled Roosevelt on 14 January. Among his witnesses was King George VI who showed a properly regal disdain for almost all his Cabinet save Churchill. "Beaverbrook . . . clearly he does not trust . . . Bevin* among the Labour crowd, talks too much . . . Attlee and Greenwood* have no real power in the Labour movement . . ."

Yet despite his admiration for the British, Hopkins knew deep misgivings. Impressed as he was by Churchill's determination to resist, he was still appalled by the lack of means to do so. Already, he felt, the British were expecting too much – Lend-Lease on an unprecedented scale, a declaration of war by Roosevelt before the summer was out. In vain Hopkins pointed out that only Congress could declare war, and many representatives were implacably hostile to this concept.

His warnings were timely. On Wednesday 15 January, two days before he dined with Churchill in Glasgow, hearings had begun in a bitter no-holds-barred debate in which a powerful caucus of men sought to avert all United States involvement in Adolf Hitler's war.

*

Long before 10 a.m., the big Ways and Means Committee Room in the new House Office building on Washington's Capitol Hill had been crowded out. Behind the horseshoe desk, puffing pipes, cigars and cigarettes, sat 23 members of the House Foreign Affairs Committee; in the centre of the curve, the chairman, little Congressman Sol Bloom, faced a semi-circle of witness chairs.

There was tension in the air and everybody felt it. The President's Lend-Lease plan, appropriately numbered House Bill No 1776, was majestically vague in its language – "A Bill to Further Promote the Defense of the U.S. and For Other Purposes" – but its purport was clear. Under this bill powers would go to Franklin Roosevelt such as no American had ever before sought.

The power to order any arsenal, shipyard or factory to manufacture

---

* Minister of Labour Ernest Bevin, Deputy Premier Clement Attlee and Minister without portfolio Arthur Greenwood were Labour MPs who had joined Churchill's coalition government in May 1940.

any defense articles the President might name, for one. The power to communicate defense information to any Government he chose, for another. Above all, a third power that might prove a political hot potato: the right to allow the British Fleet to use the harbours of New York and Norfolk, Virginia, to carry out repairs at American expense. If the Bill became law it would be a tacit non-shooting alliance with Britain and all other nations who helped to keep the war away from American shores.

In a sense the weeks of debate that would follow were a mirror image of the United States, its polarised fears and aspirations – a debate which as Roosevelt said was to rage "in every newspaper, on every wavelength – over every cracker barrel in the land". As the Committee's first witness, the Secretary of State, 69-year-old Cordell Hull, clad in a shiny blue serge suit, his face as pale as candle-wax under silver-white hair, read his prepared statement, his long slender hands seemed to tremble slightly. His voice deep with conviction as he charted the aggressions of Germany, Italy and Japan since 1931, he told the Committee flatly: "The most serious question today for this country is whether the control of the high seas shall pass into the hands of powers bent on a programme of unlimited conquest."

The early afternoon saw Treasury Secretary Henry Morgenthau Jr, flanked by seven aides, succeed to the stand. A humourless intense anti-Nazi – whose criterion for hiring a staffer was "Does he hate Hitler's guts?" – it was Morgenthau's lot to reveal for the first time in history the confidential balance sheet of another nation's finances. While the war was costing Britain $500,000,000 a day, the Secretary stressed, all British assets quickly convertible into dollars had been spent or obligated before 1 January. "Slow assets", nominally valued at £3,868,000 could not be liquidated in time to obviate the need for United States aid.

The British held virtually no gold – while dollar exchange assets available were only $1,775,000 against the annual requirement of $3,019,000,000.

This was startling news to many like the outgoing Vice President, John Nance Garner, who in a noisy whisky-flushed Cabinet oration was to charge that the British had billions to spend and were short-changing the United States. Morgenthau replied obliquely that "the British financial cow was just about dry", but the assertion was made in no mood of blind trust. As the Treasury Secretary explained to Roosevelt, secret reports from the Federal Reserve Bank of New York had monitored every financial move the British had made since Lend-Lease was mooted.

Other voices from the President's Cabinet took up the tocsin. On 16 January, Secretary of War Henry Stimson, 73, "Light Horse Harry", warned that a failure to pass the Bill would not only bring about a British defeat but plunge America into the war in 90 days. Following him on the stand, the tough ruddy-cheeked Navy Secretary, Frank Knox, produced telling statistics. America was building a two ocean Navy in 72 private yards and 11 Navy yards – but completion lay six years away. If the Royal Navy gave up the United States' strength would fall steadily behind the combined Axis fleets.

These were the authentic voices of American interventionism – whose ranks would soon include such diverse warriors as Mrs Calvin Coolidge, widow of the thirtieth U.S. President, Allen Dulles, lawyer and future head of the Office of Strategic Services in Switzerland, the department store owner Marshall Field, film magnates Darryl F. Zanuck and Spyros Skouras and Dan Tobin of the Teamsters Union.

But contrary voices were heard, not only from the witness chairs but across the length and breadth of America and through all their speeches the horror of war ran like a scarlet thread. These were the isolationists, perhaps 800,000 strong, spread among 700 separate organisations, and their sincere belief was that America could best serve the cause of civilisation by staying aloof from this war. This quarrel was not of America's making, nor did it infringe on America's security – yet Roosevelt, like Woodrow Wilson 23 years earlier, resolutely sought an international role for the United States.

Above all, the isolationists were united by a profound distrust of Roosevelt's motivation: as the first President in American history ever to serve a third term, the first to guide the nation's destiny from a wheel chair following a polio attack, would he also be the first to wage war without declaring it? On 6 January, leafing through a big black leather binder to deliver his State of the Union message to the 77th Congress he had spoken for the first time of a post-war world cleansed of Nazi-ism that would embody the Four Freedoms: freedom of speech, freedom from want, freedom to worship God in one's own way, freedom from fear. But although devotees like his Secretary of Agriculture Claude Wickard saw him as "like Atlas, in that the whole world rested on his shoulders", no Republican applause greeted his peroration.

Two weeks later, on 20 January, his 10.30 a.m. inauguration at St John's Church – a reinauguration as portentous as Caesar's – had likewise struck a chilling note. Following his speech, no high school bands or festive floats with pretty girls had taken the stage, as in happier years. Instead only U.S. Army riflemen wearing drab khaki, marched with bayonets fixed, eyes staring intently ahead under steel helmets. The rumbling of tanks, heavy military trucks and heavier guns was heard along Constitution Avenue. Then as the cold blue sky darkened, almost 300 military aircraft, silver red-tipped bodies glistening, ripped the sky above the White House and the roof tops of the quiet city.

These were more planes than most American citizens had ever seen or would ever wish to see.

Thus the isolationists before the House Affairs Committee were swift to disclaim that the war was America's business. The distinguished aviator Colonel Charles Lindbergh, darling of the American First Committee, in flatly opposing the Bill, called for 20,000 planes to defend the United States and a negotiated Anglo-German peace. General Hugh Johnson, sometime columnist and former Chief of the National Recovery Administration, claimed the bill gave Roosevelt totalitarian powers and lashed out against "humanitarian lollypopping".

Some were more forthright still. One kingpin isolationist, Senator Burton Wheeler of Montana, claimed that the President's bill would "plough under every fourth American boy" – "the rottenest statement I ever heard in public life," raged Roosevelt. Senator Bulow saw Hitler as no menace at all. "If I were as certain of a place in Heaven as I am that Herr Hitler will never invade . . . I would feel just as if I were already in God's pocket."

In contrast to the studied courtesy of the public forums, spontaneous anti-Roosevelt propaganda struck a jarring and spiteful note. Outside the British Embassy on Massachussetts Avenue, paraded lady members of the Paul Revere Sentinels and the Women's Neutrality League, brandishing placards reading: "Benedict Arnold Helped England, Too". A cartoon in Captain Joseph Patterson's isolationist *New York Daily News*, set the sour keynote: outside a walk-up apartment house, a raddled harlot labelled War accosted a doughboy: "Come on in, I'll treat you right. I used to know your Daddy."

The former Ambassador to France, William Bullitt, saw Americans as indulging in a fatal fallacy: they looked to the Atlantic Ocean as the French had looked to the Maginot Line. In Chicago, John Wheeler Bennett, head of the Research Department of the British Information Service in New York, had oral proof of this. Following a courteous reception by the American First Executive Committee, he felt emboldened to ask: "When would you find it necessary to resist a German invasion?" One man replied in all seriousness: "When they cross the Rio Grande."

The same voices rehearsing the same arguments were to drone on for many weeks to come. Although the House Foreign Affairs Committee, concluding its public hearings on 29 January, threw the House open to a formal five-day debate on 3 February, the Senate's Foreign Relations Committee began its own hearings on 27 January. Thus, on 8 February, when the House passed the Bill by a vote of 260 to 165, Hull, Stimson, Knox and others were manfully repeating their testimony in the Senate's stifling Caucus Room, packed out with 1800 citizens who had shouldered their way into a room designed to hold 500.

The surprise witness arrived on the afternoon of Tuesday 11 February. Steered by a phalanx of policemen, a rumpled bear-like figure, a lock of hair drooping over one eye, shambled through the throng from a rear door to an excited buzz of comment. Heralded by a staccato popping of photographers' flash-bulbs, the least-likely deponent for the interventionist cause had arrived to take the stand on behalf of Lend-Lease: 48-year-old Wendell Willkie, the Wall Street lawyer and Republican candidate, whom Roosevelt had soundly defeated in November, 1940.

It was an eleventh-hour appearance; only at 12.30 that afternoon had Willkie's plane touched down at Washington's National Airport. But as one whose 18-day visit to England, as a private citizen travelling at his own expense, had been publicly blessed by the President, Willkie spoke as a man fresh from the front line. "I feel that I am walking through history," he had told newsmen after talking with Cabinet Ministers, policemen, air raid wardens and Tommies, but one simple incident had impressed him above all.

Driving through London's Trafalgar Square one noonday, the air-raid sirens had sounded and Willkie learned that German daylight raiders were approaching the capital. Yet incredibly, as ack-ack guns boomed overhead, the traffic rumbled on, and in the shadow of Nelson's Column, a group of old ladies, unperturbed, had continued to feed the pigeons.

It was known, too, that Willkie had had three long private talks with Churchill – talks which had left him impressed with the Premier's implacable determination. On a visit to Dublin, Willkie told Churchill, the Prime Minister Eamon de Valera had voiced a bitter complaint: since Eire was still neutral and refused to cede the former British treaty ports of Queenstown (now Cobh), Berehaven and Lough-Swilly, Churchill had clamped down a stringent economic blockade, denying Eire not only charter shipping, food, iron and steel but even guns to ward off a possible German invasion.

Churchill had only shrugged, unconcerned. "Any nation that is used for the battlefield in a dog-fight will cease to exist," he opined. "Perhaps it will be Irish soil."

Above all, Willkie had swallowed whole the bait that Churchill, in an effort to counteract Lindbergh's propaganda, had dangled before the American people. In a transatlantic broadcast on Sunday 9 February – for which Hopkins had stood in as co-author – Churchill had assured the nation that Britain required nothing of them beyond war material. "We shall not fail or falter," he promised. "We shall not weaken or tire. Give us the tools and we shall finish the job."

Thus Wilkie, speaking fast and urgently, now told the Senate Committee in all sincerity what they most wanted to hear: that the last thing the British contemplated was an American Expeditionary Force, "this year, nor next year".

Advocating that every American bomber save training planes should be sent to Britain post-haste, along with five or ten destroyers a month, he summed up: at the worst, it was a matter of self-preservation. Should

Britain fall, "we would be at war in a month" or at most "sixty days". But with American aid, Britain would not fall.

Others would speak up as trenchantly – notably Senator Alben Barkley, who opened the ensuing debate with the immortal words of Patrick Henry: "Is life so dear or peace so sweet as to be purchased at the price of chains or slavery? Forbid it, Almighty God." But it was Willkie's appeal to the national self-interest that ultimately turned the tide.

Meanwhile the British, anxious to prove their worth, were embarking on as dubious a military venture as even 1941 would witness.

*

Both the venture – and the decision – were rooted in history. As far back as April, 1939, following Mussolini's Good Friday invasion of Albania, Churchill's predecessor, Neville Chamberlain, had guaranteed Greece British support in the event of Axis aggression, extending the pledge to Turkey and Rumania. The question had remained hypothetical – until 28 October, 1940, when Benito Mussolini, *Il Duce* of Fascism, bent on scoring off Hitler for seizing oil-rich areas of Rumania, had sent four ill-equipped Italian divisions storming into Greece.

The chivalrous Churchill's immediate reaction – "We will give you all the help in our power" – proved premature. As the Greeks fought back like tigers, the Italians, within weeks, were in headlong retreat, surrounded at the ports of Durazzo and Valona, their backs to the sea. Moreover, the Greek Premier, Ioannis "Little John" Metaxas, known as the "carpet slippers dictator", had declined Churchill's offer, fearing German intervention.

Midway through January, Churchill was still insisting and Metaxas still demurring, although perhaps to discourage further importuning he put the price sky-high: he would accept a force of 200,000 well-equipped British troops. But the British, in any case, could send no reinforcements that would decisively affect the outcome. On 2 November, Secretary of State for War, Anthony Eden, had dismissed it in a two-word diary entry: "Strategic folly".

Two events now conspired to change the course of history. On 29 January Metaxas died of blood poisoning and his successor, an immaculate banker named Alexander Koryzis, promptly agreed to accept the British offer.

This was a bitter blow, for the only troops available would be stripped from the one theatre of war where the British were conducting a triumphant campaign: Libya. In the past two months, the Western Desert Force, under Lieutenant General Richard O'Connor, had advanced 500 miles, taken 130,000 Italian prisoners, 400 tanks, more than 1,000 guns and the major fortresses of Bardia and Tobruk.

It was now that Eden – who had become Foreign Secretary* on 23 December, 1940 – made a fatal error. "A vain feminine creature," as one Cabinet colleague had dubbed him, Eden had long seen himself as an elder statesman; now his aspiration was the creation of a Balkan bloc to thwart any German move southward – "The only chance to prevent the Balkans being devoured piecemeal". Hungary and Rumania had made common cause with the Axis, Bulgaria was wavering – but might not British intervention in Greece stiffen the resolve of Turkey and Yugoslavia?

It was a fond illusion. Although the Balkans loomed as the 1941 surrogate for Belgium and the Netherlands – "all little people waiting to be eaten one by one", noted the Minister for Economic Warfare, Hugh Dalton – what they sought above all was to wall themselves into fortresses of individual privacy. In Sofia, King Boris III of Bulgaria, an amiable lepidopterist who also collected mountain flower petals, fretted that Roosevelt's provocative broadcasts might involve the whole world in war: "national socialism may be good for Germany, fascism for Italy, and bolshevism for Russia but . . . none of these is wanted by Bulgaria".

King Boris, in any case, was hedging his bets: to circumvent what the U.S. Minister in Rumania termed "a period of peaceful bullying", fourteen Bulgarian airfields were already playing host to 280 Luftwaffe aircraft, their war material ferried thence by 40 special Luftwaffe trains.

It was the same in every capital. Turkey, despite an Anglo-Turkish pact of 1939 pleaded weakness of both arms and air-power; offered 10 R.A.F. squadrons they still proved what Sir Alexander Cadogan, Permanent Under Secretary to the Foreign Office called "timorous and sticky". At Beli Dvor, The White Palace, Belgrade, Prince Paul, the Regent of Yugoslavia, although a resolute Anglophile, saw the Allied cause as already doomed; his sole ambition was to pull out in September, when his nephew, 17-year-old King Peter II ascended the throne – "he would not go on with his duties for another day", reported the British Minister, Ronald Campbell. Faced with a Foreign Office proposition for a United Balkan Front, Prince Paul, shaking with rage, berated Campbell: "This stinks of Anthony!"

But one factor could hardly be denied: a British expedition to Greece, however foolhardy, might do much to convince the United States that Britain was still a contender worth backing.

Major-General Francis Davidson never forgot his first assignment as newly appointed Director of British Military Intelligence. On the hectic afternoon of 11 February following an urgent summons from the Chiefs of Staff, Davidson and a team of experts were given exactly four hours to draw up an appreciation (with maps) of German troop strengths in

---

* A post he had previously held from December 1935 to February, 1938.

Rumania and Bulgaria. On their report would hinge a crucial decision: whether to divert troops to Greece from Egypt and Libya.

At 5.30 p.m. Davidson was given three minutes by the Chiefs of Staff – General Sir John Dill, Admiral Sir Dudley Pound, Air Marshal Sir Charles Portal – to present a digest of his information. His conclusion: on their present track record, the Germans, if they invaded Greece, would reach Athens by 21 April.

One day later, as if Davidson had never uttered, Eden and Dill departed for Cairo to sell their plan willy-nilly to the trio charged with protecting Britain's Middle East dominion by land, sea and air: General Sir Archibald Wavell, Admiral Sir Andrew Cunningham and Air Chief Marshal Sir Arthur Longmore. Later the disgusted Davidson found that Churchill had even doodled in blue pencil all over his best strategic map, rendering it illegible.

Such was the British desperation to win American approval in the dawn of 1941.

*

Both at home and abroad many men entertained grave doubts. In Whitehall, two of the first to voice them, on 19 February, were Hugh Dalton and Sir Alexander Cadogan.

Might it not be better, both men pondered, "to allow the Greeks, under pressure, to make a separate peace . . . better than having the country devastated to the last and better than putting in some of our own troops and having them not even evacuated but trapped and destroyed?".

It was a thought that Churchill, too, explored, next day with the War Cabinet – "in that case we could not very well blame them . . . we should have done our duty." Later that day he cabled Eden: "Do not feel yourselves obligated to a Greek enterprise if in your hearts you feel it will only be another Norwegian fiasco." This counsel profoundly shocked Sir Michael Palairet, the Grecophile British Minister in Athens. "I felt quite sick with horror when I read the Prime Minister's telegram," he confessed to Eden later. "I don't think I *could* have gone to the King with a message on those lines; *hara-kiri* on the Palace threshold seemed the only way out."

But Sir Michael's fears were groundless. Shuttling from Cairo to Athens and on to Ankara, Eden was bent on having his way. On 22 February, in a series of meetings with King George of the Hellenes that dragged on for forty-eight hours, Eden, backed by the Middle Eastern Commander-in-Chief, galvanised the Greeks like a high pressure armaments salesman – promising them 100,000 men, 240 field guns, 202 anti-tank guns, plus vastly inflated totals of medium guns, ack-ack

12

guns and tanks. Not surprisingly, King George and his cabinet assented readily.

Even Wavell, who had earlier feared the Greeks might crack, stressing that Crete spelt greater security for Egypt and Malta, was at last won over. "I can't help thinking," commented General Sir Hastings (later Lord) Ismay, Assistant Secretary to the War Cabinet, "that (Wavell) allowed political considerations to influence his military judgement."

All hopes of a Balkan bloc had already gone by the board. In Ankara the Turkish Cabinet proved ambivalent, despite Eden's attempts to rally them by reciting reams of Persian poetry at a ceremonial banquet. By 1 March, Bogdan Filov, the sad sick Premier of Bulgaria, racked by stomach ulcers, was to sign the Axis pact in Vienna in Hitler's presence. Prince Paul of Yugoslavia now so feared involvement that he refused even to slip away from Beli Dvor Palace to meet Eden in southern Serbia. "I can hardly grasp how I've been given the strength – so far – to stand all the strain," he excused himself, "but I can assure you that it's no easy task."

Another gravely worried man was Robert Menzies, the Australian Premier, then on a visit to London. Menzies had reason: of the 58,000 troops who were ultimately sent – barely half the number that Eden had promised – more than 17,000 would be Australians, a further 16,000 New Zealanders. Could he say to his colleagues, Menzies asked the War Cabinet, "that the venture had a substantial chance of success?"

Churchill, though equivocal, still struck at the heart of the matter. "If we forsook Greece it would have a bad effect in the United States."

Three days later, the Australians reluctantly agreed – on condition that contingency planning ensured that "evacuation (if it became necessary) could be successfully undertaken".

On 7 March, with the die finally cast, Churchill's planners felt nothing but consternation. His Director of Military Operations, Major-General Sir John Kennedy saw it as "a major error". Captain Ralph Edwards, Royal Navy, Director of Operations (Home) thought it "a very wrong policy . . . another Winston lunacy". As Minister of Aircraft Production Lord Beaverbrook set off for the Cabinet meeting that set Greece in motion, his parliamentary private secretary gave a soothsayer's warning: "Remember three words – Gallipoli – Narvik – Dunkirk."

Even Churchill felt it necessary to warn Eden: to mollify Australia and New Zealand, whose troops would bear the brunt of any fighting, the decision should be presented as one taken by Wavell and his fellow-commanders, not by the Foreign Secretary – "you have given us few facts or reasons . . . which can be presented to these Dominions as justifying the operation on any grounds but *noblesse oblige*".

In Washington, D.C., the reactions were all that Churchill might have hoped. Under Secretary of State Sumner Welles thought it "one of the wisest (decisions) taken during the war". Peppery little Harold Ickes, Roosevelt's Secretary of the Interior, noted: "Certainly the British have to stick to the end . . . They cannot afford to subject themselves to the charge of deserting their allies, as happened when the British were evacuated from Belgium." Rear Admiral Richmond Kelly Turner, Chief of the Navy's War Plans Division, agreed. "Sending British troops to Greece," he minuted the Chief of Naval Operations, Admiral Harold R. Stark, "has so weakened the British Army in Egypt that the Germans will have little difficulty in regaining all of Libya."

Yet Turner saw the entire venture as a moral necessity. "Abandoning Greece to its fate could have been an action so base and immoral that reinforcing them was necessary regardless of its influence on the future of Britain . . ."

*

In Athens, one American on the spot was less certain: Lincoln MacVeagh, the U.S. Minister and a longtime observer of the Grecian scene. If war comes to Greece, he predicted to Roosevelt, "the best that the Allies can look forward to is a succession of Thermopylaes". The Luftwaffe, he thought, would "take the place of the Persian arrows, darkening the sun, and British tenacity and Greek devotion would fight in the shades".

MacVeagh had been in no way reassured by a talk he had had with Anthony Eden during his time in Athens. "I think eventually the Yugoslavs, Turks and Greeks will all be in the fighting," he had told MacVeagh airily, "but there will be a lot of slipping and sliding before that happens."

MacVeagh was politely sceptical. Weren't the British still living mainly on efforts and hope?

Eden, he recalled, was "singularly sanguine". "Even if Germany succeeds in over-running Greece," he prophesied, "I don't see how this will help her. By that time we shall have cleaned up in the Middle East and be sitting pretty in Africa. In making war in the Balkans, Germany is only playing football in her own cabbage patch."

It was a strangely ill-timed assessment. Thirteen days earlier, General Enno von Rintelen, the German military attaché in Rome, had brought news to Benito Mussolini in his 40-roomed mansion, Villa Torlonia, that left the Duce beaming. Alarmed by Italian reverses in Libya, Hitler was coming to his Axis partner's rescue: a hastily-assembled 5th Light Motorised Division was to be despatched from Germany to serve as a "blocking detachment" in Tripolitania, Libya's northernmost province.

On 12 February, its new commander *Generalleutnant* Erwin Rommel, arrived in Tripoli.

*

Across the worn paving of Tripoli's main *piazza*, rumbled file upon file of 17-ton Mark IV Panzers, camouflaged in the newly-fashionable desert shade of sand-yellow. Motionless in their turrets, the commanders of the 5th Light Division, arrayed in olive-green tropical uniforms and peaked forage caps stared ahead of them, as impassive as the death's head badges adorning their lapels. At the saluting base, the commander of the newly-formed German Afrika Korps the stocky blue-eyed Rommel stood braced rigidly to attention beside the Italian commander in North Africa, the stooping 62-year-old General Italo Gariboldi.

Yet to Rommel's aide, *Leutnant* Heinz Werner Schmidt, the truly impressive realisation on this crisp spring morning was that his chief was as astute a propagandist as tactician. No sooner had the Panzers passed the saluting base than the column veered into a side street – and after fifteen minutes Schmidt was conscious that at least one Mark IV, with a faulty chain, had passed this way before. For the benefit of the cheering crowds – and any British agents who might be on hand – Rommel was stretching a meagre force of 50 tanks to the proportions of an armoured corps.

Deception – allied with audacity – was to play as great a part as armoured strength in the next phase of the desert battle and for this very reason, Rommel, former commander of the 7th Panzer, "the Ghost Division", who in May 1940 had time and again out-manoeuvred the British columns retreating to Dunkirk was destined to call almost every shot in the months ahead.

Three days after settling into his headquarters in Tripoli's opulent Hotel Uaddan, Rommel was fast formulating plans – plans which in no way coincided with the briefing he had received from the Army's Commander-in-Chief, *Generalfeldmarschall* Walther von Brauchitsch. The Afrika Korps' role, the Commander-in-Chief had stressed, was to be both limited and defensive. Führer Order No 22 of 11 January had made the situation plain: "The position in the Mediterranean, on strategical, political and psychological grounds, demands German aid. Tripolitania must be saved."

The German High Command, Von Brauchitsch warned, planned no decisive strike against the British in North Africa. By the end of May when the Afrika Korps was strengthened by the arrival of the 15th Panzer Division – Rommel might launch limited attacks against Agedabia, south of Beda Fomm, the site of Lieutenant-General O'Connor's last decisive victory. Later he might retake Benghazi, the seaport capital of Cyrenaica. In vain Rommel was to argue: "The Benghazi area can't be held by itself. We shall have to retake the whole of Cyrenaica." His instructions remained finite: to submit operational plans for this move to bolster sagging Italian morale not later than 20 April.

At 49, Rommel was in stark contrast to the top brass of the Army High

Command. Von Brauchitsch Rommel knew as a sensitive withdrawn patrician, who often retired to vomit after a tongue-lashing from Hitler. At times, too, Rommel had clashed with the Chief of Staff, the acerbic ambitious *Generaloberst* Franz Halder – "What did you ever do in war apart from sit on your backside in an office?", Rommel had once challenged him rashly. A schoolmaster's son lacking both money and influence, Rommel was a fighting general with an intuitive sixth sense of his enemy's weakness, dedicated to the twin concepts of speed and surprise – *Sturm, Swung, Wucht*, (Attack, Impetus, Weight) was his most quoted maxim. A virtual teetotaller and non-smoker, fascinated by military minutiae and devoted to just one woman, his wife, Lucie, he now lost no time in adapting to unfamiliar desert conditions. Would heavy tanks bog down in the sand, as Italian generals asserted? Would wheeled trucks do the same? Promptly, Rommel consulted *Leutnant* Hans-Otto Behrendt, an Egyptologist assigned to him as an Arabic interpreter and learned a desert warrior's first lesson: the secret was to drive on slightly soft tyres.

All through February, Rommel was exultant, for unknown to Von Brauchitsch, and in direct defiance of his orders, the first units of the 5th Light Division were already by 15 February, moving in convoy to the coastal village of Sirte, 300 miles from Tripoli – poised to strike, on 24 March, at the rose-red fort of El Agheila, 140 miles south of Benghazi. "we're going to advance to the Nile," Rommel boasted proudly to his staff officers.

The reasons for the High Command's caution were quite unknown to him, though to an outsider they made sound strategic sense. By slow degrees, throughout eastern Europe, three million German soldiers were massing to attack Soviet Russia.

*

Spring came early that year to the *Berghof*, Hitler's white-painted chalet-style retreat perched on the Obersalzberg, high in the Bavarian Alps. From the wide picture-windows of his pine-panelled workroom, the Führer and Chancellor of the Third Reich could see the first tender green breaking through white along the snowy slopes of the Untersberg, the sheltered sunstruck places where blue gentians and Alpine violets pierced the soil. He felt it more strongly still in his blood and bones: spring was the time when armies marched.

Now, as March dawned, Hitler was facing the most crucial decision of his life: the massive May land assault against Russia – Operation Barbarossa – that he had ordered as far back as December, 1940. Day and night now, the obsession rarely left him: the great drive to the east, embracing all the territories between the Vistula and the Ural Mountains, with a southward thrust towards the vast granaries of the Ukraine. It was the *Drang nach Osten* of which Kaiser Wilhelm II had dreamed, which Hitler himself had charted in *Mein Kampf*.

At his broad desk, or relaxed in his green-tinted bath tub, or at the breakfast table sipping China tea, spreading his toast with mountains of jam, Hitler pondered each aspect of his strategy anew. Later it would be time to set down fresh thoughts on paper: one of his confidential secretaries Fräulein Johanna Wolf or Fräulein Christa Schröder would type the draft in huge letters designed to save his eyes before Hitler slashed revisions in green, blue and red pencil.

His motives for the drive were part economic, part idealistic. To harness the vast resources of slave labour, to seize the coal-rich Donets Basin as well as the oil-rich Caucasus, to provide *Lebensraum* for Germany's millions – these made sound economic sense. But to eliminate Russia – with whom he had concluded a mutual non-aggression pact in 1939 – was in the nature of a crusade; not only would he destroy the hated cradle of Bolshevism but "England's last hope", wiping out two enemies at one stroke. In Hitler's complex global reasoning, to turn east was also to turn west.

Three unknowns bedevilled his planning: the ultimate extent of American intervention; the true intentions of his third partner Japan; the Russian capacity for resistance. But like a busy area manager, he was laying plans to convert the Balkan states into compliant satellites; small wonder that on the Balkan bourse of rumour, business had never been more brisk. Hungary, Rumania, and now Bulgaria had fallen into line – and Prince Paul was under mounting pressure to adhere to the Tripartite Pact.

Marshal Henri Philippe Pétain, the octogenarian ruler of Vichy France, was under pressure too; in due time Hitler would seek to occupy Mediterranean ports in France, as well as North Africa, as well as passage for German troops through Tunisia for an attack on the British in Libya. The one man who had tacitly refused any transit for German troops scheduled to attack Gibraltar, General Francisco Franco, *Caudillo* of Spain, had now been crossed off the Führer's list. "The man has missed a historic chance," declared Hitler loftily, but Franco was shrewder. "The Germans are trying to deal in the skin before the lion has been killed," was his assessment of Hitler's plans for Britain.

Greece was an unlooked for factor in Hitler's time-table. Angered by Mussolini's ill-timed invasion, he had formulated no plans to rescue his Axis partner, as in Africa – but now the imminent British presence brought Greece into the spotlight. From Salonika, in northern Greece, the British had launched their drive on Austria–Hungary in World War One. That must not happen again.

Thus overnight, thanks to Eden's machinations, Greece was now of paramount importance to the success of Barbarossa. To seize Greece was

17

to seal off the Balkans, especially Rumania's Ploesti oilfields – both from Russia and from the British in the Eastern Mediterranean. It would provide a staging point for German troops massing for the Russian offensive – and prevent Britain and Russia joining forces when Germany turned east.

Hitler saw one thing plainly: time was of the essence. From Finland to the Balkan passes, the Red Army was a potential threat to every economic link: Balkan grain, Rumanian oil, even the timber, phosphates, chrome ore and platinum that Russia still scrupulously transshipped to Germany under the 1939 agreement. Would Barbarossa kill not only the goose but all its golden eggs? Perhaps – but the wary Hitler knew that Russia could renege on the agreement at any time it suited her.

"What one does not have but needs, one most conquer," Hitler summed up.

Not for one moment did he dream that it would all blow up in his face like a firecracker at a party. In the end, Barbarossa would bring about the entire chain of circumstance that Hitler had sought to forestall – forcing Russia and Britain into an uneasy alliance, engaging Russia and freeing Japan, in the Far East, for a titanic onslaught on the United States. But Hitler had no inkling. In this same month, during a brief reunion with his younger sister, Paula, he told her: "Do you know it is my absolute conviction that the Lord is holding His protecting hand above me?'

Henceforth, the clocks must tick against him, but now the days and nights fled towards spring, and, for the moment, spring spelt destiny.

*

All over Europe, men and women now made unobtrusive preparations for the holocaust ahead. It was as if, sensing Hitler's brooding presence, they sought to put their houses in order, as a sudden spasm of pain might impel a man to draft a will. "Impossible to think," noted a London-based Canadian diplomat, Charles Ritchie, "without his shadow falling across our thoughts."

In Stockholm, Sweden, Harold Elvin, a 32-year-old Englishman and son of a prominent trade unionist, wrote on impulse to an old friend of his father, Sir Stafford Cripps, the British Ambassador in Russia. A rolling stone who had once worked as an art director for film producer Alexander Korda, Elvin had later opted out to spend five years cycling as far east as Leningrad, as far south as Barcelona, living as the peasants did, honing his expenses to £1 a week. Now he begged Cripps: could the Ambassador find him some niche in the Moscow Embassy?

Though Sir Stafford's reply was discouraging – the only vacancy was as an assistant night watchman, without even Foreign Office grading, paying only £4 a week – Elvin agreed readily, booking an air passage to Moscow with a stopover at Riga. He had no real premonition: it was just that Moscow seemed the place to be.

*

In Brussels, Andrée de Jongh, a 24-year-old headmaster's daughter, came to a sudden decision. All through her youth at 73, Avenue Emile Verhaeren, in the middle-class suburb of Schaerbeck, she and her sister Suzanne had been taught by their father to revere the memory of Edith Cavell, the English nurse executed by the Germans in 1915 for helping Allied soldiers to escape. Now, with two medical diplomas to her own credit – both as nurse and ambulance attendant – Andrée thought back to the six months she had worked in the Hôpital St Jean, Bruges, tending both German and British soldiers as they lay side by side on straw pallets. Often until Christmas, 1940, when German military personnel took over the hospital, the idea had crossed her mind, "How stupid to cure these British soldiers if they're going to be taken prisoner by the Germans! Why not help them escape?"

Now, having returned to Brussels, Andrée de Jongh was determined to find the answer to that question. Petite, fair-haired, galvanised by such energy that Frédéric, her father, had christened her "Little Cyclone", she and a young radio repair mechanic Arnold de Pé, hit upon a solution. Their escape line should be routed where the Germans least expected it: not through Vichy France, where loyalties to Pétain might betray them but through the northern zone of Occupied France and thence to the Low Pyrenees. It would be a conspiracy of youth, with few organisers under 25 – and ultimately the most successful of all the escape lines.

*

At Ismailia, on the Suez Canal, 64 miles from Cairo, A.C.1 (Aircraftman First Class) Marcel Gerard Comeau, a 19-year-old aerial rigger with No 33 (Hurricane) Squadron, talked things over with his mate, Ken Eaton. Three years an R.A.F. regular, the lanky irrepressible Comeau was an expert at interpreting latrine rumours – and now orders had arrived that the squadron's 21 planes were to be sprayed with dark green and brown camouflage paint. To the "erks" (other ranks) of 33 Squadron this meant one thing: they were all "for Greece".

Comeau – whose Gallic name was derived from forebears in Nova Scotia – was in no way perturbed by the fact that the R.A.F. had just posted him to Kenya; he had no intention of "missing the fun". Around 1 March – coining a brand new motto, "Put a hundred miles between yourself and the parent unit" – he stowed away aboard the troopship *Dumana*, agog for his first view of Athens. Always searching for where the action was hottest, he was to "desert" twice more before the year was out.

*

In Belgrade, the Yugoslav capital, 51-year-old Ruth Mitchell, a spirited redhead from Milwaukee, Wisconsin, was already at the scene of the action, but one question remained: How to become part of it? Twice married, with a grown-up son and daughter, Ruth and her family had long seen action as their birthright. Her father, John Lendrum Mitchell, Civil War veteran, United States Senator and banker, had built the 5,000 mile long Chicago, Milwaukee and St Paul railroad; the Mitchell family home, with its private race track, had covered the area of a full city block. Her brother Brigadier-General "Billy" Mitchell, United States Air Force, had been court-martialled in 1925, found guilty and resigned from the service after charging the War and Navy Departments with "incompetency and criminal negligence". His theory had been one that 1941 would amply validate: the aeroplane had rendered the battleship obsolete.

Following one's own bent regardless was thus the Mitchell way of life. Three years resident in Yugoslavia, as a student of Serbian folk-lore, Ruth's one-storey house in the Slavija Hill district of Belgrade had long been a cultural outpost, famed for poetry readings and spirited philosophical discussions.

A hundred-carat romantic, Ruth Mitchell looked back four months to one of the most stirring demonstrations she had ever witnessed: a column of marching men pouring down Slavija Hill to the nearby Orthodox Church. All of them wore the handsome brown black-embroidered costume of the Shumadiya peasant; their feet were shod in soundless upturned rawhide sandals and black astrakhan caps adorned their heads. Before them swayed black silver-fringed banners with a skull-and-crossbones emblem and this same device was repeated in metal on every man's breast.

These were the *Četniks*, Serbian freedom fighters loyal to King Peter, whose mystic order, formed to resist the Turkish invader, dated back centuries before the Treaty of Versailles, dismembering the old Habsburg Empire, carved a new country, Yugoslavia, from the kingdom of the Serbs, Croats and Slovenes.

Ruth had sounded out contacts. Never before had a foreigner, let alone a woman, been accepted by the *Četnik* movement, but her accomplishments – a skilled horse-woman, capable of foot-slogging thirty miles a day, with a private pilot's licence – swayed the balance. But before she could be enrolled as a despatch rider, a probationary period followed. She practised for hours with a dagger on a dangling bag of sawdust, quick

20

thrusts upwards to reach the heart. Into her coat collar she sewed a cyanide capsule, sited so that it could be chewed despite bound hands. Her name was formally inscribed in an old well-worn book.

On 3 March came the day of her initiation. Accompanied by a sponsor, she once more crossed a snowy courtyard on the outskirts of Belgrade, mounting rickety wooden stairs to a two-room office. Behind a desk sat 70-year-old Voivoda Kosta Pechanats, the *Četnik* leader, whose guerilla bands, on the Salonika front, had tied down three German Army divisions in World War One. The dimly-lit room was thronged with portraits of Serbian fighters, past and present, offset by a glittering arsenal of daggers and swords.

Now, facing an icon of Sava, her right hand firm on a crossed dagger and revolver, Ruth Mitchell looked Pechanats firmly in the eye and repeated after him: "*Do smrti za Srbiju, tako mi Bog pomogao*" (Till death for Serbia, by the help of God).

Pechanats took the old worn book then and firmly drew a line through the name "Ruth Mitchell". His explanation would have daunted a woman less determined: "When you become one of us, we consider you as good as dead."

*

For House Bill 1776, the end came almost as an anti-climax. At 3.50 p.m. on Tuesday, 11 March, flanked only by a few staffers and White House photographers, Franklin Roosevelt solemnly and silently inscribed his name on a bill that became law by a final tally of 317 to 71. In recognition of the Bill's six sponsors – among them Senator Barkley, Congressman Bloom, Speaker Sam Rayburn – the President signed his name with six pens, a few letters at a time, cleansing them with six blotters before passing them over in tribute.

News from Washington was now news for the whole world. American flags flew in the streets of London. In Sydney, crowds sang *The Star Spangled Banner*. Canada's Premier, William Lyon Mackenzie King, called the law "one of the milestones of freedom". Prime Minister Jan Smuts of South Africa exulted: "Hitler has at last brought America into the war."

Only Hitler remained unimpressed. The message from the Berghof ran: "No power and no support coming from any part of the world can change the outcome of this battle . . . England will fall."

Behind the jubilant facade, the bonds of Anglo–American amity were albeit strained almost to snapping point. In Washington, D.C., Sir Edward Peacock, King George's personal financial adviser, who feared a buyer's market, was stalling determinedly on the liquidation of British investments – notably the American Viscose Corporation, the country's largest rayon producer. When Treasury Secretary Morgenthau complained, "They don't make a god damn move on this thing," the newly-appointed Ambassador, Lord Halifax, made a childish attempt to over-awe him. "Sir Edward Peacock has very powerful friends in England," he warned, "and he is very close to the Governor of the Bank of England."

Even so Halifax, on 20 February, had cabled a warning to Churchill: Britain "should without delay hand over to America our remaining financial resource in that country". But a month later, the Premier was still temporising – "it was impossible for us to continue to make concessions at short notice to meet the exigencies of United States politics". The business "should be allowed to simmer".

In truth, it was Morgenthau who was simmering, and finally under pressure, Halifax backed down; by the end of May the American Viscose Corporation came under the hammer. "In the end," noted Harold Ickes, "the British got about $87 million for a property reasonably worth $125 million."

It was in keeping with Roosevelt's grim determination that the British must pay their way; all along he had stressed to his Cabinet his insistence on hard cash. "What mattered was dollars, not properties," noted Agriculture Secretary Claude Wickard. "Holdings of railroads in South America and elsewhere were not wanted by us."

What one commentator called " 'The White Cliffs of Dover'* stage of Anglo-American friendship" was almost a thing of the past: never far from the surface now was America's deeprooted suspicion of Britain as a rapacious colonial power looking first to her own ends. "The British are always foxy," Roosevelt had cautioned Willkie on his return from London, "and you have to be the same with them." Thus Churchill's suggestion that the United States should send a show-the-flag cruiser mission to the naval base at Singapore was rejected out of hand by Admiral Harold Stark: "Never absent from British minds are their post-war interests, commercial and military."

Churchill was profoundly shocked. Although in public he lauded Lend-Lease as "a new Magna Carta" and "the most unsordid act in history", the private realisation that the Commonwealth would pay the United States £1 million in 1941 for only seven per cent of its munitions cut him to the quick. All along he told the Ministry of Information's Harold Nicolson, he had believed "that we were exchanging a bunch of flowers for a sugar cake. But not at all, the Americans have done a hard business deal." In a mood of extreme rancour he told the Chancellor of the Exchequer, Sir Kingsley Wood: "We are not only to be skinned but flayed to the bone."

* A best-selling poem of 1940 by the American author Alice Duer Miller, celebrating the British way of life. It gave its name to a top-of-the-charts ballad (featured by Hildegarde) and later to a film (starring Irene Dunn).

In fact, both sides had little cause for complaint. Churchill's driving obsession was to bring about active American involvement; given all the "tools" in the world Britain could never have "finished the job" without American manpower and he knew it. Roosevelt saw Britain as the sole bulwark in a Nazi sea – but his avowed wish "to get rid of that silly foolish old dollar sign" was little more than a fantasy spun to divert the White House Press Corps.

Even the course of nature, it seemed, must be diverted in British interests. When Minister of Food Lord Woolton noted peremptorily that he would need fully 27,000 tons of canned salmon to titillate jaded British palates, Secretary of the Interior Ickes did the one thing possible. He extended the salmon run for five days to stock up the British larder.

What a later generation of politicians was to call the "special relationship" was at last under way – but a long and thorny road lay ahead for both nations.

"Convoys Mean Shooting and Shooting Means War"

13 March–14 April 1941

All through March Roosevelt rarely left the confines of the White House. In the shabby comfort of the Oval Office, with its soft green walls, he worked behind a desk wildly cluttered with miscellanea – gold oblong matchbook folders labelled, "Stolen from Franklin D. Roosevelt", a toy Missouri mule kicking Ol' Man Depression up the rear, cigarette lighters, a china pig, a cloth elephant. Yet there was no confusion in his thinking. Even 3,500 miles from Europe, his finger was on the pulse of history.

To London, on 10 March – one day before Lend-Lease became law – went 43-year-old William Averell Harriman, millionaire's son, merchant banker and croquet champion, now Roosevelt's newly-created "Defense Expediter" with instructions to "keep the British Isles afloat". Ahead of him, on 1 March, as the new Ambassador to the Court of St James's, had journeyed John Gilbert Winant, former head of the International Labour Organisation – charged with the task of wooing Britain's left wing, particularly Minister of Labour Ernest Bevin, should Churchill's government fall.

A slow-spoken Lincolnesque figure, described in a Foreign Office memorandum as "very earnest and very shy . . . a poor mixer and not blessed with small talk", Winant was to find his assignment taxing almost beyond endurance. During frequent weekends at Chequers, the Premier's country residence, Churchill would "have a go" at Winant, over Saturday luncheon, urging more and more Lend-Lease supplies, until 3 p.m. when he retired for a catnap. At this point an aide took up the cudgels – until Churchill refreshed from sleep, returned to badger the weary Winant into the small hours.

Already Roosevelt was striding rapidly away from the neutrality to which he publicly paid lip-service. Always he had been at pains to present Lend-Lease not as a step towards war but as a step away from it: this was a pious fiction. British ships would now be repaired in American docks; 8,000 young British pilots were to be trained on American airfields. Ten coastguard cutters were transferred to the Royal Navy. Next Roosevelt extended the American neutrality patrol zone to longitude 26 degrees west – bringing the United States' outermost line of potential defences to Greenland, 900 miles nearer to Europe, only three miles from the German war zone. Other strictly unneutral moves were in the pipeline: the Red Sea was declared open to U.S. shipping, so that arms could be taken to technically-neutral Egypt. Mindful of a probable British loss of 3,500,000 to 5,500,000 tons of merchant shipping – of which no more than 2,100,000 would be replaced by British and U.S. yards in 1941 – the President asked Congress for authority to seize all foreign shipping in U.S. harbours, including Vichy France's famous liner, *Normandie*, now quietly rusting at Manhattan's 48th Street pier.

For the time being, though, he stopped resolutely short of using American warships to convoy Lend-Lease goods. As Roosevelt had recently remarked to one visitor: "Convoys mean shooting and shooting means war."

Such moves were public knowledge – but unknown to Congress as Lend-Lease was under fire, Roosevelt had virtually smuggled a Trojan Horse into official Washington. As early as 29 January, six high-ranking British officers, all clad in mufti, had arrived unobtrusively for top-secret talks with their U.S. counterparts. Known as the A.B.C. meetings (American–British Conversations), the delegates were to huddle together on fourteen occasions between then and 29 March. Their terms of reference were an ultimate war between the United States and all the Axis powers, including Japan. The final A.B.C.–1 agreement, drawn up on 27 March, stressed one basic concept: Hitler's Germany loomed as the real enemy.

But Roosevelt was probing farther afield than England; his eyes and ears were everywhere. As his listening post inside Vichy France he had appointed as Ambassador Admiral William D. Leahy, whose official brief was to maintain cordial relations with Marshal Pétain – or, as Leahy himself put it, "to stiffen wavering Gallic vertebrae". In the third week of March, another observer, Colonel William J. ("Wild Bill") Donovan, one-time soldier and lawyer, reported back to the President, after a three-and-a-half month 30,000 mile trip through Europe, the Near East and Africa. Donovan, too, had stopped off in London – to lunch with Churchill and discuss "a relationship of mutual selfishness" – but he had ranged much farther afield: to Egypt to talk with Wavell, to Sofia, to chat with King Boris (six weeks before he joined the Axis), to Athens, Belgrade, Turkey, Palestine and Baghdad.

The drums were beating faster in the un-declared war and the mood that Donovan reported from the Balkans was one of fear – fear in Greece that too much British aid would provoke the Germans, fear in Belgrade that Prince Paul, following a mid-February parley with Hitler by his Prime Minister and Foreign Minister, would soon capitulate.

Now, not for the first time, Roosevelt was to make public promises that he was powerless to keep. On Saturday, 15 March, at a crowded dinner of the White House Press Correspondents Association, he came out with a trenchant speech that was beamed to Europe in fourteen languages: "The British people and their Grecian allies need ships. From America they will get ships. They need planes. From America they will get planes. Yes, from America they need food . . . They will get food."

This was fighting talk but specious fighting talk, falling far short of reality. One month earlier, on 14 February, Cordell Hull had told the Yugoslav Minister, Constantin Fotitć: "We can supply the materials of war to victims of aggression." In practice, Fotitć reported wanly to Prince Paul, he had looked to America for positive aid in vain. Only one armaments manufacturer had even agreed to consider an order for 96 anti-aircraft batteries – stressing that there would be an eighteen-month delay in delivery and that the prohibitive price would include the entire cost of the machines and tools.

It was as bad for the Greeks. Although Roosevelt's declaration was to be learned by rote in Athenian schools, along with the orations of Pericles, in practice no aid was forthcoming. Back in November, 1940, the Greek Minister, Constantin Diamantopoulos, had been promised 30 P-40 planes – but as 1941 dawned, the P-40s available, 300 in all, were found to have been allotted to Britain and China, now in the fourth year of her war with Japan. In January, the State Department resorted to dishonesty – denying that the November offer had ever specified P-40s. Instead, they would allot the Greeks 30 obsolete U.S. naval planes. When Diamantopoulos protested that Greece needed fighters, and 60 at least, Treasury Secretary Morgenthau told him boorishly: "Take the planes and shut up."

In February, when three-and-a-half months had passed, Assistant Secretary of State Adolf A. Berle – fearing that "to have the President's word discredited would run through the Balkans like a germ" – soothed the Minister that delivery might be expected in four weeks. On 26 March, Sumner Welles was still hoping that "a solution satisfactory to Greece will be found in the near future". Five days later, Hull cabled the Legation in Athens that planes were on their way: eight Grumman F3F-1 Navy fighters built in 1936, would proceed by slow boat to Suez. "We appear," noted one diplomat smugly, "to be well out of the woods in this matter."

Thus by degrees the suspicion was growing in Europe that Roosevelt's promises were designed to provoke token resistance by unarmed nations, in the hope of those nations finding favour with the American public. "Any nation which tamely submits on the grounds of being overrun," the President noted to Cordell Hull, "will receive less sympathy from the world than a nation which resists, even if this can be continued for only a few weeks." Obscurely he saw Abyssinia* as a case in point: "Abyssinia won world sympathy by a brief though useless resistance – and Abyssinia will be restored in some way not now foreseeable."

On 18 March, in one of his last talks with the U.S. Minister in Yugoslavia, Arthur Bliss Lane, Prince Paul was once more urged to stand firm – although with what Lane did not specify. Why not, the Minister urged, refuse to sign any pact with Hitler, keep diplomatic integrity intact and maintain Yugoslavia's reputation abroad?

Paul's reply sadly summed up the viewpoint of all the small and threatened nations. "You big nations are hard," he told Lane. "You talk of our honour but you are far away."

*

The British were now committed to a decision that had found favour with Roosevelt but would prolong the war in North Africa for two more years. The Greek expedition, finally launched on 4 March, had stripped General Sir Archibald Wavell to the bone. Cyrenaica, so recently a scene of triumph, was now "a passive battle zone", policed by a "minimum possible force" of half a division, ill-trained and ill-equipped, hovered over by one fighter squadron.

Moreover, the one Briton with a genuine intuition for desert warfare, the recently-knighted Lieutenant-General Sir Richard O'Connor, had been transferred from Cyrenaica to command rear echelon troops in Egypt. Into his shoes, as March dawned, as G.O.C., Western Desert Force, stepped Lieutenant-General Philip Neame, V.C., famous for lobbing improvised jam-pot bombs at the German trenches in 1914 – but a sapper, unversed in desert warfare. "Delay enemy's advance over the 150 miles from Agheila to Benghazi for two months," were his sole instructions from Wavell.

As Wavell was later to admit, he had mis-calculated fatally. Not until mid-March – "when it was rather too late" – visiting Benghazi, did he realise that the escarpment running south of the port, far from being defensible by a light mobile force, could be ascended almost everywhere. Nor had Wavell ever visited the salt marshes near El Agheila – which stretched twenty clear miles from the coast towards Libya's Great Sand Sea. Near-impassable to vehicles save at a few easily mined points, these could have formed "a formidable defensive barrier".

But Wavell, in any case, thought the Germans would launch no effective counter-attack earlier than May – echoing the very beliefs of the High Command in Berlin. Knowing Rommel's instructions to the letter

* Abyssinia (later Ethiopia) had been overrun by Mussolini's troops in a seven-month campaign from October 1935. The British restored Emperor Haile Selassie to his throne on 5 May, 1941.

27

through the daily intercepts of the Enigma machine,* Wavell had automatically assumed that an order to stand fast would be implicitly obeyed.

Both camps had reckoned without *General leutnant* Erwin Rommel – who knew nothing of Hitler's decision to invade Greece nor of his long term plan to launch Operation Barbarossa.

At dawn on 24 March, with the suddenness of a coronary attack, Rommel struck.

Deploying on a 1,000-yard front, scores of tanks and armoured cars of Major Imfried von Wechmar's 3rd Reconnaissance Group bored for the fort of El Agheila. Behind them groaned trucks whose drivers were obeying to the letter Rommel's canny precept: "Panzers to the head of all formations! Rear vehicles to raise dust – nothing but dust." For the first time, Rommel's desert tactics were put to a decisive test, for much of Von Wechmar's "armour" was incapable of firing a shot. Known as "The Cardboard Division" because of its Volkswagens mounted with wooden chassis, canvas coverings and dummy guns – "I won't hold it against you if you lose one or two", Rommel joked to Wechmar – their outlines in the swirling dust yet suggested a formidable fighting force. Promptly the British garrison of El Agheila fell back on Mersa el Brega, 30 miles east.

For the first, but not the last time in the desert, the British were to mistake Axis shadow for substance. At Mersa el Brega, on 31 March, the desert gate to Cyrenaica was breached by Rommel's 50 tanks – moving on a wide front to create maximum confusion, striking in concentration as battle was joined. Through the curtain of shattered white houses that the British had abandoned charged the men of the Afrika Korps chanting their newly-minted battlecry, "*Heia Safari!*" – a Bantu phrase meaning "Drive onward".

Now, as blindly as the Italians before O'Connor the British fell back without a fight – packed ignominiously 30 to a truck, nerves at breaking point from lack of sleep, faces masked with thick yellow dust like jaundice patients. Everywhere there was dire confusion. At Beda Fomm, Second-Lieutenant Roy Farran's first intimation of trouble was a convoy of British Service Corps trucks zizagging frantically along the coast towards Benghazi. Flagging them down, the astonished Farran heard from a near-speechless driver that the Germans had broken through on a wide front: the prelude to "seven of the most inglorious days in the

---

* The much discussed "Enigma" dated from 1938, when M.I.6, the British secret intelligence service, bought the secret of a German cipher machine (code-named "Enigma") from a Polish mathematician, who had worked in the Berlin factory where it was produced. His price was £10,000, a British passport and a French residential permit for himself and his wife. From an apartment on the Left Bank in Paris he created a replica of "Enigma" and a working model, codenamed "Ultra", was completed and sited at Bletchley Park, a Victorian mansion forty miles north of London. The value of the information was, of course, dependent on the British understanding the objective of any one battle.

history of the British Army". At Antelat, a panic-stricken corporal's scream "Mass retreat – the Jerries are coming", so outraged Lieutenant-Colonel Crichton Mitchell, a sapper, that he threatened to shoot the man on the spot.

In vain, Churchill had cabled Wavell: "I presume you are only waiting for the tortoise to stick his head out far enough before chopping it off." All initiative had been lost. Following Wavell's instructions to the letter – not to "hesitate to give up ground if necessary as far as Benghazi and even evacuate Benghazi if the situation demanded" – Neame made no attempt to visit the front but strove vainly to restore order from chaos with a series of desultory telegrams.

In this pell-mell 800-mile eight-day retreat, which the British with wry self-deprecation, were to christen "The Tobruk Derby" or "The Benghazi Handicap", orders and counter-orders multiplied. At Bardia, one company of Lieutenant Colonel Eustace Arderne's Durham Light Infantry were first instructed "Hold the fort" – a task once entrusted to 45,000 Italians – then, within hours, advised: "Believe you are surrounded. Blow everything." At Msus, Captain the Honourable Anthony Hore-Ruthven, told that an enemy column was approaching, blew up an entire divisional petrol dump – then, too late, recognised the "enemy" as a British patrol of the Long Range Desert Group.

At Rommel's Advanced H.Q. near the Agedabia landing ground, the air was alive with tension as runners scurried in and out with messages, and Major Georg Ehlert, the Ops officer, scrawled incisive red and blue marks on the talc of his operations map. "They're mad and now I've got them", Rommel crowed, as news of the headlong rout reached him for now, driven on by the demon of pursuit and in defiance of the High Command, he had resolved to take all Cyrenaica at one stroke. But unit after unit told the same bleak story: no more petrol.

Rommel would not be gainsaid. Promptly he ordered all the 5th Division's light trucks to be unloaded of supplies and formed into columns. Each driver was given 24 hours to return to the divisional depot and collect enough petrol, food and ammunition to see the campaign through. It was a dangerous gamble, a day and night when the division was powerless to move, becalmed in 110 degrees of desert heat – and one more chance that Neame failed to exploit.

Rommel's concept was now one of the boldest: to stage in reverse a 150-mile drive that O'Connor had launched in February across the wasteland of Cyrenaica to the tiny desert fort of Mechili. Simultaneously striking en route at Benghazi, Msus and Derna, three other columns would converge on Mechili. Later Rommel was to claim – and the Afrika Korps War Diary was to support him – that a go-ahead for this risky manoeuvre arrived at the eleventh hour from the Army High Command, thus nullifying the angry protests of General Gariboldi (nominally

Rommel's superior in this Italian theatre of war) that prior authority had not been obtained from Rome.

Yet all evidence suggests that this so-called 3 April directive was rigged. One day earlier, on 2 April, the High Command had ruled: "Even after the arrival of the 15th Panzer Division, an extensive operation with Tobruk as the objective cannot be undertaken for the time being." On that same evening Rommel confessed in a letter to his wife: "The brass at Tripoli, Rome and possibly Berlin will gasp. I took the risk against all orders and instructions because I saw an opportunity."

From Athens, Anthony Eden, disturbed by "more and more alarming telegrams . . . from Archie" had set off post-haste for Cairo – to find that Wavell, belatedly, had lost all faith in Neame's judgement and was set to replace him with O'Connor. O'Connor, though, diffident to a fault, felt that "changing horses in midstream would not really help matters". Instead, O'Connor gained Wavell's assent to a compromise. Might not he stand in as Neame's adviser until the battle front had stabilised?

As the British debated these military niceties Rommel's columns forged on for Mechili. But already despite his present successes some critical observers saw signs of a growing impetuousness which would ultimately undo Rommel. One commander, whose column was temporarily halted, was startled when a message fluttered from the cockpit of Rommel's Fieseler Storch spotter plane: "Unless you get going at once I shall come down, Rommel." To *Generalmajor* Heinrich Kirchheim, liaison officer with the Italian Brescia Division, Rommel's frenetic haste was self-defeating. Unwilling to allow his vehicles the needful two-hourly halt period to clean motors of sand, Rommel had tank after tank, truck after truck, drop by the wayside. Always insistent on keeping up with his lead tanks, he was often poorly oriented on the overall battle situation.

Even so, by 9 April, Rommel's whirlwind tactics had netted him a rich harvest of V.I.P. prisoners. At 3 a.m. on the pitch-dark night of 7 April, the big blue sedan carrying O'Connor, Neame and Colonel John Combe, of the 11th Hussars, was bogged down in a traffic jam on the outskirts of Derna. From the darkness sounded harsh voices, shouting instructions, and Neame's chauffeur volunteered: "I expect it's some of them Cypriot drivers, sir." Seconds later, the hapless brass were staring impotently into the levelled barrels of German sub-machine guns. Trapped one day later, after an encircling attack on Mechili that resembled a Sioux swoop on a stockade, was Major-General Michael Gambier-Parry, commander of the 2nd Armoured Division.

In high good humour, Rommel watched Gambier-Parry's command truck unloaded of its gear, then reached forward to annex an oversize pair of sun-and-sand goggles. "Booty – permissible I take it, even for a general," he grinned, adjusting them over the gold-braided rim of his peaked cap. The legend of the Desert Fox was born.

On this very day, a historic conference was taking place, 75 miles to the west, around a glass-topped table in the loggia of the waterfront Albergo Tobruch. Present were Wavell, Major-General J. D. Lavarack, commander of the 7th Australian Division, Major-General Leslie Morshead, commanding the Australian 9th, and his Chief of Staff, Colonel "Gaffer" Lloyd. One day earlier, on 7 April, Churchill had urged: "Tobruk . . . seems to be a place to be held to the death without thought of retirement." Now the commanders had met to decide how this might best be achieved, for so long as Tobruk held out as a bridgehead and sallyport on Rommel's flank, he could make no major advance into Egypt. His Afrika Korps would be denied the use of water supplies – and of the only suitable port east of Benghazi through which he could be supported.

Were they then, one man asked, to hold Tobruk whatever the cost?

Laconic as always, Wavell took his time replying. He took out his eye-glass, polished it, then called for a map. For a few minutes he studied it in silence, noting the thinly-garrisoned villages scattered across 450 miles of desert: Bardia, Sidi Barrani, Mersa Matruh. Then he told Lavarack drily, "There is nothing between you and Cairo."

*

It was an unlikely time and place for diplomats to gather: a dingy freight yard, hemmed in by tenement buildings, on the outskirts of Budapest. At this hour, 10 p.m. on Tuesday, 25 March, the sidings were almost deserted under sheeting rain; from across the tracks a steady shuffle of engines sounded and whistles cried in the night, a sound of horns and of hunting. On the makeshift platform, the Yugoslav Minister to Hungary, Svetozar Rašić, fidgeted uneasily flanked by his Legation staff and three men not normally welcome in Serbian company: the German, Japanese and Italian Ministers.

Minutes later, a special blue-and-gold passenger train slid into the yard, and at once Rašić boarded it, hastening through the slow-moving cars in search of his quarry, the Yugoslav Premier Dragiša Cvetković, a sallow gypsy-featured one-time financier, plagued by a liver ailment, and his Foreign Minister, the bald rotund Aleksander Cincar-Marković, known to Balkan foreign correspondents as "Stinker".

A shock awaited Rašić. Suddenly, as the train halted, Cvetković blundered from his compartment, seized Rašić by the arm and descended abruptly to the platform. "Mr President," Rašić chided, "Mr President, you must greet the Ministers."

Cvetković barely spared the diplomats a glance. "Never mind," he answered curtly, then lapsed into brooding silence. Suddenly he asked Rašić distractedly, "What could I do?"

There was no need for Cvetković to amplify. Almost seven hours

31

earlier, in the green-and-gold splendour of Vienna's Belvedere Palace, Premier and Foreign Minister had undergone their final humiliation. In the presence of the German and Italian Foreign Ministers, Joachim von Ribbentrop and the smooth amoral Count Galeazzo Ciano, Mussolini's son-in-law, both men had appended their signatures to the protocol of adherence to the Tripartite Pact.

Abruptly, still without deigning to acknowledge the diplomats, Cvetković returned to his compartment. Rašić followed behind. There he found his old chief, Cincar-Marković, fully as despondent as the Premier. For some time, the two men sat slumped at the window table, silent, apathetic. Still unregarded, the three Axis ministers waited patiently outside the Premier's saloon, ready to formally welcome the newest recruit to Adolf Hitler's sphere of influence.

"Please," Rašić urged, "at least when the train starts, look out of the window and wave your hand."

Cincar-Marković was bitter. "I would as soon wave my foot at them as my hand."

Sadly, Rašić returned to the platform: for all the good it had achieved, this meeting, scheduled for security reasons in the freight yard rather than the main railway station, might never have taken place. Then the train jerked forward, speeding for Belgrade across the rain-drenched Pannonian plain.

The signing of the Pact had been inevitable for weeks – ever since Prince Paul had returned on 5 March from a meeting with Hitler at the Berghof. All through the five-hour talk the Führer had stressed one point repeately: he could not protect Yugoslavia from a possible Italian invasion unless they signed the Pact. But Paul had jibbed; his people would never accept clauses permitting the Axis to use their territory to wage war. Hitler saw this as a trifle. He would not request passage for German troops through Yugoslavia.

On 6 March, Paul called a nine-man crown council meeting at the White Palace, in Dedinje, on the outskirts of Belgrade. But in truth there was little to discuss. The Allies had been forthcoming with nothing but calls to resist. The Yugoslav Army could hold out for little more than six weeks; after this food and ammunition would be exhausted. For two years Germany had controlled Czechoslovakia's Skoda Works, once Yugoslavia's prime source of arms.

When one man insisted that Yugoslavia should enter the war, "if only symbolically", the Minister of War, General Petar Pešić scoffed: "I'm an old soldier, but I've never heard of a symbolic war. What is it?"

Prince Paul was now a man tugged by many winds. A former graduate of Christ Church, Oxford, who held the Order of the Garter, Britain's oldest order of knighthood, he felt an instinctive kinship with the Allies; his wife, Princess Olga, was a member of the Greek Royal

32

family, while his sister-in-law was the Duchess of Kent. "But," he told the Vice-Premier, Vladko Maček, "I cannot lead (our people) to slaughter, and that is what we must expect if we precipitate a war with Germany."

On 20 March, when the full cabinet convened, only three out of seventeen ministers declared against the Pact. Rumours of a coup to be carried out by the Air Force commander, the aged General Dušan Simović, were dismissed out of hand; who had ever heard of a *coup d'état* being broadcast in advance? Ahead, for Cvetković and his Foreign Minister, lay only their humiliating 25 March rendezvous in Vienna. "Bad news from Juggery," commented Hugh Dalton ruefully.

"This," the Yugoslav Minister in London, Ivan Subotić, told the unamused R. A. Butler of the Foreign Office, 'rather archly', "can be compared to the Munich period of your policy."

That night, an almost unearthly silence descended on Belgrade. In the city's *kafanas*, the coffee houses, where Serbian patriots foregathered, men and women wept quietly and unashamedly at the shame that had enveloped their country.

One woman was not weeping; instead she was suffused by a quiet sense of triumph. Two days earlier, on 23 March, Ruth Mitchell, the newly-enrolled American *Četnik*, had watched hordes of teenage school-children stampeding through the streets, pressing leaflets on bystanders, as they chorused, "*Bolje rat, nego Pakt* – Better war than the Pact." Where children led, Ruth believed, adults would follow.

At 8 p.m. on 25 March, Ruth was dining with a group of British foreign correspondents at Belgrade's Hotel Bristol. All through the evening, knowing from her *Četnik* contacts that trouble was in the making, she had the curious feeling of "watching a play . . . calmly, politely eating while world-shattering events were brewing."

At 10 p.m., well aware that no one would believe her, Ruth yielded to temptation. "Let me tell you something," she said gently. "Within twenty-nine hours Prince Paul, Cvetković, Cincar-Marković and the whole Cabinet will be either prisoners or dead."

"They'll have to take peace even at the German price," one newsman countered. "They have no choice."

Ruth Mitchell leaned forward. "Telegraph your paper," she said, "that the Serbian peasants don't want peace at any price the Germans could ever offer. Tell England that the Serbs choose war."

The picture was to remain in her mind for years: the polite indulgent smiles of the men in the know, but still chivalrously content to humour the dinner-table caprices of a charming woman.

*

33

The first intimation of the coup came as casually as an invitation to take pot luck. On the afternoon of 26 March, Brigadier-General Bora Mirković, of the Yugoslav Air Force, paid a visit to the Zemun Airport headquarters of his Commander-in-Chief, General Dušan Simović. Mirković found that the old General was at home enjoying a siesta, though Mrs Simović, who answered his telephone call, at once volunteered to waken her husband. Mirković demurred: he had nothing urgent to say. But when the General did awake, would he drop by his own office?

Simović, a slim grey-haired man, took his time; it was 5 p.m. before he strolled in. Mirković's abrupt greeting rocked him on his heels: "I have decided to remove the traitors tonight."

Simović begged for a postponement – but in vain. As the field organiser of the coup, in which Simović was little more than a figurehead, Mirković was adamant that the hour had come. The entire Air Force, totally loyal to King Peter, already held the trump card of Zemun Airport. And other conspirators were spoiling for action: a division of the Royal Guards, including an infantry regiment, two cavalry regiments, and an artillery regiment, plus a battalion of tanks, a company of engineers, and other miscellaneous groups.

That night the streets of Belgrade were almost empty, silent and deserted under the lamplight. Only at midnight, was a steady rumbling heard along all the streets radiating off Kralja Alexandra, the city's main boulevard; grey-green Army tanks were moving into blockade positions, bulking squarely across the tram tracks, ugly 47-mm cannons restlessly traversing the darkness. On the Kralja Milana, an anti-aircraft gun, its muzzle lowered, commanded the whole street, even beyond the White Palace, to the Terazia, Belgrade's main square. Flitting shapes in Air Force blue advanced stealthily through the shadows.

At 2 a.m., a black Cadillac limousine screeched to a halt outside the home of Premier Dragiša Cvetković on fashionable Dedinje Hill. An Air Force officer, descending with a patrol of soldiers, found a guard barring his way: "The Premier cannot be disturbed."

The officer's drawn revolver was a proof of his earnest: "Nevertheless, disturb him!"

At dawn on 27 March – Belgrade – and all Yugoslavia – awoke to a sense of honour redeemed. Aboard the tramcars on Kralja Milana, early-rising commuters thronged the windows staring wide-eyed at the tanks and guns now looming everywhere. American flags and Union Jacks fluttered triumphantly from the balconies and shop fronts. On the broad boulevard of Mihilova, a voice took up the stirring national anthem, *Oi Serbia!* and thousands of lungs filled with air and took up the chant. Other voices were raised in counterpoint: *Zivala Engleska* (Long Live England) and *Petra Drugy* (Peter Our Friend).

34

In his bedroom in the White Palace, the 17-year-old King – whom the British Minister, Ronald Campbell, deemed "a pleasant boy, still rather young for his age, and immensely keen on anything mechanical" – was as much in the dark as any of his subjects. His first knowledge of the *coup* had come at 6 a.m., when his valet had shaken him violently awake to announce an urgent visit from the Commander of the Belgrade Garrison, General Kosić. Only then did the young King learn that troops had taken over General Staff Headquarters, the Ministry of War, and the General Post Office, and that all telephone cables had been cut.

At 9 a.m., as he switched on his radio, the King's confusion multiplied; what sounded like his own voice was announcing to the people that he had taken the royal power into his own hands, Prince Paul having resigned, and charged General Simović with the formation of a government.

Although these events came to pass before the day was out, the conspirators, unable to gain access to the Palace, had taken the bizarre step of calling on a young officer to impersonate his own monarch.

For thousands of citizens, the sound of freedom was the sound of breaking glass. The plate-glass windows of the German Travel Agency, with its big cotton swastikas mounted on flagpoles, were suddenly too tempting a target; rocks flew, and the wide windows collapsed in a pile of glittering shards. Across the street, the tramway workers were burning Hitler in effigy, and the innocent suffered along with the guilty. The Swedish envoy, mistaken for a German, was dragged from his car and beaten senseless.

Now the crowd advancing on the Terazia had become a broad human river, swelling to 40,000 strong, and the massed voices acquired a conscious powerful rhythm, like a Hawaiian war chant:

Bolje rat, nego Pakt!
Petra Drugy! Petra Drugy!
Bolje rat, nego Pakt!
Petra Drugy! Petra Drugy!

Inevitably that afternoon Ruth Mitchell was marching too – not with the crowds but with a 2,000-strong *Četnik* column, heading for the residence of Patriarch Gavrilo, of the Serb Orthodox Church. Standing under a heavy Byzantine arch, the old priest raised his hand in blessing, then suddenly, to Ruth's surprise, she was surrounded by other women from the column, hugging and kissing her, shedding their iron self-control to weep tears of joy that an American was marching with them. "England and America will stand by Serbia," Ruth promised them gravely, and years afterward she was to recall with bitterness, "My God, I still believed it. I believed I spoke the truth."

Common to all the crowd was the belief expressed by one Serbian officer: "Tomorrow we shall gladly die for having lived yesterday."

In London, the jubilation was intense, for the newly-created Special Operations Executive, administered by Hugh Dalton's Ministry of Economic Warfare, had for months been working towards this end, against stubborn Foreign Office opposition, funding the Serb Peasant's Party and other opposition groups to the tune of £5,000 a month – cash which was made available to them by the Legation's Air Attachés, Group Captain Hugh MacDonald and Wing Commander Tom Mapplebeck.

Dalton's one fear was that now the crunch had come the Serbs and Croats, notoriously hostile, would fall upon one another in preference to the Germans.

"Prince Paul would be so vexed if he ever found out," the Foreign Office had argued, but Dalton embodied the then fashionable British view, "Our friend has been a complete skunk. He has deceived our diplomats, as such gentlemanly skunks always do." Churchill was in complete accord. "Prince Palsy", as the Premier dubbed him, was "fit only for a life of luxurious seclusion." When Paul abdicated in favour of his nephew at 11.50 p.m. that day, departing with his wife for Greece, Churchill's conviction was only strengthened.

At the Foreign Office, the Yugoslav Minister Ivan Subotić, once more called on R. A. Butler to recall that a pledge had been kept; as First Lord of the Admiralty, Churchill had once expressed the hope that Yugoslavia would never forget her traditions. Now, his voice shaken by emotion, Subotić told Butler: *"Yugoslavie n'a pas démentie ses traditions."*

But in Berlin the storm cones were already hoisted. Hastening to the Reich Chancellery in response to an urgent summons at 11.55 a.m. on 27 March, *Generalfeldmarschall* Wilhelm Keitel, Chief of the Armed Forces, and *General Der Artillerie* Alfred Jodl, Chief of the Operations Staff, at first found the Führer making no sense. Shaking with rage, brandishing a telegram from Belgrade, his words were an incoherent torrent. He had no intention of standing for it. Now he would smash them once for all. It was time people got to know him better. He would clean up the Balkans "good and proper".

Within the hour, the storm had abated. To subdue Yugoslavia would mean a re-allocation of troops previously slated for Russia – 27 divisions in all, seven of them armoured – to strike simultaneously from Austria, Hungary, Rumania and Bulgaria under *Feldmarschall* Siegmund List, a tough brooding Swabian who had commanded the victorious Twelfth Army in the French campaign.

At 1 a.m., *Feldmarschall* von Brauchitsh and *Generaloberst* Halder arrived in the conference room, to be joined by Joachim von Ribbentrop. On fire with excitement, Hitler led them to the map table. His greeting was a challenge: "I have decided to destroy Yugoslavia. How much military force do you need? How much time?"

At Washington's old Willard Hotel, on Fourteenth and E Streets, where John Wilkes Booth had lodged on the day he shot Abraham Lincoln, the mood was festive. At 7 p.m. on Saturday, 5 April, the semi-annual white-tie dinner of the Gridiron Club had got under way in the long ballroom; all Washington officialdom, including the President, had gathered for a merry evening of speeches and lampoons.

The first news of import came when the hour was late. At the ballroom door, a *New York Times* office-boy handed a torn-off news-ticker scrap to a Secret Service guard, who passed it on to the *Times*'s bureau chief, Arthur Krock. Krock, in turn, handed it to Cordell Hull. Adjusting his pince-nez, the Secretary of State read impassively that Russia and Yugoslavia had signed a non-agression pact.

The dinner went on. Roosevelt made a fifteen-minute off-the-record speech. As he spoke another message arrived: when Roosevelt sat down, Krock passed it over. Soon after the President departed for the White House.

The time was a little past midnight on Palm Sunday, 6 April. A young moon had gone down, and Hitler had invaded Greece and Yugoslavia.

Five thousand miles away, the white city of Belgrade slept peacefully under the stars. Incredibly, there was no anticipation that Yugoslavia was doomed; with strange naiveté, General Simović was hoping for the best of both worlds. His new government wanted "to avoid discussion" of the Tripartite Pact; they would not denounce it, nor would they ratify it, for they did not wish to provoke Axis forces. The thought that Hitler was bent on revenge never once occurred to them.

A precise warning from the Yugoslav Military Attaché in Berlin, Colonel Vladmir Vauhnik, that an attack was imminent went unregarded. Was not 6 April a Sunday, the day that Simović had selected to marry off his daughter?

Ruth Mitchell's first intimation came around 7 a.m. In the sitting room of her house on Slavija Hill, Michael, her Cossack houseman, had just laid her breakfast tray, and Ruth was fiddling with the knob of her short-wave radio. Suddenly the raucous voice of Joachim von Ribbentrop seemed to fill the room with hate: "*Die bomben fallen und jetzt in diesem Augenblick steht schon ganz Belgrad in Flammen.*" (The bombs fall and already now this instant all Belgrade is in flames.)

The usual lies, thought Ruth contemptuously. Although she listened intently, a Sunday silence enveloped the streets, broken only by the soft jingle of milk carts, the shuffle of peasant feet.

The lull was illusory. From his bedroom balcony in the Hotel Srpski Kralj, foreign correspondent Ray Brock, of the *New York Times*, was conscious that a mounting uneven drone had filled the air. Seconds earlier he had checked his watch: 7.06 a.m. Now his breakfast coffee forgotten, Brock focused his binoculars and suddenly in the glinting sunlight, he saw them: sixty bombers, Heinkels, Dorniers and Stuka JU87s, sliding above the naked city. As he watched, thirty Stukas peeled from the formation, falling like falcons towards Zemun Airport. Then the bombs struck home.

A whistling ear-splitting inferno engulfed the streets of Belgrade. More than 1500 tons of bombs rained down on the city. With "a crack like a 100-yard whip", whole buildings disintegrated. Blinding flashes of flame ripped outwards, blotting out the streets in black and billowing smoke. Sticks of incendiaries clattered like tin trays, to burn with a blue-white light along the tram trucks. A torrent of bricks, glittering glass, and twisted sheet metal piled head-high along the pavements, coated with molten tar; on the Terazia, teak paving blocks torn loose by the bombs loomed like a surreal mountain.

All sound was mingled into an indescribable devil's chorus: the scream of diving Stukas, the slow, majestic cadence of church bells, the wailing of ambulance sirens, the insistent honking of car horns. Thick walls were toppling, and what seemed like waggonloads of tiles, but in the lobby of the Srpski Kralj nobody screamed and nobody spoke. On Slavija Hill, Ruth Mitchell was conscious of a terrifying wind that "drove like something solid through the house", then "a weird smooth sound like the tearing of heavy silk" as the neighbouring houses collapsed.

All over the city there were scenes of apocalyptic horror. Thus one man would recall a grocer's delivery van, impressed as an ambulance, piled high with bodies, among them a young girl wearing one silver slipper on her right foot. Her left leg had vanished altogether – "just like a fox would chew the leg of a bird".

Bombs had hit the zoo and wild animals stampeded panic-stricken through the burning streets; a polar bear, moaning piteously, hobbled towards the Sava River. Other bombs had struck the Terazia; in its centre yawned a crater thirty feet across, strewn with 300 torn and mutilated bodies. And no man who saw it ever forgot the spectacle of the Kralja Milana, the main shopping centre. As a landmine struck, more than 100 merchants had been raising their shop shutters; now outside almost every shop, as if arranged by a macabre stage director, a body lay inertly, face down in the rubble.

The horrors were not fleeting. Although the first raid lasted barely an hour, a second attack, more punitive still, began at 11 a.m. For almost seventy-two hours, waves of bombers moved back and forth across the city, like tractors ploughing a field, until 10,000 buildings had toppled and 17,000 civilians lay dead among their ruins.

Ruth Mitchell did not linger as a witness. Even as the first bombs fell she was struggling into her uniform: blue serge tunic with skull-and-crossbones insignia, a dagger and loaded automatic, black socks embroidered with roses. Soon after 11 a.m., in any case, she was forced to abandon her house forever; the building next door was in imminent danger of collapse. Already she had taken the wise precaution of sending Michael, her houseman, on ahead, with his wife, Sultana, to their little cottage on the outskirts of the city. This would be the first staging-post on her journey south.

By now, Ruth knew her instructions almost by heart. Somehow, by bus, by refugee train, even on foot, she must reach Montenegro, the smallest of Yugoslavia's constituted republics bounded by Albania and the Adriatic Sea. It would be a 160-mile journey, but all *Četnik* calculations were based on the belief that Podgoritsa airfield, on the Albanian border, would be the last stronghold to fall.

Here Ruth was to attach herself to the local *Četnik* formation, prepared for one of two roles. If the British landed in force on the Grecian coast and pushed north for Macedonia, Ruth was to act as liaison officer between the *Četniks* and the advancing British.

If they did not land, the alternative was bleaker: to discard her uniform and then, under the shield of an American passport, to begin a new life as a spy.

*

The British would not be advancing. Barely six days after Ruth Mitchell began her southern journey, two naval officers in impeccable white met over mid-morning sherry in an office on the dockside at Alexandria, overlooking the quarterdeck of the flagship H.M.S. *Warspite*. Rear-Admiral Harold Baillie-Grohman, Flag Officer Attached Middle East, had been summoned in a hurry from Cairo by the Commander-in-Chief of the Mediterranean Fleet, the pugnacious sandy-haired Admiral Sir Andrew Browne Cunningham.

The two men were old friends, and Cunningham lost no time in coming to the point. A signal from Rear-Admiral Charles Turle, the British Naval Attaché in Athens, gave only cause for alarm; the situation in Greece was deteriorating rapidly. Baillie-Grohman was to fly to Athens with all possible speed to sum up the situation for himself.

Cunningham could offer only one crumb of comfort: if an evacuation took place, offshore operations were unlikely to be hampered by the Italian Fleet. In a bloody three-minute battle on the night of 28 March, Cunningham had decisively savaged the Italians off the Mediterranean cape of Matapan – damaging their flagship, the 35,000 ton *Vittorio Veneto*, sinking three cruisers and four destroyers. From that day on, the Italian Navy would play no further decisive role in safeguarding Rommel's supply lines. For a moment Baillie-Groham stared out across the sunlit harbour, where a fresh nor'easter bellied the sails of the *feluccas*, throwing a fine spray over the bows of picket-boats plying between ships and shore.

How long, he wondered, could the British hold out?

Cunningham, as always, was succinct: "Turle thinks we shall probably have to pull out within six weeks."

*

Adolf Hitler was angry, and with reason. The Yugoslav coup, coming as unexpectedly as a thunderclap, had seen his priorities go awry. On the morning of 27 March, the Führer had been preparing to grapple with an enigma that was also exercising diplomatic minds in Whitehall and Washington: the precise intentions of Japan in 1941.

On 26 March, the Japanese Foreign Minister, Yosuke Matsuoka, had arrived at Berlin's Anhalter Bahnhof to a red-carpet reception more suited to a film-star; as he descended shyly from the train, advancing with solemn timidity on Von Ribbentrop, interpreter Paul Schmidt thought compassionately of "a child who has lost his parents at a fair".

The appearance was deceptive. Although the pipe-smoking Matsuoka, with his dapper black moustache and gold-rimmed spectacles, radiated an air of gentle bonhomie – "an English country gentleman painted yellow", one news agency summed him up – he was a formidable in-fighter for Japanese interests. In 1933, he had been the first delegate to quit the League of Nations following Japan's invasion of Manchuria – a precedent later followed by Hitler and Mussolini. Now he saw the European war as a prime opportunity for Japan to pursue expansionist policies in South-East Asia and the Pacific. Not for nothing did one wall of his Tokyo home bear the motto: "When the west wind blows, fallen leaves are piled up in the east."

Moreover, Matsuoka had journeyed by way of Moscow, for three days of talks with Josef Stalin and Foreign Secretary Vyacheslav Molotov, and was slated to return for further talks – while in Washington, D.C., a new Japanese ambassador, the one-eyed Admiral Kichisaburo Nomura, a six-footer turning the scales at 200 pounds, had arrived with five spare glass-eyes for talks with Cordell Hull.

Hitler was uneasy. What about the Tripartite Pact, whereby Japan had allied herself with the Axis as far back as September, 1940? Why had Matsuoka found it necessary to visit Stalin – and was Nomura giving the Americans verbal guarantees?

From January onwards, Ribbentrop had been pestering the head of his Political Department, Ernst Woermann, for an analysis of the "true intentions" of the enigmatic Matsuoka. A month later he was urging the new ambassador, General Hiroshi Oshima, to attack the British naval base at Singapore – although the Philippines, which enjoyed common-wealth status under the United States, should be left alone. To attack them might be the very provocation Roosevelt sought.

Preoccupied with the destruction of Yugoslavia, only on the afternoon of 27 March could Hitler turn his attention to Japan. No sooner was Matsuoka seated than the Führer launched into a long diatribe on German invincibility like a boy boasting of his toy soldiers; in eighteen months he had crushed 60 Polish divisions, 6 Norwegian, 18 Dutch, 22 Belgian and 138 French.

For once the garrulous Matsuoka, known to his friends as "Mr 50,000 Words", had met his match. As Hitler ranted on, urging the importance of a Japanese attack in the Far East, the Foreign Minister sat speechless.

His first response struck Hitler like a bodyblow: "I can give no firm promise on behalf of Japan at this moment."

With scant conviction, he sought to justify himself. Japan was cor-rupted by weakling intellectuals, both in court circles and commercial life, all people who contrived to hamstring Matsuoka – "the sort of person who would like to capture the tiger cub but was not prepared to go into the den and take it away from its mother".

For the rest of his visit, Matsuoka remained politely non-committal. All Hitler's attempts to wrench the Tripartite Pact into an offensive against the British met with failure, for Japan had signed the Pact pri-marily as an act of retaliation against the United States; in 1940, angry that Japan's war with China still dragged on, Congress had ended trade agreements that went as far back as 1911. At times the Foreign Minister fell back on a scapegoat. Nodding towards Colonel Yatsugi Nagai, who was holding a watching brief for the Japanese Army, Matsuoka replied: "You'll have to ask him."

Ribbentrop's parting shot was patronising to a degree. After suggest-ing that Matsuoka send for maps of Singapore, he added pompously: "The Führer, who must certainly be considered the greatest expert of modern times on military matters could advise Japan as to the best methods for the attack on Singapore." But Matsuoka only smiled politely.

To Mussolini, Hitler later confided that Matsuoka had combined "the hypocrisy of an American Bible missionary with the craftiness of a Japanese Asiatic". It was a verdict that Cordell Hull, with his habitual log-cabin language, had long ago endorsed. "Matsuoka," snorted the Secretary of State, was "as crooked as a basket of fish-hooks."

*

According to perspective, the threat posed by Japan loomed large or small, as in a fairground's distorting mirror.

41

In London, a momentary alarm had flared briefly on 5 February: secret intelligence alerted the Foreign Office that "Japan had warned her Embassy staff . . . to reduce their contacts with the British authorities to a minimum, and to be prepared to leave the country at short notice." Promptly, Eden had summoned the Ambassador, Mamoru Shigemitsu, for "a full and outspoken discussion"; if Japan was planning aggression in the Far East, to synchronise with a German offensive, Britain would react with vigour.

Although Australia's Robert Menzies warned the Foreign Office: "One thing the Jap won't do is lose face. He'd rather fight," his caution fell on deaf ears – "what irresponsible rubbish these Antipodeans talk!' scoffed Sir Alexander Cadogan. But by mid-February, Churchill, a committed colonialist who saw the Japanese as an inferior race, was reassuring Roosevelt: "I am not myself convinced that this not a war of nerves." Although some believed that Japan was ready to wage war on Britain and the United States, "personally, I think the odds are definitely against that."

From Washington, the view was more ominous. Since her 1937 invasion of China, Japan and the United States had been embarked on a collision course; America had for years sustained Generalissimo Chiang Kai-shek's Chinese Nationalist regime in the profound belief that China was only the first stage in a Japanese drive to over-run all South-East Asia and the Pacific.

This basic concept lay behind Hull's weekly talks with Admiral Nomura, talks which were kept strictly secret from the British. What one Washington newspaper column was to term "a long-range exercise in diplomatic futility" was to drag on over nine months, always in the Secretary's private apartment at the Carlton Hotel, later at the Wardman Park, often from 8.30 p.m. to 10 p.m., while the long-suffering Frances Hull brewed endless pots of China tea.

"There is plenty of room in the Pacific for everybody," Roosevelt had emphasised at his first meeting with Nomura on 14 February, and this was the point on which Hull laid stress, but often he wondered how much the Admiral took in. Partially deaf, with uncertain English, he was given to sudden disconcerting guffaws out of context.

Even so, Hull, who saw diplomacy as preaching morality rather than negotiation, persevered. On 9 April, he laid down four basic if long-winded principles for transmission to Tokyo: respect for the territorial integrity and sovereignty of each and all nations, support of the principle of non-interference in the internal affairs of other countries, support of the principle of equality, including equality of commercial opportunity, non-disturbance of the status quo in the Pacific.

Meanwhile, Japan kept the world guessing. Four days later, a bombshell came from Moscow: on Easter Sunday, 13 April, Matsuoka, in a creditable impersonation of Bunyan's Mr Facing-Both-Ways, had signed

42

a five-year neutrality pact with the Soviet Union. Stranger still, Josef Stalin, known widely as a recluse, arrived unescorted at the Moscow Station to bid the Foreign Minister farewell. Clad in a khaki képi and greatcoat over black boots, he bear-hugged Matsuoka three times, promising "We shall remain friends."

Then, as if amity was the keynote of this day, the dictator's glance lighted on the German military attaché, Colonel Hans Krebs. His head cocked, black eyes twinkling from a sallow face, Stalin enquired sharply, "German? German?" When Krebs assented, Stalin pumped his hand, assuring him, "We, too, shall remain friends – whatever happens."

In his fine walled villa, "The Eagle's Nest", at Hoanshan, across the Yangtse from Chungking, General Chiang Kai-shek heard of the pact with horror: would Russia now abandon the aid that they afforded him in turn for his tacit recognition of the 400,000-strong Eighth Route Army of Communists under General Chu Teh? But the word from Moscow was reassuring; if Chiang continued to resist the invaders, Soviet aid would still flow unchecked. Pact or no, Stalin would not risk a Japanese infiltration of Siberia.

But in Washington, too, the pact had struck a jarring note – and Chiang was swift to capitalise on the discord. More than once, in the past, a covert threat that he might be forced to come to terms with Japan had loosened American purse-strings. For Roosevelt, who looked to a post-war Asia dominated by a China inspired by the Four Freedoms, with America shaping the future in the Pacific, no prospect could be more alarming.

As early as February, he had sent Dr Lauchlin Currie, an ambitious economist, on a mission to patch up Chiang's fissure with the Communists, and Currie was swift to recommend a back-up team of American advisers who would iron out China's corrupt bureaucracy and implement liberal reforms. In truth, Currie had missed the point; while the Communists leaned on peasant support, the Nationalist regime depended largely on corrupt landlords. What Chiang wanted was not reforms but guns, planes and money.

Such was Roosevelt's determination to thwart Japan that these, too, would be forthcoming. In mid-April, the President signed a covert executive order authorising American airmen to resign from their services to form a volunteer group in China: the inception of the famous "Flying Tigers" under Colonel Claire Chennault, Chiang's American air adviser. China too, had qualified for Lend-Lease, and there was no lack of Washington wheeler-dealers on Chiang's payroll to lobby on his behalf. Among them were his brother-in-law, T. V. Soong, abetted by so many relatives that Treasury officials coined an acid jingle, "Sing a Song of Six Soongs", as well as Currie himself and former White House aide Thomas Corcoran, who had allegedly netted a down payment of $30,000.

Treasury Secretary Henry Morgenthau always recalled with disgust a luncheon with Roosevelt at about this time. Until now, Morgenthau had always insisted that aid be given in small, regulated amounts, to discourage currency speculation; if Chungking did not like it, they could "go jump in the Yangtse". But on this day Roosevelt had insisted: "We have to do something for the Chinese in order to save their face. I want you to make that $50 million loan right away."*

Morgenthau was aghast. "Well, Mr President, that is just like throwing it away."

Roosevelt was unyielding: "I know, but it is a question of face-saving." Reluctantly, Morgenthau gave in: the China lobbyists had beaten him to the draw.

The metaphor-of-the-month, embodying all Japan's fear of encirclement, was coined in Tokyo by an Army spokesman, Major Kunio Akiyama. "Japan," he proclaimed, "has the heart of a dove of peace, but a snake – the United States and Great Britain – has placed its egg in the dove's nest."

Urged to clarify, Akiyama was obliging: he had in mind the fortification of Singapore, the arrival of Australian troops in Malaya, the impending fortification of the Pacific islands of Samoa and Guam.

"What would hatch from the egg?" a correspondent asked curiously.

"God knows," the Major replied, "but the dove will protest vigorously."

*

In one war zone, the Germans faced a sudden setback. By mid-April, the fortress of Tobruk had become a thorn in Rommel's flesh, an obsession that was to dog him for seven months. The potential conqueror of Egypt and Suez stood halted on the threshhold of triumph by an impudent garrison. In time, looming disproportionately larger, the obsession would become fatal. Now he was in the front line day and night, flat on his belly, his mouth tight-lipped, cap perched on the back of his head as he studied the Australian lines through Zeiss binoculars: dug-outs like enormous yellow ant-hills festooned with barbed wire, silent as tombs under the burning sun.

To the 4th's Divisional Commander, *Generalmajor* Johannes Streich, Rommel insisted: "We must attack Tobruk with everything we have – before Tommy has time to dig in." So confident was he of success, he assured *Oberst* Herbert Olbrich of the 5th Armoured Regiment, "The enemy will retire immediately when your Panzers approach." Heartened by Rommel's belief in a speedy victory, one battalion even tagged its administration truck on to the rear of the assault column.

* The loan had been requested by Chiang on 17 April.

Nor did this confidence seem misplaced. At 5.20 a.m. on Easter Sunday, 14 April – an attack delayed by eight hours because the promised Italian guides failed to show up – the first wave of Streich's tanks bulled unmolested through a gap blasted in the wire. As Rommel had predicted, the Australians manning the perimeter posts made no attempt to engage them – but as the German infantry followed up, a murderous fire hit them from the rear and from this moment on men began to die. Oblivious to this, Streich's Panzers ground on. Soon they were two miles inside the perimeter – moving deeper by the minute into a deadly and elaborate trap.

Suddenly, a corridor of fire engulged the Panzers. Mobile anti-tank guns, rushed from nearby sectors and mounted on 1½ ton trucks by gunners of the Royal Horse Artillery, were firing from both flanks at a point-blank range of 600 yards. The massive turret of one 22-ton Mark IV tank was torn clean from its mountings. *Oberstleutnant* Gustav Ponath, commanding the 8th Machine Gun Battalion, who had driven brashly through the wire in his staff car, was blown to pieces by an anti-tank shell. In the terrible confusion that saw the loss of 17 tanks – at least one immobilised by an Australian ramming a crowbar into the tread sprocket – Streich's men fell back. "It was a witch's cauldron," one tank commander wrote later. "We were lucky to escape alive."

In the command truck that was his Advance Headquarters, Rommel was beside himself. "Your Panzers did not give of their best and left the infantry in the lurch," he blazed at Streich. Vainly Streich defended himself: his tanks would have reached their objectives, despite the searing fire, but deep well-camouflaged tank traps had checked them. Impatiently Rommel brushed his excuses aside. Both Streich and Olbrich, he charged, had "lacked resolution".

The entire course of the desert war was now to hinge on the struggle for Tobruk, for the fortress, Rommel well knew, was the one remaining bridgehead that could repel a mass advance on Egypt. Still he told *Generalmajor* Kirchheim, his liaison officer with the Italian Brescia Division, resolutely: "We'll be in Tobruk the day after tomorrow – and then our next goal is the Suez Canal."

But Rommel was tempting the fates. The 220 square miles that was Fortress Tobruk was now a hive of grim activity garrisoned by 23,000 determined men – Anzacs, Britons, Indians, even a Jewish transport unit with the Star of David on their trucks – commanded by an Australian fully as tenacious as Rommel himself.

Known to his troops as "Ming the Merciless", after the villain of the *Flash Gordon* comic strip, dark diminutive Major-General Leslie Morshead, 51, had been pictured by a World War One historian as "the nearest approach to a martinet among all the young Australian colonels". A onetime schoolmaster, the prickly Morshead's aim was nothing less than to convert Tobruk into a near-impregnable fortress. "There'll be no Dunkirk here," he told his brigadiers curtly. "If we have to get out we shall fight our way out. There is to be no surrender and no retreat."

Within days, the clog-shaped port, surrounded by high artillery look-out posts, was divided, like Caesar's Gaul, into three parts: the harbour zone, the inner and outer defence lines. Carved into 16 sectors – 140 strongpoints in all – the outer perimeter defences centred on the Red Line, a series of concrete dug-outs holding up to 15 men apiece. Two miles inland from the Red Line lay the Blue Line, a continuous mine-field so thickly sown that the sappers themselves lost track of them, zigzagged with barbed wire and strongpoints sited 500 yards apart. By Morshead's command, no man was excused strong-point duty unless too sick to fight.

And Morshead went further. Nothing so enraged him as the cock-a-hoop headline in one Australian daily: "Tobruk Can Take It". "We're not here to take it," he stormed. "We're here to give it." His accent was on the defensive-offensive: 20-man patrols, armed with bayonets and hand grenades, shod with sandals fashioned from old motor tyres, who nightly launched surprise attacks on the enemy lines. Soon even Rommel was aware of their deadly efficacy: approaching one Italian sector at dawn he stopped short in amazement at the sight of hundreds of discarded sun helmets decorated with the cock's feather plumes of the Bersaglieri Rifle Regiment. An entire battalion had been seized overnight. Not all enjoyed P.O.W. status. One patrol of Rajputs, warrior-caste Hindus from Jodhpur, was rebuked for over-estimating their enemy dead. Nights later they returned with two small sacks – filled with 16 right ears and 16 left ears, still oozing blood.

For 242 days and nights, the eyes of the world were focused on the men whom the Axis propagandists had dubbed "The Rats of Tobruk". More than 50,000 letters from families, even unknown admirers, poured into the port's Post Office each week. Canny Army technicians augmented their pay packets churning out Tobruk souvenirs made from the grenades and shell-cases on the workshops' lathes. In the Red and Blue Lines, one scene was common to every strongpoint; men lying doggo for 13 daylight hours on end under corrugated-iron lean-tos, fighting boredom, weak from the sun, plagued by lice and sand flies and dysentery. To stir above ground by day was to court a sniper's bullet, and mealtimes were thus turned upside down. Men breakfasted at 9.30 p.m., took a hot lunch at midnight and dined before dawn.

Camouflage became the daily key to life or death. Helmets, even windshields, were daubed with anti-glare paint: the tracks of walking men, as visible from the air as chalk lines on a blackboard, were smoothed clear with camel thorn switches. Yet normal life of a sort went on among the dug-outs. Six mimeographed newspapers flourished, from "Tobruk Truth" to "Mud and Blood", the Catholic Church held services daily, and every few weeks Morshead rotated men from the defence lines to the coastal area, to enjoy cricket matches, sea bathing and amateur talent nights.

Motionless in their dug-outs, men dreamed impossible dreams. Imaginary pails of iced beer replaced the vile brackish water, and corned beef and tinned herring vanished before T-bone steaks. Pets, if they chanced upon them, were cherished like pedigree prize-winners. One Anzac dug-out acquired Myrtle, a tame magpie. A British flak battery adopted Larry the Lamb, an ancient sheep who relished corned beef and posted a sentry each night to guard him from would-be butchers.

In truth, Tobruk was never completely blockaded, since the harbour afforded a seaward access to Alexandria, 394 miles to the east. But air cover was almost non-existent, for Tobruk lay beyond the range of Egypt-based fighters and the harbour was littered with rusting wrecks, bulging from the water like dying sea-monsters, the harvest of 437 high-level Stuka raids. It was with good reason that the W.D.L.F. (Western Desert Lighter Flotilla), who brought supplies on "The Spud Run" from an Alexandria jetty called "The Condemned Cell" was rechristened "We Die Like Flies".

On the perimeter, a consciousness of hardships shared bred a wry camaraderie between besiegers and besieged. Both sides saw as fitting a war that spared women and children and cities, and both endured the same desert privations – water which "looked like coffee and tasted like sulphur", as one of Rommel's officers noted, which rusted a blade after three shaves, and canned meat the Italians called "potted old man". There were many fleeting relaxations of tension. Private Noel Sankey, in one dug-out always recalled how the Germans listened in attentive silence to his rendering of "Silent Night, Holy Night", then responded with "*Horst Wessel Lied*". Sergeant Walter Tuit, an Anzac stretcher-bearer, seeking casualties under a Red Cross flag in no-man's-land, was impressed when a lieutenant gave him a *Reichswehr* not the Hitler-salute, and another brought him fresh lemon squash. And each night, prompt on 9.57 p.m., Britons no less than Germans tuned into Radio Belgrade, to hear Lale Andersen sing the sad and sleepy tune that was to become the anthem of all the desert warriors:

> Underneath the lantern
> By the barrack gate
> Darling, I remember
> The way you used to wait.
>
> 'Twas there that you whispered tenderly
> That you loved me, you'd always be
> My Lili of the lamplight
> My own Lili Marlene . . .

47

3

"Do Not Succumb to Provocation"

15 April–18 May, 1941

EVERYONE WAS AGREED on one thing: whatever the reverses, Winston Churchill remained in good heart. As early as the end of March, he had told the Polish Ambassador, Count Edward Raczynski: "There might have been moments when I doubted our victory; there was never a moment when I expected our defeat." Midway through April, he expressed similar confidence to the Swedish Ambassador, Bjorn Prytz. He was, the Premier said, "an optimistic frog".

Seeing Prytz' bewilderment, Churchill expounded a parable: two frogs entered a dairy window to taste the milk. But both miscalculated; leaping straight into a bowl, they found the sides too high and slippery to escape. The pessimistic frog, losing heart, at once threw up its fore limbs and sank to the bottom. But the optimistic frog, hoping somehow to survive, floundered on all night, beating at the milk, and by morning was floating safely on a thick slab of butter.

"Now," Churchill summed up to the delighted Prytz, "I am an optimistic frog, too."

It was a heartening tale – but Churchill and his people had need for optimism. News came daily from the Balkan fronts, and all of it was bad. Yugoslavia was falling fast. For long hard months, the British had nursed their hopes – making much of the repulse of the Luftwaffe, the Greeks' brave stand, triumphs in Libya – and watched them grow. Now the gains of months were incredibly threatened.

As always, the key to Hitler's *blitzkrieg* was unremitting speed. Impelled by his Directive 25, on which *General der Artillerie* Alfred Jodl had laboured unceasingly until 4 a.m. on 28 March, that speed, day and night, never dropped below fifty miles an hour. As the dust-choked Panzer columns churned on, the priorities were ruthless; ten minutes after a breakdown, any Panzer with a complex mechanical fault was nosed off the road for salvage. Traffic control was streamlined; a full Panzer division stretched for more than sixty miles of highway, and from each tank turret a black-clad crewman, signalling with a red-and-white circular disc, controlled the speed of those who followed.

In two days, the tank tracks had straddled the entire Vardar River valley, dividing northern Greece from south-east Yugoslavia; in three days, Salonika; in six, the Serbian hills and Albania.

In the thermal spa of Vranjska Banya, 200 miles south of Belgrade, the plight of General Simović was typical of the whole muddled counter-offensive; with one small portable radio set, on loan from the British, he strove to maintain contact with six separate Yugoslav armies. But the Yugoslavs, although one million strong were fatally uncoordinated; attempting to defend the entire frontier, 1,860 miles long, Simović lost everything. Time was of the essence, yet whole units were creaking into battle in ox-carts that moved at three miles an hour.

Chaos reigned on every front. As fast as Simović mobilised troops, the new Foreign Minister, Momćilo Nincić, hoping for peace with Hitler, demobilised them. In the north-western region of Croatia, it was as Hugh Dalton had feared; thousands of soldiers saw the conflict as strictly a Serbian quarrel. Many units mutinied or went home. One entire brigade, including its commanding officer, surrendered to a German bicycle company. Another unit, throwing an officers' party, halted long enough to surrender, then settled down to serious drinking.

By 5 p.m. on 12 April, the swastika flew once more over the German legation in rubble-strewn Belgrade. Five days later, finding that King Peter, Simović and Nincić, had all left for Greece, the disgraced Aleksander Cincar-Marković was the only man left to return to the capital and sign the surrender.

Now, as a nation, Yugoslavia ceased to exist. Her place on the map of Europe was succeeded by a nominally independent Croatia, under Dr Ante Pavelić, a Mussolini protégé. Serbia was to become a German fiefdom; Montenegro an Italian puppet state.

This sense of a nation divided came home poignantly to Ruth Mitchell on a refugee train going south. At first the implications escaped her: a troop train going north had drawn level, its windows packed with drunken, dishevelled soldiers, taunting and gesticulating. Suddenly Ruth understood: the soldiers had tacked blue, white and red ribbons, the emblem of Croatia, onto their peaked caps.

Ruth sat quite still, not speaking, painfully conscious of the bulky automatic in her handbag. She was bewildered too. For months she had cherished the concept of belonging, of the brotherhood of *Četnik* freedom-fighters symbolised by the uniform she wore. Now she was cut off, without finite orders, uncertain as to whether the *Četniks* of Montenegro still held out.

Suddenly she felt helpless and alone.

*

In the gardens of the Tatoi Palace, fourteen miles from Athens, the long shadows of cypress trees, striped the grass, jet-black against the setting sun. It was very close to dusk on Saturday, 19 April.

The men grouped round the long table in the Palace conference room contemplated nothing but disaster. At its head, King George II of the Hellenes, sat stiffly upright, his face drawn and haggard. By contrast, his Commander-in-Chief, General Alexandros Papagos, was slumped apathetically in his chair. The British contingent were solemn to a man: Wavell, his Chief of Staff, Lieutenant-General Sir Arthur Smith, the commander of the British Expeditionary Force in Greece, Lieutenant-General Sir Henry Maitland Wilson, and Rear-Admiral Harold Baillie-Grohman.

"We must know," Wavell said, and his voice was sharply edged, "whether the Greek Army can give effective support to General Wilson's left flank on the Thermopylae Line."

Papagos was morose. Less than twelve hours ago he had given orders for a division to proceed to Epirus, in north-western Greece, but whether they could stop the German advance, even if they arrived in time, he did not know. "What he did know," said Papagos vehemently, "was that the longer his armies continued to resist, the more defenceless Greek civilians would suffer."

Foremost in every man's mind were the tragic blunders of the last fifteen days. Eden's early discussions with the Greeks had always stressed one thing: both British and Greek troops would stand fast on the 70-mile long Aliakhmon Line, stretching from the Aliakhmon River to the Yugoslav frontier, and the Greeks would field thirty-five battalions. But all along Eden had failed to understand one crucial point: Papagos would make this stand only if Yugoslavia declared war.

Once Germany entered Bulgaria, Papagos had changed his stance; he could not risk shifting troops from Macedonia, for strafing Stukas might catch them on the move. All he could now offer for the Aliakhmon Line was three divisions – between sixteen to twenty-three battalions, as against the thirty-five promised.

In truth, Eden, who had promised 100,000 men and furnished only 58,000, had little cause for complaint; that privilege was reserved for the front-line troops. From 8 April onwards, the story of the Greek campaign became a story of punishing withdrawals, of long hard marches through mountain passes, where many men, clad only in desert shorts and pith helmets faced temperatures ten degrees below freezing, their hands and faces blue with cold.

A sense of let-down was everywhere apparent. It was small comfort to the men of the 3rd Battalion, Royal Tank Regiment, that Eden, on a visit, promised them new tank tracks before the battle began. By the time the spares did arrive the tanks had been abandoned, the links and pins of their tracks snapped like pipeclay by the harsh and rocky roads.

Supplies were a problem from the first. Incredibly, no Naval Officer-in-Charge had been appointed for the port of Piraeus; fire-fighting drill was thus non-existent. On the night of Sunday, 6 April, disaster struck. At 9 p.m., a low-level raid by German bombers blew 11 ammunition ships sky-high, shattering windows seven miles away, closing down the entire port for ten days. With this one raid, the Greek campaign was virtually lost before it had even started.

Air cover was almost non-existent. "More aeroplanes should be sent as quickly as possible," South Africa's Premier, Jan Smuts, counselled Churchill, "I am expediting another bomber squadron . . . and Beaverbrook should surely also disgorge from his hoard." But although Churchill had promised fifteen, perhaps up to twenty-two fighter squadrons, only eighty aircraft were sent, of which thirty were destroyed at a stroke in one ground attack. Thus the Luftwaffe held the sky; as King George and the British debated, the total R.A.F. fighter strength in Greece was one serviceable aircraft.

Now time was running out. On 18 April, Premier Alexander Koryzis, tormented by the fate that was overtaking his country, went quietly home and ended his life with two bullets. One day later, the swastika was hoisted on the summit of Mount Olympus. Now the Olympus Line, along with the Metaxas Line, the Aliakhmon Line, the Thermopylae Line, took its place in the rank of sad futile names that had stretched from Mannerheim to Maginot.

At Tatoi Palace, the conference room was dark now with the sombre shadows of evening; the King's master of ceremonies, Colonel Levidis, called the guards to draw the heavy window curtains. Then, as the lights were switched on and the double-doors closed, Wavell once again assured King George: as long as the Greeks fought on, the British would stand by them.

Then he added quietly, "But, your Majesty, if you and your Government wish us to leave, we will do so. The decision rests with you, sir."

Silence fell. The King held a brief whispered consultation with his Vice-Premier, Tsuderos. Then, gripping the arms of his chair, he looked slowly round the long table. "Gentlemen," he said, "we do not think there is time to reorganise our army in Epirus to give support to your left flank before the enemy attacks. Therefore it is our opinion that the British force should be withdrawn."

*

Aircraftman Marcel Gerard Comeau, who had "deserted" to Greece to get his fill of the action, was a sorely bewildered young man. Ever since his arrival in Athens at the beginning of March, Comeau had felt assured that victory was in the air. The welcome accorded to 33 Squadron's trucks as they drove through the streets of Athens had been unforgettable: waving girls packing the wrought iron balconies, excited children running to keep pace, greybeards chorusing "Bravo!", while a rain of myrtle leaves and flower petals cascaded down on the Chevrolets.

Ahead of them the morning sun shone high and bright above the Acropolis, painting the Parthenon's pentelicon marble with breathtaking light and shade. And all the way to Eleusis airfield, twenty miles from Athens, the rapturous welcome had continued.

Nor was the action that Comeau had sought lacking for long. Posted with a squadron detachment to Paramythia, a muddy Albanian landing-ground in an icy valley, he and the others had grown daily more jubilant as the small band of fighters, almost unopposed, knocked down 28 Italian planes. Soon the squadron had moved nearer still to the fighting – to Larissa, 78 miles north of Athens.

Here, too, as the pilots' successes mounted, Comeau and the squadron's "erks" found the simple friendly villagers could never do enough for them. Night after night they feasted for a few coppers a head on whole sheep, spit-roasted in the main street, linking arms with the Greeks, drinking toast after toast to "Victory" and "Long life" in the pungent resin-tasting *retsina* wine.

By 6 April, when Hitler at last struck, Comeau had been posted yet again – this time to No 11 (Blenheim) Squadron at Almyros landing ground, on the eastern edge of the Thessalian plain. Put in charge of 100 women from the village of Exinopolis, who were constructing a dispersal road for the bombers, the young airman had a sneaking feeling that the war was being run for his benefit – "the happiest weeks of my life . . . eggs by the bucket-load and stewed octopus with beans."

All too soon this idyll ended. By 13 April, news came that the Greeks were crumbling. At Almyros, Comeau and the others listened uneasily to distant gunfire, eyes probing the skies for a Luftwaffe that had so far left them in peace. But on 15 April, they watched a tall black corona of smoke pulsing from Niamata airfield, over the hill. A Luftwaffe attack had destroyed every single Blenheim of the newly-arrived 113 Squadron.

On the evening of 16 April, Air Vice Marshal John D'Albiac, R.A.F. theatre commander, had ordered most squadrons to fall back on Athens.

From that moment on, the retreat was a spectacle familiar to any Dunkirk veteran. Along the rocky roads leading from Stylos to Lamia, from Lamia through Daphne, five-gallon petrol tins piled thirty feet high flared like beacons in the night as the British set fire to them. At least 8,000 vehicles – along with 209 aircraft – would be wrecked and left behind; the air was loud with the roar of engines racing at top speed, heavy with the smell of overheated cylinder blocks.

In little ports like Nauplia Bay and Myloi, the scene was familiar too: the long patient line of troops silhouetted at the shore line, motor barges, black and low-slung, chugging from the water's edge towards waiting corvettes and destroyers, the muttered interchanges between captains and beachmasters: "*Hyacinth* – I can take a hundred – tell them to get a move on."

As the ill-starred British Expeditionary Force pulled out, a wry jest passed through the ranks: the initials B.E.F. really stood for "Back Every Fortnight".

For Aircraftman Comeau, scrambling aboard the infantry assault ship *Glenearn*, the lump in his throat came close to choking him. Even at Nauplia, his last glimpse of Athens was still fresh in his mind; in the chilly evening, the streets had been deserted but the few old men loitering outside the taverns had still clapped their hands with great dignity, calling out "Bravo!" as the trucks groaned past. On 22 April, Greece had surrendered; five days later, the swastika flew from the west wall of the Acropolis. Where had it all gone wrong? Comeau wondered. Now he was bound for the island of Crete – but when the time came could the B.E.F. put up any better showing there?

*

It was perhaps no more than coincidence – yet in Churchill's darkest hour something impelled his long-standing pen-friend, Franklin Roosevelt, to seek more than a meeting of minds across the Atlantic Ocean. Quite suddenly the idea came to him: he wanted to trade ideas and aspirations face to face.

On the stifling hot Sunday of 20 April, with the thermometer trembling in the eighties, the President was entertaining an old friend at Hyde Park, his house on the Hudson River, 60 miles upstate from New York city. William Lyon Mackenzie King, the Canadian Prime Minister, was responding to a pressing invitation to discuss the war situation in Europe.

Coatless and tieless, in a white linen shirt, the President lounged comfortably on the verandah of the small cottage he had built facing the river. To Mackenzie King he seemed in thoughtful mood; he spoke of the "pretty tough time" he was having, of the "defeatist attitude" so widespread in America. Reverses in North Africa, the Yugoslav capitulation, the situation in Greece had "made everything look very dark for the present". There was only one thing to do, the President thought – "to let the people realise that it was only part of a larger plan".

That "larger plan" Roosevelt confided, now seemed to call for an urgent meeting with Churchill, with whom he was already in constant touch. ("We have been writing each other love letters for some time," was the way Churchill later put it to King.) It was now that Roosevelt began a measured review of likely meeting places.

Bermuda? That seemed too far away, and dangerous besides. Iceland

53

was likewise too distant for a man confined to a wheelchair and so was Greenland. Then how about Newfoundland? "That," said the President thoughtfully, "seems to me to be the best place."

The Atlantic Charter – which history would record as the world's first summit meeting – was now in the making.

*

The British had need of such friends. As May dawned, their grasp on the world's trouble spots grew ever more tenuous.

In late March, Rashid Ali el-Gailani, a small, swarthy pro-Axis former premier of Iraq, where the British maintained two air bases, staged a coup with four colonels known as "The Golden Square", wresting power from the pro-British Regent, Amir Abdul Illah. On 3 April, hearing that four doctors, armed with a death certificate from heart failure, were prowling round his Baghdad palace, the Regent fled, huddled under rugs in the car of the U.S. Minister, Paul Knabenshue, and was flown to Basra, on the Persian Gulf.

For the British, the situation was alarming. Not only were their two air bases, at Habbaniya and Shaiba, vital staging posts for India and for Egypt; much of the allied war effort relied on the oil-rich areas around Mosul and Kirkul. If the Axis gained control of the pipe-line running from Haditha on the Euphrates River, south through Transjordan and Palestine to Haifa, their plight would be desperate.

Early in April, an intelligence source, code-named "MICE", reported to the War Office: "Rashid is being driven hard by the Axis and seems determined to go ahead. Is using Axis gold to bribe officials and is rapidly reorganising administration in external districts to eliminate Regent's supporters . . . Basra reports indicate conviction is growing there that British intend to take no action . . ."

Nor did they, for at this stage of the desert war Wavell was like a juggler balancing too many coloured balls: Greece, the Nile Valley, an imminent attack on Crete all loomed larger in his thoughts. To the horror of the British Ambassador in Egypt, Sir Miles Lampson (later Lord Killearn), the Commander-in-Chief had even contemplated asking Rashid Ali for "his terms". "I am aghast at the probable results of this climb-down," Lampson cabled Eden and three days later stressed again, "A crawl to Iraquis would be political disaster."

No man was more in agreement than Lieutenant-General Sir Claude Auchinleck, then Commander-in-Chief, India; he too, had warned Sir John Dill of the perils of ignoring Iraq. "Turkey, Iraq, Iran, Afghanistan and even Saudi Arabia will be involved in a general rot. If, on the other hand, we can hang on to this bastion we will always have a good chance of retrieving the situation."

As it was, Auchinleck's urgency saved the day. Towards the end of March he flew to Basra for a personal meeting with Wavell, to convince him that "bold action" was essential. Wearily, Wavell assented – though until then he had seen Iraq as no more than "a nuisance area on (his) eastern flank". "His credit is fast falling," noted Deputy Premier Clement Attlee. "He still thinks in terms of defending a line or a perimeter."

In truth, the Axis involvement in Iraq was half-hearted. Although Rashid Ali had long been a hat-in-hand supplicant of Hitler's, he was "driven hard" only by Ribbentrop, hopeful of fomenting an anti-British rising; the Führer was too deeply preoccupied with Greece, Yugoslavia and Barbarossa. The Chief of Staff to the Luftwaffe, General Hans Jeschonnek, was notably unresponsive; the Luftwaffe could spare few planes to transport arms to Iraq. Later Rashid Ali complained that such Axis arms as he did receive were so sub-standard as to be useless. Once Ribbentrop had talked grandly of a one million Reichsmark subsidy, but two instalments of £10,000 in gold were all Rashid received.

Nonetheless, Auchinleck's troops – one infantry brigade of the 10th Indian Division – were en route from Bombay to Basra and more were to follow. Ostensibly they were in transit to Palestine, and at first, in accordance with an existing treaty of alliance, Rashid Ali agreed to their landing. But soon, under pressure from the Iraqui Army, he modified his stance. No further troops must land until the first contingent had crossed the Palestine frontier.

When the Ambassador, Sir Kinahan Cornwallis, made it plain that more troops would arrive notwithstanding, the Iraquis, on 30 April, laid siege to the British Embassy and to Habbaniya airfield.

Although Rashid Ali grandiloquently proclaimed the thirty-day confict that ensued as "a Holy War", it was at best a holy skirmish. There were many ludicrous undertones. Habbaniya might boast its own polo ground and swimming pool, but most of its 80 aircraft – which included 32 Audaxes and 29 Oxfords – were better suited to an R.A.F. museum. When the few capable of take-off flew low over the city, dropping placatory leaflets in Arabic, they were greeted by a spatter of machine-gun fire. Promptly the airmen retaliated by showering down the leaflets parcel by parcel – still wrapped.

Inside the Embassy, where some 350 Britons had taken refuge, life under siege was a far cry from beleaguered Tobruk. Persian gardeners still tended the green lawns, and the Oriental Counsellor sent a daily list of supplies to the Iraqui Foreign Office. Each morning such creature-comforts as fresh lettuce, ice and apricots – along with face powder for the ladies – were delivered through the postern of the main gateway. The bar opened daily at 6 p.m., and Sir Kinahan Cornwallis settled to a few rounds of clock golf.

In the best Victorian tradition, help was on the way: a motley Palestine-based relief column, 2,000 strong, known as "Habforce", equipped with 500 vehicles and twelve days rations to cross 300 miles of desert. For one unit of the column, the 1st Cavalry Division, it was demeaning, to say the least; every officer had brought his own hunter from the English shires, yet now they were reduced to a role of truck-borne infantry. Along with them marched men of the 1,000 strong Arab Legion, under John Bagot Glubb, "Glubb Pasha", long-robed Bedus with ringleted hair and kohl-rimmed eyes, known as "Glubb's Girls" although their cross-belts of pointed bullets and silver-handled daggers showed that they meant business.

The need for "Habforce" had passed before the column ever assembled – the Habbaniya garrison having dispersed the besiegers with one sortie – but true to tradition they marched anyway, though it was 1 June before they reached Baghdad. Their commander, Major-General George Clark, visiting the Embassy, felt that it all smacked of another century, as indeed it did – "the scene there reminded me so much of what might have happened at Lucknow . . . the same Union Jack, the same garden and compound filled with British refugees, the same indomitable spirit".

But by then Rashid Ali had also conformed to tradition and escaped to Iran; his flash-in-the-pan rebellion was over, and the threat to British interests eliminated.

Even here, the British had profited from American friendship; not only had the U.S. Minister, Paul Knabenshue, helped the Regent escape, he had sheltered more than 130 Britons inside his Legation. Now the problem arose of how to reward him, a diplomatic headache that finally filled an entire Foreign Office file.

Could he be awarded a K.C.M.G? (Knight Commander of the Order of St Michael and St George). It seemed the State Department frowned on their diplomats accepting knighthoods. A gift of silver plate? This, too, was contrary to American protocol.

It was midway through July before an acceptable solution was found, and Knabenshue at last received his richly-earned gift: a signed photo of King George VI.

*

By 15 April, the imminent loss of Greece, with all its fighter fields had prompted Wavell to brood once more over the "Worst Possible Case" file he had opened in June, 1940. Now, fearing that Egypt would become untenable under air attack from Greek bases, allowing Rommel to advance unchecked, Wavell pondered the fall of Alexandria and Cairo, the ultimate abandonment of Egypt and Libya. It was a concept that angered Churchill more than any that his generals had yet propounded. In a towering rage, the Premier shouted at his Director of Military Operations, Major-General John Kennedy: "Wavell has 400,000 men. If they lose Egypt, blood will flow. I will have firing parties to shoot the generals."

But on 30 April, as Wavell had all along feared, Rommel, repulsed once but still undaunted, struck again at Tobruk.

It was an attack more lethal than any the Germans had yet launched – or, ultimately, encountered. In seventy-two hours of thrust and counter-thrust, Stukas, artillery and machine-gun fire flayed the battlefield – a barrage so intense that one Anzac signalman, crawling on his belly and mending severed barbed wire as he went, took $4\frac{1}{2}$ hours to cover the one-and-a-quarter miles between his company's post and Battalion H.Q. Red tracer criss-crossed the defence lines like Morse code come alive, and Rommel moved tirelessly everywhere, cursing, exhorting, even snaking on his belly like any front-line infantryman into the first trenches captured. "What the British risk in broad daylight," he tongue-lashed his engineers, "you can't even manage in the dark!" Angered that the Italians had not pressed home their attack, Rommel coldly warned their liaison officer, General Count Giorgio Calvi di Bergolo, the tall aquiline son-in-law of King Vittorio Emmanuele: "In future I shall expect the immediate execution of officers who show cowardice in the face of the enemy."

There was little doubt that Rommel was in earnest. His troops might adore him; his officers found his relentless goading a sore trial. One general, caught breakfasting as late as 6.30 a.m., was at once returned to Germany. On 1 May, a tank battalion commander who burst into tears of frustration in the last vain attack on Tobruk, was summarily court-martialled. Soon after Rommel dismissed *Generalmajor* Johannes Streich, with the curt comment: "You were far too concerned with the wellbeing of your troops."

"I can imagine no greater words of praise for a division commander," was Streich's rejoinder.

In the frenzied chaos of this battle, few men grasped with certainty who was winning – or for how long. One German doctor, approaching the wire in an ambulance furiously berated the Anzac who drew a bead on him; convinced that Rommel had taken Tobruk, he had arrived to treat the German wounded. (Seized as a P.O.W., he treated both sides impartially.) Corporal Bob McLeish and a team of Australian Bren gunners found themselves marooned in a trench under heavy fire, along with some German infantrymen. Their sergeant told McLeish reasonably "I don't know who'll be the prisoners – you or us. We'd better wait awhile until the shelling stops." At length, as the guns grew silent, more Germans entered the trench. "You're the prisoners," beamed the sergeant.

57

Few Germans fought the battle under such adverse conditions as *Leutnant* Bucher of the 104th Field Artillery Regiment and his runner, *Gemeine* Wievelhofe – in civilian life, both school-teachers. Racked with dysentery, they had removed their trousers to sponge their soiled seats with a mugful of coffee. A mortar shell blasted the garments to rags; until 4 May, when Rommel withdrew, both men were forced to fight a war in their underpants.

On hand to witness this systematic slaughter was *Generalleutnant* Friedrich Paulus, acting chief of the Army High Command, the curt icy disciplinarian who two years later was to surrender at Stalingrad. Three days earlier, Paulus, who dismissed Rommel as no more than "a thick-headed Swabian", had arrived on an urgent mission from *Generaloberst* Halder: somehow to hold "The Desert Fox" whom Halder stigmatised as "this soldier gone stark mad", in check. Now Paulus was appalled by what he saw. "The troops around Tobruk are fighting in conditions that are inhuman and intolerable," he told his conducting officer, *Leutnant* Heinz Werner Schmidt. "I am going to recommend to Berlin that we withdraw to a strong position at Gazala" – a fort 30 miles to the west.

Paulus saw one thing as plain: Rommel's brilliant but disobedient advance to Tobruk had not only failed to bring about a decisive victory, it had added another 700 miles to his already extended supply lines. All told, his Afrika Korps, the Luftwaffe, Italian troops and civilians in Libya needed a mind-boggling total of 116,000 tons of supplies a month – yet the port of Tripoli could handle 45,000 tons a month at most.

As Rommel hesitated, too stubborn to admit the truth of his defeat, a furious once-for-all halt order, transmitted on 3 May, arrived from von Brauchitsch, berating Rommel for his reckless disregard for life – in two days he had suffered over 1,900 casualties. Von Brauchitsch categorically forbade him to attack Tobruk again, or even advance into Egypt. Rommel was to hold his position, conserve his forces, and launch no further attacks. Sourly Rommel conceded to *Oberst* Hanshenning von Holtzendorff, commanding the 104th Field Artillery Regiment, "For the moment the siege of Tobruk will have to be abandoned." To Lucie, his wife, he confided his future pattern for disobedience: "The reports I send back, stating the conditions as they exist, don't suit their book. The result will be that we'll keep our mouths shut and report in the briefest form."

For the first time in the desert – or in any World War Two theatre – the Germans had been forced on the defensive, and with Rommel this realisation rankled bitterly. Other Afrika Korps reactions were more philosophic. One officer confessed in his diary: "What we experienced in Poland and on the Western Front was only a promenade compared with this." Another took the longest of long term views. "Ah well," he noted, "the Greeks also spent ten years before Troy."

*

Josef Stalin knew him as "Valter" but that was only one of his many aliases. In the Zagreb suburb where he lived with his common-law wife, Herta Has, and their baby son, Aleksander, they called him Engineer Slavko Babić; on the other side of the town he was Engineer Tomanek. Friends nicknamed him *Stari* (The Old Man), although in 1941 Josip Broz was only entering his forty-ninth year. Sometime in the 1930s, he had begun using another alias, common in his native Croatia, which the world would come to know: Tito.

Tito had been an organiser for the illegal Yugoslav Communist Party for seventeen years now. In Zagreb's Corso Kavana, his favourite café, he had long been a familiar sight to the waiters: a well-dressed stockily-built man with blue-grey eyes and a strongly-marked jaw, always in the same window seat, sipping strong coffee. As he studied his regular newspaper, *The Croat People*, he chain-smoked cigarettes in a strange holder shaped like a miniature pipe.

On 7 May, the ex-locksmith Tito had bade a long farewell both to Herta Has and the Corso Kavana. The time for action had come, though first certain precautions must be taken. Croatia was now a Fascist protectorate, and all private cars were being requisitioned; to hand in his Ford, Tito thought, might draw undue attention to himself. He called in some friendly masons; within hours, the car had been bricked up in his garage.

That evening, armed with a forged identity card and forged permits, Tito boarded the night train for Belgrade, 240 miles away. Travelling in another compartment was a girl communist; her task, when they reached Belgrade's Zemun Station, was to walk ahead through the police controls, ensuring that no special checks or changes in papers were required that day. Tito left nothing to chance.

Once past the controls, Tito knew he was safe. In Belgrade, he had almost as many accommodation addresses as aliases: a flat at 16A, Rumunska Street, another at 5, Doticeva Street, rooms in the Gladstone Street house of a wealthy party sympathiser, Vladislav Ribnikar, proprietor of the liberal newspaper, *Politika*. In Ribnikar's bathroom, a secret door in a cupboard behind the wash-basin led to a hiding place below the roof, housing a cache of sixteen hand grenades and two revolvers. Tito would never yield without a fight.

Once there, his first task would be to reactivate his secret radio link with Georgi Dimitrov, Secretary General of the Comintern in Moscow, whose code name was Deda (Grandfather). There was no time to lose. Tito had news for Deda that Josef Stalin at present refused to credit: all units scheduled for the invasion of Soviet Russia must be fully operational by 15 May.

59

All that year, the messages had flooded in, small alarming clues and pointers, as mosquito-shrill as static in the ether. It took a stubborn man, with a deeply-ingrained suspicion of Western motivation to ignore them. But Josef Stalin, it seemed, was such a man.

The first warning had come as early as January, when Sam E. Woods, the genial American commercial attaché in Berlin, received a tip-off from a German anti-Nazi with connections in high places. Plans for an attack on Russia, he told Woods, had been in the making since August 1940, and Hitler had boasted that he would have "only my soldiers from Vladivostok to Gibraltar". As details of the plan were firmed up, Woods and his contact were soon meeting regularly in the darkness of Berlin cinemas, where scribbled notes of the latest developments were slipped into the attaché's pocket.

Cordell Hull, fearing a "plant" passed this news to J. Edgar Hoover's Federal Bureau of Investigation, but Hoover thought the material authentic. Thus, on 20 March, Sumner Welles took the precaution of warning the Soviet Ambassador, Constantin Oumansky. Oumansky "turned very white", but promised to forward the information to the Kremlin.

Almost simultaneously, the American military attachés in Berlin were reporting that 15 million German soldiers were under arms, posing the question: Who were they going to fight?

Midway through February, Berlin buzzed with rumours. A conscience-stricken printer called at the Russian Consulate with one sample of a large newly-placed contract: a German–Russian conversation manual. There was little doubt as to its purpose. Printed in the Russian language were such disquieting gambits as "Where is the *kolkhoz* (collective farm) chairman?" "Are you a Communist?" "Hands up! I'll shoot!" "Surrender!"

April brought a fresh alarm from Berlin, this time from the Embassy's First Secretary, Valentin Berezhkov. During a cocktail party at the American Embassy, a Luftwaffe Major had told him frankly: "My squadron was recalled from North Africa yesterday and has received orders to transfer to the East – to Lodz." Many other detachments, he told Berezkhov, had made a similar move. "I do not know what it means, but I personally would not like anything to happen between our two countries."

Berezhkov lost no time in transmitting this information to Moscow.

It was not only rumours gleaned by diplomats that Stalin spurned; carefully-documented reports sent in by the Soviet Union's most brilliant spies received equally short shrift. From Tokyo, 45-year-old Doctor Richard Sorge, a hard-drinking womaniser who for eight years had functioned as a Moscow agent, was amassing a formidable dossier of German intentions. Ostensibly a representative of the German daily *Frankfurter Zeitung*, the Russian-born Sorge had entirely won the trust of all the German Embassy officials who counted – notably the Military Attaché, *Oberst* Max Kretschmer. After skilfully pumping Kretschmer, Sorge had reaped yet more damning evidence from a special envoy of the German War Ministry, *Oberst* Ritter von Niedermayer.

By 15 May, Sorge had obtained the precise date of Barbarossa – 22 June – from an old friend, *Oberst* Scholl, en route to Bangkok as Military Attaché. All this – even down to a copy of Hitler's fateful Directive 21, which had set preparations in motion – had been trans-mitted to Moscow by W/T from the end of April onwards. Yet only silence followed, and Sorge was to lament despairingly: "Why has Stalin not reacted?"

Week by week, the warnings grew more clamant – from Rudolf Rössler, known as Lucy, an agent operating inside Switzerland, from Viktor Sukulov-Gurevich, alias Kent, in Brussels, above all from the doyen of Soviet agents, Leopold Trepper, otherwise known as "Mon-sieur Gilbert" or "Le Grand Chef".

Identified by the call-sign PTX Moscov, Trepper, a dapper fastidious gourmet, Polish-born and Moscow-trained, had by degrees evolved a spymaster's dream: a network known to all *Abwehr* (German military intelligence) agents as "The Red Orchestra" yet one with a perfectly legitimate front. Operating from two offices – Simexco on Brussels' Rue Royale and Simex on the Champs-Elysées, Paris – their cover was near impregnable. Both firms supplied cement and construction materials to the German Organisation Todt, responsible for *Wehrmacht* military construction.

All but four Trepper employees were frontmen, convinced they were working for a sound business concern; one with Nazi leanings, even lent credibility to the establishment by barking "*Heil Hitler!*" when he lifted the phone. Soon the Principals of Simexco and Simex were receiving *Ausweis* or passes which opened every door to them. Over Black Market meals at Paris restaurants like Chez Kornilov, Trepper saw to it that his German guests drank deeply – ensuring his own sobriety by swallowing olive oil, which checks alcohol from acting on the system – and listened hard. At one such meal, Ludwig Kainz, a Todt engineer recently re-turned from the east, told of working on fortifications on the German–Russian border in Poland.

After that, Trepper had worked fast. As professionals, he and his agents never traded reports in cafés or restaurants but only in public places: lavatories, the Metro, or the Tuileries Gardens. Soon their in-formation was too convincing to be gainsaid. In February, Trepper sent Moscow a detailed dispatch of all the divisions being withdrawn from

France and Belgium and sent to the frontier. By May, he had confirmed both Tito's 15 May readiness date and Sorge's date of attack.

It was in vain. On 20 March, Marshal Filipp Ivanovich Golikov, Director of Red Army Intelligence, had minuted his subordinates: "All the documents claiming that war is imminent must be regarded as forgeries emanating from British or even German sources."

On all important dispatches, filed by Sorge, Trepper and others, Golikov sedulously noted in the margin: "Double agent" or "British source".

This scepticism was, on the surface, readily encouraged by Josef Stalin. In April, a Czech agent named Shkvor, operating from Berlin, confirmed German troop concentrations, reporting that the Skoda Works in Prague had been ordered to halve deliveries of military equipment to Russia. On the margin of this report, Stalin minuted in red ink: "This is merely an English provocation. The perpetrator should be sought out and punished."

Yet, the surface impression was misleading. Stalin accepted the physical evidence as valid enough – but fatally miscalculated Hitler's true intentions. The Führer, he thought – and his secret police the N.K.V.D., were in full accord – was indulging in a gigantic bluff of sabre-rattling. Germany's threatening military moves would soon be followed up by blunt demands for economic, even territorial, concessions.

As a result, Stalin switched overnight to a policy of blatant appeasement – what U.S. Secretary of the Interior, Harold Ickes, called "a series of cuddles in the direction of Germany". Though the prices of material delivered were upped by 40 percent, supplies crossed the border at a frenetic rate: manganese, grain, chrome, crude oil, even 4,000 tons of rubber. And Stalin made further propitiatory moves – severing diplomatic relations with such German adversaries as Belgium, Norway, even, only a bare month after signing a non-aggression pact, with Yugoslavia.

All these were one-sided concessions which Hitler had not even sought.

For those waiting impatiently on the side-lines, it seemed that fear was the keynote. From Russia's south-west frontier, one corps commander, Marshal Rodion Malinovsky, a Spanish civil war veteran, begged for clarification: "Can we open fire if the enemy invades our territory?" The reply seemed strangely supine: "Do not succumb to provocation and do not open fire."

From the British Embassy, Moscow, Sir Stafford Cripps voiced a bitter complaint: the Foreign Office had given him no cards whatsoever to play. But, as Hugh Dalton commented accurately, "Whatever cards he had, he could not play them to effect . . . when the Russians were terrified of Germany."

Like many another ruler, Stalin had read the danger signs correctly –

but he somehow sought to postpone history. On 5 May, at a Kremlin reception, the dictator spoke for forty minutes to hundreds of young officers, new graduates from the military academies. Nor did he mince his words. The situation was extremely serious: a German attack in the near future was not to be ruled out.

But at this moment the Red Army was not strong enough to smash the *Wehrmacht*. Modern tanks were lacking, and, so, too, were modern planes. Thus the government was doing all it could, by diplomatic means, to stave off an attack until the autumn.

His conclusion was unwarrantably optimistic. Almost inevitably a war with Germany would be fought – but in 1942, under conditions by then far more favourable for the Red Army.

*

Another man was striving to swim against the current of history. Night after night he had lain sleepless in the bedroom of his house on Harthauser Strasse, in the Munich suburb of Harlaching. On the wall at the foot of the bed was pinned a giant map of a momentous 850-mile journey. Hour after hour he had lain propped up by pillows, a single reading lamp directed like a spotlight on this map, the room cloaked in darkness as he absorbed the details: distance, points of orientation, the course of his journey.

Walter Richard Rudolf Hess, Deputy Führer of the Third Reich, the trusted friend who had worked with Hitler on Part One of *Mein Kampf* in a cell in Landsberg Gaol, had pondered this mission for almost a year now. Time had only strengthened his convictions: the Barbarossa attack which Hess had long urged, would at last involve Germany in a two-front war. But Hitler, he believed, was far from seeking this, merely an understanding with England. And surely the English would never tolerate a Soviet victory over Germany?

But for the English to comprehend Hitler's intentions, someone had to make the first overture. This was the scenario that Rudolf Hess had drafted for himself – "a Parsifal", as one man saw him, who dreamed of a "great mediating act to save the Reich for Germany . . . and . . . for Hitler, his idol".

If he reached England, Hess knew exactly whom to contact. His close friend, Dr Albrecht Haushofer, son of the famous geo-politician who had been Hess' mentor, had long sought to establish friendly contacts with a group of powerful Britons – among them R. A. Butler, Under Secretary of State to the Foreign Office, Lord Dunglass, Neville Chamberlain's Parliamentary Private Secretary (later Lord Home of the Hirsel), above all, with the Duke of Hamilton and Brandon, Scotland's Premier Duke, and Lord Steward of His Majesty's Household.

Haushofer, who had met the Duke briefly at the 1936 Olympic Games, had formed the intriguing notion that part of a Lord Steward's duties must be to wait on King George VI at dinner. In the autumn of 1940, he had even written the Duke a friendly letter, routing it via Lisbon, though no reply had been forthcoming. Haushofer could not know that his letter had been intercepted by the censor, and had not been shown to the Duke until March 1941.

If only he could reach the Duke's country estate at Dungavel House, Lanarkshire, Scotland, Hess reasoned, he had only to produce Haushofer's visiting card to gain an audience with King George VI.

On the morning of 10 May, Hess knew that weather conditions were as good as he could hope for. Twice before he had attempted this lone mission, and twice, he had been forced back – once by inclement weather, once by a jammed aileron. Now the subterfuges of months were to pay off: the ME 110, which he had tricked Professor Willy Messerschmitt into modifying, grumbling about its limited range until the engineer fitted two auxiliary tanks, holding 700 litres each, into the wings; the twenty trial flights he had made to point out alleged defects; the top secret maps of forbidden air zones he had bespoken from Hitler's personal pilot, Hans Baur.

Those closest to him were uneasy, not quite knowing why. Hess had not confided in Ilse, his wife, but his constant trips to the Messerschmitt airfield at Augsburg could not pass unnoticed. Nor could the mysterious telephone calls relaying weather reports at regular intervals to Hess' secretary, Hildegard Fath. His adjutant, *Hauptmann* Karlheinz Pintsch, more in the secret, was even less reassured. Forced to confess his purpose, after his second abortive flight, Hess had claimed the Führer knew everything – but in that case, why had Hess entrusted him with a letter to Hitler to be delivered if the flight succeeded?

At 2.30 p.m., Ilse Hess was more puzzled still: her husband had arrived in her bedroom to take tea, as was his custom, but wearing the uniform of a *Hauptmann* in the Luftwaffe: light blue shirt, dark blue tie, blue-grey breeches, and high airman's boots. He offered no explanation, mentioning only a sudden summons to Berlin, which entailed another side-trip to Augsburg.

Unknown to Ilse, the last message she would receive from him for eight months was tucked unobtrusively away among their four-year-old son, Wolf's toys.

Shortly before 6 p.m., the Deputy Führer's Mercedes arrived at Augsburg airfield. In an ante-room of the administration building, Hess changed into a jacket matching his Luftwaffe trousers and fur-lined flying overalls. A silver-grey ME 110 had been man-handled from a hangar and lined up on the tarmac.

Now, climbing briskly into the Messerschmitt's cockpit, Hess completed the take-off drill, grinning and giving the thumbs-up sign to the airfield's research manager, Herr Piehl. Hunched against the slipstream, Piehl slipped the wooden chocks from the wheels and the little plane headed into the wind.

"How long will he be gone?" he asked *Hauptmann* Pintsch. "I've got better things to do on a Saturday than hang around here."

Pintsch stared at him unseeing. In his pocket he fingered the letter he must deliver to Hitler if Hess had not returned in four hours. "I've no idea," he said.

*

At Bentley Priory, the headquarters of Fighter Command, Royal Air Force, twelve miles north of London, the mood was one of grim expectancy. By 6.15 p.m. on 10 May, the moon was at the full – and the cold spring nights had now assumed a sinister significance in the calendar of *Reichsmarschall* Herman Göring's Luftwaffe.

On the night of 16 April, almost 700 bombers had attacked London for close on eight hours; three nights later, 400 bombers had made the two-way trip. In truth, the raids were designed to foster the illusion of an impending invasion, a smokescreen to divert attention from Operation Barbarossa, but as yet the British could take no comfort from this fact.

At 10.45 p.m., as British radar stations showed the first blips dancing forty miles into France, Squadron Leader Cyril Leman, in Fighter Command's Ops Room, rang his Commander-in-Chief, Air Marshal Sholto Douglas: "There's something big on tonight, sir."

Next door, in the underground Filter Room, Squadron Leader "Dickie" Richardson, the Junior Controller, was struggling to sort order from chaos. Below Richardson, who was perched in the Controller's gallery, a tense team of plotters, tight-packed round a giant map of the coastline from Penzance to Aberdeen, kept in nightly contact, using head-and-breast sets, with radar stations girdling the coast.

In the Ops Room, as hushed and subdued as a city counting house, Sholto Douglas and Cyril Leman were also watching from the circular gallery; across the map of England, the W.A.A.F. plotters with the long-handled plotting rods eased an urgent thicket of red metal arrows towards the capital. On the gallery's wall map, the suffused lighting round the London region changed from yellow to red: danger imminent.

More than 500 bombers were heading for the capital, and soon Canewdon on the Thames estuary and other radar stations en route could report only "mass plots" to the Filter Room – so many aircraft winging west that the dancing white scallops on the radar screens fused into one colossal "blip". Section Officer Sadie Younger, who covered the estuary corner, was to recall: "We worked only four-hour shifts but that was enough . . . a night like that sent you cross-eyed."

But the Filter Room's knottiest problem had arisen as early as 10.23 p.m. The W.A.A.F. plotting the northern sector of coastline had a sudden call: one of the radar stations showed a single plane crossing the coastline north-east of Alnwick, Northumberland. "Hey," Sadie Younger heard an irate plotter call, "What's that type doing up there? They should have told us there were some more coming in."

But as the minutes ticked by it seemed there weren't: merely a lone aircraft crossing the North Sea coastline at 300 m.p.h. Two fighters, trying to intercept it, had as promptly lost it.

Squadron Leader Richardson rubbed his eyes. It made no sense. A quick glance at the Movement Control Sheet confirmed what he really knew; no friendly aircraft was scheduled within miles of the spot. Yet no German bomber could touch above 180 m.p.h. His chief, Air Commodore Tom Webb-Bowen, came to the only decision possible: "Stick an 'X' on it."

This stamped it as doubtful, to be watched but left alone; there was little else to do. To mark it "Hostile" automatically called the local guns and fighters into action – and just conceivably it could be a friendly fighter in trouble.

Next door, in the Ops Room, Air Marshal Sholto Douglas became curious. He told Squadron Leader Leman: "Find out what it is – what it's doing." On the Ops Room control table the plane was marked by a red metal arrow; as Douglas watched, the W.A.A.F. plotters, ear-phones attuned to each fresh course the Filter Room gave, were slowly easing the plane north towards Edinburgh.

But Leman had one ace up his sleeve that the Filter Room could not play: the dozen-odd Observer Corps posts scattered across the moorland between the Northumbrian coastline and Edinburgh. If someone could catch a glimpse of the plane the whole problem might be solved. At 10.30 p.m. came bewildering news from Post A 3 at Chatton: "We've got a visual at 100 feet – it came from behind cloud. It's a Messerschmitt 110."

Sholto Douglas shook his head: "Impossible. No Messerschmitt would have the fuel to get to Edinburgh and back. Get another fix on it." Again Leman uncradled the phone, convinced in his own mind that Hitler had developed a new bomber. Within minutes came confirmation from Jedburgh. It was indeed a Messerschmitt, now hedge-hopping as low as fifty feet.

Sholto-Douglas made a snap decision: "Get the fighters up after it." Then a strange thing happened. For a while the plane became confused with the track of an R.A.F. Defiant flying in the same area. At 11.09 p.m. before the fighters had had time to make any contact, the observer post from Eaglesham came on the line. The plane had been shot down at

Bonnyton Moor, a few miles south-west of Glasgow. But with more phone calls the mystery deepened. No. 14 Group, R.A.F., controlling all fighters in Scotland, knew nothing about it.

The minutes passed but no more news came of the Messerschmitt. Douglas felt a strange sense of disquiet. Why had it made that lonely northern run – and who had shot it down? At 11.20 p.m., a W.A.A.F. removed the red metal arrow from the board; the pawn was out of play. But at 11.30, everyone was more preoccupied by that one mystery plane than by the hundreds now milling over London.

*

As the anti-aircraft batteries hammered from London's Regents Park, a group of Cockneys bedded down in a shelter by King's Cross Station, chorused, "Good, we're giving it to 'em." District Warden Rob Connell paused in a count of heads to ask curiously: "But s'pose a Jerry baled out in your back garden – what then?" Again, the reaction was unanimous: "Oh, that's different – offer the poor lad a cuppa char."

Four hundred miles away, at Floors Farm, near Eaglesham, south-west of Glasgow, Mrs McLean, a 64-year-old crofter's widow, was doing precisely that. For all the family it had been a hard day and by 11 p.m. she and her daughter Sophia were already in bed; David, her ploughman son, was in the next room also preparing for sleep. Suddenly, as from a long way off, Mrs McLean heard a strange droning; it went on and on as if half a dozen planes were circling the house. By this time David McLean had snuffed out the oil-lamp and dashed to the window – too late to see the plane rip violently into the ground 200 yards away but in time to see a parachutist drifting gently down.
flames.

Grabbing a hay-fork McLean dashed to the scene, to find an aviator in full flying kit alternately nursing a hurt ankle and fumbling with his parachute harness. When Mrs McLean saw David struggling back to the cottage, supporting a handsome black-browed stranger who admitted he was a German she felt "none too friendly" – but Scottish hospitality won the day. The poor man looked pale and tired and his ankle was so swollen that she just had to get the kettle boiling and offer him a cup of tea.

"Thank you, I never drink tea as late as this. I'll only have a glass of water," was the stranger's courteous reply.

So the McLeans and their visitor settled down to chat – as strange a tea-party as existed anywhere that night. The stranger gave his name with disarming frankness – Horn, *Hauptmann* Alfred Horn of Munich. Almost diffidently, David McLean explained that he had asked a farm worker, William Craig, to call in the military. "Please," said the visitor, "I think that would be best." Later he pulled out a pocket-book to

67

produce a snapshot: "That's my son. I saw him this morning. God knows when I shall see him again."

Still the visitor sat chatting, seeming grateful for the comfort of a peat fire. He was so obviously a gentleman that Mrs McLean was fascinated – by his fluent English, his gold watch and bracelet, his easy manners. His one apparent concern was his parachute: "I should like to keep a piece as a souvenir. I am very lucky to be alive."

Presently, in answer to David's summons the tiny kitchen was boiling with people – two signallers from the Royal Signal Corps, who had arrived unarmed, a special constable on part-time duty, a Home Guardsman brandishing a World War One revolver. Asked if he was armed, the stranger spread his hands in a gesture: "You see all I have. My plane was unarmed also."

As the soldiers searched him, the McLeans stood silent and embarrassed; it was as if through no fault of their own the hospitality had gone sour. But there was little to find: a box of German matches, a thick wad of papers, capsules of homeopathic medicine. The one thing that struck them was the number of photographs of himself and his family that the visitor seemed to carry. To the end he remained calm and smiling; when the time came to go, he bowed stiffly to Mrs McLean, thanking her profusely. As if to atone for the formalities of the search, one of the young signallers presented him with a bottle of milk which he had brought for his guard duty.

By 12.30 the McLeans had washed the tea-mugs and retired to bed – a little dazed by the night's drama, unaware that they had done anything more unusual than entertain an unlucky German airman.

Others were swiftly embroiled in the bizarre scenario. In the small hours of Sunday, 11 May, Wing Commander the Duke of Hamilton, commanding the R.A.F. fighter sector at Turnhouse, East Scotland, was roused from sleep by his Sector Controller. The pilot of a German plane that had crashed near Eaglesham had asked for the Duke by name.

At 10 a.m. the Duke along with Flight Lieutenant Benson, the R.A.F. Interrogating Officer for South Scotland, looked in on the prisoner – now in a private room at the Maryhill Military Hospital, Glasgow. When the German asked if the junior officer could withdraw, the Duke gave consent.

Once alone, the German relaxed, remarking conversationally, "I am sorry to have missed you in Lisbon." Then, seeing the Duke's look of bafflement, "I do not know if you recognise me, but I am Rudolf Hess." Gathering confidence he explained that he was as close to Hitler as any man alive. He had plans for a negotiated peace with England which he knew Hitler would regard as a basis for discussion. The Duke decided to temporise. "If it's a question of peace plans," he replied, "I think I should return with an interpreter." His one idea was to get out of the hospital as fast as might be, saying nothing to anyone until he had made personal contact with Sir Alexander Cadogan.

It was now 11 a.m. At the Foreign Office building on London's Whitehall, the only man the Duke could contact was Nicholas Lawford, one of Eden's private secretaries. But his allusions were veiled, and as Lawford struggled to make sense of a story "like an E. Phillips Oppenheim thriller", Churchill's Private Secretary, John Colville, strolled in. Cupping his hand over the receiver, Lawford whispered: "This may be a lunatic. He says he is the Duke of Hamilton, that something extraordinary has happened . . . he won't say what it's all about . . . I think he's a lunatic."

Suddenly Colville recalled a waking day-dream of Göring descending by parachute over London. Taking the phone, he asked with emphasis: "Has somebody arrived." After a long pause, the Duke replied: "Yes."

Intrigued, Colville called the Premier at Ditchley Park, the eighteenth-century Oxfordshire mansion of his friend Ronald Tree, where security decreed that the Premier spent all weekends when the moon was high. Partly curious, partly irked, Churchill kept asking: "Well, *who* has arrived."

"I don't know," Colville repeated patiently for the fourth time. "He won't say."

"It can't be Hitler," Churchill ventured.

Since Colville didn't think so, there was only one way to settle the matter; the Duke was bidden to fly south and report to the Premier.

Worn-out after a gruelling day, the Duke did not reach Ditchley until late that evening: owls were dipping like moths in the moonlit park and the great stone hall was cloaked in darkness. Inside, Churchill and a mixed party of thirty guests were just finishing a leisurely dinner; the premier was in expansive mood. The previous night's punitive raid on London had cost the Luftwaffe thirty-three bombers;* moreover, as a fervent film fan, Churchill was about to enjoy a private screening of *The Marx Brothers Go West.*

Later the Duke would always recall his meeting in camera with Churchill and the Secretary of State for Air, Sir Archibald Sinclair – both men seemingly incredulous at the news. "Do you mean we have got the Deputy Führer of the Third Reich in our hands?" Churchill asked with sonorous relish.

That, Hamilton replied, was what the prisoner had claimed. Suddenly, seeming to lose interest, Churchill remarked: "Well, Hess or no Hess, I am going to see the Marx Brothers."

The truth was that Churchill and his Cabinet were profoundly embarrassed. Ever since 1941 dawned, they had striven to impress America with their resolution to beat Hitler; even their disastrous showings in

* A figure later amended to fourteen.

Greece and Libya had been all to that end. Now Hess' arrival – whether speaking for the Führer or himself alone – was bound to unleash a floodtide of speculation: were the British prepared to contemplate a peace offer?

For the secret could hardly be kept. By 13 May, Hess's gaunt beetle-browed face glowered out from every front page – and the rumours multiplied. Had he come via Spain after discussing a peace deal with the appeasement-prone British Ambassador, Sir Samuel Hoare? Had he arrived to assassinate Churchill – or to make love to Unity Mitford?* Meanwhile, those who cherished puns enjoyed a field-day. Was he a Trojan Hess – or suffering from Hessteria? The answer to both was inevitable: Your Hess is as good as mine.

Churchill was appalled by what he deemed the irresponsible press coverage. Feature writers vied with one another to stress Hess's good looks, his clean living, his devotion to his wife and son. "The general effect of what had been published," the War Cabinet noted, "had been almost laudatory, and there had been no reference to Hess's record, which was as bloody as that of any of the Nazi leaders." Some journalists shared this conviction. Mollie Panter-Downes, London Correspondent of *The New Yorker*, commented: "The public was justly a bit muzzy as to whether it was reading about Hitler's right-hand man or Gary Cooper."

Within the Cabinet, argument raged: how could this imbroglio be turned to sound British advantage? At first, Ivone Kirkpatrick, a former First Secretary in Berlin, who could positively identify Hess, was flown north, there to question him on four separate occasions. Then, Churchill, having digested the trend of Hess's thinking, proposed quoting some excerpts in a House of Commons statement. Eden objected; the Germans should be kept guessing. He himself drafted an alternative statement – one approved by Lord Beaverbrook but opposed by Minister of Information Alfred Duff Cooper. In the small hours of Thursday, 15 May, Churchill flew into a tantrum; he would make his own statement or not at all.

"Then," Eden replied firmly, "no statement." "All right," Churchill raged, slamming down the phone, "No statement."

But was Hess in a fit mental state to negotiate a peace offer? Relays of psychiatrists who examined him, in Scotland and elsewhere, seemed to doubt it; one man compared him to "a caged ape, oozing hostility". Angered at being treated as a prisoner-of-war rather than as an envoy to King George VI, Hess had grown sullen and rancorous. Now the psychiatrists adjudged the German was suffering from hysterical amnesia, claustrophobia, paranoid schizophrenia, psychogenic disturbances,

* Unity Mitford, one of the six daughters of Lord Redesdale, and a former close associate of Hitler's. She had been returned to Britain from Germany in January 1940, suffering from an undisclosed injury.

70

hypochondria and delusions of persecution. It was small wonder that one man added a rider: Hess also had an inferiority complex.

On 17 May – the day after Hess was moved from Scotland to the Tower of London – Churchill thought it apposite to send Roosevelt a note of reassurance. "This is the old invitation to us to desert all our friends in order to save temporarily the greater part of our skin," he wrote soothingly. "Here we think it best to let the Press have a good run for a bit and keep the Germans guessing."

Roosevelt was sceptical. "I wonder what is really behind this story," was his only laconic comment.

One Foreign Office specialist, T. W. Whitehead, adviser on American affairs, shared the President's misgivings. "Our failure to publish any news about Hess has been turned to our disadvantage," he wrote. "The Germans have spread the idea that Hess has come over to England with a peace offer, and that our continued silence is evidence that the Cabinet are seriously considering the offer."

Even so, the German policy was one of snatching at straws. On the Obersalzberg, Hitler's interpreter, Paul Schmidt always recalled, the news of Hess's defection came "as if a bomb had hit the Berghof". Hitler's architect, Albert Speer, who had called with some sketches, remembered too, "the inarticulate almost animal outcry", as the Führer opened the letter brought by *Hauptmann* Karlheinz Pintsch. "Oh, My God! My God!" he burst out to Göring's representative, General Karl Bodenschatz. "He has flown to Britain."

In this moment, Hitler's fears were manifold – the fear of a threat to troop morale on the impending Barbarossa front, the fear that Mussolini would desert the Axis alliance to make his own peace terms with Britain, the fear that Hess, under a truth serum, would reveal the plans for the Russian attack. And supposing the wily Churchill induced Hess to broadcast over the B.B.C.?

Expert advice had been sought – including that of General Ernst Udet, World War One fighter ace and now technical chief of the Luftwaffe. Could Hess have reached his goal? Udet thought not: given the prevailing side winds he would probably have flown past England. Momentarily Hitler's spirits rose: "If only he would drown in the North Sea!" Ribbentrop, who was also consulted, fell back on his British affairs adviser, Fritz Hesse. Supposing Udet was wrong, was there any chance of the British making peace? Hesse thought it out of the question. Ribbentrop's lament was heartfelt: "If only the Führer wouldn't always be taken in by fools who trick him into believing there can be an easy peace with England."

Scapegoats were singled out on all sides. Not only Adjutant Pintsch but many of the staff of Augsburg airfield were arrested and locked up and, for good measure, since Hess had long dabbled in the occult and fringe medicine, scores of astrologers and naturopaths. Meanwhile Hitler himself oversaw the wording of the press release which announced to the world that Hess was mad: "The National Socialist Party regrets that this idealist fell prey to tragic hallucinations."

Some Germans, though, found the news less than surprising. The alarums past, interpreter Paul Schmidt returned home to Berlin and found himself discussing the contretemps with his gardener. The old man seemed quite unperturbed. "Didn't you know," he asked innocently, "that we're already governed by madmen?"

4

"He'll Never Beat Men Like These"

19 May–28 May, 1941

THE QUAYSIDE WAS bathed in the golden light of evening. The little group of men strolled slowly, laughing and chatting, drinking in the last of the sun. Once their host, Viggo Axelssen, ship's chandler, bachelor and *bon-viveur* of Kristiansand, Norway, did pause, borrowing a friend's spy-glass to scan the horizon, but too briefly to cause comment.

Eight miles away, beyond the Oksøy lighthouse, a group of ships was steaming west at high speed. Two were quite obviously camouflaged German warships, aircraft circling above, destroyers ahead, as they headed for the Norwegian fjords.

After eighteen months of war, it was a common sight for the subjugated Norwegians; no one even gave it a thought. And when Axelssen mentioned dropping by his office to fetch something, only a burst of laughter followed. That night the ship's chandler was giving a dinner party at the Kristiansand Club to celebrate the launching of a new boat; the "something" could only be a bottle of schnapps.

But once in his office near Vestre Strand-gade, Kristiansand's town centre, Axelssen worked fast. Scribbling a twelve-word message he pocketed it, setting out for the club. Now as his way led him past the bus station, he stopped off to trade gossip with Arne Moen, a grave-faced man wearing a peaked cap and a shiny serge uniform. Within the hour, as Axelssen was calling for a third round of drinks in the club's Red Room, Moen's bus was already grinding up the narrow road towards the port of Flekkefjord, sixty miles north-west.

The message which Axelssen had written, and which Moen had not even scanned, was now secure in a pocket of the bus's engine casing.

In his roomy grocer's shop on Flekkefjord's main street, the proprietor, Tor Njaa was still open for business. When Moen walked in, Njaa raised a silent eyebrow; although the bus driver ostensibly called for a packet of ersatz coffee, his presence always spelt urgency. Not pausing to remove his white jacket, the grocer stuffed Axelssen's message into his pocket, crossing the street to the dairy where Sofie Rørvik worked.

Once Njaa had left, Sofie took the crumpled paper, carefully smoothing out the wrinkles before easing it into the top of her stocking, flat against her thigh. It was now around 6 p.m. on 20 May. The long summer night stretched ahead; not until after midnight would darkness fall.

Sofie's way out of town lay uphill, through a steep valley fringed with yellow catkins and giant oaks, a 10-mile cycle ride to the farm of young Gunwald Tomstad at Helle. The farm, six acres of arable, more than eighty acres of moors and woods, would never make Tomstad rich, but it was still an ideal centre for a spy ring. All sea traffic rounded Lista lighthouse, at the mouth of Flekkefjord, coming close in to obtain the protection of the German coastal batteries, and could thus be easily monitored.

Axelssen, Moen, Njaa, Sofie Rørvik, Tomstad himself, had one thing in common: all of them were secret agents in a coastal network that stretched 360 miles from Oslo to Stavanger. Tonight they were about to achieve their biggest coup in the entire war. The quarry that Axelssen had sighted was Germany's mightiest warship, the *Bismarck*, outward bound, along with the cruiser *Prinz Eugen*, on a three-month cruise to ravage the Atlantic convoys.

At Helle Farm, just as she had expected, Sofie found Tomstad closeted with his chief, Odd Starheim, a curly-headed shipowner's son who had escaped to Britain in 1940 to become one of the first Scandinavian agents of the Special Operations Executive. Returning to Norway in a British submarine on New Year's Eve, 1940, armed with a radio transmitter, Starheim's brief had been to set up a network based on Kristiansand, Norway's third largest port and now a German naval base.

This evening Axelssen's message had reached its fifth and final link. As Sofie waited, the two men set to work coding it.

Although they had known for some hours that the valley was encircled by German listening posts, both were too engrossed to realise that troops armed with special equipment were at this moment crossing the open spaces between the farm buildings.

Starheim was aware only of the need for urgency. Conceivably this message was the most important that his mission – with the unromantic code-name "Operation Cheese" – might ever accomplish. The two men mounted to the musty attic of the farmhouse, and Tomstad, opening an old suitcase, removed a small compact transmitter. Crouched in a cubbyhole, Starheim began calling Home Station, London.

Methodically, his fingers stabbed at the keys: "A battleship . . . probably German . . . passed Kristiansand . . ."

Outside the attic, on a stairway smelling of old timber and dust, Tomstad was standing guard, the muzzle of his automatic pistol trained on the stairs that led to the first floor. Faint far-off shouts were reaching him from the farmyard; the direction finder signals were now recording at maximum strength. If they broke in he would shoot and keep shooting, to ensure that the message got through.

This was the time of year when Helle was at its loveliest, when patches of blue anemones and bog cotton splotched the heath surrounding the farm. Would it soon be the time when all three of them had recourse to their cyanide capsules, ensuring death in nine seconds at the most, three if lucky?

". . . passed Kristiansand . . . heading west . . ."

To Sofie Rørvik, waiting below, the coded dots and dashes seemed as loud as hammer blows, resounding all over the house. Suddenly they stopped – so abruptly that Sofie and Tomstad himself had to bite their lips to stop themselves from crying out loud.

Starheim had completed the last three words of the message: ". . . escorted by three destroyers".

Tomstad had just one hope that his farm would go unmolested. Early that year, for love of country, he had deliberately assumed a pariah's role. Summoning courage, he had walked into Flekkefjord town hall and asked to join the Norwegian Nazi Party, the *Nasjonal Samling* (N.S.). He wore the Party's black uniform at rallies, and hung a framed portrait of their leader, Vidkun Quisling, in his hall. Now every villager and neighbour looked through him as though he were dead – but the N.S. leaders had come to trust him.

Now all of them would have to bluff, because their lives depended on it. Starheim must depart in broad daylight, a man with nothing to hide, and Sofie must go with him to help him past the control posts – the two of them walking like lovers, arms entwined, oblivious to everyone.

Armed with paint brush and tin, Tomstad mounted a ladder to an outhouse roof and watched them go. Soon they were a long way down the valley. Though a few Germans stopped and stared, calling out lewd suggestions, nobody barred their passage. Tomstad kept on painting until they were out of sight. Some soldiers crossed his yard just then, along with a Gestapo man, but seeing him they only smiled broadly and waved; they had no time to stop and chat.

Still painting, Tomstad felt his legs trembling. His cover had held; it was going to be all right. No one would come to question him; that same evening the great hunt was joined. But it had been close – very close.

*

Unknown to Starheim and his agents, their signal had now placed the *Bismarck* in double jeopardy.

Soon after midnight on 21 May, Commander Norman Denning, of Royal Naval Intelligence, had been roused from sleep in The Citadel, the ugly concrete headquarters of the Operational Intelligence Centre in

Whitehall, hard by Nelson's column. The British Naval Attaché, Captain Henry Denham, was cabling from Stockholm: the Swedish cruiser *Gotland* had spotted the German squadron's course and a friendly source had at once tipped Denham off.

The report had been graded B3 – source good, information possibly, but by no means certainly, correct.

Starheim's report, coming hard on the heels of Denham's now lent a new aspect of urgency. At 3.30 a.m. R.A.F. Coastal Command were alerted to scour the Norwegian coast from first light until the ships were located and identified. By early afternoon, the risks run by Starheim's agents were vindicated. A Spitfire of the Photographic Reconnaissance Unit had pinpointed *Bismarck* and *Prinz Eugen* in Korsfjord, the entrance to Bergen Harbour.

Events now moved swiftly. Aboard the new flagship of the Home Fleet, *King George V*, moored in Scapa Flow, a green telephone linking Scapa with London rang insistently. The Admiralty were briefing the Commander-in-Chief, Sir John Tovey, a small compact sea-dog with blue twinkling eyes, that trouble was imminent. Promptly Tovey ordered the cruiser *Suffolk*, patrolling the Denmark Straits, to keep a sharp look-out; her sister ship, *Norfolk*, was despatched from Iceland to relieve her.

Now a subdued buzz of rumour ran through Scapa's ships – men guessing something was afoot, yet unable to pin down details. Aboard the E-Class destroyer, H.M.S. *Electra*, Lieutenant Frank McLeod, the Chief Engineer, received the order: "Raise Steam". In fact, this was a routine signal, allowing the ship four hours to prepare for sea, but McLeod did not waste a moment; the force of those rumours was too potent. Within minutes came an order more imperative still: "Raise Steam With Despatch!"

This cut the preparation time to two hours – a sure sign of impending trouble. But soon another order halved the time-span yet again: "Raise Steam With All Despatch!"

Admiral Tovey faced a dilemma. The weather was changing by the minute and mist and rain were drifting; now he was beset by the fear that the Germans were already en route for the Atlantic, where eleven allied convoys lay at their mercy. By 9 p.m., as darkness fell, he came to a decision. Vice-Admiral Lancelot Holland, in the battle-cruiser *Hood*, was to take the battleship *Prince of Wales*, with the destroyers *Electra*, *Anthony*, *Echo*, *Icarus*, *Achates* and *Antelope* and proceed to Iceland for refuelling. Then they must take up a watchful stance south-west of the island.

Aboard every ship that formed this vanguard there was a pleasant tingle of expectancy. In *Electra*, Lieutenant McLeod cast a sharp but confident look over the organ loft of pipes that made up his engine room then reported to the captain, Commander Cecil May: "Steam for twenty knots, sir . . . third boiler will be ready in the next half hour." Simultaneously, the First Lieutenant, Richard Jenner-Fust, also reached the bridge: "Ship secured for sea, sir . . . Slip Rope wove."

It was the same on every ship. Only forty minutes had elapsed since Tovey's signal, yet now only the Slip Ropes – slim wire hawsers – secured the destroyers to the buoys.

Towards midnight on 21 May they slipped their moorings, one by one, forming line ahead to pass through the Switha Gate, heading for the Pentland Firth and their rendezvous with *Hood* and *Prince of Wales*. Now all hands were furiously preoccupied with the preliminaries for action – priming depth charges, arming torpedoes, checking guns, manhandling "ready use" ammunition.

One mood was common to all: a calm and absolute confidence. Aboard *Electra*, when the Captain's steward asked Gunnery Officer Timothy Cain, "Think we'll have luck, sir?", Cain was buoyant. "We won't *need* luck, not with the *Hood* for company." In *Prince of Wales*, all ranks felt the same. With an audible click the loud-speakers switched on and Captain John Leach, a stocky much-loved West Countryman, hailed the ship's company: "The odds are that they are making for the Atlantic to prey on our convoys . . . What we have to hope now is that we intercept them and bring them to action."

As the tannoys clicked off, there was an audible sigh of relief. It was the real thing at last and nothing could stop them. Midshipman Kenneth Townsend-Green still recalls, "We enjoyed the invincibility of it all," a sentiment echoed by Petty Officer David Hunter. "She was a great ship – unsinkable."

These were comforting illusions – yet totally unwarranted. Although all naval men took a fierce and irrational pride in "the mighty *Hood*", she was now, after twenty-two years in service, an obsolescent hybrid. Despite her eight 15-inch guns she was a warhorse from another age, built for speed but not for slogging, her deck protection, at maximum, no more than three inches thick.

Ironically, the same truth held good both for the *Prince of Wales* and her German quarry. Laid down on New Year's Day 1937 as Job No 3968 at Cammell Laird's shipyard, Birkenhead, it was not until 4 May, 1939, that she had gone down the slipway, launched by the Princess Royal. With her 1,612 crew – 110 officers, 1,502 ratings – she was virtually a floating town; Ordinary Seaman Gerald Cooper still recalls, "It took you several weeks to find your way round." Although she displaced 35,000 tons, fully 15,000 was accounted for by armour plating, but this luxury was to be paid for in gun power and speed. At best the *Prince* could muster 28 knots against *Bismarck*'s 30.

Her special pride was her ten new-type 14-inch guns, designed for greater penetration and a higher rate of fire, but two of the new-type turrets were still giving trouble and tonight she was sailing with more than 100 civilian contractors still aboard her, desperately trying to locate the faults. Even so, Churchill, who had twice served as First Lord of the Admiralty, looked to her as "something that could catch and kill" for he believed as implicitly as Roosevelt, one time Secretary of the Navy, that in 1941 sea power would decide the world's fate.

Although Hitler had private misgivings, the *Kriegsmarine* took as fierce a pride in the *Bismarck* – not for nothing had the *Prinz Eugen* ungrudgingly dubbed her "Big Brother". One sixth of a mile long, 120 feet wide, displacing more than 50,000 tons fully laden, she was the mightiest warship afloat. Her armament – eight radar-controlled 15-inch guns, with landing space for six aircraft – was as formidable as the statistics that naval enthusiasts loved to quote: a crew 2,400 strong, a wiring system so complex it comprised 28,000 miles of electrical circuits, Krupp armour, thirteen inches thick, fashioned from specially hardened Wotan steel that protected her sides and turrets. Commissioned in February, 1941, and thus a novice alongside the newly-built *Prince*, who achieved it on 19 January, she had one factor in common with her British pursuer: both were deemed unsinkable.

At 11 p.m. on 22 May, on receipt of the code-word REBEL, Tovey, in *King George V,* along with four cruisers, six destroyers and the aircraft carrier *Victorious*, moved out of Scapa to join in the pursuit. Twenty ships now made part of the hunt that Odd Starheim had set in motion.

Yet the most formidable adversaries the *Bismarck* faced pointed a cogent moral for all naval powers in the months that lay ahead: the nine near-obsolete Swordfish torpedo-bombers of No 825 Fleet Air Arm Squadron, unwieldy single-engined biplanes fashioned from wood, fabric and metal struts, lashed down on the heaving flight-deck of H.M.S. *Victorious*.

*

One Allied spy was less lucky. For Ruth Mitchell, her *Četnik* crusade was over almost before it had begun.

In the weeks since leaving Belgrade, she had followed a tortuous 160-mile route – by refugee train to Chacak, thence to Ujiće, where King Peter and his ministers had briefly encamped, finally after sixteen hours in a cattle truck to Sarajevo, where the seeds of World War One had been sown. From Sarajevo she had boarded a baggage car to Mostar, then on to Herzegnovi beside the blue Adriatic. At long last she had reached Montenegro.

It was here that Ruth knew a brief temptation. A Serb she had known in Belgrade, on the staff of the British Legation, warned her there was no time to lose. Those British diplomats still left were making for Risan, 13 miles down the coast, in the hope of a last minute evacuation by seaplane and submarine. "Will you go now?" he urged. "Tomorrow may be too late."

Ruth Mitchell thought long and hard. Her ties with England were longstanding; once, in another life, as the wife of Stanley Knowles, a housemaster at Tonbridge School, she had become deeply attached to the English countryside and the English way of life. Her son by her first husband, John Lendrum van Breda, was at this moment a Pilot Officer in the Royal Air Force, serving in the Western Desert. It was three months – the time when Rommel arrived in North Africa – since she had heard from him.

Her other choice was a thornier road: on the run by day and night, the broiling sun of a Balkan summer giving place to the soaking rains of winter, cold rocks for a bed, hard black bread, cheese and an onion for food.

But finally she realised she had already chosen – on the day when Pechanats drew the line through her name in the old time-worn book. She was a Četnik. The question was: where should she go to best serve the Četnik cause?

Logic suggested the port of Dubrovnik. As the largest city on the Montenegrin coast, it would certainly house Italian military headquarters. A spy with an American passport might do useful work there – though the passport, Ruth realised with a sudden sinking of the heart, was no longer valid. She had been due to renew it at the American Legation on Monday 7 April – the day after the great bombardment of the city. All she could hope was that the Italians would find the bold American eagle, stamped in bright gold on the cover, too impressive to be looked at askance.

Luck was with her; two Yugoslav naval officers, heading down the coast, agreed to give her a lift. With her Četnik uniform now stowed inside her grip, Ruth, conventionally attired in dress and head scarf, reached Dubrovnik around 20 April.

Once there she lost no time in putting the past behind her. Her uniform and insignia she concealed under bomb rubble in the garden of her first staging post, the run-down Hotel Gradats. An old friend from America, Laura McCullaugh, who passed each spring at the Pension Ivy, hid Ruth's Četnik pass in a sponge bag and buried it in a flower bed.

By early May, when Dubrovnik, under Italian tutelage, had been rechristened Ragusa, Ruth had settled into a small hotel near the naval base at Gruzuh, two miles from the city. Armed with a large-scale map of the port, a capacious marketing basket and a pair of dark glasses, she set out each morning along the cliffs to "shop" for gun emplacements.

By degrees she was amassing a sizeable dossier of information – but how could she transmit it to those who most needed to know?

Again, luck seemed to be with her. On 17 May, in the dappled half-light of a grape trellis behind a provision store, she held a brief whispered rendezvous with a *Četnik* agent named Vaso, a Montenegrin frontier policeman she had met on her journey south. Vaso had electrifying news: A *Četnik* rising was planned for 28 June, the anniversary of a great Serbian battle, and Ruth was needed at headquarters. Vaso himself would meet her 31 miles inland, in the tiny town of Nikšić, and guide her to the new leader, Colonel Draža Mihailović.

Ruth was bewildered. Had Pechanats renounced the leadership? But Vaso just scowled and answered evasively; only later did Ruth learn with shame that Pechanats had sold out to the Germans.

But at last she had made the longed-for contact. At dawn on 23 May, she would leave to join Mihailović.

The afternoon of 22 May was warm and sunny. Towards 5 p.m. Ruth enjoyed a leisurely swim, then dried off on the beach. Then, donning a shirt and grey flannel slacks, she headed for the deserted hotel dining-room, a large glassed-in terrace overlooking the bay.

In cheerful mood, whistling softly, she noted the setting sun throwing a rose-gold glow on the white wall opposite the window. The glow had entrapped her shadow, and now, for the fun of it, still whistling, Ruth began to gyrate, a slow rhythmic waltz movement, intrigued by the shifting shadow patterns on the wall.

Abruptly Ruth stopped. Her shadow was now hemmed in by two other shadows, one long and thin, the other smaller. Turning, she faced two rubber-shod men in plain clothes.

She knew at once who they were. "Ruth Mitchell? We are the Gestapo. You will come with us at once."

*

Aircraftman Marcel Gerard Comeau had a strange sense of foreboding. As early as 19 May – three days before Ruth Mitchell's arrest in Dubrovnik – Comeau had the uneasy sensation that the debâcle he had experienced in Greece had been only the dress-rehearsal for a greater disaster in Crete.

What Comeau had witnessed as the assault ship *Glenearn* limped into the main harbour at Suda Bay had scarcely suggested grim preparedness. He himself tramped down the gangplank to the jetty but on other ships men were less fortunate; as the Stukas screamed low over the water, some leapt overboard in mid-harbour, swimming for their lives to dry land. But once ashore, they found no permanent accommodation to house them and few tents; most slept in their clothes among the olive trees. Transport was non-existent. While Comeau foot-slogged the twenty miles to Maleme airfield, other landing grounds were further-flung – thirty miles to Retimo, sixty-five to Heraklion.

The troops that he passed along the way seemed in sorry shape – dishevelled, unshaven, their nerves at snapping point after the constant strafing. They were embittered, too, by the lack of air cover and Comeau's blue uniform brought a barrage of taunts and catcalls: "R – A – bloody F – Rare as Bloody Fairies." It was a bitter pill to swallow.

Of the 44,000 men – 29,000 British and Dominion troops, 15,000 Greeks – flung together as an improvised defence force, only 8,700 had come fresh from the Middle East; others demoralised or wounded in Greece, lacked even rifles. Typical of the square pegs plugging the round hole of Crete were the men of the 1005th Dock Operating Company. Impressed as stevedores because they hailed from British ports, all of them were in fact shipping clerks, fresh from office stools. Following one day's Stuka bombardment, almost 100 men reported sick, suffering from "nervous prostration". On 3 May they were replaced by Australian volunteers.

Although the newly-appointed Commander-in-Chief, Major General Bernard Freyberg, V.C., a battle-scarred New Zealander and a veteran of Gallipoli, had not seen fit to accept the offer, one stout-hearted body of men might have served him as well. As May dawned, they had petitioned him en masse:

> We wholeheartedly put ourselves under your service, dangerous or not, provided that the cause of our Allied effort is fulfilled . . .
> Respectfully yours,
> The convicts of the Island of Crete.

But so many supplies had been left behind in Greece, even seasoned troops would have found the going hard. One New Zealander, Second-Lieutenant Charles Upham, of the 20th (N.Z.) Battalion always recalled it as "a pauper's campaign" from first to last – no entrenching tools, "mortars without baseplates, Vickers guns without tripods". One unit even improvised artillery sights from slivers of wood and chewing gum. Most Australians used herring tins for dixies and whittled spoons from olive wood, but many men, like Comeau himself, never saw hot food during the entire campaign. One doctor, Lieutenant Theodore Stephanides, attached to the Cyprus Regiment, found drugs so short he fell back on a knowledge of botany – decocting herbal draughts from plantains, mallows and mulberry leaves.

Even so, Comeau knew contentment of a kind. Realising that No 11 (Blenheim) Squadron would make little headway against the Stukas, the youngster had "deserted" yet again – re-attaching himself to the Hurri-

81

cane ground crews of No 33 Squadron of Maleme. Wedged between the sea and the coast road, the airfield lay at the base of the wooded 340-foot Kavkazia Hill; here, at least, Comeau enjoyed the shelter of a tent, though there were only duckboards to sleep on and a warm reunion with old friends like Ken Eaton, Tubby Dixon and Paddy Rennie.

Innocent of the battle plan, they wondered idly: How would Crete be defended when the time came?

Few men realised it, but Crete was virtually indefensible from the start. Although the island was 170 miles long, only one major narrow road followed the northern coastline. So limited were its port facilities that at Suda only two ships could berth at a time; at Canea, unloading was feasible only by lighter. Anti-aircraft, artillery and tanks were woefully short; of the twenty-one tanks that Wavell could spare, all proved defective, lacking cooling systems for the guns and even wireless communication. No air cover was possible from North Africa, 400 miles away; in theory, the island would be self-supporting.

But only in theory. On 19 May, no more than six aircraft – three Hurricanes, three obsolete Gladiators – were left on the entire island, too few to serve any useful purpose. On this same day they were flown back to Egypt.

For a long time Comeau and his mates wandered round the air strip, then drifted listlessly back to their tents. It seemed strange to be aircraftmen without any aircraft to repair – when the battle had not even started.

*

On the morning of this same day, in an ornate rococo suite on the second floor of the Hotel Grande Bretagne, Athens, a group of junior officers had gathered for an eleventh-hour briefing. For maximum security, the room had been hermetically sealed and shuttered against the sunlight, but the secret was not kept for long. Suspended from a gilded cornice, they espied a giant map of Crete.

For a moment there was a burst of excited comment and chatter, until General Kurt Student, the genial crop-headed commander of the Seventh Air Division, hushed them with a soft, *"Mein Herren, Ich bitte Sie."*

Then, in what Baron Friedrich von der Heydte, commanding the 1st Battalion, Third Parachute Regiment, recalled as "a quiet but clear, slightly vibrant voice", Student outlined his plan. The concept was both bold and unprecedented: to capture an entire island, 100 miles from the Greek mainland, by air attack and vertical assault. Although Hitler had finally assented – persuaded that seizing Crete would ensure his dominion in the Aegean, negate a threat to Rumania's Ploesti oil-fields and ensure Turkish neutrality – the project was originally the brainchild of

Hermann Göring, determined to revenge the reverses of the Battle of Britain.

But Student, a dedicated professional had worked for the plan until it had become part of his life. Now he shared his secret with the men who must make it a reality: the island was to be attacked by paratroops at four different points simultaneously. The target of the Assault Regiment, dropping to the west, was the airfield at Maleme. The Third Regiment was to seize Canea, Crete's capital. While the First Regiment struck at the town and airfield at Heraklion, the Second Regiment was allotted identical targets at Retimo.

The logistics were staggering. As 10,000 parachutists were drifting from the sky, a further 750 would be landing by gliders, both DFS 230s, carrying ten men, and Gotha 242s, holding up to twenty-five. A back-up force of 5,000 would travel by JU-52 transports, the old Luftwaffe workhorses known as "Auntie Ju". For mopping-up operations, a seaborne force of 7,000 men would land on Day Two.

Nothing had been left to chance. Each paratrooper would carry three days' emergency rations: specially prepared *Wittler* bread, sliced and wrapped in cellophane, processed chocolate, tartaric acid, sugar, biscuits, thirst-quenchers, cigarettes, phonetic phrasebooks, even contraceptives. Each man's wrists and ankles would be heavily padded, to lessen the risk of sprains.

Security was absolute. Paybooks were replaced by identity cards, giving no hint of the bearer's unit. Parachute sing-songs were to be strictly forbidden. Even the proud badge of the paratrooper – a plunging eagle in an oval garland of oak and laurel leaves – must be removed for the duration.

A colour code for parachutes would streamline the operation further still – black for other ranks' supplies, red for officers, white for ammunition, yellow for medical supplies. On landing, each section leader would fire a white Very light if all was well, a red Very light if trouble threatened, a cluster of three white lights to signal, Objective Gained.

As the conference broke up, each battalion commander was conscious of one vital factor: unless at least one airfield was seized, and seized early, enabling follow-up troops and supplies to be flown in, what the Luftwaffe had styled "Operation Mercury" would swiftly grind to an ignominious standstill.

*

"I cannot feel that there was any real grip shown by Middle East H.Q. upon this operation," Churchill was to comment irascibly. "They regarded it as a tiresome commitment . . . No one in high authority seems to have sat down for two or three mornings together and endeavoured to take a full forward view of what would happen . . ."

There is no doubt that Churchill was right. Since November, 1940, six different commanders had briefly held sway in Crete, but in six months no one had given them any positive directives as to what was expected of them. Freyberg, the seventh, had taken over on 30 April, but as First Secretary Harold Caccia reported from the British Legation in Athens: "As far as I could see no serious attempt to prepare defences had been made until a few weeks ago. Even barbed wire on the beaches was being improvised."

Yet on the morning of Tuesday, 20 May, as he breakfasted serenely in his dug-out headquarters near Canea, Freyberg's mood was one of buoyant optimism. "Am not the least anxious about an airborne attack," he cabled Churchill on 5 May, for in anticipation of a major assault from the sea he had positioned many of his troops at forward strongpoints along the coast.

Yet by strange irony, Freyberg this morning was better briefed than almost any World War Two commander to date. Precise details of Hitler's Directive No 28, including troop strengths, times and dispositions had long been available to him through the Ultra intercepts; to this end Hut No 6, which housed the duty cipher watch at Bletchley Park, had been working overtime for weeks. Although Freyberg was never privy to the existence of the "Enigma" machine – the information, he thought, came from a disgruntled stool-pigeon in Berlin – he knew exactly what the Germans planned for Crete.

Yet one simple truth eluded him: the airfields were the prime target. Unaware that German paratroop strength was limited – 10,000 men were the maximum available – and convinced that the JU-52s could crash-land on any stretch of beach they saw, it was a seaborne attack Freyberg feared above all.

To counter the attacks, he had thus split his command into four semi-independent bodies, functioning from Maleme, Retimo, Heraklion and Suda. Yet communications were so primitive each command was virtually on its own, operating in the dark. One hundred field wireless sets, one man argued later, might still have saved Crete. One runner, journeying the 45 miles from Retimo to Freyberg's H.Q. took six days to do it, memorising three separate passwords as he went.

Freyberg, though, was certain that a diversified command could cope with all eventualities. Towards 7 a.m., as the first gliders loomed silently overhead, the Commander-in-Chief, with the satisfied air of a man finding his dinner guests punctual, remarked, "They're dead on time."

All over the island, at this moment, men stood mesmerised by the most naked display of air power that they had ever seen. Rarely in a modern battle had such a host of visual impressions been registered: the JU-52s moving sluggishly over Heraklion, "huge black beasts with yellow noses", the silvery tapering wings of the gliders, passing "as silently as ghosts with just a swishing sound", the puffs of french chalk drifting on a light breeze as the parachutes snapped open.

The similes that men conjured up bespoke the depths of their emotions. For Major Geoffrey Cox, a New Zealander, the sound of Bren gun bullets clipping rocks and branches as the Allies opened up was "like the clatter of a million lawn-mowers all at once". Strangely, the impressions were often festive. To one man, the drifting parachutes, billowing open as low as 300 feet recalled "the balloons coming down at the end of a party". To another the spilling hordes of troopers were "like handfuls of confetti in the bright sunlight".

Most men were stunned by the precision of the exercise. As the gliders ploughed relentlessly on, slicing through olive trees, bushes, shallow stone walls, bombers moved in their wake, softening up the opposition "with the methodical monotony of coolies planting rice". Everywhere the valleys were littered with discarded parachutes "like huge discarded mushrooms", though not all Germans made it to the target. One JU-52, caught by lethal Bofors fire, erupted in flames, its occupants scrambling for safety "like plums spilled from a burst bag".

Marcel Comeau, who had thirsted for action, suddenly had all he could handle. Busy searching for his pipe, which he had mislaid, he let the others go ahead of him to the mess tent; only in the moment of finding it was he aware of a throbbing crescendo of engines. Ducking through the tent flap he saw overhead a vast glinting armada of planes, JU-88s, Heinkels and Dorniers, showering bombs on the R.A.F. lines and the New Zealanders' camp at the base of Kavkazia Hill. For thirty minutes on end the bombs tore at the soft soil "until it hung in the air like a blanket, blotting out the sun".

Grabbing a rifle, Comeau had just dived headfirst for a foxhole when the sound of rushing air filled his ears. Open-mouthed he saw a glider, swooping low through the curtain of dust, disappearing towards the west. Then, with a snapping crack of olive branches, another glider appeared, careering straight towards him. Before Comeau had time to duck it had bulldozed into the tent he had just vacated, slewing half round, spraying him with loose dirt. Then it stopped dead in its dust cloud, one wing dug into the bank behind Comeau.

Doubling under its wing, "feeling pretty scared", Comeau scrambled up the bank, heading for higher ground. At that moment, the glider door opened to disgorge a dazed-looking German and Comeau, at almost point-blank range, shot him dead. The man spun backward onto a second paratrooper – a time-span long enough for Comeau to eject and re-load. The second man was holding his head in his hands as Comeau fired again, toppling him in a heap to block the darkness of the doorway.

Hastily the airman ejected the empty cartridge case but the next round jammed; sweating and cursing he wrestled with the bolt but could not budge it. Now, from the corner of his eye, he saw the remaining Germans piling from the glider, and more men racing through the trees from a second glider which had landed. With bursts of rapid fire tattooing the soft earth ahead of him Comeau raced for Kavkazia Hill, along with a motley group of New Zealanders who had survived the bombing.

The German plan seemed simple now: to take Kavkazia Hill, to silence the Bofors guns surrounding the landing field and thus secure Maleme. If Kavkazia was held, the allies stood a chance. Comeau and the others were determined that it should be held.

"The enemy entered Crete as a conquering power," the Chiefs of Staff were to assure Churchill later, but the Germans had no such impression. Some paratroopers, jumping too soon, landed in the sea off Maleme; others misled by green jump masters, hit drop zones far from their planned positions. Private Melville Hill-Rennie, of the 20th (N.Z.) Battalion, saw one German plane that had plainly misjudged its height. Although he counted thirty-five bodies tumble from the plane, not one parachute had opened before the men struck the ground.

In some gliders that remained on course, landing without damage, only silence prevailed; every man was dead in his seat, his neck snapped by the impact. Another, landing at 75 miles an hour, ripped itself apart against the ironwork of a bridge. The 3rd Battalion of the 1st Assault Regiment, landing east of Maleme, were mostly caught and killed within minutes of landing; by dusk only 200 out of 600 men remained alive. Asked if he needed help in mopping up, a New Zealand commander replied curtly: "They'll all be dead before you can get a man here."

Top commanders proved as vulnerable as privates. *Generalleutnant* Wilhelm Sussmann, commanding the Centre Group, was killed soon after take-off when his glider crashed on an island within sight of Athens. *Generalmajor* Eugen Meindl, who headed the Maleme operation, was seriously wounded soon after landing. Even men who landed securely felt cut off and at a loss for orders. Baron Friedrich von der Heydte found himself suspended from a fig tree like a latter-day Absalom, without one of his battalion in sight. Heydte finally caught up with his headquarters company at their rendezvous point, Galatas Jail, but although radio contact had been made with four companies, only one company had made fleeting contact with the British. "We felt we were all alone in this valley," Heydte recalled later.

Of the thousands who dropped this morning, the plight of 18-year-old *Fallschirmjäger* (Paratrooper) Walter Goltz, of the Assault Regiment's 3rd Battalion, somehow emerges as typical. Aboard his JU-52, Goltz was fourth in line to jump, but as he made to leave the plane, the transport's nose was peppered with bullets. Next a shell burst under the port wing; as Goltz jumped the plane was out of control and banking steeply.

As the full force of the wind hit him, Goltz's goggles were ripped from his face; the Junkers had been flying too high and he took a long time to land in a deep valley south-east of Kavkazia Hill. Tramping through an olive grove, he found no sign of life, either British or German; the dozen men who comprised his "stick" had all been killed.

Later that morning, he met four more survivors and all of them remained in hiding until late afternoon. Then, venturing forth along the dried-up irrigation canal encircling the hill, they chanced on another twenty Germans – half of them wounded. Using old ladders for stretchers they finally brought their wounded to a communal field hospital by the Tavronitis river, east of Maleme.

Only that evening – some twelve hours after landing – was Goltz given finite orders to take up a defensive position west of Maleme.

By dusk on 20 May, it was plain that Student had fatally miscalculated. By striking at too many airfields simultaneously – a move urged on him by Hitler – he had failed to secure any of his objectives at all. Although casualty figures have always been in dispute – 4,500 men by some counts, more than 6,000 by others – the effort had cost him dear. The loss of aircraft was phenomenal – although estimates again ranged from 271 to close on 400.

"The days of the parachute troops are over," Hitler told Student testily, following an exhaustive inquest on Crete; from this time on German paratroopers were deployed only as elite infantrymen.

Then, at 9 p.m., one commander took a decision which turned the whole campaign upside down. All that day, Lieutenant-Colonel Lionel Andrew, V.C. commanding the 22nd (N.Z.) Battalion, had been under withering mortar fire in his headquarters at Maleme. Wounded by a shell splinter, Andrew was at his wit's end; for hours now he had lost all signal and runner contact with three of his five companies, and the conviction grew on him that they had been overwhelmed. Knowing he could not hold the airfield and the slopes of Kavkazia, with only 200 men, Andrew decided he must withdraw.

Three miles east, in Platanias village, the Brigade Commander, Brigadier James Hargest, had heard nothing but success stories all day. When Andrew made radio contact at 9 p.m., seeking permission to withdraw, the wireless battery was fading fast; Hargest could barely hear him. In any case, he assumed that Andrew was merely adjusting his perimeter. As he replied, "If you must, you must," the wireless went dead.

By 2 a.m., Andrew had pulled out his remaining men away from Kavkazia Hill to a point nearly two miles east of Maleme – unaware that the three missing companies were still holding out, both on the airfield perimeter and on Kavkazia. And as the New Zealanders moved out, the Germans of the Assault Regiment began a slow wary night trek along the undefended slopes.

Student tried a bold gamble. By first light, the Assault Regiment had taken most of Maleme and the high ground to the south. Then, at 8 a.m., as three and a half companies of paratroopers landed in a drop zone out of British range, a JU-52 risked a perilous touchdown on the beach. By 8.10 a.m. another had landed – this time on Maleme. By 5 p.m., an air shuttle service from Greece was throwing in troops at a breathtaking rate; one day later, planes ferrying in forty men at a time were landing every three minutes.

Now it would be only a matter of days. With the loss of Maleme, Crete was lost.

Marcel Comeau didn't know what to make of it. In the small hours of 21 May, one of Andrew's missing companies – "D" Company under Captain T. C. Campbell – realising they had been abandoned, decided they too must pull out. By chance they awoke Comeau and a handful of "erks" on the summit of Kavkazia. Now, dazed with sleep, weighed down by a Lewis gun on his shoulder, Comeau made part of their retreat – a nightmare journey through rocky defiles and tall stands of Aleppo pines, over tumbled piles of German bodies, smelling of blood and *ersatz* coffee, past bloated shapes, still twisted in their harnesses, suspended from darkened trees.

It was some time before the full irony of the retreat came home to Comeau: victory had come to Student not by a stirring feat of arms but by the failure of a wireless battery.

*

In Europe, the British were daily losing ground. Soon, apart from the two and a half square miles of Gibraltar, not one inch of continental European soil would be under British military control. But in the North Atlantic, their luck was holding.

All through 23 May, two among the twenty ships dogging the battleship *Bismarck* kept in determined pursuit, closing the gap at a steady 60 miles an hour. Then at 7.22 p.m., the starboard after look-out on the bridge of the cruiser *Suffolk* achieved a first sighting: the black mass of the *Bismarck,* with *Prinz Eugen* in attendance, looming from mist on the starboard quarter. "Two ships bearing Green One Four Oh," came his excited shout.

Fifteen miles away, the cruiser *Norfolk* was steaming through drifting wraiths of fog; her captain, Alfred Phillips, was munching cheese-on-toast in his sea cabin when his Yeoman of Signals arrived in haste with news from the *Suffolk* – "One battleship one cruiser in sight bearing 020 degrees distant 7 miles. Course 240 degrees." At once Phillips increased speed, heading for open water but misjudging the direction. Emerging from fog, he saw *Bismarck* only six miles ahead, coming straight for him.

88

Five orange-brown salvoes had straddled the oily swell before *Norfolk* regained the safety of the fog.

It was not a combat that the Germans sought. This Atlantic sortie was, in fact, a piecemeal deployment of their forces: the *Tirpitz*, the second giant battleship in the *Bismarck* class still had four months crew-training ahead of her, the battleship *Scharnhorst* was undergoing repair to her boilers, the 30,000 ton *Gneisenau* was out of service for six months following damage by a British aerial torpedo. Although a bold attempt to shake the Royal Navy's control of the Atlantic had seemed necessary, the Fleet Commander, Admiral Günther Lütjens, had received due warning from the Commander-in-Chief, *Grossadmiral* Erich Raeder. "Needless to say," Raeder had stressed, "you will have to operate with prudence and care."

It was an admonition Lütjens would obey to the letter. A dour taciturn veteran, whose whole life was the Navy, Lütjens had seen too many Fleet Commanders dismissed after tangling with the *Kriegsmarine* – among them his old friend and predecessor, Admiral Wilhelm Marschall. "I know what they want," he had told Marschall just before sailing, "and shall carry out their orders."

"The primary objective is the destruction of the enemy's carrying capacity," ran his *Kriegsmarine* directive. "Enemy warships will be engaged only in furtherance of this objective, and provided such engagement can take place without excessive risk."

Raeder, too, had displayed a similar prudence. Mindful of Hitler's innate scepticism regarding the deployment of capital ships, it was not until 22 May, on a visit to Hitler's private apartment in Munich, that he broke the news that *Bismarck* had sailed.

Hitler was alarmed. He recalled that on 5 May, when he inspected *Bismarck* in Gotenhafen, Lütjens had expressed reservations about British torpedo-aircraft. Now he asked Raeder point-blank: "*Herr Grossadmiral*, can't we fetch the ships back?" But Raeder was adamant: any such move would have an adverse effect on naval morale.

Accordingly, Hitler backed down – but from 24 May on, his every fear was to be justified.

Late on 23 May, the sighting reports from *Norfolk* and *Suffolk* had reached *Hood* and *Prince of Wales*, 300 miles away. Thus all through the Arctic night the chase continued, through the snow squalls and ice floes of the Denmark Strait, then on through the white walls of Atlantic spindrift. "We had a 'white out' every two minutes," Sub-Lieutenant Michael Buxton remembers from *Prince of Wales*, "so hit with tremendous spray you couldn't see anything – the whole ship was just white."

At 5.35 a.m. on 24 May, Vice Admiral Lancelot Holland, in *Hood*, first sighted his quarry. At once, not waiting to gather cruisers or destroyers. Holland hoisted his flag signal, "Blue Pendant Four" to *Hood*'s yardarm, then turned towards *Bismarck*.

The Germans were ready. As early as 4.35 a.m., *Prinz Eugen*'s second gunnery officer *Korvettenkapitän* Paul Schmalenbach had ordered, "War-watch stand by!" The listening plot had reported the sound of ships' screws from two fast-moving turbine ships at 280 degrees. Simultaneously, aboard *Bismarck*, the officer of the watch, *Kapitänleutnant* Werner Nobis, ordered, "All hands to action stations! Clear the decks for action!" All over the German ships alarm bells rang stridently, and the iron deck plates vibrated to the rhythm of thousands of sea-boots as men doubled to take up battle positions.

Now, in these last moments, men focused their minds on anything rather than the battle that lay ahead. Sub-Lieutenant Michael Buxton swivelling his field-glasses aboard *Prince*, sighted one of the rarest of all migrant birds, the Great Northern Diver. Promptly he called up his friend, Sub-Lieutenant Esmond Knight, actor and ornithologist, sited in the Air Defence Position above the bridge: "There she is – you have a look at her." Knight was delighted – unaware that the bird was almost the last thing he would ever see.

On the bridge of *Prince of Wales* Captain John Leach had sent a last minute summons to the Chaplain, the Reverend W. G. Parker. A prayer he imperfectly remembered – that of Sir Jacob Astley before the battle of Edgehill in 1642 – might be apposite at this moment. It was a timely inspiration. Many men still recall that as the battleship closed in for action, Parker's voice was resounding in every corner of the ship from crow's nest to engine room: "O Lord, Thou knowest how busy we must be today, if we forget Thee do not Thou forget us; for Christ's sake. Amen."

Then, at 25,000 yards range, with a storm of sound that almost knocked her gunners senseless, *Hood* opened fire.

From this maelstrom of sound, few retained more than swift traumatic impressions. As *Hood*'s first four shells, weighing a ton apiece, screamed from the muzzles at 1,600 miles an hour, an agitated petty officer on *Prinz Eugen*'s bridge called out: "He's fired." *Kapitän* Hellmuth Brinkmann replied quietly, "Of course he's fired, man. Now let's see what comes of it."

What came of it was disaster for the British. *Hood* was still striving like *Prince of Wales*, to find the German range; in any case, half of *Prince*'s heavy armament, including her rear turret, was inoperative through jamming, but the German guns were dead on target from the first.

Hood was hit and tall leaping flames were seen to spread amidships; warned of a fire in the Ready Use lockers, Admiral Holland was heard to say, "Leave it till the ammunition is gone." But it was too late. Around 6 a.m. *Hood* was straddled again, and abruptly she blew up, vomiting

Carley floats and seamen, lockers and portholes, fuel tanks, guns and 42,000 tons of steel plating in a pillar of orange fire that rose 1,000 feet high.

"My God," Marine Peter Dunstan heard Captain Leach shout, "The *Hood*'s blown up!", but within three minutes she had wallowed from sight; most men's impressions were subliminal. Dunstan's C.O., Captain Derek Aylwin, saw only "an amazing orange glow and bits and pieces falling through the air". In *Bismarck*, the majority were below decks, and the news came only by intercom; one man always recalled the long drawn out shout of the gunnery officer, *Freggatenkapitän* Adalbert Schneider, "She's blowing *uuuuup!*" Aboard *Prinz Eugen*, it was the war artist, *Leutnant* J. C. Schmitz, a trained observer, who carefully noted an "ashen-grey cloud . . . glowing red at the rims," finally transmuted to a "sinister fir-tree shape".

"The mighty *Hood*" had gone – and with her 95 officers and 1,324 men, all save three of her company.

Few men aboard the *Prince of Wales* could really credit it. In the S 4 turret, Boy Seaman Edward Grindley heard someone ask incredulously, "Gone? Where to?" Petty Officer Frederick Kenshole, in the Y Engine Room, chided his informant: "Don't start rumours." Able Seaman Charles Wright believed it, but felt "as though Buckingham Palace had been laid flat". Leading Telegraphist Bernard Campion had to repeat the news twice to his mate, Leading Telegraphist Priddle. Following an ominous silence, Priddle remarked weakly, "I'm changing me knickers".

In England, the news was heard with consternation. Despite her age, *Hood* had been venerated like few others; a showpiece of naval reviews, the ship that always showed the flag when it was needed, her picture featured in school books and on the walls of private homes. In London, the First Lord of the Admiralty, A. V. Alexander, was so overcome he retired to his private sanctum to play "O God, Our Help in Ages Past" on his harmonium. Churchill seemed less perturbed. William Averell Harriman, weekending at Chequers, the Premier's country retreat, was awoken at 7 a.m. to find Churchill, wearing a yellow sweater over an abbreviated nightshirt, standing beside his bed. "Hell of a battle going on," he ground out. "The *Hood* is sunk. Hell of a battle."

Churchill, for his part, had high hopes that a U.S. navy ship might be in the offing, prompting *Bismarck* to open fire and bring America into the war.

It was now the *Prince of Wales'* turn; the range had closed to 18,000 yards and both Germans were out to cripple her. Twelve minutes after the battle commenced, they achieved their aim; she was straddled by four of *Bismarck*'s heavy shells, three from *Prinz Eugen* – one of which, failing to explode, lodged beside the oil tank. But others wrought appalling havoc, slicing clean through her bridge, wrecking her compass platform, the echo-sounding gear, the radar office, the aircraft recovery crane, all the boats and several cabins.

Below decks, few were conscious of the carnage. Stoker Norman Portlock, in X Engine Room, felt the battleship "keel hard to port, like a motor bike turning" but those aloft knew unimaginable horrors. Sub-Lieutenant Esmond Knight remembered the last salvo as "a great rushing cyclone" that doomed him, in the space of seconds to the ranks of the warblinded, never to perceive anything but dim shapes again. Leading Telegraphist Bernard Campion, in the Remote Control Office below the bridge, was appalled to see blood pouring down the voicepipe, saturating his signal pads. Sub-Lieutenant Michael Buxton hastened from the Main Armament Directory Control Tower to find "no bridge – nothing but hairs on it, like dog's hairs, and blood – all one's friends".

Holed below the waterline, shipping 400 tons of water, the *Prince of Wales* was in no shape to carry on the fight. Leach now reached a sensible decision: the moment had come to break off action, make smoke and join the shadowing cruisers until the damage was repaired and the guns overhauled. At 6.13 a.m. he disengaged to the south-east.

It was left to *Hood*'s destroyers, among them the *Electra*, to search for *Hood*'s survivors and for two hours, in line abreast, they steamed hard southwards. Yet search as they might the sea lay empty – nothing but patches of oil, tangled piles of wreckage, a lone marine's hat. Then they espied them – two men swimming, one on a raft, but no other sign of life.

Incredulously, the Chief Engineer, Lieutenant Frank McLeod voiced what all of them felt: "But there *must* be more of them – there can't be only *three* of them. Where are the others?"

But there were no others – only a remarkable trio of three survivors. The first man helped aboard, Able Seaman R. E. Tilburn, shook himself like an angry dog and cursed officers and ratings impartially: "And what's up with you – you poverty-stricken crowd? Ain't you got no bloody boats?"

The second, Ordinary Signalman A. E. Briggs, asked eagerly who his rescuers were then let out a disgusted groan: "Now isn't that just my rotten luck – to be picked up by a *Chatham ship*."

The third, Midshipman W. J. Dundas, confronted the First Lieutenant to apologise with a sunny smile, "So sorry I can't salute sir – I'm afraid I've lost my cap."

As the trio were led off to the Sick Bay, *Electra*'s captain, Commander Cecil May, smiled for the first time that day. "There's one thing the Hun forgets," was his patriotic prediction. "He'll never beat men like these."

*

Captain John Leach and his crew were barely aware of it but *Prince of*

Wales had done better than they knew. Of the eighteen salvoes she had loosed off before disengaging, three 14-inch projectiles had done irreparable damage – holing *Bismarck*'s fuel tanks, lowering her bow by one degree, slowing her to 28 knots.

Minutes later, *Kapitän zur Zee* Brinkmann, on the bridge of *Prinz Eugen*, received an urgent signal from *Bismarck*'s commander, Ernst Lindemann: "From the *Bismarck*, Captain to Captain. Please see if I am leaving a trail of oil." A rating on the cruiser's bridge soon confirmed that fear: "There is a dark patch below the starboard hawser! A hit!"

As the flagship turned to starboard, ahead of *Prinz Eugen*, the men lining the cruiser's decks fell silent: a broad snakelike irridescent band of oil, shimmering in rainbow colours, was travelling in her wake. Any contact unit, any cruiser, any aircraft needed only follow that to keep its quarry under constant surveillance.

Aboard *Bismarck*, both Lütjens and Lindemann saw only one course of action: the battleship's Atlantic foray was over almost before it had begun. *Prinz Eugen* could be detached for independent cruiser warfare – but with one boiler room out of action, serious flooding and a steady drain of fuel, *Bismarck* needed repairs. Her one hope now was to reach the Normandy dock at St Nazaire, almost 1,500 miles away on the coast of Brittany.

"Intend to shake off enemy as follows," Lütjens signalled Brinkmann at 2.20 p.m. "During rain showers, *Bismarck* will move off on westerly course." But the enemy would not be shaken, and as the day wore on Lütjens' signals to the *Kriegsmarine* grew increasingly despondent. At 7.14 p.m. he admitted: "Enemy maintains contact." At 8.56 p.m.: "Impossible to shake off enemy owing to radar. Proceeding directly to Brest owing to fuel situation."

For the hunt was now on with a vengeance, and to square accounts for *Hood* warships were being vectored towards intercept over thousands of square miles of ocean. Admiral Tovey, in *King George V*, was already en route from Scapa Flow, along with four cruisers, six destroyers and the aircraft carrier *Victorious*, but now others were swelling the pack: Force H from Gibraltar, under Admiral Sir James Somerville brought *Renown*, *Sheffield* and the carrier *Ark Royal* into the fray. The battleship *Rodney*, en route to Boston for a refit, was about-turned in mid-Atlantic, along with the destroyers *Somali*, *Tartar*, and *Mashona*. Soon the 4th Destroyer Flotilla, under Captain Philip Vian, whose rescue of the *Altmark* prisoners had made headlines in 1940, were hastening to the scene.

Soon after midnight, Lütjens' worst fears were realised; for the first time the British struck from the air. All that day the carrier *Victorious* had battled northwest at 30 knots. Now at 10.14 p.m., nine Swordfish biplanes of 825 Squadron, each with an 18-inch torpedo slung from its belly, took off from the rain-lashed flight deck, across a heaving 32-foot swell. Diving through a curtain of flak, they saw one torpedo strike home on *Bismarck*. The damage was minimal – but a precedent had been set.

Then, around 3 a.m. on 25 May, *Bismarck* contrived to evade her pursuers. Now, for fully thirty hours, she steamed hard, undetected, for the south-east. Following thirty-six hours at action stations, officers and men relaxed, thankful at last to wash and shave and relish hot food. For Lütjens, who was fifty-two this day, a brief telegram arrived from his Führer: "Best wishes on your birthday. Adolf Hitler."

But Lütjens was feeling far from festive. Almost a thousand miles of ocean lay ahead and the meteorologist, Dr Externbrink, held out no prospect of merciful fog on the voyage to France. At noon, when the admiral addressed *Bismarck*'s crew over the loud-speaker system, his mood was sombre. "The British are massing their forces to destroy us," he told them bluntly, "and we shall have another battle with them before we reach home."

Then he added: "It may well be a question of victory or death. If we have to die, let us take with us as many of the enemy as we can."

It was a blow to morale from which few men fully recovered. The third gunnery officer, Burkard, the Baron von Müllenheim-Rechberg, who had not heard the speech, was aghast when a petty officer offered him a free translation: "The admiral says we haven't a hope, sir, the whole British Fleet is after us and they are bound to find us." The engineer officer, *Korvettenkapitän* Gerhard Junack, going on watch below, found his men equally disheartened. Worse, some of Lütjens' staff officers had now taken, in defiance of regulations, to wearing their life-jackets under their uniforms.

But not until 10.30 a.m. on 26 May, was *Bismarck* sighted again – this time by a Catalina aircraft on loan from the U.S. Navy, with an American co-pilot, Ensign Leonard B. Smith. Her position lent new urgency to the quest. She was now 690 miles north and west of Brest, drawing hourly closer to the Luftwaffe's air umbrella.

Just as Hitler had feared, air power proved decisive. Towards 9 p.m. on 26 May, fifteen Swordfish from the carrier *Ark Royal* took off from a flight deck whose up-and-down movement was now 56 feet – the height of a four-storey house. Twisting and turning like snipe from port to starboard, they struck at *Bismarck* for fully thirty minutes, and this time their blows were decisive. One torpedo, striking under the turn of the bilge aft, jammed her port rudder in a hard-over position.

Now *Bismarck* was slowed to 8 knots, veering in sluggish circles, a sitting target for the British. At 9.40 p.m. Lütjens acknowledged this in a signal to Berlin: "Ship unmanoeuvrable. We fight to the last shell. Long live the Führer."

Dawn on 27 May brought only the inevitability of death. At 8.47 a.m.

Admiral Tovey at last arrived in *King George V*, *Rodney* in consort, their grey sides glinting in the morning sun. At 16,000 yards range both ships opened fire, brilliant orange flashes from the heavy guns followed by white fountains of spray. "Get closer, get closer," Tovey ordered repeatedly, "I can't see enough hits." But the shells were striking home on *Bismarck*'s foremast and fire control platform with deadly accuracy. In *Rodney*'s cordite-handling room, Petty Officer Glue, making chalk crosses on a hopper door to signify salvoes, notched up twenty almost before he had realised it.

In these last hours, men's feelings were inextricably mixed. Aboard *Tartar*, a young sub-lieutenant, Ludovic Kennedy, thought compassionately of wolves closing in on their prey. Sub-Lieutenant Eryk Sopocko, of the Polish Navy, serving in *Rodney*, thought of his ravaged homeland and felt no such pity. As he watched Rodney's gun crews, dripping with sweat, smeared black with cordite, he told himself: "Justice, you still exist."

To some it was the most stirring battle ever known; in the destroyer *Sikh*, one excited rating fired a third torpedo before the first and second had even hit the water. For many below decks, the issue was still in doubt. In *Rodney*'s "X" turret, a Marine captain, sighting *Bismarck* through his periscope, yelled excitedly, "She's on fire from stem to stern." Back came a query from the shell-handling room: "Who, sir, us or them?"

Bismarck was doomed and all aboard her knew it. *Ark Royal* was over the horizon, impatient for another strike, *Norfolk*, who had dogged her from the first, was standing by, and now Vian's destroyers and other ships ringed her on all sides. But there was no thought of surrender. For forty minutes her guns blazed back defiance, though Tovey found it incredible that any ship could stay afloat after such a beating. "Somebody get me my darts!" he barked, irascibly. "Let's see if we can't finish her off with those!"

But *Bismarck* would decide her own fate. At 10.15 a.m. *Korvettenkapitän* Gerhard Junack, in the mid-ships engine room, heard *Freggatenkapitän* Walter Lehmann on the telephone: "Prepare for Measure 5." That meant, place explosive charges with time fuses in the cooling water intakes and open the seacocks. As they evacuated the engine room, once this was done, Junack rallied his men, "We'll all meet again on the Reeperbahn" – the red light district of Hamburg.

They acted just in time. Three minutes later, the cruiser *Dorsetshire* ranging from port to starboard hit her with three Mark VII torpedoes from 2,600 yards range. By now, her entire hull was swarming with black ant-shapes, men scurrying in frantic haste to evade the icy sea. At 10.57 a.m., 400 miles off Brest, she heeled to port, sinking very fast by the stern.

Her survivors were tragically few. Of 2,400 men aboard *Bismarck*,

95

Dorsetshire picked up eighty men, *Maori* another twenty, but a sudden alarm that a U-Boat was hovering prompted both captains to ring down for full speed. Hundreds of men, clawing frantically at the paintwork as the sides slipped by, were cut to pieces by the churning screws.

Later the Ministry of Information was to roundly condemn a B.B.C. account of *Bismarck*'s last hours as "nauseating and sentimental", but the men who had brought her to bay felt differently.

"She had put up a most gallant fight against impossible odds," Tovey told the Admiralty unrepentantly, "worthy of the old days of the Imperial German Navy. It is unfortunate that 'for political reasons' this fact cannot be made public."

*

For one group of men, the news brought a sense of vindication. A thousand miles from the scene of action, in the Red Room of the Kristiansand Club, Norway, Viggo Axelssen, the ship's chandler, was drinking quietly with a group of friends. Word of the *Bismarck*'s fate had just reached them, and now Axelssen recalled vividly the message he had scribbled only seven evenings ago, the journey that had begun with Arne Moen's bus and ended in the farmhouse attic at Helle.

"Gentlemen!" he said, raising his glass, and all of them stood as one. "Thirty-five thousand tons."

They drained their glasses, repeating the figure solemnly. It signified the *Bismarck*'s "official" tonnage, given out to comply with the 1936 Anglo-German Naval Treaty, limiting the displacement of capital ships. Then Axelssen opened the connecting door to the dining room, where other members had already begun their evening meal. They, too, were asked to rise and drink the same toast.

Every man rose silently, raising his glass, but nobody said a word.

*

"She's sunk!"

In the Oval Office of the White House, Franklin D. Roosevelt had just had word from the Navy Department. Hanging up the phone he turned to his speech-writers, Samuel I, Rosenman and Robert E. Sherwood with as much satisfaction as if "he had himself fired the torpedo".

The news had come at a grimly appropriate time. That same evening, in a speech to the Governing Board of the Pan-American Union, to be broadcast to the world by international hook-up – what he liked to call a "Fireside Chat" – the President was moving another step forward in his undeclared war. He was about to proclaim a state of unlimited national emergency.

As always, there were factors that it would be impolitic to spell out. For the State Department, Cordell Hull had vetoed all mention of the fact that Admiral Harold R. Stark, Chief of Naval Operations, had with great misgivings transferred three battleships, one carrier, four cruisers, and two destroyer squadrons from the Pacific to the Atlantic – leaving the Pacific Fleet at Pearl Harbor, Hawaii, in every major respect inferior to the Japanese. To be both aggressive in the Atlantic and peaceful in the Pacific was, as Roosevelt saw it, no easy task.

Typically Roosevelt was keeping abreast – but never ahead – of American public opinion. "I am waiting to be pushed into the situation," he told Treasury Secretary Morgenthau in mid-May, but what the British Ambassador, Lord Halifax, called "his policy of gradualness" drove some of his colleagues to distraction. When Roosevelt maintained mildly that Atlantic Patrols were a step in the right direction, Secretary of War Stimson snorted: "Keep on walking, Mr President – keep on walking!" One week earlier, his former Ambassador to France, William C. Bullitt, told Roosevelt pointedly, "There is a desire (by the nation) to know the facts *from you*."

From London's front line, the need seemed more urgent still. "When the Gallup poll shows 19% for war now," wrote Averell Harriman in a letter which found its way to Roosevelt, "and 68% for war if necessary to save the British, America must be a nation of ostriches. Don't they read the newspapers or listen to the radio? Are we to continue to hide behind the skirts of these poor British women who are holding up the civil defence here?"

Roosevelt was less certain. To be sure, two isolationist newspapers, the St Louis *Post-Dispatch* and the Detroit *Free Press*, had announced a change of heart – "the die is cast," said the *Free Press*, "we are in the war" – and defence was still a popular and non-controversial issue. The cost of defence had upped the income tax rate from 2.2 per cent to 6.6 per cent, and few had grumbled; federal excises for defence now accounted for eight cents on every pack of cigarettes, $4 per gallon of liquor, 25 cents on a gallon of gasoline. Yet war, by contrast, was still an emotive issue. Only recently, isolationists in Congress had protested bitterly when the Army bespoke "overseas caps" from the textile industry: the very word suggested another American Expeditionary Force.

Under the relentless goading of Harry Hopkins, whom one admirer christened "Generalissimo of the Needle Brigade", United States production was at last gathering momentum – for defence, if not for war. Steel was short, and so was aluminium, but from March onwards the target had been set: 2,400 planes, 951 tanks would reach Britain before the year was out. Letters routed to Government departments now took on the aspect of a litany – "My dear Mr Secretary, I find that the defence of the United Kingdom is vital to the defence of the United States" – and a floodtide of supplies followed: 100,000 cases of evaporated milk, 11,000 tons of eggs, 6,000 hogsheads of tobacco, 200,000 gas masks, service, 18,772 drawers, cotton, ankle-length, 43,002 jerkins, felt.

Fully $5 million had been earmarked for aviation bases, and three million new workers had swelled the ranks of heavy industry; red, white and blue banners, looming above the assembly lines, warned, TIME IS SHORT. But there was another side to the coin and Roosevelt knew it: other assembly lines were still producing five million private automobiles a year, the highest total in United States history.

Hence the President's declaration of a state of emergency – to instil a sense of urgency many citizens were far from feeling.

On the hot and stifling night of 27 May, his black-tie audience gathered in an incongruously genteel setting: the East Room of the White House, lavishly decorated with small silver bowls of pink roses. As the President faced a battery of microphones his audience waited apprehensively, perched on small gilded chairs once used for White House musicales. The French windows were flung wide to combat the heat, and the scent of honeysuckle drifted from the south portico.

But Roosevelt was not really addressing this audience – the Ambassadors and Ministers from the twenty Latin-American republics – at all. His words were aimed at the world – at the neutral, the enslaved, above all to the uninvolved, disinterested people of America, where a quarter of all homes still lacked running water, a third were without flush toilets, and the largest single cause of ill-health was malnutrition. Of what concern was Hitler's Europe to them?

"Some people seem to think," Roosevelt began, by way of explanation, "that we are not attacked until bombs actually drop in the streets of New York or San Francisco or New Orleans or Chicago. But they are simply shutting their eyes to the lesson that we must learn from the fate of every nation that the Nazis have conquered."

By now, he reasoned, Americans must realise that "it would be suicide to wait until they are in our front yard". Old-fashioned commonsense called for the use of a strategy that would prevent the enemy gaining any such foothold – which was why he proposed to add more ships, more planes, to the North and South Atlantic patrols.

"Our Bunker Hill of tomorrow," he warned farsightedly, "may be several thousand miles from Boston."

Just as he had anticipated, the speech drew only a polite spatter of applause. The guests drifted out on to the South Lawn, to sip fruit punch and lemonade by the light of Japanese lanterns. Roosevelt relaxed happily as Irving Berlin launched into a piano rendition of "Alexander's Ragtime Band", later retiring to bed. It was here that Sherwood found him in seventh heaven, the coverlet littered with more than a thousand telegrams that had poured in since the broadcast.

"They're 95 percent favourable!" Roosevelt exulted. "And I figured I'd be lucky to get an even break on this speech." The United States, it seemed, was at last coming alive to the peril.

Outsiders were less convinced. Soon after, Sir James Dunn, an astute Canadian banker, sent a measured assessment of the state of the nation to his old friend and fellow countryman, Lord Beaverbrook – a view which "The Beaver" hastened to pass on to Churchill.

"The states of Michigan, Wisconsin, Minnesota and the Dakotas form an isolationist bloc under Lindbergh and *The Chicago Tribune*", Dunn opined. "John L. Lewis* is a Communist bent on smashing the Capitalist system. Philip Murray† thinks that this is Labour's chance and does not feel that the Hitler menace is real."

"The U.S.A." Dunn concluded, "is not yet frightened enough to get the representatives behind Roosevelt."

---

* John L. Lewis, leader of the United Mine Workers' Union, had called out the soft coal miners for a month-long strike in April. He had already branded Roosevelt as a warmonger.
† Philip Murray of the Congress of Industrial Organisations (C.I.O.) had likewise opposed Lend-Lease.

5

"No Peace, No Rest, No Halting Place, No Parley"

29 May–21 June, 1941

THE LONG NIGHT marches had begun again, and the mountain passes echoed to the trudging feet of weary men. In places, the white rocky roadsides resembled an open-air quartermaster's stores; in the bitterness of defeat, men were abandoning rifles, bandoliers, packs, blankets, gasmasks, hand grenades, even empty water bottles. "The limit of endurance has been reached," Freyberg signalled Wavell on 26 May. "Our position is hopeless." The end in Crete was very near.

Wavell himself was close to despair. "I have never seen him so gloomy!" the British Ambassador in Cairo, Sir Miles Lampson, cabled Eden. "Archie was in the depths of depression – especially concerning equipment – 'All right,' he said against the ice-creamers, but useless against the 'Boche'." Even now, the lesson of Crete had escaped the Commander-in-Chief: whoever did not command the air above the sea faced annihilation or unacceptable loss. Faced with a 30 to 1 air superiority, the British had never stood a chance.

The R.A.F.'s new Commander-in-Chief, Middle East, Air Marshal Sir Arthur Tedder, saw this clearly. "Root of situation is secure air bases," he signalled the Chief of Air Staff on 30 May. "This campaign is primarily a battle for aerodromes."

At the last, Crete had become a series of small swirling actions – gallant in themselves, yet lacking all cohesion. One force dislodged Student's paratroopers from a village strongpoint by dropping a beehive down their chimney. Near Galatas, Captain Michael Forrester, attached to the Greek Military Mission, charged into battle wearing shorts and a long yellow jersey, leading a posse of 100 Cretans, many of them women armed with ancient fowling pieces, one man with a serrated breadknife fastened to the end of a shotgun.

A young New Zealander, 33-year-old Second Lieutenant Charles Upham, of the 20th (N.Z.) Battalion proved a one-man task force in himself. On 21 May, though racked by dysentery and subsisting on condensed milk, Upham had led a counter-charge at Maleme airfield, destroying a machine-gun nest of eight men. Wounded in the shoulder, he still led his platoon with his arm in a sling – striding up and down a ridge to draw German fire, picking off two more Germans by propping his rifle in a tree fork. Then, after leading a final rearguard action up a 600-foot ravine, Upham took time out to free some tethered mules – to be led, weeping tears of frustration, aboard a Navy destroyer. His was the sole Victoria Cross to be awarded in the Cretan campaign.

The true reality was now inglorious evacuation. On 28 May, the Navy prepared to live up to their Dunkirk tradition of one year back: regardless of loss, the troops must be moved out. "It takes the Navy three years to build a new ship," Admiral Sir Andrew Cunningham reasoned. "It will take three hundred years to build a new tradition."

Thus for three days the evacuation continued – under relentless low-level strafing that cost them three cruisers and six destroyers, badly damaging a further seventeen. Aircraftman Marcel Comeau saw it from the seaside village of Sfakia, almost too weary to walk another step. Yet somehow he forced himself to toil back up the ravine; the knowledge that rescue was conditional on bringing back all the walking-wounded and stretcher cases lent a magical power to his legs. At 3 a.m. on 29 May – the last day but one of the evacuation – Comeau scrambled aboard the destroyer *Killearn*, en route for Alexandria.

But many men, like Lieutenant Theodore Stephanides, a medical officer with the Cyprus Regiment, had cause to wonder. "I knew that I was taking part in a retreat," he recalled later, "in fact I wondered if it could not be called more correctly a rout." For the first time in his service career, Stephanides was conscious of seeing naked panic that came close to breaking point, and of small shabby subterfuges that shocked him deeply. More than one man, he knew, had thrown away his steel helmet, tied on a field dressing and claimed Red Cross evacuation as "walking wounded".

It was with some justice, the doctor reflected, that a bitter gibe had been coined on the sandy beaches: that every man taking part in the Cretan evacuation would soon receive a medal inscribed, EX CRETA.

*

In England, the angry inquests began within days. At Church House, Westminster, the temporary debating chamber for Members of Parliament following crippling bomb damage to the House of Commons, the Ministry of Information's Harold Nicolson noted that Churchill was unusually diffident as he entered the chamber on Tuesday 10 June. As he passed along the front bench, he stooped to ask a Cabinet colleague, "Where is the ladies' gallery?"

Nicolson knew why: in the flaring debate that followed, Churchill needed the solace of knowing that Clementine, his wife of more than thirty-two years, was seated comfortably and within his view.

There was much to debate – news, wrote the U.S. Military Attaché, General Raymond E. Lee, "of the sort that would have made Kipling wince". True, some 15,000 men had been ferried to safety, but the losses were staggering – 11,835 prisoners, 1,742 killed or missing, 1,737 wounded. The R.A.F. had lost 46 planes – while Cunningham's Mediterranean Fleet was reduced to two battleships, two cruisers and thirteen destroyers ready for service. Many citizens were fast accepting the view of the military historian Liddell Hart; British hearts of oak were being betrayed by their leaders' oaken heads. "Greece and Crete," noted Mass Observation's weekly report, "have put people back into a state of doubt worse than Dunkirk."

But more powerful voices than Britain's M.P.'s were airing trenchant criticisms. Of the troops left behind in Crete, 3,000 were Australians, more than 800 New Zealanders, and many Australian Labour Party supporters were clamantly accusing the United Kingdom of "cold blooded murder" in sending green ill-armed troops to be "butchered" in Crete. In one secret session of Parliament, the Minister of the Army, Percy Claude Spender, saw the country's morale as now so low that "one hostile armoured division would be sufficient to conquer Australia".

In Wellington, New Zealand, Prime Minister Peter Fraser felt the same sense of betrayal. "I would strongly urge in the name of the New Zealand Government," he had pressured Churchill on 24 May, "that all possible additional support by air and sea be immediately provided, especially additional air assistance that can be released from all other quarters including United Kingdom." To this broadest of hints, the Premier responded tartly: "Suggestion that we are holding back air assistance for the sake of the United Kingdom is really quite unfounded."

For a rift was opening that would never quite be healed. From Cairo Sir Miles Lampson reported: "It is being freely said . . . that at best there has been tragic mismanagement and at the worst criminal lack of care for men's lives." In Alexandria, Admiral Cunningham admitted to "considerable odium . . . and scraps ashore", for many airmen had been mercilessly worked over by the Anzacs in the bars of the port. The demand for air cover at all times was now a near-pathological obsession. As Chief of the Air Staff, Portal spoke out frankly to General Ralph Royce, the U.S. Air Attaché: "AOC-in-C, Middle East under intense pressure from both Army and Navy for air support and protection . . . getting standing patrols for the defence troops . . . which is an unusual and uneconomical practice."

The truth was that Churchill, anxious to impress America at all costs, was fast alienating his Dominion Allies. All along, policy in Greece and south-east Europe had been wholly decided in London, without reference to Wellington or Canberra. When Churchill's Secretary of State for Dominion Affairs, Lord Cranborne, pressed him to confide in them

102

more freely, the Premier, paternalist to a fault, disagreed. "Frankly, I do not see the object of spouting all this stuff out – some of it injurious, if it leaked – unless it is thought that the Dominions require to be frightened into doing their duty."

"There was a curious element in the British make-up," complained Lieutenant-General Sir Thomas Blamey, the Australian Commander-in-Chief, "which led them to look on the Dominions as appendages of Great Britain." Many Australian Labourites were more forthright; the British were looking on the Dominions as a prime source of cannon fodder. Nor was Churchill the only Briton mortally to wound Australian susceptibilities. Premier Robert Menzies, meeting Lieutenant-General Sir Henry Maitland-Wilson, fully expected a tribute to the Anzac rearguard in Greece. Instead Wilson, with ill-concealed distaste, told him, "Your . . . soldiers are terribly badly disciplined and cause a great deal of trouble."

On 12 June, at St James's Palace, speaking to a massed audience of diplomats and Dominions High Commissioners, Churchill gave a rousing pledge that Britain would "fight on till life is gone or victory won", and that Hitler would find "no peace, no rest, no halting place, no parley". But from this time on, Churchill would find the Dominions resolved on one thing: the British must bear their share of the fighting or take the consequences.

This would prove a major setback in the months to come, for Britain sorely needed Commonwealth support. Canada was unavowedly staunch, with 65 percent of her national income earmarked to meet war obligations, but South Africa posed more of a questionmark. Despite Churchill's longstanding friendship with her Premier, Field Marshal Jan Smuts, the country had entered the war by the slim margin of 80 votes to 67. Many Afrikaaners, descendants of the stubborn Dutch farmers who had waged the Boer War, saw this as a British, not a South African quarrel – a sentiment fanned by Dr Josef Göbbels' nightly propaganda broadcasts from Zeesen. From among two million whites only a volunteer force of 150,000 had signed on for service "anywhere in Africa", adopting the orange-red shoulder flashes known as *rooi lusses*.*

The irony was that America was now as dissatisfied with the British war effort as the Dominions. Following a Middle East inspection, the air attaché, General Royce, summed up the attitude prevailing there: slovenly, shiftless, apathetic, and Luddite when faced with unfamiliar machinery. Although an old friend, Averell Harriman still had to be blunt with Churchill; the waste of equipment by British troops was "incredible". From his vantage point at the Ministry of Economic Warfare, Hugh Dalton saw the danger signs; disquieting stories were current in America concerning Churchill and his entourage.

---

* A figure later increased to 186,218.

Harriman was growing daily more disillusioned, and so, too, was Winant. "There is much comment on Crete and our failure to provide air cover," Dalton noted. "It is said that many important decisions are taken over here late at night in a state of sozzlement" – a reference to Churchill's interminable small-hours meetings with his Chiefs of Staff, liberally fortified by brandy and soda.

Despite their outward unity, rumour had it that Churchill and his ministers were now irrevocably at loggerheads. For once, rumour did not lie. At one luncheon for industrial correspondents, Beaverbrook, soon to become Minister of Supply, astounded the company by launching into a tirade against all his colleagues save Churchill, Eden and the First Lord, A. V. Alexander. Then weeping brokenly, he blundered from the room. It was no lone example. Minister of Information Alfred Duff Cooper, "a little flushed before (lunch) and more flushed afterwards," devoted one Press Conference to berating the entire Cabinet. "I don't know why you think *I* have any information for you," he sneered. "Nobody tells me anything."

Beaverbrook was a red rag to many colleagues; before War Cabinet meetings, Minister of Labour Ernest Bevin always slipped his false teeth into his pocket, lest he bite through his tongue in sheer annoyance. Others distrusted his influence on Churchill – in his presence, one man noted, "Winston is like a chicken in front of a cobra." Beaverbrook was likewise anathema to the Minister of Works, Lord Reith – "to no one is the vulgar designation shit more appropriately applied".

Beaverbrook, for his part, never ceased his efforts to discredit Bevin with Churchill: Bevin's threat, in 1940, to prosecute him for allegedly overworking juveniles in aircraft factories still rankled bitterly. It was a campaign that had the warm support of Brendan Bracken, Churchill's redhaired crony and later Minister of Information – though "not fit to be a Minister" in the view of Lord Privy Seal Clement Attlee.

Dalton's own guns were trained on Alfred Duff Cooper – "This little pig" – while reserving a spatter of grapeshot for Eden; the Foreign Secretary was "a nervy fusser", with the manner of "a peevish child seizing all the toys". For good measure, the Chancellor of the Duchy of Lancaster, Lord Hankey, denounced the entire War Cabinet: "They struck me as a set of 'yes-men', leaving the running of the war entirely to Churchill."

"All this ridiculous business of personal relations will be seen in retrospect as quite fantastic," Dalton was to record sadly. "We were supposed to be fighting the Germans, but a large number of the participants were really fighting each other, intriguing, back-biting and feeling injured and jealous."

*

104

In one respect, at least, Churchill's Cabinet were fully in accord: their profound distrust of the men who ruled unoccupied France from the little spa town of Vichy. "A Turkish bath planted with trees," as one man described it, Vichy with its rambling turn-of-the-century hotels, crammed with potted palms and rattan chairs, was somehow symbolic of the weary languor that had settled upon France.

Their distrust focused primarily on two men: 84-year-old Marshal Henri Phillipe Pétain, whose luncheon table at the Hôtel Parc et Majestic was hidden from the faithful by a wicker screen, and 59-year-old Admiral Jean François Darlan, an able ambitious schemer, who travelled everywhere in a personal train equipped with two bathrooms and a 24-piece naval orchestra.

While Pétain harboured no great love for the Germans – "I am a prisoner," he would quaveringly assure Roosevelt's ambassador, Admiral Leahy – Darlan unashamedly embraced the concept of Nietzschean superman. "British and American soldiers demand beef-steak," he told Leahy patronisingly. "The Germans can live on a few prepared pills." And anticipating a German victory Darlan was mindful that France should be on the winning side. With this end in view, on 10 February, he had annexed no less than four Ministerial portfolios – Vice President, Minister of Foreign Affairs, Minister of the Interior,* and Minister of Information.

Early in May, Darlan had found himself courted by Germany. Syria, over which Vichy France held a mandate, was needed as a staging post for German planes abetting the short-lived Rashid Ali rising in Iraq. In return, the Führer might make concessions on such factors as daily occupation charges and the return of German-held French prisoners.

Darlan now saw a chance for France to escape from armistice constraints and assume a voluntary neutral role in Hitler's New Order. Promptly he agreed. By 9 May, German planes and technicians were touching down at Aleppo airport.

This gesture of compliance was to cost him dear; at one and the same time Darlan was to destroy all world sympathy for Vichy France and ultimately to lose Syria.

In vain did Cordell Hull warn the French of the dangers of transit. "Vichy had gone straight into the arms of the German Government," he accused Pétain's ambassador, Gaston Henry-Haye. His condemnation of Pétain was more scathing still; the transit was "a gratuitous act of vast military aid to Hitler".

Unlike the British, who had no official diplomatic relations with Vichy, Roosevelt had always been careful to maintain a dialogue with Pétain and Darlan. The advantages seemed manifold: to ensure that Darlan maintained control of the French Fleet and kept the Germans from French

* A Ministry he later ceded to Pierre Pucheu.

North Africa, to block collaboration with her colonies and prevent economic collapse. For these reasons, Robert Murphy, a craggy affable diplomat in Algiers, had established a liaison with General Maxime Weygand, Pétain's Delegate General in French North Africa.

To Hull, British intransigence over France seemed counterproductive: lacking support from Britain, what incentive did the French have to resist Germany? Although he cautioned Henry-Haye to "play down his controversial utterances . . . both alike suffer from clashes that arouse feeling", Hull also took Lord Halifax to task. Unless the British showed flexibility, allowing American goods to reach France, Darlan might yield up the Fleet – "Lazarus, in a state of great hunger, felt extremely grateful to the rich man when he was permitted to pick up a few crumbs that fell from his table".

Unknown to Hull, though, Eden had his own private pipeline to Weygand: a Polish engineer, code-named "Lancelot", who shuttled between Cairo, Lisbon and Tangier. Weygand needed both wheat and petrol and a tacit "gentlemen's agreement" had thus been reached; both sides would proclaim overt hostility, to lull Hitler's suspicions, and supplies for North Africa would filter discreetly through the British blockade.

If the French were ever to fight again as Allies, Churchill believed, it would be on North African soil or not at all.

Originally the Premier and Wavell had hoped that General Henri-Fernand Dentz, who commanded 30,000 French troops in Syria, along with local levies, would resist the German incursion. But by mid-May, some 70 Axis bombers and fighters, and forty transports, had made use of Syrian landing fields. Plainly Dentz was obeying Pétain to the letter.

Now one man saw his chance. For almost a year General Charles André Marie de Gaulle, leader of the Free French forces, had been a man consigned to the wilderness. Although the British were backing him to the tune of £8 million a year, not more than 50,000 Frenchmen had flocked to his banner – some in England, more in French Equatorial Africa and the Cameroons. From the first, the British had treated him with cautious reserve; he was acknowledged as chief only of those "who rallied to him".

"Why have you brought this lanky gloomy Brigadier?" Churchill had asked Major-General Edward Spears, his personal liaison officer with the French, when the two returned to London in June, 1940, and Spears had to be honest. "No one else would come." But by December, 1940, after an Anglo-de Gaulle attempt to seize the port of Dakar, Senegal, had been ignominiously beaten off, Churchill was spoiling for a change.

Privately, Pétain told Leahy, Churchill had sent him word that "de Gaulle had been of no assistance to the British cause", which left the Marshal wondering "why the British do not eliminate him". The truth was Churchill had tried and failed. Since de Gaulle's attempt to rally all French possessions below the Sahara under his banner had fallen through, the Premier had tried to inveigle Weygand into supplanting him – and been tersely rebuffed.

To play second fiddle was intolerable to the larger-than-life de Gaulle. A 6 ft 4 in ramrod, ascetic and humourless – "a head like a banana and hips like a woman", commented Dalton unkindly – the General saw himself, like the Sun King, Louis XIV, as the embodiment of French honour. At one Savoy Hotel luncheon, he charged Harold Nicolson that the Ministry of Information was "Pétainist". When Nicolson protested that the Ministry was working "for all France", the outraged de Gaulle trumpeted, *"La France entière? C'est moi!"*

From Brazzaville, on the Congo, capital of the Free French colonial empire, the British Consul, Robert Parr, strove to clarify de Gaulle's viewpoint: "If Great Britain attaches so little value to the moral side of the movement . . . instead of fostering it by all possible means she weakens it by complaisance towards Vichy . . . he (de Gaulle) must decide what is his fundamental duty for France, for whom he is trustee."

But the British, for the most part, were more in accord with the advice Hoare offered from Madrid: "If our propaganda gives the impression that everybody left in France is a traitor and only the émigrés are patriots, we shall push France not only temporarily but permanently into the Axis."

De Gaulle, though, was not easily gainsaid, and this was his hour. Wavell, warned by Sir Miles Lampson that speed was essential, was "not particularly communicative or responsive", but found he had no choice. A German foothold in Syria would prove intolerable. With Churchill's blessing de Gaulle flew from London to Cairo with instructions to map out a Syrian campaign.

At one stroke de Gaulle had achieved all he had fought for: his own private war in which his Free French would face the Germans, at one and the same time avenging the shame of Vichy, ensuring his own position as leader and weakening Roosevelt's insidious link with Pétain.

Even this early, Churchill was finding de Gaulle a sore trial. A resolute trencherman, he bitterly resented the French leader's habit of interrupting his meal-times with long impassioned phone calls. On one such occasion, at Chequers, Churchill refused the call, but de Gaulle persisted so assiduously that Sawyers, the valet, begged the Premier to yield. Cheeks crimson, his napkin crumpled, Churchill strode from the dining room.

Ten minutes later, returning to rapidly cooling soup, Churchill, still crimson, was enveloped in mulish silence. Suddenly he burst out: "Bloody de Gaulle! He had the impertinence to tell me that the French regard him as the reincarnation of Joan of Arc."

As always, Churchill had had the last word. "I found it very necessary to remind him that we had to burn the first!"

*

Even by 1941 standards, it was a bizarre campaign. Security was totally lacking, and so, too, were shock tactics; at 2 a.m. on Sunday, 8 June, the forces that crossed the frontiers of Syria in a three-pronged drive from Palestine, Iraq and Trans-Jordan, advanced boldly in bright moonlight, to the resounding strains of Free French bands blasting out *La Marseillaise*. As if to emphasise the strange dichotomy, even their banners were at cross-purposes: before a shot was ever fired, a white flag of truce was hoisted alongside the *Tricouleur* as they marched.

Hasty improvisation was evident from the first. The Free French, 6,000 strong under their Field Commander, General Paul Louis Le Gentilhomme, had been augmented by the only forces the hard pressed Wavell could muster – two brigades of the Australian 7th Division, the 5th Indian Infantry Brigade, and those veterans of the relief column, "Habforce" – "almost as many sprigs of the nobility as Henry V had led to Agincourt", one man recalled, their ranks later swelled by Prince Aly Khan and 1,000 Ismaili horsemen raised from his father's followers.

Military hardware was conspicuously lacking. For their part, the Free French could muster exactly eight guns and ten light tanks; while some fought from astride camels, others were on horseback or in armoured cars. Some British troops – to the appropriate strains of "We are Fred Karno's Army" – moved up in old ramshackle omnibuses with patched roofs or in citrus trucks still slippery with orange peel. Air cover for the entire striking force was sixty aircraft, many of them manned by pilots straight from flying school.

Courtesy and conciliation were the keynotes from the first. The Australians were under orders to wear slouch hats, not steel helmets, until actually fired upon; at Tibnine, ten miles beyond the frontier, the mayor approached one column led by Lieutenant-Colonel A. B. MacDonald, with a novel request. Could he telephone to Tyre, their next objective, to enquire if the invaders would be welcome? Only when the answer was affirmative did the column press on.

The question was, welcomed by whom? For the one factor normally indispensable to a battle – a determined enemy – was missing from the first: within hours of the frontier crossing, the Germans had written Syria off. From all the airfields, the German ground staffs were hastily flown back to Europe or evacuated by train through Turkey. As the columns forged on in search of them, hundreds of Germans and Italians were passing peacefully through Ankara.

The way now lay open to a tragic situation: a civil war, in which

Frenchmen for the first time raised their hands against Frenchmen. It was a situation de Gaulle had never remotely foreseen; the advance of de Gaulle troops, he believed, would meet an onrush of Vichyites who had seen the light, eager to embrace his cause.

It was a fatal error. Only one prominent Frenchman, Colonel Philibert Collet, commanding a troop of fair-skinned Muslim Circassians, led his forces over the frontier – but of the ten squadrons that rode with him all but three changed their minds and rode back. It was Collet who broke the daunting news to General Georges Catroux, de Gaulle's Commander-in-Chief: even Vichyites feeling sympathy with the Free French would resist their invasion on principle.

"What fine fellows the Free French are," General Spears, now heading a Mission to de Gaulle, wrote to Brendan Bracken, "but alas! Dr Göbbels himself could not make them (the opposition) believe it." The Syrians were equally disenchanted. "All the inhabitants loathe French in any form," Lampson cabled Eden, "Free French just as much as Vichy."

Both Pétain and Darlan hoped for bitter resistance – "the demonstration of loyalty to Germany . . . can improve the position of metropolitan France" – but their hopes were barely realised. Many Vichyites did fight gamely, but as the war rumbled on for thirty-four days over dry chalky highways, through squalid stone villages, the tragedy of fratricide was more often averted. One Free French unit captured a hill by advancing with their rifles slung over their shoulders; the Vichyites who held it refused to open fire. In one battle, two men poised to lob grenades at one another, suddenly realised that they were brothers. Collet's Circassians, meeting up with their own kind, fell on their necks with tears of joy.

One unit of the 6th *Demi-Brigade*, Foreign Legion, ambushed a patrol of the 13th *Demi-Brigade*, and took them prisoner. Then their C.O., ordering the guard to present arms, made an oddly moving little speech: "You are firstly *légionnaires*, secondly you are prisoners of war, and only in the end are you my enemy."

War correspondents hastening to the front for a scoop found an almost pastoral peace. Cecil Brown, of C.B.S., heading for Beirut, pictured swarms of tanks and guns and thousands of men milling up the coastal road. Twelve miles from the city he caught up with the advance post: four near-naked Australians, splotched with purple antiseptic skin dye, lying behind a barbed wire barrier, fronted by a double row of land mines. To Brown's chagrin, not a tank or a gun was in sight.

All along the front, fighting instinct was fast waning. Lieutenant-General John Evetts, newly-appointed British commander, assessed the mood swiftly, then called the Australian divisional commander, Major-General J. D. Lavarack, at Advance Headquarters, Nazareth. "The Free French forces are extremely tired," he reported frankly, "and have little or no desire to go on killing their brother Frenchmen . . . it is doubtful whether they can be persuaded to advance even against feeble resistance.''

Thus, by 20 June, the Vichy French were as anxious to evacuate the Syrian capital, Damascus, as Evetts was to seize it. One day later, at 1.30 p.m., watched by thousands of silent Moslems, Damascus "fell" before an onslaught of two Free French colonels, two Australians, a British major and two armoured cars. The allied army, following up later, had to by-pass the main street – not because of war or barricades but because the authorities were renewing the tram tracks. Their triumphal entry into the city wound, to spirited applause, through the heart of the brothel quarter.

There had been needless tragedies, even so. At Kisweh Fort, outside Damascus, British ack-ack hit a Vichy transport plane; of the three men aboard, only the sergeant-pilot lingered long enough to unburden himself to Major Bernard Fergusson, British liaison officer with the Free French. Squeezing Fergusson's arm, the dying man twice asked him plaintively: "*Pourquoi nous combattons? Pourquoi?*"

Fergusson did not think to answer that they were fighting because of one man's obsession that he alone was the soul of France – an obsession that by 12 July had caused more than a thousand deaths on either side.

For it was at 0.01 hours on that date, following the thrice-repeated code-word "Robert-Robert-Robert", that the cease-fire came into effect on all fronts – and for de Gaulle another bigger battle was then beginning.

*

They were days as terrible as a nightmare, yet as exciting as a dream. One unwary move, one rigid adherence to, or departure from, orders could bring the three great uncommitted powers – Japan, Russia, the United States – closer to war.

At 5 a.m. on 21 May – before the ships pursuing the *Bismarck* had even readied for action – one man made such a move. That morning the submarine U-69 was surfaced on the oily swell of the South Atlantic, 750 miles off Freetown, Sierra Leone, and the mood aboard her was sullen. "The Laughing Cow" which grinned from her conning tower, an emblem selected at random from a French cheese carton *La Vache qui Rit*, was belying her nickname. Despite sunny weather, it was weeks since the U-boat had sighted an enemy masthead. Worse, her commander, *Käpitänleutnant* Jost Metzler had just committed the unforgiveable crime of shaving at sea – a sure omen of bad luck.

It was not long in coming. Metzler, who had passed the warm tropical night on the bridge, had just retired below when the cry rang out, "Commander to the bridge." Grabbing his hat and scaling the steep iron companionway, Metzler soon saw why. Three miles away, the look-out had sighted the navigation lights of a 5,000 ton freighter.

Metzler was at once suspicious. The merchantman might be a neutral – but unusually she bore no illuminated flag aft and neither her national colours nor the name of her country were painted on her hull.

As U-69 turned towards the ship, closing to 1,000 yards, another strange factor became apparent. The freighter's cargo, stacked on her after-deck, consisted primarily of top-heavy crates. "Either she's got aeroplane parts on board," surmised *Leutnant zur Zee* Auermann, the First Lieutenant, "or else she's a Q-ship."

Every submariner was justly wary of Q-ships – armed merchantmen with concealed guns such as had been used to trap submarines in World War One. "Ask for her name," Metzler ordered, and Bade, the helmsman, bent to his Morse lamp. The answer blinked back through the grey dawn: *"S.S. Robin Moor."*

Now Metzler grew more dubious. A quick check with *Lloyd's Register* and *Groener's Shipping List* revealed no such vessel. As was customary, Metzler ordered the freighter to stop and lower a small boat, bearing the captain and his papers.

But the rowboat that pulled towards them around 6.30 a.m., crewed by eight sailors, brought no captain and no papers – merely the Chief Officer standing nonchalantly in the bow, a cigarette gummed to his lower lip. By now it was light enough for Metzler to see the legend "S.S. Exmoor, New York" on the freighter's stern, and the Stars and Stripes, though unilluminated on her hull. The Chief Officer's explanation seemed perfunctory, to say the least. The freighter had been sold two weeks back to the Sea Shipping Company and renamed. There had been no time to repaint her.

Metzler was in a quandary. Time and again, *Konteradmiral* Karl Dönitz, the submarine chief, had reiterated Hitler's orders: incidents with United States vessels must at all costs be avoided. This cautious naval policy, spelt out on 25 April, was to be stressed again on 9 June and 7 July: Roosevelt must be given no cause for provocation. Acting on advice from Dr Hans Thomsen, the chargé in Washington, German newspapers were to refrain from attacking Roosevelt and from overtly endorsing isolationists like Lindbergh.

Fully as anxious to placate Roosevelt as Stalin was to placate Hitler, the Führer's view of the United States was a strange one, fostered by his genial incompetent Military Attaché, General Friedrich von Boetticher: the country was split between sober, moderate, patriotic and pro-German General Staff and a rabble of warmongering politicians and pressmen, dominated by international Jewry.

Apart from an abortive 1924 attempt to screw Nazi Party funds from the motor magnate, Henry Ford, Hitler had dismissed America from his thoughts. Convinced that the country harboured 13 million unemployed and that the wrong side had won the Civil War, he decried the American way of life "as a concept . . . inspired by the most vulgar commercialism". Unless sorely provoked, such "a mongrel society" could never threaten Germany.

Hence Jost Metzler's dilemma on the sultry morning of 21 May. He had erred in stopping an American ship – but plainly the *Robin Moor*, in contravention of the Neutrality Act, was carrying contraband. Although the Chief Officer would admit only to motor cycle parts and tractors, bound for Capetown, Helmsman Bade, a onetime Merchant Navy loading officer, was sceptical. "Aircraft, *Herr Käleunt*," was his estimate, "if they were really car parts, then they must be omnibuses."

Metzler came to a decision. The crew had twenty minutes to abandon ship and take to the lifeboats: after this *Robin Moor* would be sunk. Her captain must report to "The Laughing Cow" with all despatch, bringing his papers and bills of lading.

Still Metzler worried. He was acting contrary to orders – but just as surely *Robin Moor* was carrying contraband by which German lives would be forfeit. When Captain E. W. Meyers boarded U-69, saluting politely as he came, his papers were so obviously genuine that Metzler gave him one last chance. "Your ship is carrying contraband and I have to sink it," he explained. "Have you anything to say?"

Meyers made no attempt to deny it, merely spreading his hands. "I'm sorry, I can't help it," was all he said.

Soon after, Metzler felt a sense of vindication. One torpedo hit *Robin Moor* amidships: thirty three shells from U-69's 8.8 cm deck gun finished the job. But as she sank wearily by the stern, to the gunners' excited cries of "La Vache qui Rit", a tell-tale carpet of flotsam was bobbing on the oily water: the broken fragments of aircraft wings, huge aircraft tyres.

Now a complication arose. In their haste to abandon ship, *Robin Moor*'s 38-strong crew, along with eight civilian passengers, had neglected to stock up on food – and Metzler had been forced to deplete his own stores of bread, butter, brandy and medicine. To ensure their safety he took the ship's four lifeboats in tow for several hours, only casting off when a gentle current would steer them to the African shore. That evening, under cover of dusk, he radioed U-Boat Command headquarters, at Lorient, of the plight of the castaways. Neutral steamers would now be on the alert.

Although Metzler could not know it, lifeboats carrying eleven of the survivors were soon after caught in a contrary current and swept out into the Atlantic; it was not until 11 June that the Brazilian steamer *Ozorio* which had sighted them, landed them at Pernambuco. (The remaining 35 reached Capetown two days earlier.)

Aboard U-69 the hapless Metzler was now given no respite at all. From his Lorient headquarters, 'The Big Sea Lion,' as Dönitz was known, followed one furious and peremptory signal with another: "Report immediately why *Robin Moor* was sunk". Only by degrees did the U-Boat commander realise that he was at the storm centre of an international incident.

For Roosevelt's reaction had been violent and immediate, and his condemnation echoed round the world. In a ringing message to Congress he spoke of "the acts of an international outlaw", of "a policy of frightfulness and intimidation", of "conquest based on lawlessness and terror on land and piracy on the sea". It was a message Sumner Welles swiftly passed on to the Chargé, Hans Thomsen, though ending with due regard to protocol: "Accept, Sir, the renewed assurance of my high consideration".

And Roosevelt took other steps, much farther reaching. On 14 June, just as Treasury Secretary Morgenthau had urged for months, he froze Axis assets in the United States, along with those of other European countries not then frozen. He closed down all twenty-five German consulates. Following reports of German submarines in Iceland's coastal waters, he accepted Churchill's invitation to take over from the British garrison that had been holding Iceland ever since its mother country, Denmark, had been overrun in 1940.

Churchill was delighted, envisaging the liberation of another division for his beloved Middle East. Long before 7 July, when the 1st Brigade United States Marine Corps took over Camp Alafoss, 15 miles from Reykjavik – "Rinky Dink" to the Marines – the Premier was assuring Roosevelt: "I am much encouraged by . . . your Marines taking over that cold place."

Roosevelt, too, was in high good humour. "When I took Iceland the market went up two points," he reminded Morgenthau skittishly. "There are a lot of places I can take. I can take the Azores for you. Just let me know . . ."*

The one man who viewed the take-over with real trepidation was Admiral Harold R. Stark, Chief of Naval Operations. "There is so much potential dynamite in this order," he wrote to Hopkins, "that I feel it should have his (Roosevelt's) O.K. before I send it over to you . . . I will wait the final "execute" until I get word from the President."

The far-reaching implications of Metzler's action were chilling indeed, Stark felt – "I realise that this is practically an act of war."

*

* At the end of March, this had been Portugal's most earnest hope. Fearing a German invasion, 10,000 crack Portuguese troops had been transported from Lisbon to the Azores, where the destroyer, *Lina* was standing by to steam for Lisbon and rescue Dr Antonio Salazar, the dictator, and his government, if need be. Portugal, Hull was informed, would accept United States "protection".

In the silence of his study at No 10 Downing Street, Churchill was hunched in his favourite leather chair. With growing disquiet, he studied the cable before him, which Wavell had despatched from Cairo on 30 May. Due to the inferiority of tanks and armoured cars, the Commander-in-Chief hazarded, prospects in the Western Desert were in no way bright. Uncradling the phone, Churchill called Field Marshal Sir John Dill to outline the gist of the despatch. "That," Churchill contended, "is the message of a tired and beaten man."

Initially Wavell had opposed an intervention in Greece, and since then Churchill's dissatisfaction with him had grown. As early as 19 May, he had debated exchanging him with Lieutenant-General Sir Claude Auchinleck, India's commander. Following Crete, Attlee, too, had been sharply critical of Wavell – "I do not think he has really freed his mind from the Maginot Line complex. Everything outside the Egyptian peri-meter he regards as commitments not opportunities." On 28 May, made fretful by Wavell's inaction, Churchill once more took him sharply to task: "Now . . . is the time to fight a decisive battle in Libya and go on day after day facing all necessary losses until you have beaten the life out of General Rommel's army."

But Wavell's pessimism did not abate. On 12 May, a convoy code-named "Tiger" had reached Suez with 238 tanks; by sailing the risky Mediterranean route forty days had been saved. But many of the "Tiger Cubs" as Churchill christened them, were in the sorriest shape – gear-boxes cracked, tracks unserviceable, all of them lacking sand filters. Action before mid-June, Wavell warned was out of the question – "even tigers have teething troubles." Churchill received the news without com-ment, but the calm was illusory. Wavell's days were numbered.

So were the days of many of his men, for the task allotted the "Tiger Cubs" was daunting: a three-pronged 150-mile attack launched from Mersa Matruh, designed to destroy all enemy forces east of Tobruk. Most vital target of all was the German-held Halfaya Pass, a 300-foot gash in the coastal escarpment running parallel with the Mediterranean shoreline, for through it must pass not only any advance into Egypt but any westward invasion. He who held Halfaya held the Tripoli-Alexandria road.

At 2.30 a.m. on 15 June, the move to the front began. Soon, on a scale never before witnessed, almost 500 tanks would clash. But as the red pinpoints of rear lights inched forward in the darkness, it was as if Wavell's sense of foreboding pressed in upon his troops. "There is battle in the air tonight," one man wrote in his diary. "It lies thick upon the tongue." Only Brigadier Ian Erskine looked further than the morrow: his under-strength 22nd Guards Brigade had been beefed up with a battalion of Durham Light Infantry to upset all his plans.

To Major-General Frank Messervy, the wiry irrepressible commander of the 4th Indian Division, Erskine complained: "Light Infantry march at a much faster pace than the Guards. What the hell am I going to do when the Brigade has to march on a ceremonial parade in Cairo?"

In his command post on the rim of Halfaya Pass, *Hauptmann* Wilhelm Bach, commanding the 1st Battalion, 104th Field Artillery Regiment, anxiously awaited news of the British. Clad in an open-necked shirt with pale blue braces supporting voluminous khaki shorts, puffing contentedly on a cigar, the portly 50-year-old Bach was a far cry from the Afrika Korps stereotype. Known to his troops as "The Pastor of Halfaya" – in civil life he had been pastor of the Evangelical Church at Mannheim – Bach, calm and paternal, still commanded the unswerving loyalty of the die-hards the British knew as "the seven-day men". These were the men who manned Halfaya's machine gun nests and gun emplacements, victualled with food and water for seven days at a time, knowing they must fight to the last bullet and the last drop of water.

On the night of 14 June, Bach's field telephone rang. He listened, then told his deputy *Leutnant* Friedl Schmidt, "Something's in the air. It's tonight or early tomorrow morning."

Towards 6 a.m. on 15 June, the faint throb of motors was borne towards the pass. Through powerful field glasses, Bach and the "seven day men" now saw on the horizon tiny black dots trailing a giant plume of dust. The British were perhaps two miles away. "Under no circumstances fire," Bach passed the word quietly. "Let them come on."

Slowly the tanks advanced. On paper, at least, this attack, codenamed "Operation Battleaxe", seemed feasible for Wavell had a four to one advantage in tanks, a two to one advantage in troops. By degrees the early morning silence was broken by the sharp crack of artillery as the British guns opened up. Shell craters pitted the biscuit-brown heights and columns of smoke arose. Still Bach's men, and the Italian battery under Major Leopoldo Pardo, held their fire.

At 9.15 a.m., Lieutenant-Colonel Walter O'Carroll, of the 4th Royal Tanks, heard with satisfaction the radio code-message, "Pink Spots": the action was under control and going well. Then the appalled last words of Major C. G. Miles, in the lead tank, burst in his eardrums: "Good God! They've got large calibre guns dug in and they're tearing my tanks to pieces."

It was true. From concealed emplacements all along the cliffside, Rommel's most deadly weapon had for the first time come into devastating play: Flak 88 anti-aircraft guns, used now in an anti-tank role, firing 22-lb shells that could tear holes as big as basket-balls in a Matilda a mile distant. As the whiplash crack of high-velocity shot sounded, three tanks stopped dead to burst asunder in billows of crimson flame and black oily smoke. In these moments, as eleven out of twelve tanks took fire like blowtorches, the fate of Halfaya was decided.

Due to lack of air cover – caused by wireless breakdowns and poor coordination between air and ground troops – the carnage was absolute. Stukas swooped unopposed from the sun, and General Messervy, sitting on the fender of a three-ton truck awaiting a mug of tea, saw a stick of bombs blast his Indian mess-waiter to fragments. British *sang-froid* to the fore, Messervy called, "Will someone be good enough to get me another cup? And I'm afraid you'll have to find another chap to bring it." Around now a dispatch rider arrived at Messervy's H.Q. with a strangely inappropriate message from Churchill to the troops: "The eyes of the world are on you, and Britain knows that her sons will conquer." On his own initiative, Captain Donald Bateman stuffed it unbroadcast into his pocket.

Five times the British sought to storm the pass, and five times Bach's men, swigging on water spiked with aniseed to slake their thirst, repulsed them. As supplies ran low, Major Pardo collected old Italian artillery shells, had them polished and greased, then fired them. Everywhere men clung like limpets to the dour slopes, and every ridge and bone-dry watercourse took its toll. But at last, at 11 a.m. on 17 June, Messervy, lacking word from the G.O.C. ordered Western Desert Force to withdraw on his own initiative to escape annihilation. Halfaya would be "Hell-Fire" Pass to the British from this time on.

Shortly, on the desert airstrip, Messervy confronted a grim-faced Wavell. "I thought he was going to sack me," Messervy recalled later, for Wavell stared at him for long minutes before breaking silence. "I think you were right to withdraw in the circumstances," was all Wavell said finally, "but orders should have come from H.Q. Western Desert Force."

*

In England, Wavell's terse admission of defeat – "Am very sorry for failure of 'Battleaxe'" brought only consternation. How many tanks "Battleaxe" had cost the British was always open to doubt – estimates ranged from 80 to 99 – but what hit hardest was the knowledge that in 12 days Rommel had achieved everything save Tobruk's fall, that had taken O'Connor 50. Sir Alexander Cadogan best summed up the mood of disillusion: "Wavells and suchlike are no good against (the Germans). It is like putting me up to play Bobby Jones over 36 holes."

The outcome was inevitable. Early on the morning of 21 June, Wavell's Chief of Staff, Lieutenant-General Sir Arthur Smith, arrived at his chief's house on Cairo's Gezira Island. Wavell was in the bathroom shaving, cheeks daubed with lather, razor poised. Quietly Smith read out a signal which had just arrived from Churchill: "I have come to the conclusion that public interest will best be served by appointment of General Auchinleck to relieve you in command of armies of Middle East . . ."

116

Wavell stared ahead. With no emotion, no regret, he said, "The Prime Minister's quite right. This job needs a new eye and a new hand." Then he went on shaving.

*

Harold Elvin, the footloose young Englishman who had felt that Moscow was the place to be, was having second thoughts. From all the war fronts the news flooded in daily – the sinking of the *Robin Moor*, the conflict in Syria, the debacle at Halfaya – but the British Embassy, a sprawling pile built by a sugar-beet baron on the Sofiiskaya Embankment, overlooking the Moscow River, was an enclave of funereal silence.

After three months Elvin's routine as assistant night watchman had become almost second nature. Every other night, at 9 p.m., he left his room in the West Wing to take up his post in the main hallway, a canopied seat lit by a single reading lamp. There, until 8 a.m. next day, he was almost a fixture – browsing through piles of *Punch* and *Country Life* borrowed from the English Church Library, breaking off to patrol his rounds, sometimes repairing to the kitchen to brew tea.

Sometimes, in the small hours, the chief watchman, Sergeant Bill Eldredge, a cheerful Cockney veteran of the Indian Army, would join him for a schoolboy feast of egg and onions on toast. But often, as on 9 June, there was only brooding silence as Elvin surveyed the familiar nightly scene: the life-size oil paintings of Edward VII and Queen Victoria, offset by linenfold panelling, the immense expanse of red carpeting that stretched beyond the hall to the giant oak staircase, on to the 15 foot landing window.

Mostly Elvin welcomed this solitude. With a staff of twenty sobersided bachelors, Embassy life by day was often oppressive. Though all were English, Elvin, as a lowly night watchman, was treated as beyond the pale; on duty journeys in an Embassy car, Elvin rode in front with Bumagin, the chauffeur, ignored by the career diplomats riding in the back. Following Embassy pressure, even his old schoolfellow from Southend Grammar School, the Reuter correspondent Maurice Lovell, told him shamefacedly, "I want to keep my job here, so I can't afford to mix with you".

As often in the past, Elvin fell back on the resources of the country. Time off meant hours spent at the Bolshoi Ballet, or watching the crowds in Gorki Park, eating ices served by waitresses in pretty blue embroidered blouses. At other times he strolled in Red Square, with its bowls of blood red carnations and neat blue balustrades, or among the pavilions and food stalls of the Ermitage Gardens. With a pang he felt closer to Savalief, the Ambassador's butler, or Fedor, the porter, than to his own class-ridden compatriots.

117

As an old friend of his father's, Sir Stafford Cripps proved a democratic exception – but in one respect he, too, had proved a sore disappointment. On the April day that Elvin first met him he had come up with a prophecy so hare-brained that even on this June night, three months later, the sense of disillusion still persisted.

Gesturing at the huge wall map in his book-lined study, Cripps had predicted suddenly, "Germany will flood through Europe this way – and they will next amass their forces here," pointing to the Russian border. "Of course," he went on, "they will send out a feeler towards Moscow and Leningrad but more serious will be hundreds-of-miles encircling movements, which will surround both in pincers".

Elvin remained silent. A trade unionist's son, he had admired the Socialist Cripps for more than a decade – yet now his idol was voicing "the biggest load of craziness I had heard from any worthy". Cripps, he had since heard, had laboured equally hard to convince the Kremlin – and been rejected out of hand.

Hadn't Germany enough enemies already? Elvin had asked himself ever since that day. Could they be so insane? Of course they could not. In a year's time Moscow would be as peaceful and inviolate as she was tonight, silent under a late pall of snow.

But in the small hours of 9 June, a small voice had begun gnawing like conscience in Elvin's mind: And yet . . . and yet . . .

*

Another man was similarly beset by doubts. Amid all the panoply of that summer afternoon, 21-year-old *Fähnrich* (Ensign-Cadet) Peter Neumann found his mind constantly straying from the goal he had so long awaited: his graduation from the S.S. *Junkerschule* (Officer Cadets Training Unit) at Bad Tölz, in the Bavarian Alps, south of Munich.

Neumann had been anticipating this day for three years now: the moment when he stood braced rigidly to attention, along with all the others on the parade ground, hearing the roll of thunder as the band crashed into *Deutschland über Alles*, absurdly proud that he now made one of the *Schutzstaffeln* (SS), the elite unit of Hitler's assault troops with their jet-black uniforms, silver death's heads adorning their caps, the twin lightning flashes on the right lapels of their tunics.

The setting was perfect for such a moment: the great black S.S. banners and swastikas flapping against the white walls of the school, the buzzards wheeling in a clear bright sky above the Karwendel Alps, the dark motionless columns of youngsters as far as the eye could see.

It was no day for doubts, Neumann recognised. And yet . . .

Like all young Germans who had embraced the Nazi Party, Neumann had been truly indoctrinated in his teens. He could recite all the injustices

1a Harold Elvin in Moscow

1b Major James Devereux, defender of Wake Island

1c Ruth Mitchell

1d Andrée de Jongh in 1941

2a Aircraftman Marcel-Gerard Comeau, survivor of Greece and Crete

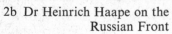

2b Dr Heinrich Haape on the Russian Front

Invasion of Crete. The second wave of German parachutists descending and grouping on the ground

3b Evacuation of Greece. Weary Tommies asleep on board a troopship

3c Bombing of allied shipping in Suda Bay, Crete

4a President Roosevelt and Churchill (seated left) at a service on board HMS *Prince of Wales* in August

4b Harry Hopkins and Sir Alexander Cadogan on board HMS *Prince of Wales*

5a General Catroux, General Le Gentilhomme and their Staff entering Damascus through deserted streets on 26 June

5b General de Gaulle inspecting a Guard of Honour of Free French at Beirut on 29 July

6a As the *Prince of Wales* sinks the crew scramble aboard HMS *Express*

6b The wreckage of the Messerschmitt 110 fighter plane in which Rudolf Hess flew to Scotland

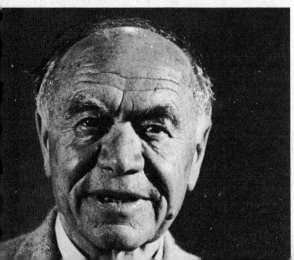

6c Lord Beaverbrook

7a Field-Marshal Rommel

7b Australians in the caves where they lived in Tobruk

8a HMS *Hood* blown up off Greenland, as seen from the *Prinz Eugen*

8b Yosuke Matsuoka, Japanese Foreign
Minister, returning from his visit to
Europe

8c Marshal Tito

9a The siege of Leningrad. Nevsky Prospekt during shelling

9b Lake Ladoga road of life

10a General Guderian at an airfield on the Russian Front briefing his staff

10b Marshal Timoshenko

10c General Zhukov

11a Russian peasants fleeing before the German advance on Moscow

11b General Dovator's cavalry units on their way to defend Moscow

12a Russian Front: a German tank rumbles over a slit trench with Russians cowering underneath

12b Red Army men dislodging Germans from a village

13a General Douglas MacArthur

13b American and Philippine troops surrender to the Japanese at Bataan

14a The crematoria at Buchenwald concentration camp in which the corpses of those gassed, at the rate of 2,000 an hour, were burned

14b Lager Nordhausen camp where the bodies of hundreds of former slave workers were discovered by the U.S. army in 1945

15a USS *California* sinking after the Japanese attack on Pearl Harbor

15b The wreckage at the Naval Air Station, Pearl Harbor

16 British troops marching along the road to Cyrene with the ancient town behind them

that had brought "Adi", as the cadets called Hitler, to power: the monstrous inequity of the Treaty of Versailles, the six million unemployed queueing at the soup kitchens, the ten million Germans who had turned in despair to Communism. Above all, the lasting harm that the Jews had done to Germany and to all Europe.

The Jews were the subject of all Neumann's niggling doubts.

A ticket collector's son from Wittenberg, south of Berlin, he had first found the Nazi ideology heady stuff – a prospect of grandeur, an escape from his father's peevish whining, from the steamy kitchen at 37 Heiligengasse, where his mother, her arms always damp and red with scrubbing, seemed to toil from morning to night.

At first in the 27th Troop of the Wittenberg Hitler Youth, Neumann had seen only the glory: that great day of the oath-taking, in the forest of Havel, when Baldur von Schirach, their leader, had arrived to address them in the Opel Käpitan bearing his grey and gold flag. On that day, hundreds of them, clasping the daggers engraved in gothic lettering *Treue bis auf dem Tod* (Faithful unto death) had sworn that fidelity to their Chancellor, Adolf Hitler.

In pursuit of that ideal, Neumann had gone on to tread a rougher road. The Holstein *Reichsnational Politische Schule* (Reich National Political Training College), with its harping on racial purity – "the Führer has said that the mixing of races was unacceptable" – had been heavy going at times, but it was nothing to the endurance tests that followed. Posted to Vogelsang Castle, near Aachen, where all the Nazi elite were trained, Neumann had mastered strange skills for a nineteen-year-old. He learned to overpower half-starved Alsatian dogs that had been trained to go for the throat, to break in wild Arab colts without using a saddle.

Before he was twenty he had learned to run a mile and a half, then wash in an icy stream. "Iron discipline. Perpetual obedience" ran the Party slogan, and to this end Neumann and the other cadets were ordered to forfeit half their meals for an entire month. On one visit of inspection Reinhard Heydrich, chief assistant to the S.S. *Reichsführer*, Heinrich Himmler, promised them "a war of liberation", but not all of them lived to fight it. Now the training had grown tougher still; they doubled to overcome strongpoints under a barrage of live ammunition. No man lived if he failed to dig a foxhole and burrow for shelter within twenty minutes; a Benz armoured car, advancing relentlessly, ground him into the mud. In one month the rate of accidental deaths rose to thirty-two.

But Neumann had survived it all; he was now a fully-fledged S.S. officer. One by one now the cadets were moving forward, mounting the steps of the tribunal to receive their brevets from the Commandant, *Sturmbannführer* (S.S. Major) Richard Schultze. To each man he murmured a word of congratulation, but Neumann barely heard. In his ears once again, there echoed the voice of Professor von Arensdorf, his mentor at the Berlin War Academy.

"It is our national duty, it is a matter of life and death, to exterminate the Jew. We must either strike him down or he will murder us . . ."

There lay the core of his doubt: the verb "exterminate". Neumann believed implicitly that Jews must be eliminated from certain professions. And never again should Jews gain control in matters vital to Germany.

But exterminate? Eliminate? Perhaps it was just a question of semantics, after all.

*

On Sunday, 30 March, more than 200 senior German commanders and their staff officers had assembled in the small panelled chamber of the Reichchancellery's Cabinet Room, settling themselves in gilded chairs bespoken from the nearby Propaganda Ministry. Hitler had summoned them, but nobody knew why. Promptly at 11 a.m. the audience rose smartly to their feet; the Führer had entered by a rear-door, making his way to the speaker's lectern mounted on a small rostrum.

It was a wide-ranging speech, which followed, lasting almost three hours; as Hitler broached topic after topic – Mussolini's misfortune in Libya, the iniquities of the Churchill clique, the partitioning of Yugoslavia – many a man found his attention wandering.

But interest quickened immediately when he switched to Operation Barbarossa. It was now, he confirmed, set for 22 June. "We have the chance to smash Russia while our own back is free," he avowed. "That chance will not return so soon. I would be betraying the future of the German people if I did not seize it now!"

His next words struck a vague chord of alarm; in many minds a warning bell rang, presaging the monstrous genocide to come. It would be a very different war from that fought in the west, Hitler warned them. Now it would be a clash of ideologies, shorn of chivalry. "The war against Russia will be such that it cannot be fought in a knightly fashion! This struggle . . . will have to be conducted with unprecedented, merciless and unrelenting harshness." In the East, cruelty now would be "kindness for the future". All Russian commissars instantly recognised by the red stars enclosing a golden hammer and sickle on their sleeves, were criminals and must be liquidated – "it is not our job to see that these criminals survive".

Did Hitler sense the instinctive repulsion felt by almost every man present? At all events, he tacitly acknowledged it. "I know the necessity of making war in such a manner is beyond the comprehension of you generals," he told them loftily, "but I cannot and will not change my orders and I insist that they be carried out with unquestioning and unconditional obedience."

"They sat there before him in stubborn silence," *Oberst* Walter Warlimont, of the Führer's Operations Department, recalled the scene later. "Otherwise not a hand moved and not a word was spoken but by him."

But no sooner had Hitler departed than many words were spoken, angry and embittered words that crowded to every man's lips. The honour of the German Army was at stake, and all of them knew it. Hemming in the Commander-in-Chief, *Feldmarschall* von Brauchitsch, they gave vent to a storm of protest, led by the three Army Group commanders on whom the invasion devolved, Gerd von Rundstedt, Fedor von Bock and Ritter von Leeb. What each man had envisaged as a legitimate theatre of war was now to become a vast laboratory, transforming the master plan of the Third Reich into nightmare reality.

At the Posen headquarters of Bock's Army Group Centre, his Chief of Staff, *Generalleutnant* Hans von Salmuth and his Operations Officer, *Generalmajor* Henning von Tresckow, pronounced the order "a disaster"; both men sought ways and means to "persuade at least the divisional commanders by word of mouth to try to circumvent the order". As Tresckow put it, "If international law is to be broken, let the Russians break it first and not us." The commander of the Thirty-Ninth Corps, General Rudolf Schmidt, called for the order to be rescinded; it was important "to show the Russian people that they had some hope for the future". The Seventeenth Armoured Division's *Generalmajor* Ritter von Thoma later admitted that no commissar captured by his division had ever been shot.

Since only twelve copies of the "Commissar Order" were transmitted, many commanders, like *Generalleutnant* Fritz Erich von Manstein, commanding 56 Panzer Corps, took the easy way out; they failed to pass the message down the chain of command. *Generaloberst* Heinz Guderian, leading Panzer Group Two, was barely aware the order existed, since Bock had never told him. "The Army High Command wants to turn professional soldiers into clergymen," was Hitler's angry reaction later.

But one group of men would know no such luxury of choice, for the oath of loyalty they had sworn placed obedience to Hitler's commands above God, above mercy, above humanity. Wherever killers were needed, 3,000 black-clad S.S. men on Russian soil would always fulfil this role.

Neumann did not know this.

*

It was the shortest night of that year, the summer solstice. Yet to many men the twilight hours of Saturday 21 June seemed the longest night of all their lives. Under the pale floodlight of a hunter's moon they waited, as hour followed hour, in fear and expectation.

Adolf Hitler, the impresario who was mounting this extravaganza, had adjourned as always after dinner to the salon of the Berlin Reichchancellery. It was a haven of deep easy chairs and shaded lights, and outwardly Hitler seemed calm and confident. His architect, Albert Speer, found that the Führer had even taken care of the musical effects, playing a few bars of Liszt's *Les Préludes* on the gramophone. "You'll hear that often in the near future, because it is going to be our victory fanfare for the Russian campaign."

Inwardly, he veered between total self-assurance and gnawing doubt. In a moment of frankness, he admitted: "We know absolutely nothing about Russia. It might be one big soap bubble, but it might just as well turn out to be very different." "A door opened before us," was how he described the suspense later, "and we didn't know what was behind it". In a letter to Mussolini, dictated on this day, he revealed something of the strain he had undergone: ". . . months of continuous nerve-racking waiting are ending in the hardest decision of my life . . . I have . . . finally reached the decision to cut the noose before it can be drawn tight."

Along the 3,000-mile border stretching from Petsamo to the Black Sea, few Russians realised that the hour was at hand. Seventeen years of Stalinist oppression had stifled almost all initiative; even the most senior commanders were wary of interpreting signs and portents. Although 170 divisions were distributed throughout five military districts – Leningrad, Baltic, Western, Kiev, and Odessa – no emergency mobilisation had been permitted even now, in the hope of placating Hitler. In Moscow, the Chief Marshal of Artillery, Nikolai Voronov, had plucked up courage to raise the build-up of German troops with the Deputy People's Commissar of Defence, Marshal G. I. Kulik. But Kulik refused to discuss it: "This is big politics. It's not our business."

Other men were noting small signs that suggested trouble. General Ivan Rediuninsky, commanding the 15th Rifle Corps in the Kiev Military District, heard of the strange conduct of many German border sentries; until a week ago they had saluted Russian officers on sight, but now they churlishly turned their backs. In Sevastopol, headquarters of the Black Sea Fleet, Captain N. G. Rybalko, the officer of the day, was conscious of another disturbing factor. The three German freighters that plied the Black Sea had all withdrawn to Rumanian and Bulgarian ports.

At Minsk, Colonel I. T. Starinov, a mining expert, sat in on a phone call between the district commander, General Dmitri Pavlov, and an unknown informant. In a palpable effort to keep his temper in check, Pavlov kept repeating "I know it has been reported. I know. Those at the top know better than we. That's all!" Then he slammed down the receiver.

Earlier that day Pavlov had received an urgent message from Major-General V. E. Klimovskikh, his Chief of Staff, reporting, "From the woods, sound of engines." This, too, he had shrugged off; Pavlov was to pass this Saturday evening in a box at the Minsk Officer's Club, watching a popular comedy, *The Wedding at Malinovka*.

In the thicket of yellow government buildings and frescoed palaces that made up the Kremlin compound, a strange ambivalence prevailed. Towards 2 p.m. this day, General I. V. Tuilinev, commanding Moscow Military District, received a call from Stalin himself. The dictator told him: "Note that the situation is uneasy, and you should bring the troops of Moscow's anti-aircraft defence to 75 per cent of combat readiness."

Yet on this same afternoon, responding to a Tass news agency flash of 14 June that the war scare was "clumsy cooked-up propaganda", thousands of Russian soldiers were proceeding on leave – many of them to the Black Sea resort of Sochi.

On the German side of the border, there was uncertainty, too. If every man knew his objective and what was expected of him, there were still small last-minute qualms: Shall I be afraid? Supposing I am wounded? This last thought was especially prevalent in the 4th Company, Panzer Lehr Regiment, encamped in a dense pine forest at Pratulin, on the Polish bank of the River Bug. Although extra comforts had been issued – including a bottle of brandy for every four men – scarcely anyone touched a drop. In spite of sulfonamide, the spectre of a stomach wound haunted them.

Among those curious as to how he would comport himself in battle was *Assistenzart* (Assistant Surgeon) Heinrich Haape, medical officer of the 800-strong 3rd Battalion, Infantry Regiment 18, attached to the 6th Division of Bock's Army Group Centre. At 31, Haape was in the unique position of being both the battalion's oldest officer and the most junior member of the mess. In twelve months of Army life, he had witnessed some strange anomalies. Although a fully-qualified doctor on the staff of The Kaiser-Wilhelm Hospital, Duisburg, it was weeks before the Army had handed back his stethoscope and scalpel. First he must learn to dig a field-latrine and administer a bed-pan.

Now, in a camp near the Lithuanian border, Haape thought back to a question posed by his medical non-com *Oberfeldwebel* Wegener, "Do we have to give the Russians first aid too?" Haape had replied firmly, "We're not the judges, Wegener – our job is to help the wounded, Russians and Germans alike." It was a conviction that he held profoundly – and one that would be put sternly to the test in the months that lay ahead.

All along the moonlit frontier, men lay in hiding. For six nights now they had trailed like a parade of ghosts through the pale light, digging narrow anti-tank slits within sight of the border, retreating to quarters before dawn. Now at last they were ready. Some whiled away the last hours with a game of Skat. Others settled to last-minute chores – writing letters home, washing up their mess-tins, polishing their boots or the brass belt buckles inscribed *Gott mit uns*.

Some had travelled a long road already. In units like the *Leibstandarte Adolf Hitler*, every truck bore the likeness of the Parthenon painted in white lead on its bonnet, a proud record of past campaigns like a luggage label tacked on a suitcase. Others were wondering just how far this journey would take them. In the 3rd Battalion of the 39th Panzer Regiment, a curious non-com asked *Oberleutnant* Weidner: "What's it all about, *Herr-Leutnant*? Are we having a go at Ivan? Or are we driving through Russia to get to the Tommies in Iran?"

Many still recall how the rivers stank. In the damp June evening, the smell of silt permeated men's tunics and the manes of the baggage horses; the smell of the Black Sea shores was the mingled odour of attar of roses and horses' urine. But more than anything it was the small sounds that men remembered from that night. War correspondent Gunther Heysing, covering the front at Biala Podlaska for the *Berliner Borsenzeitung*, treasured the tinny resonance of a mouth organ solo of *Antje the Blonde*. *Gemeiner Soldat* Reinhold Pabel, an infantryman with the 6th Division, marvelled at a woman's soft voice from a far-off field, singing an Ukrainian folk song. To thousands more, the overture to battle would always be the deep plaintive night-long croaking of the bull frogs along the banks of the Bug.

At 11 p.m. an urgent code message was routed from Berlin to all commanders waiting in the East: "Dortmund, Mohn, Kresse, Aster, Aster." The die was cast; and the attack was on. Slowly, inexorably, the minutes ticked away, leaving three million men poised on the edge of eternity.

6

"We Have Only To Kick In The Door"

22 June–30 July, 1941

SOON AFTER MIDNIGHT, a train whistled mournfully. On the Fourth Army front, between Brest-Litovsk and Lomza, the sound came unexpectedly, fretting nerves already tense. Then, in the pale light, the locomotive was suddenly visible, shuffling over the frontier bridge from Russian to German territory: the international Moscow–Berlin express, a long freight train filled with grain clanking behind it. Josef Stalin was making his last delivery to his erstwhile ally, Adolf Hitler.

At 1 a.m. the move to battle stations began. The forces were advancing to their start-lines: 186 divisions, including 154 German, 14 Russian and 18 Finnish. Now was the time for each separate Army command to transmit its call-sign indicating full and final readiness – "*Wotan*" from Von Rundstedt's Army Group South, near Jassy, "*Kyffhäuser*" from *Feldmarschall* Gunther von Kluge's Fourth Army on the Bug. In their tents and office buses, the staff officers, bent over maps and written orders, conversed only in undertones.

The luminous minute-hands of their synchronised watches crawled slowly towards zero hour: 3.15 a.m.

Suddenly it was as if a master electrician had thrown a switch. One minute there was only absolute silence, then, along 3,000 miles of frontier, the order passed from post to post, "Troop, open fire!" Then the guns of Barbarossa spoke.

With an ear-splitting earth-shaking roar the front erupted in flame. More than 7,000 guns poured a storm of fire onto the Russian positions. On the Ninth Army front, north of the Pripet Marshes, crouching German troops saw the high wooden Russian watch towers collapse in shaking yellow flames. Dimly audible through the inferno came the frantic baying of frontier guard dogs.

Caught up in a kind of frenzy, men surpassed their own expectations. As the first salvoes screamed into space, *Oberleutnant* Zumpe, of 3rd Company, 135th Infantry Regiment, leaped from the ditch by the Brest–Litovsk railway embankment, with a frantic yell of "Let's go!" Steel helmets mushroomed from the tall grass behind him, and men raced like torch-bearers for the bridge. As they doubled along the high parapet, the guns drowned out the clatter of boots on planking; one burst of sub-machine gun fire and the Soviet sentry toppled. Then Zumpe, sliding a green shield over the lens of his flashlight, waved it like a berserk stationmaster towards the German side of the bridge.

The first armoured scout cars jolted forward. It was 3.17 a.m., and far overhead the tail lights of the German fighters were winking towards the east, the first of more than 2,000 planes that would strike this day.

Not all crossed so easily as Zumpe. *Gemeine* Reinhold Pabel of the 6th Army, was only one of many infantrymen paddling for dear life across the Bug in a rubber dinghy, weighed down by light anti-tank guns and heavy machine guns. Behind them sappers set to work erecting pontoon bridges.

On the face of it, the assault plan was working to perfection. Von Leeb's Army Group North was forging from East Prussia towards Leningrad: Von Rundstedt's Army Group South driving for Kiev from Lublin; Von Bock's Army Group Centre advancing on either side of the Minsk–Smolensk–Moscow line. Through the stands of waving grain, stitched with purple mallows, through a glowing Van Gogh landscape of sunflower fields the grey legions of *Wehrmacht* and *Waffen* S.S. swept on. On this first day, surprise was total: 10,000 prisoners were taken, 1,200 aircraft destroyed on 66 Belorussian airfields.

Like a vast travelling workshop, the columns rolled on, trailing a pungent blue vapour of Panzer exhausts in their wake; streaking ahead of the streams of horse-drawn wagons came a steady chain of trucks, their drivers bawling peremptorily, "*Weg! Weg!*" (Make way). On the horizon, the rhythmic boom of guns pulsed like a giant piston. By the wayside, white acacia-wood crosses marked the graves of those who had fallen to snipers' bullets.

By order of the fanatical *Feldmarschall* Walter von Reichenau, every junior commander in Sixth Army was forced to inscribe the legend, "Pursuit without rest" above his mapboard – but it was the same on every front. Despite the choking clouds of yellow dust, the speed was relentless: a steady unwavering 22 miles a day on roads that were little more than rutted cart-tracks.

"Keep going, keep going," *Generalleutnant* Erich von Manstein exhorted his panzers. "Never mind about your flanks. Never mind about cover." Like other commanders, Manstein sensed that Russia could never be conquered and occupied: only bold incisive forays might overthrow the regime and paralyse its potential. Four days and five hours after zero hour, Manstein had completed a non-stop 200-mile dash through Russian territory.

Guderian, too, lancing for Smolensk, the gateway to Moscow, with Panzer Group Two, knew the same urgency. To combat a log-jam of traffic threatened by 87,000 vehicles, he set up a three-category priority system – with fighting men taking precedence over all. When the commander of the Herman Göring Luftwaffe Communications Regiment complained bitterly about his No 3 priority, Guderian asked tersely, "Can telegraph posts shoot?" When the man shook his head, Guderian retorted, "And that's why you'll keep No 3 priority."

The speed brought hardships in its wake. Now the Panzers were moving so fast, the supply wagons could not keep pace; one unit survived for three days on tinned tomatoes and mineral water. Some took to living off the land like old-time mercenaries. Helmut Pabst, and his 9th Army signals unit, after breakfasting, lunching and dining off dry bread, fell back on onions and turnips plucked from the fields and milk from peasants' churns.

Even top commanders enjoyed no mess privileges. "Heat, gnats, dust," Guderian wrote to his wife, Gretel. "I am missing my bath." Manstein hailed a roast chicken dinner as manna from heaven; his usual evening fare was smoked sausage and rye bread smeared with margarine.

But the pace could not continue. Slowly, even now, the Russians like a patient awakening from an anaesthetic, were taking the decisions that had to be taken to turn the tide.

*

In the Russian lines, total confusion had reigned. Nobody knew what was happening or what to do. At 11 p.m. on the Saturday, the Naval Commander-in-Chief, Admiral of the Fleet Nikolai Kuznetzov, was working late at his Moscow headquarters when Marshal Semeon Timoshenko, People's Commissar of Defence, telephoned abruptly. "There is very important news," he said. "Come to my office."

Along with his deputy, Rear Admiral Vladmir Alafuzov, Kuznetzov set off down Frunze Street, for a small building located opposite the Defence Commissariat. Climbing to the second floor, they found Timoshenko, a bald hard-eyed man of 46, in conclave with his Chief of Staff, General Georgi Zhukov. Though a breeze stirred the heavy magenta curtains, the heat was stifling; Zhukov, working on a pile of telegraph blanks, had his tunic unbuttoned.

Naming no sources, Timoshenko told the naval officers that an attack by Germany was now considered possible. The fleets must be ordered to combat readiness.

"In the event of attack, are they allowed to open fire?" Kuznetzov asked promptly. The appeasement tactics of recent months were still fresh in his mind.

Timoshenko said yes. "Run to headquarters," he told Admiral Alafuzov, "and send a telegram to the fleets immediately." Then, as Alafuzov hesitated, "Run!"

It was no time to stand on dignity. At a brisk jog-trot, Alafuzov set off up the sultry canyon of Frunze Street. It was already past midnight on 22 June.

Back in his office, Kuznetsov came to a decision: telegrams could take time, and time was pressing. Uncradling the phone, he called the commanders of the Baltic, Northern and Black Sea Fleets to pass on Timoshenko's message. Every man's reaction, he noted, was the same as his own: But can we open fire?

His task discharged, Kuznetsov stretched out on a leather divan, courting sleep. But already at 3 a.m. the yellow light of dawn filled the sky and sleep would not come. Then the phone rang shrilly, and answering Kuznetsov heard the excited voice of Vice Admiral Filip Oktyabrsky, the Black Sea Fleet commander.

"An air raid has been carried out against Sevastopol," he stammered. "Anti-aircraft is fighting off the attack!"

Oktyabrsky did not add that the Chief of the Fleet Anti-Aircraft Defence I. S. Zhilin, had been bitterly reluctant to comply. "Keep in mind that you bear full responsibility," he cautioned the Duty Officer, Captain Rybalko. "I am entering it in the combat operations log." Incensed at the shilly-shallying, Rybalko shouted, "Write what you want, but open fire on those planes."

In Moscow, others were proving harder to convince. At Naval Headquarters, Kuznetsov received an irate call from the Secretary of the Party's Central Committee, Georgi Malenkov: "Do you understand what you are reporting?"

"I understand," Kuznetsov replied patiently. "War has started."

The trouble was Malenkov did not believe a word of it. He at once called Sevastopol to check, only to hear Oktyabrsky assure him sharply, "Yes, yes, we are being bombed." At that moment, the Commander-in-Chief could scarcely hear Moscow; mammoth explosions were shaking the walls and windows of his room.

But already a virus of indecision had fatally infected the men whose rapid decisions were needed. Moscow's Military District Commander, General Tiulinev, looked in on Zhukov soon after 3.15 a.m. to see the Chief of Staff replacing his phone. "German aircraft are bombing Kovno, Rovno, Sevastopol and Odessa." Zhukov announced. Then he added, "We reported that to Stalin but he continues to regard it as a provocation by German generals."

To the men on the spot, the strange lethargy of the High Command was almost too frustrating to bear. One border unit signalled frantically, "We are being fired on. What shall we do?" Back from headquarters came a chilly rebuke: "You must be insane. And why is your signal not in code?"

At Bialystok, General Ivan Boldin, deputy commander of the Special Western Military District had no less than four agitated telephone calls from Marshal Timoshenko. Despite his earlier alerting of the fleets Timoshenko was now stressing that "no actions are to be taken against the Germans without our consent". Beside himself, Boldin shouted back, "Cities are burning, people are dying . . . Comrade Marshal, we must act . . . this is no provocation . . . the Germans have started a war!"

But it was not a war which Moscow acknowledged. The mining expert, Colonel Starinov, reached the town of Kobrin in a lull between air raids, hoping desperately for some bulletins from the Defence Commissariat. Instead he found the main square black with refugees piling into trucks, heedless of the loudspeakers blasting out Radio Moscow's 6 a.m. Keep-fit class: "Stretch your arms out, bend! Livelier! Up down, up down . . ."

A few men strove to restore order from chaos, but finite instructions were few. At Minsk, General Dmitri Pavlov, convinced that trouble threatened, did transmit the code-word GROZA – signifying full combat readiness – but many units never received the signal. Major-General Potaturchev, commanding the Soviet 4th Armoured Division, seeking orders from his superiors, was told mysteriously, "We've got to wait."

At 5 a.m., two hours after zero hour, an order did come – "Occupy envisaged positions" – but no military manoeuvre was thus implied. Instead, the division was to melt into the vast forest east of Bialystok and go into hiding. Seven days later, there was no division to hide; shot up by Stukas, picked off piecemeal by Panzers, the proud 4th Armoured was a scrapheap of smoking wreckage.

Those who looked to the Kremlin for leadership looked in vain. Although Stalin, on 6 May, had assumed the Premiership – with Vyaches-lav Molotov doubling as Deputy Premier and Foreign Commissar – the new Premier remained obstinately mute. At noon, on 22 June, it was Molotov's voice that Muscovites heard from rooftop loudspeakers all over the city: "Brothers and sisters, our cause is just. The enemy will be beaten. We shall triumph." Later Nikita Kruschev was to charge that for four days Stalin had retreated to his second-floor office, locking himself in and refusing to see anyone. A despairing cry burst from him: "All that Lenin created we have lost forever."

The first heads were swift to roll. Both Lieutenant-General P. V. Rychagov, Air Commander of the Baltic District, and Major-General A. A. Korobkov, Fourth Army commander, were ordered to Moscow and shot. Lieutenant-General Kopets, chief of the Soviet Bomber Command, escaped this fate only narrowly; faced with a loss of 800 bombers, he committed suicide on 23 June.

But as the beaten armies fell back, it was plain that more positive measures were needed to stop the rot.

On the baking hot afternoon of 27 June, the trans-Siberian express came to an unscheduled stop in the little railway station of Novosibirsk, 900 miles east of the Ural Mountains. Hastening along the train, the stationmaster and a military official at length located the special compartment of Lieutenant-General Andrei Eremenko. A squarely-built former Red Army N.C.O., Eremenko heard their message impassively: "Comrade General, the Defence Minister requests you to leave the train and continue your journey by air."

One day later, on the evening of 28 June, Eremenko was reporting to a cold and angry Timoshenko at the War Ministry. Timoshenko was succinct; the new arrival was to replace General Pavlov, as Commander-in-Chief of the Western Front. "What is the task of that front?" Eremenko asked precisely.

Timoshenko answered him in five words: "To stop the enemy advance."

*

It was the mining expert, Colonel Starinov, who saw the shape of things to come. On the day that he arrived in Minsk, General Pavlov and his principal commanders were taken out and shot. Now Starinov had come to render a report to one of the few senior staff officers who had kept his job.

But as he entered the man's office an extraordinary transformation took place. The man turned deathly white. His hands were shaking, and a nervous tic convulsed his entire face.

Suddenly he began to stammer pitiably, "I was with the troops . . . and I did everything . . . I am not guilty of anything . . ."

Wonderingly, Starinov now realised that the man was staring not at him but beyond his shoulder – to the two green-capped N.V.K.D. (secret police) officers who travelled with him to ensure his safe conduct from zone to zone.

That fear would dominate the whole campaign from this time on, Starinov realised. Any failure, any breach of duty, however unintentional, would always trigger the nightmare vision of a call from the men with the green caps.

*

At Hitler's headquarters, the news of the Russian defeats was received – for more reasons than one – with unrelieved delight.

As often with a major campaign, Hitler had relocated his headquarters staff close to the battle zone. At 2.45 p.m. on 23 June, a special train had borne them away from Berlin-Grünewald to the area designated Security Zone One – which Hitler called the *Wolfsschanze* (Wolf's Lair) – in the Forest of Görlitz, a few miles from Rastenburg, East Prussia.

It was a setting to daunt the stoutest heart: a huddle of wooden

130

blockhouses, humming day and night with the rattle of electric ventilation, its every window facing north to humour the sun-hating Hitler. Invisible from the air, through camouflage netting suspended at tree-top height, the site was dotted with marshy ponds and stagnant mosquito-infested lakes – "a cross between a cloister and a concentration camp", was Jodl's dour summary. Silence reigned eternally, save for the gunshot crack of a breaking branch or a sudden explosion as a fox touched off a mine.

Every man thus had high hopes that his sojourn here would be brief.

At first, such hopes seemed feasible. "We have only to kick in the door," Hitler had summed up the Russian enterprise to Jodl, "and the whole rotten structure will come crushing down!" His generals, so dubious regarding the 1940 campaign in the west, now saw the Führer as near-infallible. On Sunday, 29 June, they had ample proof; twelve Special Announcements, or victory bulletins, were broadcast every fifteen minutes of the day, preceded by a blast of trumpets and Hitler's chosen Liszt prelude – "Like a county fair side-show", one listener commented in disgust.

It was Hitler who had insisted on a whole week of waiting to maximise the impact, despite Göbbels' sarcastic comment, "If the announcements are held up much longer the public will think the troops have reached the Indian frontier."

But such was Hitler's initial euphoria that his staff was carried on the floodtide. Certainly the Führer could have no doubts as to the outcome, for he had despatched a special engineer team to blow up the Kremlin. Then, too, there was his forward-looking approach in allotting "Oil Brigades" to each army group, special detachments to exploit the first oil-rich territory captured – even though the units would have to cover the 1,400 miles between the frontier and Baku on the Caspian Sea before winter approached. "It would probably be no exaggeration," Halder noted in his diary, "to say that the campaign against Russia has been won in the first fortnight."

To Hitler's architect, Albert Speer, this seemed no less than the truth. Already, in anticipation of victory Hitler had extended his list of German cities slated for reconstruction to twenty-seven – and contracts to the value of thirty million Reichsmarks had been awarded to granite companies in six different countries. Barely three weeks before Barbarossa was launched, Hitler had founded his own transport fleet and set up shipyards in Berlin and Wismar – with plans to build 1,000 cargo boats to transport the granite on order.

And didn't it seem likely, the generals reasoned, that the British would at last see sense? Hitler, at any rate, had made it plain that all western Europe could be theirs in return for a free hand in the east. On 22 June, the German Ambassador in Ankara, the canny Franz von Papen, had put this proposition through a novel intermediary, the Turkish Foreign Minister, Sükrü Saracoglu – who passed it on, as intended, to the British Ambassador, Sir Hughe Knatchbull-Hugessen.

But there was one essential proviso: neither Great Britain nor the United States should associate themselves with Russia in the war that had now begun.

"Do you mean that they should not contract a marriage?" Saracoglu asked.

"That is my meaning," von Papen replied, primly.

*

"When Barbarossa begins," Hitler had predicted as far back as February, "the world will hold its breath and make no comment." It was strangely wishful thinking. Before 22 June had run its course, the world was commenting as never before since World War Two began.

Anthony Eden, weekending at Chequers, always associated Barbarossa with the most unpalatable before-breakfast gift he had ever received: a mammoth Cuban cigar on a silver salver presented at 7.30 a.m. by Churchill's valet, Sawyers. "The Prime Minister's compliments and the German armies have invaded Russia." ("We savoured the relief," Eden related, "but not for me at that hour the cigar.") Within the day, Churchill was broadcasting to the nation a statement in part reprinted by *Pravda*: "No one has been a more consistent opponent of communism than I . . . I will unsay no word that I have spoken about it. But all this fades away before the spectacle which is now unfolding . . . Any man or state which fights on against Nazidom will have our aid . . . we shall give whatever help we can to Russia and the Russian people."

Even in the Axis camp, many were aghast at the news. Benito Mussolini, awoken at 3 a.m. in his bedroom at Villa Mussolini, on the Adriatic Coast at Riccione, had the word from his son-in-law, Count Ciano, calling from Rome: Hitler's letter had yet to reach him. His black eyes squinting against the harsh light of the bed lamp, the Duce told his wife matter-of-factly: "My dear Rachele, that means we've lost the war."

An implacable anti-Communist like Pope Pius XII, in Vatican City, might hail the war as a crusade, "high-minded gallantry in defence of the foundations of Christian culture," but most Italians shared the Duce's view, notably his Minister of Currency and Exchange, Raffaele Riccardi. "At this stage of affairs," Riccardi recorded sourly, "the one thing that might yet surprise me would be finding a pregnant man."

Some saw the widening of the combat, like Churchill himself, in terms of sorely-needed reinforcements. In Algiers, General Maxime Weygand, the Commander-in-Chief, French North Africa, had long looked askance at the faith of the State Department's Robert Murphy: if Britain would win in the end, as Murphy believed, who would furnish the extra divisions? On that day, summoning Murphy to his villa, the excited Weygand told him: "Now I know where they will come from – Russia!"

Others, long opposed to the conflict, knew a change of heart. Along with Herbert Agar and Dorothy Parker, fellow interventionists, the playwright Robert Sherwood arrived to address a Fight for Freedom Rally at the Golden Gate Ballroom on Lenox Avenue, Harlem. Outside the usual pickets jeered and taunted them, brandishing Communist-inspired banners that proclaimed them "tools of British and Wall Street Imperialism". Ninety minutes later, they had vanished; word had reached the picket line that it was now a workers' war, too.

A few were openly sceptical. At a party given by his Ministry of Propaganda that Sunday afternoon, Dr Josef Göbbels reiterated his prophecy that it would be an eight-week campaign at most. Turning to the film star, Olga Tschechowa, Chekhov's niece, he said, "We have a Russian expert here. Will we be in Moscow by Christmas?" Irked by his manner, the actress replied, "You know Russia, the endless land. Even Napoleon had to retreat." Ten minutes later, an adjutant approached her. "I imagine, madame, you are ready to leave. The car is outside."

At the British Embassy, Moscow, it was close to midnight on 22 June. Harold Elvin had just set off on the first of his nightly patrols when Fedor, the porter, came hastening after him. An anonymous Russian was on the phone with a strange request; he wanted to speak to an Englishman – any Englishman. As the only staff member on duty, Elvin accepted the call.

"We fight together, I think?" were the unknown's first anxious words, and in this moment Elvin felt curiously moved: a man whose face he would never see was seeking reassurance, a sense of comradeship, in a world that was disintegrating before his eyes.

"Yes, I think so," he replied, trying to infuse his voice with confidence, but the Russian was too disturbed, or knew too little English, to carry the conversation further. "I shake your hand," was all he said before ringing off.

*

But across the world many men and women had grave misgivings. A compact with Russia seemed as incompatible as a working agreement with Hitler: could the free world consciously opt for a choice of tyrannies? A London businesswoman, Hilda Neal, summed up in her diary what thousands, perhaps millions, felt: "I want no alliance with a nation steeped in blood."

Those like her were thunderstruck by Churchill's emotional impulsive pledge. Franco's ambassador in London, the Duke of Alba, reported to Madrid a rumour that *The Times*, at the eleventh hour, had had to scrap a

133

leader attacking a Russian alliance after hearing the Premier's broadcast. There was not, and never could be, an alliance, Eden took pains to reassure Alba, but ordinary citizens were sceptical. When the Reverend Philip Russell, vicar of Lythe, near Whitby, Yorkshire, called for prayers for Russia from the pulpit, his cousin, Nurse Kathleen Phipps, mused, "Philip is nothing if not up-to-date." But back at her hospital, the matron set her firmly to rights: "Stalin is not a nice person, Nurse – one has to be very careful these days."

Many shared these sentiments. Sir Stafford Cripps might urge from Moscow, "We must not try and play too safe on information if we want the Russians to fight our battles all out," but others saw the connection as anathema. On 8 July, when the first Russian trade mission arrived at London's Euston Station, the Vice Chief of the Imperial General Staff, Lieutenant-General Sir Henry Pownall, warned his adjutant: "Don't let any of those photographers take me shaking hands with the Russian general." At a private dinner party, the new Minister of Aircraft Production, Lieutenant Colonel John Moore-Brabazon, expressed a hope trade unionists were swift to condemn once the news leaked out: let the Russians and Germans destroy one another while the British Commonwealth built up her forces. In the United States, Senator Harry Truman of Missouri struck a similar note: "If we see that Germany is winning we ought to help Russia and if Russia is winning we ought to help Germany and that way let them kill as many as possible . . ."

Roosevelt, as so often happened, was content to let Churchill take the lead. Cautious and oblique as always, he went no farther than to unfreeze Soviet dollar funds, thus enabling them to buy weapons, at the same time declaring that the Neutrality Act would not be invoked against Russia, thus permitting American shipping to enter ports like Vladivostok. For the rest he was content to await the Russians' shopping list and on 8 July he got it: a staggering two billion dollars worth of requirements, including 3,000 pursuit planes and 3,000 bombers.

The concept outraged as many Americans as it pleased. Ex-President Herbert Hoover proclaimed: "It makes the whole argument of joining the war to bring the Four Freedoms a gargantuan jest." The *New Republic* columnist John T. Flynn, demanded: "Are we fighting to make Europe safe for Communism?" Others scoffed at "Packages for Petrograd" or what wits called "Lenin-Lease"; the *Wall Street Journal* stated frankly: "The principal difference between Mr Hitler and Mr Stalin is the size of their respective moustaches." The isolationist Congressman Hamilton Fish proposed – not entirely in jest – that Roosevelt should invite Stalin to Washington, to have him baptised in the White House pool.

Then, as later, Roosevelt was curiously impervious to Russia's potential for evil. "Dear Bill," he wrote to Leahy in Vichy on 26 June,

". . . Now comes the Russian diversion. If it is more than just that it will mean the liberation of Europe from Nazi domination . . . I do not think we need worry about any possibility of Russian domination." As a former Ambassador to the Soviet Union, William C. Bullitt did give the President clear warning of Soviet imperialism, but Roosevelt would have none of it. "I think if I give him (Stalin) everything I possibly can and ask nothing from him in return, *noblesse oblige,* he won't try to annex anything." In vain Bullitt pointed out that "when he talked of *noblesse oblige* he was not speaking of the Duke of Norfolk but of a Caucasian bandit whose only thought when he got something for nothing was that the other fellow was an ass".

Hopkins, who flew to Moscow on 30 July for two meetings with Stalin, backed the President's judgement. "Give us anti-aircraft guns and the aluminium and we can fight for three or four years," the dictator told him confidently, giving the impression of "talking to a perfectly co-ordinated machine, an intelligent machine". "I would hardly call Uncle Joe a pleasant man, although he was interesting enough," he wrote to Ismay later, "and I think I got what I wanted but you never can be sure about that. . . ."

In the end the priorities of *realpolitik* prevailed. If the first job was the extirpation of Hitler, then Russia must be aided, and few interventionists then saw Soviet power as a threat to the Western democracies. Even hitherto isolationist journals were united on that score. "The two English-speaking nations," prophesied the St Louis *Post-Dispatch*, "will exercise the decisive voices at the peace table." "An awakened democracy," thought the Dallas *Morning News*, "will now take steps after Hitler is beaten to make sure that the Russian brand of political communism stays home."

As Oscar Cox, of the Office of Emergency Management's Division of Defence Aid, summed up in a memo to Hopkins: "Our main objective in spending billions on defence is to see to it that Hitler does not rule the world – including us." It was left to Assistant Secretary of State Adolf A. Berle, on the eve of Hopkins' departure for Moscow, to view this new and uneasy alliance clear-sightedly.

"The Russian hatred of Britain," he minuted Hopkins, "is if possible more deeply implanted than the Russian hatred of Germany, though Fate puts them on the same side for the moment.

"Eastern Europe is looking out for itself: not for the British or for us. We can be of help to one another now . . . but we cannot bet our whole shirt on the continuance of the relationship."

He ended on a bleak note of caution: "Therefore, for God's sake, tell the sentimentalists to watch themselves."

*

135

Benito Mussolini summed it up as aptly as any man: "This war has now assumed the character of a war between two worlds."

The Duce spoke the truth. On 22 June, the one military enigma remaining was Japan. Thousands who had stood on the sidelines until this moment were now rallying to Hitler as the great anti-Bolshevik crusader. "The destruction of Russian communism is now inevitable," General Francisco Franco, who had wanted no part of the war, told the American Ambassador, Alexander Weddell, and to hasten its end he offered a volunteer force of 18,000 strong to fight on the Russian front, the famous Blue Division under General Múñoz Grandes. On 27 June, after planes with Russian markings had bombed the frontier town of Kassa – allegedly a plot cooked up between the German Air Attaché in Budapest and the Hungarian General Staff – the Regent, Admiral Nicholas Horthy, weighed in with ten divisions.

General Ion Antonescu, chief of Rumania's fascist "Iron Guard" had been delighted to enter the fray. "Of course, I'll be there from the start," he told Hitler, after promises of Bessarabia and other territory, "When it's a question of action against the Slavs you can always count on Rumania."

Although Europe's two staunchest neutrals – Switzerland and Turkey – stayed staunchly neutral, others felt too keenly to remain uninvolved. Denmark severed relations with Moscow, like Vichy France, closed down its one communist newspaper and rounded up all known Reds: soon the Regiment Nordland, made up of Danish, Dutch and Norwegian Nazis, took their place on the Finnish front, along with Regiment Westland, sympathisers from Belgium and Holland, augmenting eighteen Finnish divisions. Sweden, while walking a tightrope of neutrality, still yielded to pressure; on 25 June, the *Riksdag* in Stockholm sanctioned the passage of the *Wehrmacht*'s Engelbrecht Division from Norway across Swedish soil to the front in Finland.

The strangest participant was Italy. Despite his instinctive reaction that the war was lost, Mussolini never ceased in his attempts to transform the volatile Italians into a nation of scowling humourless warriors. Although Hitler had not asked for troops, Italian honour – which Mussolini equated with his own – demanded that they should be made available. Promptly he offered four divisions three of infantry, one of cavalry – plus ninety planes lacking an anti-freeze system.

Outfitted with the same summer uniforms and cardboard shoes that had served them in the French campaign of 1940, these troops were to die cursing their Duce in temperatures 36° below zero. But Mussolini's ego was mortally wounded that Rommel's men had redressed the balance in Libya, so go they must.

To flaunt his unity with the *Wehrmacht*, Mussolini reviewed his Russian Expeditionary Force at Verona accompanied by only one man –

General Enno von Rintelen, the tall aquiline Military Attaché in Rome. As the Duce took the salute, bolt upright in his car, the German in the back seat struggled with conflicting emotions – pity for the marching men in their threadbare uniforms, the slap of their broken shoes on the stone flags drowned only by the drum-beat, and amazement that any man as intelligent as Mussolini could so delude himself.

As the last contingent, to a fanfare of brass, wheeled towards the waiting troop trains in Verona Station, the Duce turned to von Rintelen, his eyes misty. "There," he told the speechless General, "go the finest troops in the world."

*

Whatever their nationality, these men had one factor in common: a determination that Communism must be destroyed root and branch. *Fähnrich* Peter Neumann, by contrast, a youngster trained to kill, was still beset by fear and indecision.

After the passing-out parade at Bad Tölz, Neumann had been posted overnight – to the headquarters staff of the *Standartenführer* (S.S. Colonel) of the Nordland Regiment, attached to the 5th Waffen S.S. (Viking) Division. At Lublin, he found the regiment already on the move; tank engines were revving up, whistle blasts and orders echoed all over the courtyard of the old Polish barracks. All night the sky throbbed with the droning of Dorniers, Focke-Wulfs and Stukas, wave after wave of them flying eastward.

A little before noon on 28 June, *Standartenführer* Willi Schleyer called his officers together in a large draughty hangar for a final briefing. "Gentlemen," he told them, his voice low-pitched and serious, "we advance on Kremenetz. We move off at dawn tomorrow." From the large plan spread on the floor before him he made the position plain: attached to *Generaloberst* Ewald von Kleist's right wing they would advance east-south-east as a unit of Rundstedt's Army Group South.

Schleyer paused then, as if to gauge their reactions. Then, eyeing them fixedly, he announced, "We have also received special instructions concerning the Russian People's Commissars, captured in action or arrested in the occupied territory. In no case are we authorised to take them prisoner. The order is explicit! They must be killed at once. . . ."

Attempting a smile, he made a vague gesture with his hand. "That's all, gentlemen."

It came home to Neumann that all the derring-do manoeuvres of the past years were over. He was in the S.S. and the S.S. was at war.

Yet on the following days, as the division swept forward towards the vast Ukrainian granary, Neumann knew no fear – only a strange exhilaration. Through Wisnia, its blackened buildings "hollow and empty as stage

137

sets", they passed on to open country, through charred wheatfields and abandoned farms, suffocated by the smell of hot oil and petrol, the dust forming a hard thick mask on their hands and faces.

Suddenly the leading tank formations ground to a halt, their guns belching fire. The cry rang out "*Kampf Verband! Los, Los!*" ("Battle formation, at the double!") Almost before he realised it, Neumann had jumped from his armoured T.C.V. (troop-carrying vehicle) and was racing into action behind a group of anti-tank gunners.

Ahead of them, Russians were doubling in short sudden spurts, trying not to be seen in the forest glades, and Neumann, his finger on the trigger of his machine-pistol, emptied a whole magazine in their wake. The manoeuvres at Vogelsang came vividly back to him, and he, too, ran in short bursts, dropping flat every few yards. Dimly he glimpsed a group of panzer grenadiers staring at him dumbfounded: an ensign racing into battle, yelling like a simple private.

Now the Russians were giving up: fifteen of them had risen from the ground, casting their rifles far from them, raising their hands in surrender. A hail of bullets cut them down like saplings.

Neumann stood rooted to the spot. Something had now gone very much awry. They were prisoners, weren't they, prisoners who had surrendered?

But he had not been afraid. He had seen a man take aim at him, fired first, and seen his adversary's head burst open. It was him or me, Neumann thought, the first man I ever killed, but I was not afraid.

Standartenführer Schleyer was fatherly: "Seems you got on all right in your first skirmish . . . carry on the good work and we may make something of you yet." His best friend, *Fähnrich* Franz Hättenschwiller, ribbed him mercilessly, but there was no mistaking the pride in his voice: "Running hell-for-leather to get his head shot off at the first sound of gunfire! For God's sake, man, you should have kept down. It wasn't your job to run after the Russkis like a greyhound!"

Secretly pleased, Neumann mumbled: "I saw everybody jumping out from the trucks . . . I thought the Reds were making a mass attack."

Next day, 30 June, in a small village outside Lwow, he was more frightened than he had ever been.

On this Monday morning, Neumann was attached to *Untersturmführer* (S.S. Second-Lieutenant) Scholtzberg, commanding the light corps of panzer grenadiers; as a new boy, he must become familiar with different forms of combat. But a determined Russian resistance, backed by a heavy Voroshilov 12 mm machine gun aimed from a second-storey window, stalled their advance. Calling a halt, Scholtzberg had just sent for two tanks to winkle the Russians out when an S.S. man doubled up.

"Sir, we've caught about ten Bolsheviks and two of them are civilians. What'll we do with them, sir?" Scholtzberg ordered, "Bring them here."

They were the first Russians Neumann had ever seen at close quarters, all of them bearded, with shaven heads and waxy skins. The two civilians wore gold stars on their sleeves: Commissars. Then Scholtzberg caught his eye and nodded. "They're all yours, Neumann! You deal with them."

Sweat was suddenly coursing down his body, as if he stood naked in a shower bath. They had to be shot, *Standartenführer* Schleyer had said so, but not by him, please God not by him.

Scholtzberg was understanding. "You'd rather not? Relax, Neumann. Libesis will handle this little formality!" He signed to *Rottenführer* (S.S. Lance-Corporal) Libesis, a cheerful Tyrolean peasant who had twice won the Iron Cross in battle, and Libesis quietly, casually, as if he had all the time in the world, approached the Commissars.

"*Narodnii Komissar li voui?*" ("You are a People's Commissar?"), he asked each man.

"*Da. Potchemo?*" ("Yes. Why?") they replied, surprised.

With agonising slowness, Neumann saw Libesis take his Mauser from his holster, loading it before the Russians' eyes. Then he aimed at each shaven head in turn, squeezing the trigger.

Suddenly there were no more People's Commissars at all. Neumann stood quite still, not moving, not speaking. Later it struck him that he never again saw the eight Red Army prisoners.

At least, he thought dully, they had been spared the tortures of a long captivity.

*

On Army Group Centre's front, driving hard for the River Memel across the Lithuanian plains, *Assistenzart* Heinrich Haape had also discovered that it was a war which gave no quarter.

Haape would never forget the trauma of his first two days in the field. In a hollow near an old farmhouse he had found the still warm bodies of six men: a medical officer from another battalion, clutching a blood-stained Red Cross flag, his stretcher bearer and four patients. A horrified eye-witness filled in the details: the doctor had been treating the men when the Russians opened fire on the hollow, and at once he had leaped up, waving the flag frantically, but still the Russians had fired and kept on firing until nothing moved.

Haape was silent for a long time, then abruptly he tore off his Red Cross armband. "It means nothing to the Russians," he said bitterly. "There's no Geneva Convention here. I'm a soldier like the rest of you now."

It was all a far cry from the Kaiser-Wilhelm Hospital, Duisberg. In brief moments of respite, Haape tried to capture the flavour of his new life in letters to his fiancée, the opera singer, Martha Arazym. Jolting up and down the columns, sometimes in his Mercedes, sometimes on horse-back, a doctor ate on the march, as and when he could, mostly goulash and peas from the field kitchens – "Never pass up a goulash cannon," was the sage advice of the Regimental commander, *Oberst* Becker.

Each day brought problems that a civilian doctor never remotely encountered. The battalion crossed the Memel without a single casualty, but next day the march was slowed to a crawl. Eight hundred men who had bathed their burning feet in the river, were hobbling on cruelly blistered soles.

Haape's next battalion order had a novel ring: unless no marching was envisaged for twenty-four hours all soldiers were forbidden to wash or bathe their feet. "Instead . . . it is recommended that the feet be rubbed with dripping or deer fat." The battalion would stink to high heaven from this time on – but at least they would march unimpeded.

How did you stop soldiers drinking from peasants' wells, thus risking dysentery? It was Haape's orderly, *Gefreiter* Mühler, who solved this problem: a subtle rumour was passed through the ranks that the Russians were poisoning the water. The first two dozen men who fell in for "treatment" were promptly dosed with charcoal and castor oil. After that they gave the wells a wide berth.

Week by week, as the battalion moved on through stifling dust, Haape grappled with fresh problems. Bitter experience taught him to forbid a morsel of food for six hours before a major battle: even one slice of bread caused extra blood to flow to the intestines, increasing the risk of internal haemorrhage in the event of a stomach wound. He saw to it that every man had a green camouflaged mosquito net; no fighting soldier could give of his best after a night of torment from the vicious Pripet Marsh gnats they nicknamed "Stukas".

"Everyone has to be a soldier here," Haape argued, when his courage was praised, but the 3rd Battalion saw him as "a real fighting man's doctor". On 14 July, when the battle of Gomely loomed, Haape left his stationary casualty post in the rear, moving up with one orderly to set up a dressing station in a foxhole on the battlefield itself. There, in the nine hours that it took the battalion to pierce the 1,100-mile long Stalin Line, a ribbon of redoubts stretching east of the Pripet Marshes, Haape, armed with a small Braun-Melsungen blood transfusion apparatus, saved many lives.

That night, along with *Leutnant* Jakobi, of the battalion's 12th Company, Haape drank a solemn toast in captured vodka: "Here's to the liberation of Russia and Christmas in the Kremlin!"

"I don't want to be a soldier," Haape confided. "I'd go home and marry Martha tomorrow." For both men had the feeling that night that the war might soon be over. Moscow, they knew, was "just over the horizon" – some 300 miles north-west.

Then, on 30 July, a million men heard a near-incredible order: "Prepare for defensive positions." From Velikiye Luki southwards to Roslavi, 400 miles of line became static. Panzers, motorised units, pioneers, artillery, infantry – all were frozen in their tracks.

It was then that Haape took thought of Hitler's lowly combatant status in World War One – "The corporal's wand waved over Army Group Centre and turned it to stone".

*

In the barracks and blockhouses of the *Wolfsschanze*, there was consternation. Barbarossa was barely five weeks old, and Adolf Hitler had twice seen fit to meddle with his generals' strategy. The results were to prove catastrophic.

As early as 26 June, 56 Panzer Group's bold 200-mile dash to the town of Daugavapils had paid off; all Manstein's instinct now was to forge on towards Leningrad. Plainly, with the Russians hopelessly confused, the thrust cried out for exploitation. But Hitler, as so often in a campaign's early stages, felt his confidence ebbing. He ordered Manstein to stand fast until the infantry caught up with him.

"This was certainly the 'safe' staff college solution," Manstein acknowledged later, but equally it destroyed all element of surprise. In the six days that Manstein was halted, General Fedor Kuznetzov, commanding the Special Baltic Military District, was working day and night to plug the breach, hurling in reserves from Minsk, Moscow, Pskov. Unwittingly Hitler had helped Leningrad to buy time.

"Perpetual interference by the Führer . . . is becoming a scourge which will eventually be intolerable," Halder noted in his diary on 14 June; on 28 June, he wrote despairingly, "He's playing warlord again," and with reason. On 30 June, overruling Halder and Brauchitsch, Hitler switched priorities. Both men agreed with Bock and Guderian that Moscow was probably within their grasp, and with it decisive victory. Hitler disagreed: Moscow could wait. Instead Guderian was to be diverted south, to aid Rundstedt's Army Group secure the fertile land of the Ukraine, Panzer Group Three, under *Generaloberst* Hermann Hoth was moved up to help Leeb's Army Group North subdue Leningrad, the cradle of Bolshevism.

For Hitler, as his closest associates saw, was racked by doubts. On 27 June, he made a sober admission to Ribbentrop, who was paying a visit: "If I had had the slightest inkling of this gigantic Red Army assemblage I would never have taken the decision to attack."

What had gone wrong? As Hitler was to admit to Mussolini, "for the first time since the beginning of the conflict, the German military intelligence had failed". Overweening confidence that Russia would crumble – "this clay colossus with a head", Hitler had sneered – had resulted in a woeful lack of planning and preparation. As a result, no winter clothing had been allotted for the troops, only three months supply of fuel was scheduled for the advancing armies, and fully a third of Germany's divisions remained in the west.

The reassuring reports of Hans Krebs, the Military Attaché in Moscow, that Russia was twenty years behind the times had helped foster this illusion, but Krebs was a young man on the make, adept at telling Hitler what he wanted to hear.

To be sure, the reconnaissance planes of *Oberst* Theodor Rowehl's Special Purposes Squadron had violated Russian air space scores of times, flying as low as 2,600 feet, their cameras turning over. But even diamond-clear prints could not reveal the existence of the Russians' T-34 tank, which was now taking the field, a 27 tonner whose armour plating was impervious to everything save the Flak 88s Rommel had employed at Halfaya. Nor could photographs reveal that the Soviet Air Force had in excess of 8,000 aircraft or the astonishing rate at which Soviet industry was churning out replacements.

Even in mid-July, when Germany had knocked out 8,000 Russian tanks, they still came on, a lumbering non-stop chain; by 30 July, this figure had been upped to 12,000 but still they came. As with the tanks, so with the men. "At the start of this war, we reckoned with about 200 enemy divisions," Halder noted. "So far we have already counted 360."

On 4 August, visiting Army Group Centre, Hitler was to let fall an admission that for the first time gave the men in the field a hint of things to come. "Had I known they had as many tanks as that," he told Bock and Guderian ruefully, "I'd have thought twice before invading."

*

In the Officers' Mess of No 82 (Blenheim) Squadron, R.A.F. Bomber Command, they remembered him as "Ten Minute" Jenkins. It was an obituary of a kind: he had been posted to the squadron and taken off from Bodney, in Norfolk, on his first operational flight. Ten minutes after crossing the Belgian coast he was dead.

It remained a record, even among the seventeen squadrons of Bomber Command, but only marginally. As the summer of 1941 wore on, no bomber crew, for the best of reasons, could precisely define a tour of operations: no one had ever completed one.

The losses were inextricably linked with Marshal Timoshenko's frantic efforts to turn the German floodtide in Russia. As early as 27 June, Ivan Maisky, the bearded irrepressible little Russian Ambassador, had urged the creation of a Second Front on a notably receptive Lord Beaverbrook – and been as coldly rebuked by Eden. The idea had been Maisky's own, but by 18 July Stalin had taken up the cudgels. What he sought from

Churchill was primarily an offensive in Northern France to divert Hitler's armies from the east – or, failing this, twenty-five to thirty British divisions to fight on the Russian front.

They were demands that Churchill was powerless to meet – yet it was vital to convince both Stalin and Roosevelt that Britain was still in earnest. In Washington, as Hopkins told Churchill frankly on 24 July, criticisms of Britain now had a cutting edge. To most Americans, the Premier's preoccupation with the Middle East smacked of "colonialism" – "The American public had never heard of Benghazi and were really not quite sure whether the Nile flows north or south." The British, many felt, were resting on their laurels; of the 43 per cent of Britons who welcomed the Russian attack, Mass Observation reported many as complacent – "It will keep Germany busy and give us a rest," or "A good thing somebody else is carrying the baby."

Such sentiments were reported from as far away as the Balkans; from Budapest, Roosevelt's Minister, Herbert Pell, relayed the belief that "they (the British) are seizing the opportunity of a temporarily distracted German attention to take tea and go on weekends while someone else fights for them".

To counter such rumours, Churchill and his Cabinet saw only one answer: a non-stop offensive by the 500 aircraft of Bomber Command, backstopped by Lend-Lease supplies. "Our entire hope of building up a decisive margin of hitting power . . . rests on the achievements of a great expansion of heavy bomber output in the United States," the Secretary of State for Air, Sinclair, wrote to Hopkins. ". . . anything that can be done to secure additional releases of B17s and B24s now would have a direct effect on our ability to hit German and Italian targets . . ."

But overnight the British found the honeymoon was over; from now on they must take their place in the queue. Priority on Lend-Lease goods, Averell Harriman explained firmly, was a thing of the past; as a frontline combatant, Russia would claim her fair share of what U.S. aid was available. In Washington, the Russian Ambassador, Constantin Oumansky, put it more bluntly: the Russians were doing "ninety per cent of the fighting and should get ninety per cent of the stuff".

Even so, a showing must be made, and the onus rested squarely on Bomber Command. "My bombing offensive is not a gamble," Portal declared, as Chief of Air Staff. "Its dividend is certain; it is a gilt-edged investment." But as the five-man crews of Bomber Command soon discovered, the most certain dividend was death.

Day after day, through June and July, the gallant suicidal sorties continued. On 4 July, Wing Commander Hughie Edwards, a 27-year-old Australian, led 15 Blenheims from 105 and 107 Squadrons in loose vics of three from the Norfolk coast, skimming low over the water towards the German port of Bremen. Three aircraft, unable to keep up the 200-knot pace, turned for home before Bremen was even sighted – a bowl of smoky haze, its harbour mouth criss-crossed by a lethal tangle of barrage balloons and deadly cables. Flying through a lethal rain of flak, they sowed an inferno of fire and hissing steam and paid the price. Although Edwards was to win the V.C. for his leadership, five out of twelve planes did not return – "equivalent to a serious reverse, which no amount of propaganda can turn into a success," Göbbels commented.

It was the third attempt to cripple Bremen in four days, an aim which had become an obsession with the ruthless Air Officer Commanding No 2 Group, Air Vice Marshal Donald Stevenson. Although such daylight strikes took a terrible toll – the Blenheims, with scant fire-power, were almost 200 m.p.h. slower than Luftwaffe fighters and were within their range for ninety minutes after crossing the coast – Stevenson would not let up. "Churchill wants it!" he stormed at one dissident, hurling his inkwell at the wall.

Most bomber-types available in 1941 were almost as vulnerable. The Wellington, its guns unable to traverse to a full right angle with the aircraft, was thus helpless against a beam attack; lacking self-sealing tanks, it needed only one unlucky hit to become a flying furnace. Its Mark 7 bombsight called for a rock-steady commercial airline approach to the target – certain suicide again. The Whitley's oxygen supply was always inadequate for long flights; its generators so uncertain that the wireless operators spent most of their trip dismantling and reassembling their sets.

On night flights, the ostensible targets were Germany's seventeen synthetic oil plants. But in reality this mattered little, for by August, a survey of 633 photographs taken by 500 bombers over a two-month period revealed a staggering deficiency. Only one-third of the bombers had got within five miles of the target; over the smoke-laden Ruhr, the total was one-tenth. At negligible cost to the German war effort or to civilian morale, 41,000 tons of bombs would claim 914 aircraft – one aircraft lost for every 45 tons of bombs dropped. But so long as the Red Army fought on, the bombing would continue.

So, too, would the daylight fighter sweeps pursue their policy of "leaning forward into France", until 426 pilots had been killed or taken prisoner, among the latter such Battle of Britain aces as Douglas Bader and Whitney Straight.

If the entire policy was in doubt, the airmen's courage never was. On the night of 7 July, 13,000 feet above the Zuider Zee, a Messerschmitt 110 rose from the darkness, to blast a Wellington bomber returning from a raid on Munster with cannon fire. The starboard engine took fire, fed by petrol from a split pipe; soon flames threatened to engulf the entire wing. Disaster was only averted by Sergeant James Allen Ward of No 75 (New Zealand) Squadron. Climbing out on to the fuselage, secured only by a rope round his waist, Ward descended three feet through howling darkness to the wing. Smothering the flames with a canvas engine cover, he somehow contrived a cautious return along the wing, back into the aircraft.

It was an exploit that merited not only Bomber Command's second V.C. of that summer, but an experience that Ward found infinitely more terrifying: a personal summons to No 10, Downing Street, to meet Winston Churchill. Ward was to die before the month was out, but the meeting was a trauma until the end: the long ticking moments of silence before Churchill finally entered his study, impeccably dressed as always in a short black coat and striped trousers, with a polka-dotted bow tie, as pink and groomed as if he had just stepped from a bath.

At first, Ward was struck dumb with stagefright, until Churchill asked him gently, "You feel very humble and awkward in my presence, don't you?" Even then Ward could venture nothing further than, "Yes, sir."

"Then," said Churchill, more gently still, "you can imagine how humble and awkward I feel in yours."

7

"At Last – We've Gotten Together"

DAY AND NIGHT, the knocking echoed insidiously. At times it was thin and repetitive, as if a too-zealous carpenter was at work. At others it was as loud as a creeping barrage, engulfing all Occupied Europe. Phonetically it was rendered as tat-tat-tat-too, three short bars and one long one, the "fate-knocks-at-the-door" motif of Beethoven's Fifth Symphony. Symbolically, to millions chafing under Hitler's yoke, it represented a phrase that was to echo round the world: the Morse signal that spelt out V for Victory.

Its conception had been inauspicious. In January, the head of the B.B.C.'s Belgian Service in London, Victor de Laveleye, had urged his countrymen to chalk V (for *victoire*) in all public places, a sign of their confidence. Few had responded – until June, when a mystery voice on B.B.C. short-wave radio, identified only as "Colonel Britton" broadcast a Europe-wide call for daily harassment of the Germans.

"You are asked to join a disciplined army," the "Colonel" – in reality Assistant European News Editor, Douglas Ritchie – told his listeners. "It is a strange army, but one to which it is an honour to belong. It is an army which the Germans fear . . . the night is your friend, the V is your sign . . . splash the V from one end of Europe to the other."

It was as if a clarion call had sounded. All over Europe, as July ended, the realisation had come that the German advance through Russia was bogging down – hampered in part by torrential rains that slowed the pace from 22 daily miles to eight, in part by stiffening resistance spearheaded by a formidable trio of Marshals, Klimenti Voroshilov, defending Leningrad, Semeon Timoshenko, before Moscow, and Semeon Budyonny at Kiev. The message was not lost on Occupied Europe: resistance could become a way of life.

From the North Cape to the Pyrenees, the V-sign resounded. It was a tattoo beaten out on cafe tables to summon waiters, hammered on the front door knockers of friends, blasted by impatient taxi horns, shrilled by freight train whistles. Diners-out in restaurants set their knives and forks in V-formation; householders set the hands of stopped clocks at five minutes past eleven. In every language, the message was the same:

victory, *victoire, vryheid* (freedom in Dutch), *Vitezstvi* (victory, in Czech) *ve vil vinne* in Norwegian.

As a symbol the V crossed all frontiers – scrawled in lipstick on the backs of German officers' great-coats in Oslo, smeared in boot-blacking on the walls of German premises in Athens, etched on dustcoated German vehicles in Copenhagen. For every citizen who scrawled it had become aware of one truth: while they themselves could not win the war, they could help Adolf Hitler lose it.

Putting a brave face on things, Josef Göbbels claimed the V for his own countrymen. V did indeed stand for victory, a German victory – *Viktoria*, an obsolete word, unknown to most. A V flag was hung from the Eiffel Tower and painters were set to work stencilling Vs on German box-cars. It was a subtle mistake; if the V-sign was not *verboten*, the occupying troops must make the best of it.

Other tokens of liberty abounded – in the tricolor scarves and Cross of Lorraine handbag fastenings sported by Parisian *midinettes*, in the Statue of Liberty buttonhole favours worn by young Danes. A new readiness to provoke the German ire had become apparent. In Prague, lamp-posts in the square surrounding the Gestapo H.Q. were ominously placarded *zadano* (reserved). A cheeky Copenhagen newsdealer advertised a new textbook: LEARN ENGLISH BEFORE THE TOMMIES ARRIVE. Ordered to remove the placard, he replaced it with another: LEARN GERMAN BEFORE OUR FRIENDS THE GERMANS DEPART.

Going slow, to sabotage the German war machine, had become almost second nature. Belgian coal miners, idling down the pits, reduced productivity by 36 per cent; at Bergen, other miners took two entire months to complete six feet of a fortification tunnel. Norwegian workers constructing a strategic German military highway put in "two hours for Hitler and six hours for King Haakon."

To bored Britons, the conquered lands now existed as little more than eight national anthems* played in rotation after Sunday's 9 p.m. news bulletin but those who had stayed behind cherished the memory of their exiled royalty. In Amsterdam, traffic lights turning orange – signifying WAIT – were always cheered lustily, a reminder of their beloved Queen Wilhelmina and the House of Orange. Norwegian street car conductors approaching streets named after the King, loudly and formally intoned, "His Majesty King Haakon Street".

In the wake of defiance, violence was swift to follow. In Holland, students of the closed-down universities at Delft and Leiden resurrected *Les Gueux* (The Beggars), a secret society formed in the sixteenth century to harass the Spanish overlords. "*Moffen*" (slang for German)

---

* An exception – until January 1942 – was the *Internationale* which Churchill sternly forbade, forcing the B.B.C. to compromise with the Kutusov 1812 March. Eden finally persuaded him to change his mind.

cocktails doctored with sulphuric acid, were served up so freely that few German troops now drank in public bars. Other favourite devices were poisoned pencils jabbed into German thighs in crowds or in darkened cinemas, and strychnine crystals dropped into plates of food from under the fingernails.

The lethal precedent had been set, and soon others joined the battle lines. On 12 August, an alarmed Marshal Pétain took to the air to share his fears with the public: "Frenchmen! . . . from several regions of France I have sensed for some weeks the rising of an evil wind. Worry is winning minds and doubt is seizing souls. The authority of my government is being questioned." The Marshal's fears were justified, for from 18 July onward and far into November, twenty-two major incidents were reported from all over France. In Paris, Bordeaux and Nantes, German military personnel were gunned down, and even Frenchmen were not immune – among them former Vice-Premier Pierre Laval and the collaborationist editor, Marcel Déat, although both men survived.

Soon the volleys of firing squads were beating like doom in all the cities of Europe. Paris, Belgrade, Warsaw were all to know the same relentlessly accelerating tempo of stabbings, shootings and booby-trap bombs, followed by their inevitable corollary: the mass trials, the clamped-down curfews, the execution of hostages by the hundred.

But the insistent V for victory drumbeat would never diminish now. An idea was fighting an idea.

*

In Yugoslavia, V stood for *vitestvo* (heroism), and certainly Josip Broz Tito's guerillas battled against heroic odds. As early as 1 July, Georgi Dimitrov, Secretary-General of the Comintern in Moscow, had passed the word to Tito's hideout on Belgrade's Gladstone Street: "The hour has struck when Communists must launch an open fight against the invaders."

Though Tito himself stayed in the capital until mid-September he lost no time in despatching lieutenants to the field – there to organise what he called "partisans", the name for the irregulars who had operated behind Napoleon's lines in Spain and Russia. It was to be all-out war from the first. On 5 July, speeding Milovan Djilas, a heftily-built student, to his native Montenegro, Tito enjoined him, "Shoot anyone . . . if he wavers or shows any lack of courage or discipline!" Rodoljub Colaković, a staffer on the Communist journal *Bomba*, bound for western Serbia, had similar instructions: "Use all possible means to terrorise the enemy."

Their beginnings were impressive: by mid-July, when he blew the vital Ralja railway bridge south of Belgrade with thirty-five kilos of ecrasite, Colaković had fully eighty armed men and a stolen machine-gun. None wore Communist badges, for their aim was to draw the entire nation into the struggle, but each man took an oath of loyalty. Day after day as new recruits flooded in, the same scene was enacted: thick knots of men standing bareheaded in a woodland clearing, the cold summer rain soaking their breeches and jerkins as they recited in chorus: "I, a son of the Serbian nation, swear on my honour . . ."

No man who swore that oath had an easy war ahead. Discipline was rigid and unrelenting; strong drink, even *slivovitz*, was forbidden, while looting or desertion merited the death penalty. Their life-style was primitive: a fortunate few had blankets or ground sheets but most bedded down in the bracken each night, awaking drenched by the morning dew. If breakfast was often blackberries, supper might be a slice of maize bread and a handful of wild damsons.

They moved covertly, by night, their raids marked by angry red explosions as barracks and workshops took fire, then withdrew as stealthily; low-pitched whistles signalled their progress through the woods.

Couriers came at regular intervals with letters from Tito. Always his instructions were virtually the same: undertake actions every day, seize arms and munitions, keep recruiting volunteers. This last was easy – "not everyone agreed to Communist leadership," Djilas exulted in Montenegro, "but no one was strong enough to challenge it."

If life was hard, they envied those who had it harder yet. "Over there on the Eastern front, that's the real war," one man told Djilas enviously, "where whole divisions burn up like matches."

In Valjevo, western Serbia, Colaković had word of a Četnik force, reputedly 40,000 strong under Colonel Draža Mihailović, a mild-mannered staff officer, operating from Mount Ravna Gora. At first he debated joining forces, but the detachment commander, Sergeant Zdravko Jovanović, was scornful. Three days with Mihailović had been enough for him; his men were *gibanicari*, a pejorative phrase meaning guzzlers of creampudding, most of whom went home to sleep at nights, instead of bivouacking under the stars.

In truth, Mihailović, fearing reprisals against civilians, had confined his followers to military targets: *Četniks* must not wage war against German personnel. Although Tito later, offered to serve under his command, the royalist Mihailović, more fearful of Communists than Germans, demurred. Soon his *Četniks* were to engage in all-out civil war against the partisans.

They proved no match for Tito's ruthlessly streamlined organisation. Whole villages rallied to Tito, risking German patrols to bring apples and hard boiled eggs to their woodland camps. Peasant wives joined together to wash and patch their linen. Even the children stood watch as daytime lookouts – "only a wild bird could fly over our village," one commander boasted.

As autumn drew on, even shelter would be forthcoming; the partisans slept in farmhouses perfumed with apples and newly-baked bread, at worst in peasant hovels smelling of mutton-fat and mould. But they remained hard and merciless and they took pride in it, for pity could have no place in the war they were fighting now.

At Žagarac, in Montenegro, partisans once brought bitter news to Milovan Djilas; his brother Aleksa had been gunned down in ambush by militiamen the day before. In true partisan spirit, Djilas feigned total indifference. "You can't," was his callous comment, "have a wedding feast without meat!"

*

It was a life that Ruth Mitchell herself would have relished, within the *Četnik* ranks – but from the day that the Gestapo seized her in Dubrovnik, her sole problem had been to survive.

In one respect, she was lucky. The *Četnik* badge and cap insignia which would have been her passport to Mihailović had been hidden beneath the floor of her bedroom closet; the Gestapo never found them. She was lucky, too, in preserving her illusions; for thirteen months she remained in ignorance of the bloody civil war which rent Yugoslavia apart.

All her life now hinged on patience – that and the ability to think fast. After two nights in a hot stuffy gaol cell in Dubrovnik, with only crusts of dry bread to eat, there followed a strangely courteous interrogation by *Sturmbannführer* von Nassenstein, the district Gestapo chief. Ruth, whose German was fluent, used all her wiles to disarm him. She was an American, writing a travel book, her family credentials impeccable. Of what could they possibly suspect her?

Von Nassenstein was non-committal. Her main interrogation would take place in Belgrade; a Croat detective would escort her there by train, but funds would be provided for her to travel there in comfort, first-class.

Another gaol *en route*, this time in Sarajevo, a small barred window, high up under sloping boards that formed a communal bed, with a stinking brimming drain for a lavatory. There were no blankets; along with fifteen other women, mostly small-time prostitutes, Ruth squatted on the floor. After darkness fell she spent that whole first night frantically crushing bedbugs.

At Gestapo H.Q., on Belgrade's Terazia, *Sturmbannführer* Seidl, a tall sallow S.S. officer, proved omniscient. On his desk a dossier twelve inches high listed everything there was to be known about Ruth Mitchell – her family, her friends, her kindergarten, her schools, every Balkan journey she had made, her *Četnik* contacts – even her photograph, wearing a *Četnik* cap. Ruth made light of it. She had interviewed "that old dotard Pechanats" in his cups, such good copy for her book, and he had pressed the cap on her as a souvenir.

On the fourth day of interrogation, the three-man panel assembled in Seidl's office reached their verdict: "We have complete proof that you are an agent of the British Intelligence Service."

Ruth Mitchell saw the warning light. She must lie as if her life depended on it – as indeed it did.

"I will say this," she said slowly. "If I die – it is certain that many German women will weep."

Aware that she had all their attention, she went on: Admiral Richard Byrd, the Polar explorer, and United States senator Harry Flood Byrd were both her brothers-in-law. (In truth, they were distant connections by marriage and Ruth had never met either of them, but her life was at stake.)

"Germany is straining every nerve and pouring out millions upon millions of marks trying to keep America out of the war," she reminded them. "If you shoot me when I am not guilty you may be sure my relatives will throw themselves with energy into working against Germany . . . my death might even be the actual small first cause of America entering the war against you."

Each man exchanged silent glances; she knew that for the moment at least her fate was deferred. Such was Hitler's determination to avoid provoking Roosevelt, her case must be referred to Berlin.

"*Meine Herren*," she concluded, "*zu sterben ist manchmal eine Ehre*" (Gentlemen, it is sometimes an honour to die).

But Ruth Mitchell was not to be accorded that honour. For two months she was penned in a 15 by 20 foot cell in the Gestapo prison, along with fourteen Serbian women. Once, perhaps in an effort to shake her resolve, she was shifted to the condemned cell – then returned as if nothing had happened.

At 7.30 a.m. on 3 August, she was transferred first to Austrian then to German soil. Graz, Vienna, Munich, Salzburg, Ulm, Berlin-Spandau – she passed in turn through all these gaols before finally joining the British women internees at Liebenau Internment camp, Württemberg, near Lake Constance.

Not until 30 June, 1942, after top-level diplomatic pressure, did she arrive back along with 900 other American citizens, on the last exchange ship to steam into New York harbour. It was hard to focus the Statue of Liberty on that clear bright morning; the tears were flowing too fast.

By then she had recognised the bitter truth of a prophecy made by a gypsy fortune-teller, Maroosia, in the one night she had spent in the gaol cell at Sarajevo. In many ways it summed up her entire Serbian idyll and the way it had gone awry. "You are going on a long journey . . . you will be . . . neither quickly free nor quite dead . . . pain and sorrow, great sorrow, but at the end the sea. Wide is the sea, very wide, but it is far away – and bitter the road to the sea."

*

In 1941, the underground war knew no respite. Even as Ruth Mitchell was passing through Zagreb in a prison train, *en route* for Austria, another woman, twenty-seven years her junior, was completing the last lap of a 700-mile journey that made resistance history.

Ever since February, Andrée de Jongh, the young Belgian girl who had determined to found her own escape line for Allied Troops, had resolutely explored ways and means. Back in the spring, she had even sold her jewels and borrowed unrepentantly from friends so that her fellow-conspirator, Arnold de Pé, could make a reconnaissance journey back to Bayonne, 20 miles from the Spanish frontier. After working there as a radio repair mechanic, he had known smugglers from Spain, who would act as guides – at a steep price of £12 a head.

By June, Andrée – who had taken the code-name "Dédée" – had been ready to go. Already, de Pé had established the links in the long chain down which the fugitives must pass: a train journey to the Belgian frontier at Quievrain; a crossing of the Somme near Amiens, to by-pass German checkpoints; a train to Paris; the night train to Bayonne; then a bicycle ride to the "safe" house of Elvire de Greef, mother of a family of Belgian refugees at Anglet. But there was farther yet to go: a tramp to a farm in the frontier village of Urrugne, followed by an all-night forced march over the Pyrenees to the British Consulate at San Sebastian, in northern Spain.

There were many willing passengers. All over Belgium, Britons lay in hiding in attics and barns: airmen who had been shot down in recent raids, soldiers who had still contrived to evade the Germans almost a year after Dunkirk. But few of them could speak French and eternal vigilance was necessary: a safe passage could hinge on the faulty tilt of a beret or an unfamiliar way with clogs. Meanwhile, in Brussels, the organisation now some twenty strong, was taking shape, Andrée was using her former skill as a poster designer to forge French ID cards. A brave teenager, 16-year-old Elise Maréchal, vetted all potential evaders who were channelled their way by doctors and priests, checking out possible Gestapo stool-pigeons. With an uncanny ear for English regional accents, she met each man separately inside a Brussels church, confirming his knowledge of Mae Wests and ditching procedures in the Channel – even letting drop a four-letter word to see if the listener blushed.

The first batch of "parcels", as Andrée called them, had left Brussels in early June; she and de Pé travelled with them. All had gone well until the party, eleven Belgians and an elderly English spinster, reached the

Somme – to find campers had pitched a tent near the rowboat de Pé had arranged to have hidden. Yet the river must be crossed – and only four of the party could swim.

Andrée was not deterred. Waiting until nightfall, she obtained a long coil of wire and an inflated inner tube from a nearby farm. Then, stripping off her clothes, she swam the forty yards to the French bank, securing the wire to a tree. For the next two hours she swam eleven times in succession across the dark river, helping the fugitives cling to the tube, which was threaded to the wire by a running noose.

By the end of June, the party had reached Elvire de Greef's house at Anglet. Elated, Andrée and de Pé returned to Brussels.

Now, in the first half of August, Andrée de Jongh had grown ambitious. To set up a regular liaison with the British she had decided to accompany the "parcels" every step of the way.

At No 30, Gran Via, the British Consulate of the old seaport of Bilbaó, the Vice-Consul, Arthur Dean, was at a loss for words. His junior, Vyvyan Pedrick, had entered his office with a highly dubious story: a girl who claimed she was Belgian had come all the way from Brussels bringing two Belgian volunteers and a Scottish soldier. Pedrick himself had questioned the Scot, Private Jim Cromar, of the 1st Battalion, Gordon Highlanders, who had been on the run ever since the battle of St Valery in June, 1940, and his story seemed to stand up.

Dean, a taciturn pipe-puffing ex-naval officer, was far from reassured. Since December 1939, a special branch of military intelligence, M.I.9, had existed to handle the escape and evasion of Allied Troops in Europe; by August, 1940, their task had been eased by the offer of M.I.6, the secret intelligence service, to set up an escape line from Marseilles to Spain. What more likely than that this girl was a German agent briefed to infiltrate the network?

True, Andrée's first appearance in his office was disarming. Dressed in a plain white blouse and tartan skirt, and flat shoes with white ankle socks, she radiated nothing so much as ardent determination.

"How long did your journey take?" Dean asked her.

"I have told you. About a week."

Dean was incredulous. "How did you cross the Pyrenees?"

Andrée's blue eyes sparkled with the memory of it. Her friends near Bayonne had procured a guide, a smuggler named Tomas, and she had pestered him unmercifully until he agreed to take all four of them. They had marched all night, eight hours at a stretch, with only a hunk of bread apiece, resting briefly in an abandoned watch-tower beset by swarms of fleas.

Once in Spain, another contact of Elvire de Greef, Señor Aracama, a garage proprietor, had lent her money and sheltered her party in his house at San Sebastian. Now, to put her escape line on a business basis,

153

she needed funds to reimburse him – and the friends who had lent money to pay the guide.

Dean was non-committal. Only the Consul, William Graham, could decide on that. Andrée must return tomorrow.

Five days passed. Each day Andrée trudged to the Consulate from the small pension where Aracama had found her a room; each day she met the same dusty answer, "Come back tomorrow". Andrée grew desperate. Aracama was paying her keep – but how could she find the pesetas to pay him back?

Unknown to her, Andrée was already at the heart of a top-level diplomatic wrangle. Cables winged from Bilbao to Madrid, and from Madrid to M.I.9 in London. The Deputy Director of M.I.6, Sir Claude Dansey, was highly suspicious, for one: the girl was an obvious plant. When Bilbao insisted stubbornly on her integrity, Dansey shifted his stance. Genuine or no, a woman had no business mixing herself up in resistance work.

It was M.I.9's front man, Michael Creswell, an urbane 31-year-old Second Secretary at the Madrid Embassy, who turned the tide. Creswell had already worked with other embryo escape lines, ferrying British evaders and escapers across Spain; once he had gathered enough of them together to hire a coach and send them all down to Gibraltar disguised as students. On her next visit to the Consulate, Graham told Andrée thankfully: "Mr Creswell will now take the matter in hand."

Their rapport was immediate, the first of many warm meetings over a late supper. Money Creswell could supply in plenty; at any one time M.I.9 had a float of up to £5,000 in foreign currency. Give priority to airmen, he instructed her, the men best able to resume the battle against Hitler on their return. Above all, a regular routine must be established. "Each time you get to San Sebastian", Creswell told her, "phone me. We shall send the diplomatic car to a place nearby and take your 'parcels' to Madrid."

But on one point Andrée was adamant: her organisation must remain entirely Belgian, completely independent from London, with no professional agents, no radio contact, and few helpers over twenty-five. It had begun as a young people's network, and thus it would continue.

"When do you think you can come back with another party?" Creswell asked her on the last day.

"In three or four weeks time!"

"Then bring three more men with you."

Andrée was delighted. The British had accepted her and her escape line, and on her own terms: the "Dédée (later the Comet) Line." And Creswell had christened her "The Postman", too. Now it was up to her to ensure him a regular supply of "parcels".

Aboard H.M.S. *Prince of Wales*, at Scapa Flow in the Orkneys, the rumours – "buzzes", the lower deck called them – had been rife for days. Following her brief but decisive encounter with the *Bismarck* in May, the battleship had returned to Rosyth for much-needed repairs; action had been sorely lacking. Now word was afoot of a new and secret assignment, and the quantities of hams, turkeys and chickens arriving aboard suggested a V.I.P. mission of some moment.

Tantalised, the wardroom had even organised a shilling sweepstake to determine their new role, but most were sorely wide of the mark. "Taking Hess back to Germany" and "Taking some chorus girls to North Africa" were two prime favourites; even Sub-Lieutenant Alan Franklin's guess, "Taking the Grand Duchess of Luxembourg to Canada" seemed more on the cards than the unknown officer who hazarded: "Taking Winston Churchill to see Roosevelt."

Towards 11 a.m. on Monday, 4 August, they knew. Steaming fast through a grey veil of mist between Hoy and South Ronaldshay came the destroyer *Oribi* and as the battleship's crew mustered on her decks, the bosuns ramrod-straight beside the gangway, a familiar figure was suddenly visible on the destroyer's bridge: a chunky blue-suited figure sporting a yachting cap, a cigar clenched truculently between his jaws. Not a word was spoken but lips moved, and a whisper seemed to travel the whole length of the ship: "*It's Winston!*"

At that moment Churchill himself had eyes only for a man who stood alone on the battleship's fore-deck, a brown tweed overcoat draped loosely about him, his face as pale as a man close to death. "Ah, my dear friend, how are you?" Churchill greeted him. "How did you find Stalin?" and Harry Hopkins, weary beyond belief, after a nightmare twenty-four hour air journey through gale-force winds, replied, "I must tell you all about it".

The meeting that Roosevelt had mooted to Mackenzie King as far back as April was at last to become a reality. Events in the Balkans and North Africa had long made such a meeting impracticable, but now Hitler's eastern offensive had given them a breathing space. In the sheltered harbour of Placentia Bay, off the coast of Newfoundland, along with their advisers and chiefs of staffs, President and Premier would hold their first summit meeting, quite unknown to the world's Press.

The agenda featured urgent business. Midway through July, Japan had entered the war game in earnest; purely for "defensive purposes", she had pressured Vichy France to accept land, sea and air forces 50,000 strong in southern Indo-China. Darlan had temporised, but not for long. By 21 July Japanese transports were already steaming into Saigon harbour, preparing to take over bases on a long strip of Annamese coastline fronting the South China Sea, and the fine naval base on Camranh Bay. Now the Japanese Navy were only 750 miles from the British naval base at Singapore – while their airfields near Cape Cambodia lay barely 250 miles from Kota Bharu, the railhead of the Federated Malay States.

As always Darlan had blamed not himself but the United States. "I hoped the news would send squadrons of United States ships steaming into Saigon Harbour from Manila," he told Admiral Leahy ungraciously. "It is always the same story; the United States is too late."

In other respects, though, Roosevelt had acted swiftly. On 26 July, he clamped down an order freezing all Japanese assets, estimated at $131 million, in the United States. On 1 August, his embargo went further: the President banned the export of all aviation and motor fuel and other petroleum products to Japan.

Although Churchill was bound for Newfoundland, to urge the use of "hard language", on Roosevelt, the President had already struck the Japanese a body-blow. Japan could supply only 10 per cent of her own oil, with a further 10 per cent from the Dutch East Indies; the remaining 80 per cent had always come from the United States. Her own resources would last her three years at most – and now the Dutch East Indies, emboldened by Roosevelt, had reneged on their contract.

But Churchill gave no sign of preoccupation as the *Prince of Wales* churned at a steady 30 knots for Placentia Bay. Ensconced in the Admiral's sea cabin on the bridge, he was revelling in the trip like a Caribbean tourist. He challenged Hopkins to backgammon – and lost seven guineas in four days. He buried himself in C. S. Forester's best-seller, *Captain Horatio Hornblower, R.N.* Midshipman Michael Pruett, assigned as his escort aboard, was fascinated by the Premier's life-style – everything from his lilac siren suit to the cases of brandy, champagne and vintage wine that had accompanied his party, £450 worth all told. Sub-Lieutenant Michael Buxton was intrigued by his direct approach. At any given moment, Churchill might appear, on the bridge of all places, to demand: "Is there no one on? I've rung my bell for the last ten minutes. Where's my brandy and soda?"

Surgeon Lieutenant-Commander Dick Caldwell, summoned to treat Churchill for a ricked back muscle, found him in a high good humour despite the discomfort. "Do you allow your patients to smoke cigars?" he enquired, puffing defiantly away, and Caldwell was tact itself: "I think it would probably depend on the cigar, sir."

"All this ozone is making me sleepy," Churchill complained to his personal aide, Commander C. R. Thompson. "I have difficulty in driving myself to two hours work a day." Hopkins, for one, was delighted. "The Prime Minister failed to work yesterday for the first time in his life," he wrote gleefully to Ismay on 7 August, and he marvelled at the harmony of

156

the trip: "There is never a cross word between any of the services. They know better than to discuss Crete in mixed company."

Harmony or not, they were working apace – as if preparing themselves after twenty-three months of war for some exalted game of Consequences. Sir Alexander Cadogan debated how to present Britain's viewpoint to his opposite number, Sumner Welles. General Sir John Dill, Admiral Sir Dudley Pound and Air Vice Marshal Wilfred Freeman, standing in for Portal, laboured on Joint Chiefs of Staff papers in the hope of impressing General George C. Marshall, Chief of Staff, Admiral Harold R. Stark, and General Henry Harley "Hap" Arnold, Chief of the Army Air Corps.

But it was at night, after dinner at 9 p.m., that Churchill most came into his own. No sooner was dinner over and the tables cleared in the 60-foot long wardroom, dominated by an irreverent Gillray caricature of the Prince Regent, than Royal Marine servants in white mess-jackets began moving chairs and couches from anteroom to diningroom. Soon Churchill would enter with his advisers, wearing the mess dress of the Royal Yacht Squadron, a navy-blue jacket, with brass buttons and blue trousers, to beam a benediction on the company. Ranged in serried ranks on chairs they made a curiously impressive sight under the brilliant lighting – their stiff winged collars and black ties offset by the gold lace of their cuffs threaded with colours that bespoke their calling; the surgeon's red, the paymaster's white. Then as the lights dimmed Churchill settled in his armchair for his bedtime story – the nightly film show.

Whatever the choice, he entered into the spirit of it. He thrilled to Leslie Howard carrying off refugees from Nazi Germany in *Pimpernel Smith*. He chortled at Hedy Lamarr and Clark Gable in *Comrade X* and at Jean Arthur in *The Devil and Miss Jones*. Humphrey Bogart in *High Sierra*, hurtling to his death down a mountainside, produced a ribald, "And a good time was had by all!" Somehow he sandwiched in two showings of Laurence Olivier and Vivien Leigh in *Lady Hamilton* – which he was seeing for the fifth time – sobbing without constraint on each occasion.

Only one anxiety troubled him at times: would he and Roosevelt achieve a true meeting of minds? "I wonder if he will like me," he had asked Harriman in trepidation, when the trip was first mooted, and Hopkins, too, noted this constant preoccupation as the days wore on – "you'd have thought he was being carried up into the heavens to meet God".

The doubt was soon resolved. On the morning of Saturday, 9 August, the *Prince of Wales* slowed to come about at her berth in the dark waters of Placentia Bay. At that moment the early summer mists parted as if by magic, and the battleship, her White Ensign hoisted, was suddenly surrounded by a log-jam of American warships, the Stars and Stripes aloft, their decks lined with cheering crews. Beyond a wavering coastline of desolate beaches and coves the land rose by degrees to dark fir-clad hills.

High on the outside platform of the Admiral's bridge, his sandy hair still ruffled from sleep, Churchill watched and waited anxiously. It was 9 a.m. and all the sixty-seven years of his life had pointed to this moment: his first faraway glimpse of a man in a Palm Beach suit, sitting patiently in a wheel chair on the quarterdeck of the heavy cruiser *Augusta*.

*

"At last – we've gotten together."

"We have."

As Roosevelt's Secret Service bodyguard, Mike Reilly, recorded it, the greeting between the two leaders, after a bosun had piped the Premier aboard *Augusta* and the bands had crashed into the national anthems, was strangely banal – yet in the space of three days history would be made.

On the face of it, those days were one long orgy of hospitality. A buffet luncheon in the cabin of Vice-Admiral Ernest J. King, the Atlantic Fleet commander, was merely an appetiser for the dinner that Roosevelt staged that night for Churchill aboard *Augusta*. Heavy silver, wavering candles and the sheen of inlaid panelling provided a gracious setting for a hearty meal of vegetable puree, broiled spring chicken with buttered peas, candied sweet potatoes and mushroom gravy, followed by spinach omelette and chocolate ice cream. Since American warships were, by tradition, "dry", the guests made do with the heady wine of Churchill's oratory.

Nor were the lower decks forgotten. On the Saturday afternoon, a shining chain of U.S. motor boats brought a pyramid of 1,502 cartons to *Prince of Wales'* gangway; with Roosevelt's compliments and best wishes, each carton contained an orange, two apples, 200 Lucky Strike cigarettes and half a pound of cheese for every rating. Next day, Sunday, aboard *Prince of Wales*, Churchill hosted a luncheon worthy of a Lord Mayor's banquet in peacetime, although to stage it had been touch-and-go: caviar with vodka (which Hopkins had brought as a present from Stalin), turtle soup (which Commander Thompson had salvaged from the basement of a London grocer) and roast grouse (as the season had been advanced to 1 August, the Chief Steward had picked up a dozen brace in Inverness). A Royal Marine Band lilted through music ranging from *The Student Prince* to the *United States Marine Hymn*. That night, not to be outdone, Roosevelt feted Churchill all over again.

Beneath the convivial surface, the formal toasts, both leaders were cautiously feeling their way, hoping for common ground. After the Saturday night dinner, Churchill gave a bravura performance as he

158

reviewed the whole panorama of 1941 to date – now hunching forward, now braced against his chair back, slewing his cigar from cheek to cheek, stressing Britain's valour – and the need for American intervention – with all the force at his command. Roosevelt listened intently, fiddling with his pincenez, doodling with a burnt match, but plainly impressed for all that.

What, he asked Churchill at one point, did he think of Hitler's chances with Barbarossa? "I think," the Premier answered resonantly, "that he made a mistake, that his ego is about to strangle him."

It was plain, too, that Roosevelt was feeling his way not only with Churchill but with the American public. "I shall never declare war," he confided in a curiously revealing phrase. "I shall make war."

It was at Sunday's church service that Churchill saw his biggest chance for a break-through. "I have chosen some grand hymns," he confided to all within earshot, and like a busy stage-manager he worked in with the sailors helping to arrange the *Prince of Wales* quarterdeck – shifting chairs to right and left, fussing with the folds of the Union Jack. The true significance of this morning was not lost on him. As Roosevelt, in a blue doublebreasted suit, crossed a narrow gangway from *Augusta* to the destroyer, a cane held in his right hand, assisted by his son Elliott on his left, it was plain that he was attempting perhaps his longest walk since stricken with polio. Moving slowly, the full length of the ship, to his place of honour on the quarterdeck, flanked by a guard of 250 U.S. Marines and sailors, he stood rigidly at attention for both national anthems. Now Churchill was visibly moved. Fiddling with a handkerchief, he feigned a head cold, but the tears were not far away.

It was an unforgettable scene: the two leaders side by side, in the centre of a hollow square, the Union Jack and the Stars and Stripes draped together on the pulpit, the British and American sailors close together, white caps doffed, as they bent over their hymn sheets and the first of Churchill's hymns, *O God Our Help in Ages Past* soared out across the silent bay. Following Royal Naval custom, Captain Leach read the lesson, its text from Joshua hand-picked to suggest amity – "I will not fail thee nor forsake thee. Be strong and of good courage" – before the chaplains offered prayers for Roosevelt, for King George VI, for all those in invaded countries. Other hymns spoke of war and of a common plight and resolution: *Onward Christian Soldiers*, and *Eternal Father, strong to save*.

"The same language, the same hymns, and, more or less, the same ideals," Churchill mused later. "I have an idea that something really big may be happening – something really big."

But Churchill was in some measure doomed to disappointment. Already, on the Saturday afternoon, Welles and Cadogan had spent three hours thrashing out almost all the points the leaders would discuss aboard *Augusta* on Monday 12 August: the Azores, Vichy and French

159

North Africa, the Far East, the main points of the joint statement known to history as the Atlantic Charter. The divergency of opinion had been apparent even then: while Churchill had journeyed to Placentia Bay to wrest commitments from Roosevelt, the President had come determined to evade them.

There was still common ground for agreement. If Britain occupied the Canary Islands, pre-empting a German attack through Spain, she could not live up to her promise to defend the Azores. In this case – provided Portugal requested the move – Roosevelt agreed to do so in her stead. On Japan, despite the "hard language" Churchill urged, the President proved more wary. "Leave that to me," he told Churchill. "I think I can baby them along for three months." To save Japan's face, his instinct was to parley: to drag out the talks between Hull and Nomura, in the hope that Tokyo would see the light and pull out of Indo-China.

Foremost in Roosevelt's mind was the intention of delaying any show-down until his Army and Navy were stronger and public opinion more receptive. "Shooting?" he had echoed to his Cabinet, when the risk of convoys to Iceland was raised. "Well, a little shooting might arouse this country from its lethargy and help in passing the extension of the (Selective Service) Act." His instinct was sure: on 12 August, as the full-dress conferences were held, the Act, which on 16 October, 1940, had seen the registration of all American males between twenty-one and thirty-five for the first peacetime conscription, was renewed by just one vote.*

Roosevelt was not surprised; for months the graffiti "O.H.I.O." had been scrawled on the walls of training camp latrines all over America. It referred not to the Buckeye State but to "over the hill in October": if the draftees were not released and sent home they would desert.

In the teeth of such opposition, Roosevelt was profoundly disturbed when Churchill told Hopkins: "I would rather have an American declaration of war now and no supplies for six months than double the supplies and no declaration." "That is a hard saying," Roosevelt said, his face clouding over, when Hopkins passed this on.

All through that August Monday, the Americans were finding Britain's war priorities woefully unrealistic. In their main appreciation, the British Chiefs of Staff had stressed: "It is in bombing, on a scale undreamt of in the last war, that we find the new weapon on which we must principally depend for the destruction of German economic life and morale." Even before discussions opened, General "Hap" Arnold had scrawled a large and eloquent marginal query beside this item. On coming face to face

* A press conference at which Wavell's successor, General Sir Claude Auchinleck, had told U.S. correspondents, "We are certainly going to need American manpower, just as we did in the last war," had not helped the Bill's passage. On 11 July, Churchill had rebuked Auchinleck: "I fear your remarks will be exploited by the isolationists and will be an impediment to the end we all desire. Mr. Winant tells me . . . that your remarks will be unhelpful."

160

with Air Vice Marshal Freeman, Arnold was stunned: this mooted campaign was based on the assumption that America could furnish 6,000 more bombers than she was then producing.

Bitterly aggrieved, Freeman dashed off a memo to Hopkins: "I must let you know how depressed I am that it is impossible for me to state our case for increased production of the heavy bomber . . . it was made clear to me at my first meeting with Arnold that, far from getting more, we were going to get considerably less."

There were other trenchant criticisms. General George Marshall, normally temperate, saw British preoccupations with the Middle East – to which the Americans assigned No 4 priority, well below the United Kingdom, Singapore and the ocean trade routes – as making little sense. Now the Russian front was paramount, the British should abandon the theatre or downgrade their effort. Admiral Harold Stark agreed; the British should re-evaluate all their priorities.

Yet progress of a kind had been made. Churchill had seen how hamstrung Roosevelt was by American memories of World War One and the League of Nations, the ever-present thundercloud of isolationism – "the mid-West is our problem", the President told one of Leach's officers, "They have never seen a ship and they know nothing about war." Roosevelt had glimpsed the Premier's deep attachment to Dominions and Empire; to Welles' chagrin, Churchill had roundly refused to amend the Ottawa Agreements of 1932, when Britain and her Dominions had met the threat of Depression by building a closed economic unit, shutting out many items of American trade.

It remained only to draft a Joint Declaration: a commitment isolationists were swift to condemn as ranging a technically neutral country alongside a belligerent power. So hastily did Churchill act to clear it with his War Cabinet that Clement Attlee roused from his bed after midnight, called a Cabinet meeting for 1.45 a.m. and was cabling back suggested amendments to Churchill by 4 a.m.

In truth, the declaration was little more than a patched-up press release, replete with high minded phrases. Britain and America sought "no aggrandisement" and "no territorial changes" that did not accord "with the freely expressed wishes of the people concerned": they respected the right of all peoples to choose their own form of government; they sought to secure for all "improved labour standards, economic advancement, and social security". After "the final destruction of Nazi tyranny", they hoped to "see established a peace which will afford to all nations the means of dwelling in safety".

World reactions, for the most part were disillusioned; the abiding hope of the Allied nations, that America would now enter the war, had not been fulfilled. Oliver Harvey, Eden's Private Secretary, thought it "a terribly woolly document, full of all the old clichés of the League of

Nations period". In Moscow, Sir Stafford Cripps dismissed it as "no bloody good at all – it means nothing to the Balkans or the Baltic". At Buckingham Palace, a puzzled King George VI noted "It said all the right things but how are we going to carry them out? Most of the peoples of Europe will have forgotten that they ever had a government of their own when the war is over." In Washington, the German chargé, Dr Hans Thomsen, scoffed: "The fools have learned nothing in twenty years."

Late on 12 August, the time had come for Premier and President to part. As the *Prince of Wales* steamed out of Placentia Bay, Roosevelt was there to bid her farewell, standing bareheaded on *Augusta*'s quarterdeck: the wistful strains of *Auld Lang Syne* rolled out across the waters towards the fir-clad hills. Both men could at least take comfort in one truth: each had found a comrade and an ally in the struggle that lay ahead.

"I am not a religious man," Churchill blurted out in one of their moments together, "but I thank God that such a man as you is the head of your government at a time like this." It was his bodyguard, Detective-Inspector Walter Thompson, who broke it to him later that the President felt the same.

"How is he standing up to it, Thompson? How is he really?" Roosevelt had asked the detective, and Thompson could reassure him: the Premier had deep reserves of energy, replenished by constant catnaps. "Is he hard to handle?" Roosevelt asked curiously, and the Special Branch man had to admit it: "Yes, sir. He is reckless and self-willed. Restraint of any kind is unendurable."

"Well, take care of him," Roosevelt counselled, then pronounced the verdict that Churchill would always treasure, "He's about the greatest man in the world." "In fact," he added, after reflection, "he may very likely be *the* greatest."

8

"Shoot Everyone Who Shows A Wry Face"

13 August–30 September, 1941

WAS JOSEF STALIN's staunchest ally Adolf Hitler himself? On Saturday 23 August, *Generaloberst* Heinz Guderian, commanding Panzer Group Two, had cause to wonder.

Before 10 a.m. that day, Guderian's Fieseler Storch touched down at Borisov airfield; minutes later, a car was bearing him to the headquarters of Bock's Army Group Centre. The commanders of the Fourth, Ninth and Second Armies – *Feldmarschall* Gunther von Kluge, *Generaloberst* Adolf Strauss and *Generaloberst Freiherr* von Weichs – had also just arrived. Each man was keenly awaiting a visitor from Hitler's headquarters: *Generaloberst* Franz Halder, Chief of the General Staff.

His arrival, at 11 a.m., came in the nature of a shock: Halder looked ill and depressed. In tired measured tones he came straight to the gist of Hitler's Directive No 34, dated 21 August: "The Führer has decided to conduct neither the operation against Leningrad, as previously envisaged by him, nor the offensive against Moscow, as proposed by the Army General Staff, but to take possession first of the Ukraine and the Crimea."

After a moment of stunned silence, Guderian burst out: "This can't be true."

Halder was fatalistic. "It is true. We spent five weeks wrangling for the drive on Moscow."

Now *Feldmarschall* von Bock broke in: "What can we do against this decision?" Halder shook his head resignedly. "It is immutable."

Guderian was persistent. In the warm discussion that followed he made his views plain: a drive for Kiev, the Ukrainian capital, would inevitably see the tanks bogged down in a winter campaign long before turning north and reaching Moscow. By then the roads and supply conditions would be appalling. His own Panzer group had not known one day's respite since Barbarossa was launched.

Von Bock came to a decision. Since Guderian argued so persuasively, he should accompany Halder back to the *Wolfsschanze*, request an interview with the Führer and try to win him over. But late that afternoon, before Halder's JU-88 took off over the endless fields of white

163

shocked corn, von Bock recalled to Guderian the apocryphal words of an officer of the guard at Worms when Martin Luther set off to justify his faith to the Emperor Charles V: "Little monk, little monk, yours is a difficult road".

It was dusk before the plane landed Halder and Guderian at Lötzen airfield, East Prussia. Their way to the *Wolfsschanze* led them through groves of tall oak trees, through clusters of low grey huts, their roofs camouflaged by shrubs that flanked the asphalted road, ending at the "Führer Hut" – surrounded by a double fence, bristling with sentries. Here only special yellow passes gained entry to the inner sanctum.

For two hours Guderian waited in suspense. The cool Baltic air drifted through the fine mosquito netting covering the open windows, and with it the stench of petrol; waging war on the midges that Hitler detested, the engineers were spraying every pond in the neighbourhood, but still the insects persisted. It was dark before the summons came to Hitler's map room.

Guderian began circumspectly, feeling his way. Hitler had no inkling of why he had sought this interview and Halder, moreover, had not been invited to sit in. Guderian was on his own, and he knew it; little support could be expected from Keitel, leaning negligently against the map table, or from Jodl, studiously taking notes. Overtly his intention must be to report on Panzer Group Two: engine breakdowns, supply problems, a balanced realistic view.

It was Hitler himself who supplied his cue: "Do you consider your troops are still capable of a major effort?"

Guderian sensed all of them watching him intently. "If the troops are set a great objective," he answered deliberately, "the kind that would inspire every man of them – yes."

"You are, of course, thinking of Moscow?" Hitler countered.

"Yes, my Führer. May I have permission to give my reasons?"

Hitler seemed open to conviction. "By all means, Guderian. Say whatever's on your mind."

Guderian seized his chance. "Moscow cannot be compared with Paris or Warsaw, my Führer. Moscow is not only the head and the heart of the Soviet Union – it is also its communications centre, its political brain, an important industrial area, above all the hub of the transport system. The fall of Moscow will decide the war."

Hitler said nothing. Guderian was warming to his subject. Stalin knew that the fall of Moscow would mean his final defeat, he insisted, and for this reason he would deploy his entire military strength before the capital. It was thus before Moscow, and only there, that the *Wehrmacht* could destroy the flower of the Red Army, and once Moscow was taken all else would follow.

Striding to a map, Guderian stabbed his forefinger at the Yelnya bridgehead, barely 250 miles from the city. That bridgehead, he explained, was still open at this moment; routeing instructions, transport schedules, even signposts denoting the mileage to Moscow were all in readiness. The panzers could move off that very night to smash Timoshenko before Yelnya. "Let us march towards Moscow," Guderian pleaded, "we shall take it."

It was now that Hitler joined him at the map table, but his finger hovered not over Yelnya but above a region more than 300 miles to the south: the Ukraine. "My generals have all read Clausewitz," he announced sharply, "but they understand nothing of wartime economics." One by one he ticked off the commodities he sought: "We need the grain of the Ukraine. The industrial area of the Donets must work for us, instead of for Stalin. The Russian oil supplies of the Caucasus must be cut off . . . above all we must gain control of the Crimea . . . this dangerous aircraft carrier operating against the Rumanian oilfields."

Guderian stood silent. Now the weeks of planning and scheming with his chief of operations, *Oberstleutnant* Fritz Bayerlein, had gone for nothing. What could he, a field commander, say to a politician who thought not like a Clausewitz but like a colonialist – in terms of coal and oil, wheat and eggs?

All soldiers could do now was obey orders – or perhaps die trying.

*

In a large ornately-furnished room on Tehran's Ferdowsi Avenue, overlooking a lush semi-tropical park, the Minister of the Third Reich, Dr Erwin Ettel, was drafting a cable. It would be bitter news for the Foreign Ministry in Berlin, but Ettel was duty bound to pass on the tip given to him by Zoulfikar Pasha, the pro-Axis Egyptian Ambassador: Iran was one oil-rich region Hitler would never occupy. The British and the Russians were planning to seize it first.

The source was King Farouk of Egypt himself, no friend of the British, who stressed that with Barbarossa a *fait accompli* Iran – most especially the British-subsidised Anglo-Iranian oilfield – was now vulnerable to an attack from Russian soil. Then, too, the 870-mile-long trans-Iranian railway was the one practicable land route to carry war supplies from the Persian Gulf to the Caspian Sea. These were prizes Russia and Britain could not afford to yield.

The ostensible bone of contention was the 2,500-strong workforce of German civilians employed by Iran's railway and telegraph systems, and in industrial plants. To the British, they were a latent fifth column, but since Churchill was cool on invasion what the War Cabinet called "firm but friendly demands" to deport them were pressed on the Iranian government. The result was a skilful exercise in diplomatic foot-dragging.

165

At first claiming that only 700 Germans were involved and that deportation would be "unneutral", the Prime Minister, Ali Mansur, next agreed to banish twenty-four forthwith, later upping the figure to thirty per month. On 8 August, the British were still patiently negotiating; they wanted "a drastic reduction" before the month ended, an eighty per cent reduction by mid-September.

The Russians were of sterner mettle. On 13 August, the Ambassador to Iran, A. S. Tehernikh, delivering his *aide-memoire*, followed up with a verbal message: the Soviets would require an answer within three days – "almost, but not quite, an ultimatum and . . . rather disquieting," to the British Foreign Office. It was now on the cards that Russia, contrary to her undertaking, would beat the British to the start-line.

It was a risk the British could not afford to take. At dawn on 25 August, the first khaki-clad columns were rolling across the border from Iraq; Indian troops, landing at the port of Bandar Shahpur, secured the world's largest oil-cracking plant at Abadan. Simultaneously, down the shores of the Caspian Sea, came the mechanised Cossacks of General Max Sinenko, their western column closing on Tabriz, their eastern on the port of Bandar Shah.

On 30 August, after eighty hours of combat – and one day after the Iranians sought an armistice – a yellow cyclone of dust extending for hundreds of miles through the horse-shoe bends and passes signalled that the British and Russian columns were converging. At Kazvin, 90 miles north-west of Tehran, they joined up to pump hands in the main square, the British to marvel at the loose grey smocks, blue breeches and old-style needle-type bayonets of the Russians, the Russians to goggle at the Gurkhas' khaki shorts.

One man had been outraged by the proceedings from the first: 65-year-old Reza Pahlavi, His Imperial Majesty, Shah in Shah (King of Kings), Shadow of the Almighty, Vice-Regent of God and Centre of the Universe. A one-time Colonel of the Persian Cossack Brigade, who had seized power from the effete Quajar dynasty in 1921, Reza was a despot of the Haroun-al-Raschid school, who detested both British and Russians alike. On learning of the invasion, his first step was a frantic cable in French to Roosevelt: in a manner "brusque et sans préavis", his frontiers had been violated. After a full week's pause for reflection, Roosevelt replied blandly: "I hope Your Majesty will concur with me in believing that we must view the situation in its full perspective of present world events. . . ." He had, he added, asked both countries to state publicly that they had no designs on Iran's independence.

This was cold comfort for the Shah, a fanatic nationalist who in 1935 had re-christened "Persia" "Iran" after the nation which dated back before Cyrus, Darius and Xerxes. Since then he had waxed rich both on British royalties and German technological skills, and until now his rule had been absolute. His moody rages were notorious; for "tiresome gabbling" he once booted 21-year-old Crown Prince Muhammad Reza into a fountain but a jockey who lost a race merited a kick in the groin, a train driver arriving late was dragged from the footplate and trampled senseless. Now, incensed by the ineptitude of his armed forces in halting the Anglo-Russian tide, he sought out scapegoats. Summoning his War Minister, General Ahmed Nakhchevan, to the Palace, he slashed him about the head and face with a sabre, screaming "Throw that carrion into prison!" The General survived the ordeal, unlike the Chief of the Air Force, who was shot out of hand.

The Shah's one thought now was to keep his seat on the Peacock Throne, and to safeguard his position he dispatched twenty-seven truck-loads of gold and jewels to Isfahan, 150 miles south.

But Axis puppets would merit only ruthless treatment from this time on, as the British were making plain. To Sir Reader Bullard, the mild-mannered old Ambassador, who liked to read Dickens aloud to his guests, Churchill cabled harshly: "Dismiss from your mind any idea of a generous policy towards the Germans to please the Persians or anyone else." Next day, 4 September, he told the War Cabinet unequivocally: "It is important that we should have complete control over Persia during the war." The British G.O.C., Lieutenant-General E. P. Quinan, was left in no doubt as to his role: if the Shah tried to leave for Isfahan to set up an independent government, he "should be seized and held".

Unknown to the Shah, a bizarre attempt at king-making was soon to take place at the Boulestin Restaurant, a haven for gourmets off the Strand in London. Trifling with the idea of restoring the Quajar dynasty to the Peacock Throne, Harold Nicolson, of the Ministry of Information, and Horace Seymour of the Foreign Office, had invited Prince Hassan Quajar to lunch.

A devoted Anglophile, who was studying the English classics at Rhyll University, the Prince proved a disappointment from the first. Perhaps his son, Drummond Quajar – "*c'est un nom écossais*" – might prove eligible; after graduating from Worcester College, Oxford, the lad was at a loose end. "Does he speak Persian?" asked Nicolson hopefully. "*Pas un mot*," the Prince replied delightedly, "*Pas un seul mot.*"

It was with some relief that Nicolson, on 16 September, heard that the Shah had abdicated and that the *Majlis*, Iran's 136-man National Assembly, had approved the Crown Prince, Muhammad Reza Pahlavi, as his successor.*

Three weeks later, the U.S. Minister in Tehran, Louis G. Dreyfus, passed two pleasant hours beneath the cool white pillars of the Shah's

---

* Who, on 16 January, 1979, was driven from his country by the elderly fanatic Ayatollah Khomeini to seek refuge successively in Egypt, Morocco, Mexico, the United States and Panama. He died in exile in Cairo on 27 July, 1980.

summer palace, conversing on world affairs in French. In the light of later events, his report to the State Department had a certain irony: "Shah . . . voluntarily espouses democratic cause because he is strongly against totalitarian doctrines . . . after remarking that his father had been unfortunate in being surrounded by bad advisers, he said he would govern constitutionally and look after the welfare of his people.

"He closed the conversation by referring warmly to the United States, which he thought would play an important role in the peace. He said he would be very happy to be an ally of America."

*

It was the first notable instance of whole-hearted Anglo-Soviet co-operation – and Rudolf Hess was baffled.

On 22 June, Hess, who weeks earlier had been moved to Mytchett Place, a secluded manor house near Aldershot, Hampshire, had heard the news of Barbarossa with a strangely wry smile. "So they have started after all," was his only comment, and it was plain that he saw a German victory as only weeks away. Yet as the months dragged by and the Russians held out, Hess grew increasingly more puzzled. What could imperialist Britain hope to gain by alignment with Communist barbarians?

By degrees he had set down his thoughts in a 12-page memorandum, a strange mixture of threats and cajolery, which he hoped would find favour with the British government. In part it read:

> Germany, for her part, wishes a reasonable peace. She is ready to conclude this without victory over England. . . . The question then, is whether the difference in aims is so great that all the sacrifices involved in a continuation of the war *must* be made – that is, all sacrifices of human beings, buildings, of irreplaceable works of art, destroyed factories, wharves, port installations, ships, of national wealth. . . .
>
> I can give an assurance that Germany has not in mind the capitulation of the British Isles. . . . An occupation of the whole island – for any length of time – be it either before or after its capitulation, does not come into the question – for Germany would be burdened with the feeding of the population.
>
> It must not be forgotten that the longer the war lasts, the more will the balance of power between England and America move in favour of the latter. . . .
>
> In conclusion: England might ask herself whether it pays her, at great sacrifice, to make the most precarious effort to conquer the Axis, and into the bargain, to strengthen with certainty Bolshevik Russia as an immensely more dangerous opponent to her Empire.

At 7.30 p.m. on Tuesday, 9 September, in the seclusion of his bedroom, the Deputy Führer spent an inconclusive hour talking over the
memorandum with an old acquaintance from pre-war days, Lord Beaverbrook; the Iranian coup seemed to lend new urgency to his appeal. As the
new Minister of Supply, Beaverbrook was shortly to depart on a trade
mission to Stalin but whether Hess knew this – or that in talks with the
Russians Beaverbrook would disclaim all notions of a peace treaty – is
unclear. For security reasons, the Special Branch men who bugged their
conversation gave Hess his usual code-name, "Jonathan" while Beaverbrook was "Dr Livingstone".

When Beaverbrook referred bitterly to the war – "the whole thing is
bloody" – Hess was swift to respond. "Yes, the whole thing is bloody, but
we can use our blood for better things. You can use your blood in your
colonies and for your Empire, and we can use our blood for the East. We
need ground for our population."

To the end he was bitter that his peace mission had been slighted: "I
thought I can come here and find a certain commonsense."

Beaverbrook's reply summed up the whole embittered paradox of
which 1941 was fast becoming the embodiment: a world in which men
killed and must go on killing as if by reflex action. "Very difficult, you
know, to find commonsense when a war is on," he told the German. He
added ruefully: "Once you get into the blood and the guns and the
sacrifices, then reason goes."

*

Nearer to the battlefront, the perspectives were different. At the British
Embassy in Moscow, Harold Elvin felt closer to the Russian people with
every day that passed.

As early as 27 June, Sir Stafford Cripps had returned from London,
with a full-scale Military Mission, under Lieutenant-General Noel
Mason-MacFarlane, in tow, but the attitude of some of its members had
shocked Elvin profoundly. One army Captain had remarked cynically:
"Of course we have to keep most of our arms back to fight this country
when Germany is finished."

Yet Elvin could only marvel at the spirit of the people. Like the
Londoners of 1940, the Muscovites had been swift to adapt. Now, at
dusk, Red Square was almost deserted; only black flocks of rooks cawed
over the Kremlin walls, circling the square red block that was Lenin's
mausoleum like scraps of charred paper. But behind closed doors and
darkened windows, a fierce activity prevailed. At the factory benches,
couples were working side by side; husbands were teaching their jobs to
their wives before departing for the front. Teenagers patrolled at twilight,
warning householders of faulty black-outs, checking sandbags and water

169

pails in case of incendiary raids. All younger children had been evacuated from the city – placed in the care of Moscow's manicurists, who now had sterner tasks to perform. At the National Hotel – where portraits of Hitler and Mussolini had only lately replaced those of Neville Chamberlain and the Archbishop of Canterbury as the architects of World War Two – women workers had now replaced the men as waiters and dishwashers.

Camouflage loomed everywhere. The gold onion domes of the Kremlin vanished beneath a coating of battleship-grey. The façade of the Great Palace was screened by a net festooned with green branches. The Bolshoi Theatre was hung with canvas, painted with false entrance doorways. Anti-aircraft batteries, screened by leaves, lay secreted in the clusters of pine and birch dotting the city. Each night, 750,000 people bedded down beneath the blue-and-gold mosaic ceilings of the Moscow subway stations – "exactly what Metro-Goldwyn-Mayer would think an air-raid shelter should look like", sniffed the noted film director Sergei Eisenstein.

Moscow's first air-raid warning came to a shrilling of whistles and a wailing of sirens on the night of 21 July, followed by the mighty roll of the ack-ack barrage, the crump of explosions. Soon the raids had become a siege, and Elvin was fire-watching at the Embassy every fourth night in addition to his other duties. At dawn he retired to his bedroom in the West Wing groggy with lack of sleep.

It was at 2 a.m. on 11 August when his deeper involvement began; the cheerful cockney, Sergeant Bill Eldredge, called him to the switchboard. He explained that a girl had rung the Embassy, wanting to "gab Russki." But it turned out that Eldredge was wrong: a Russian girl was feeling a desperate need to talk English.

To Elvin it would always be the strangest of all his Moscow encounters, symbolic of the lonely immensity of the land, her people's infinite capacity for suffering. He heard the girl's first words with a chill of foreboding.

"I've lost both mother and father at Minsk in the war. I heard tonight. I'm alone. My name is Tamara. I was mad to know what to do. I can't sleep . . . I'm absolutely alone. I thought I'll ring up the British Embassy, maybe I could speak with an Englishman for an hour . . . will you speak to me for one hour?"

That night it was Bill Eldredge who made the tea and brought it to the switchboard. Hardly realising what he said, Elvin talked on for fully two hours, striving to understand, to bring comfort. The next night, she called again at 2 a.m. Another two hours went by. Soon it had become second nature, talking for hours night after night to a girl whose face he had never seen, a fixture at the switchboard in the main hallway, only the harsh light of the single reading lamp probing the shadows.

They met only twice: once in the Tretiakov Art Gallery, timorously at first, each wondering what the other would be like. The second time was on 11 September, at an all-night dance at Moscow University, where Tamara was a student. Later, in a darkened classroom, they made love until dawn.

After that everything went wrong. In the small hours of each night, the telephone link was maintained, but Elvin, laid up with synovitis in his left knee, was confined to his bedroom, watching the barges slide down the Moscow River, past the high red crenellated walls of the Kremlin. On 23 September, she phoned for the last time.

For weeks now she had been a volunteer, digging trenches outside Moscow, but at last, after repeatedly nagging the authorities, her wish had been granted: she was heading for the front line. Elvin was appalled. "To do what?" he asked her.

Tamara was vague. "Red Cross, digging trenches – do you think they might let me fight?" Her voice was tender and puzzled by turns. "My English friend . . . Room 10, Tretiakov Art Gallery, I will always remember." Suddenly she asked, "Tell me something, I keep asking myself . . ."

"Yes, Tamara?"

"You know my mother and father were killed by the Germans?"

"Yes, Tamara," Elvin said again.

"*Why?*"

Long after, Elvin would remember with pain that he had found no answer to that question.

*

Churchill was disgruntled as September dawned. Despite his new-found rapport with Roosevelt – and a timely success in Iran – the war for the first time in months had reached stalemate. Moreover, a groundswell of enthusiasm for all things Russian – and thus a tacit acceptance of Communism – was sweeping Britain.

Already intellectual left-wingers had created a thousand committees and societies to promote the Soviet cause, blithely brushing aside long-held reservations about Stalinist oppression – "why worry about the colour of the fireman's socks during a fire?" was one Briton's pithy appraisal. Mass Observers reported the widespread "feeling, again obscure and often incoherent, that Russia was a working man's country" – and that 60 per cent of people, nagged by a vague guilt that Britain's role was now secondary, felt that more help should be given her. They noted, too, "a kind of secure cheerfulness . . . unknown since the fall of Greece" – and that Stalin's appearance on a newsreel was a signal for prolonged applause.

To Churchill it seemed that the Russian cause now loomed larger than that of the Empire. In September, a "Tanks for Russia Week", launched by the canny Beaverbrook as Minister of Supply, saw an unprecedented response; in one Kent railway works, 1,000 freight waggons for Russia were completed within ten weeks, despite seventy-six air-raid warnings. At Birmingham, where workers daubed "Marx" "Lenin" and "Another for Joe" on their finished products, the Ambassador, Ivan Maisky, was hoisted high on to a tank while workers sang the *Internationale*.

That winter the august Athenaeum Club on London's Pall Mall elected Maisky to its membership.

As sales of the *Soviet War News* climbed to 50,000 weekly, and British Communist Party membership neared an all-time level of 65,000, a subtle propaganda campaign to heighten British workers' guilt-feelings was early apparent. Until now, men and women had felt themselves hard done by, given their daily short commons, a clothes rationing system of 66 coupons a year, with even jam and honey restricted by a points system. Now they were assailed by posters plastered on doors and hoardings that proclaimed: RUSSIAN WORKERS FIGHT FOR US! RUSSIAN WORKERS BURN THEIR HOMES FOR US!! DO WE REALISE? DO WE CARE? That early graffiti on railway arches, STOP THIS IMPERIALIST WAR, had soon given way to SECOND FRONT NOW. In one instance, a Party poster's blatant politicisation prompted the censor to step in: below the slogan THE RED ARMY'S FIGHT IS YOUR FIGHT loomed the parrot-cries, Remove pro-Fascists from high places – End Employers' mis-management and waste – Restore T.U. (Trade Union) Rights and *Daily Worker*.*

This was not Churchill's only cause for disquiet. If he grieved that the spirit of Empire was waning much of his Empire, even this early in the war, was already bent on secession.

From 16 August on, Article III of the Atlantic Charter had caused a ferment that would not be stilled. In final form, it read: ". . . they respect the right of all peoples to choose the form of government under which they will live; and they wish to see sovereign rights and self-government restored to those who have been forcibly deprived of them."

At once the able and progressive Governor of Burma, Sir Reginald Dorman-Smith, warned that the Burmese, under their ambitious Premier, U Saw, would use this lever to push for full post-war self-government; many nations under British rule felt as enslaved as Norway or Belgium. This in turn alarmed the Colonial Secretary, Lord Moyne; how could he countenance self-government for Gibraltar, Aden, The Gambia, Hong Kong, to name but a few? On 4 September, the War Cabinet decided firmly that the Charter was concerned solely with Nazi-dominated European nations. It had no connection with the British

* The *Daily Worker* had been banned by the Minister of Home Security, Herbert Morrison, from 21 January, 1941. It was not re-licensed until 26 August, 1942.

Empire's internal affairs – or with relations between the United States and the Philippines.

Nonetheless, facing the House of Commons on 9 September, Churchill phrased things more subtly. The Charter had no connection with people who owed "allegiance to the British Crown" – since Britain was already pledged to help India, Burma and other countries obtain equal partnership in the Commonwealth once the war was ended.

This promise of jam in a far-off tomorrow incensed many nationalists – among them Mahatma Gandhi, one of the few leaders of the Indian National Congress who remained at liberty, for in eleven months 5,000 Indians had been clapped into jail for civil disobedience, among them the former President Jawaharlal Nehru. Their argument had some cogency: if Britain was really fighting for democracy, she should prove it by granting India Dominion status.

America should not aid Britain without guarantee, Gandhi maintained now. "She should ask what will happen to India, Asia and African possessions. She should withdraw any help unless there are guarantees of human liberties. . . ." U Saw, who had convinced Dorman-Smith of this – but not Churchill – was rash enough to appeal to Roosevelt over the Premier's head. Urging him not to "regard the case of Burma as a domestic issue for the British Empire", U Saw warned "The world's faith in the genuineness of the war aims enunciated by you and Mr Churchill will depend on the view you take on this point."

It was in vain. "The Prime Minister of Burma lacks authority to treat with foreign governments upon his own initiative," Hull advised the President, who did not even bother to acknowledge the letter. On the strength of a brief parley he held with the Japanese, Churchill was to jail U Saw too.

Visitors to the Far East were well aware of the danger signs. The Commander-in-Chief, Air Chief Marshal Sir Robert Brooke-Popham, after passing through Calcutta, reported to Ismay of "a difference between the bazaars and the business quarter" too marked "to please a defender of democracy"; he found the Europeans "too plutocratic, too well-dressed, and seemed very far-removed from the war". Profits took priority over all; since one practice air-raid warning had cost the jute manufacturers 40,000 rupees (about £2,500) in lost man-hours it had not been repeated. In Dutch East Indian cities like Batavia, the ace Filipino reporter Carlos Romulo found the Javanese leaders ready and waiting to collaborate with any Japanese invasion. Had not Queen Wilhelmina also denied that the Atlantic Charter applied to them?

Such aspirations Churchill would never fully grasp. "As regards India," the Secretary of State, Leopold Amery lamented, "(he) has never got beyond the early Kipling stage." At times brutally dismissive – "what those people need is the *sjambok*", he once told Dorman-Smith

173

– at others he saw the Empire through a rose-tinted haze recalling a Victorian Durbar. "If the Japs were to invade," he confidently predicted, "it would make the Indians loyal to the King Emperor for a hundred years."

It was already much too late. Throughout almost all of Asia now, the white man was truly hated; the sky was black with chickens coming home to roost.

*

Roosevelt apart, Churchill was increasingly at odds with all his erstwhile allies. The reason was not hard to find: neither British factory workers, Asian nationalist leaders or Dominions generals saw the prime objective of the war as the preservation of the British Empire.

"The P.M. is interested only in victory and not in the purposes of victory," the Labour pundit Harold Laski wrote to Justice Felix Frankfurter of the Supreme Court, an intimate of Roosevelt's, "He will seek to preserve 'traditional Britain' at all costs . . . he has set his face backwards and not forward in the concepts of the post-war world."

Another man galled beyond endurance by Churchill's imperialist stance was General Charles de Gaulle. As the Syrian campaign had ended de Gaulle had been enraged to find that his doughty Free French, having served their purpose, had been coolly set aside; in the twenty-two clauses of the armistice treaty signed between Britain and Vichy France no mention had even been made of them. His private war had been fought in vain – for while the British guaranteed Syria ultimate independence, they were keeping a tight hold on the terrain for the duration.

"White with suppressed passion," de Gaulle invaded the Cairo office of the Minister of State Oliver Lyttelton both denouncing the treaty and refusing to accept it. When he thrust forward a document withdrawing all Free French Forces from the Middle East Command, Lyttelton promptly tore it up.

In the end though, Lyttelton saw the justice of de Gaulle's complaints; he reversed many Armistice clauses in favour of the Free French, who now took over all war material and both Syrian and Lebanese levies, as well as recruiting 6,000 Vichyites to their own ranks. But between Cairo and London de Gaulle left what Churchill was to call "a trail of Anglophobia" behind him; the gulf between the two men was widening daily.

In Churchill's eyes, de Gaulle's cardinal sin was an interview he granted the *Chicago Daily News* on 27 August in Brazzaville. Hinting that Britain's tenuous relationship with Vichy was a means of maintaining contact with Hitler, the General next broached the idea of offering West African naval bases to the United States. Nor would he seek destroyers in return – a sneering reference to Britain's ceding of eight crucial Atlantic bases in 1940 in return for fifty over-age U.S. destroyers. Churchill's explosion of rage when he heard resembled an old-time vaudeville comedian; tearing his cigar from his mouth he first hurled it on the floor then jumped on it. He had been waiting for three months for an excuse to get rid of the General, he trumpeted – "de Gaulle was to feel the draught the minute he arrived".

And that he did. Four days later, when he reached London, even the Spears Mission was forbidden to contact him; any request for a meeting was to be summarily refused. Broadcast facilities, if sought, must be withheld by the B.B.C. Nor was de Gaulle free to leave the country again; M.I.5, the British counter-intelligence agency, was to dog his footsteps night and day.

De Gaulle promptly saw the red light. In a noonday meeting with Churchill on 12 September, he proved the soul of conciliation. "While he, de Gaulle, was yet an infant in politics," he told the Premier, and "that what he said had sometimes been directed to individuals who deserved it," fundamentally he had always been, and always would be, loyal to Churchill. Without demur, he agreed to the formation of an eight-man Free French National Committee which, on paper at least, diluted his dictatorial powers.

Only much later did Churchill realise that de Gaulle's apparent readiness to comply had been prompted as always by the same unswerving ambition: the official recognition by Russia and all the refugee governments in London that he alone was the true leader of the Free French.

Churchill's other problems were less easily resolved. The rift with the Dominions, so noticeable after the fall of Greece and Crete, was now an outright impasse. On 28 August, faced with a vote of no-confidence by his Labour opposition, the Australian Prime Minister, Robert Menzies, resigned; his successor, Arthur Fadden, took office with a bare majority of one. At this point, the demands of Lieutenant-General Sir Thomas Blamey, the Australian C-in-C in the Middle East, became insistent. By 29 August, the 18th Australian Brigade had been withdrawn from Tobruk. Now Blamey sought to strip Tobruk of all the Anzacs remaining – and the reassembly of all Australian forces under his sole command.

It was a move Churchill mightily opposed – but in view of mounting Australian pressure he had little choice. On 11 September, he had reluctantly agreed – "irrespective of the cost entailed and the injury to future prospects" – if the Australians insisted. Three days later, Fadden did insist. The Australians had held Tobruk against Rommel since April, in the most gruelling climate that Allied troops had yet endured.

On 18 September, Churchill's Most Secret cipher telegram to Auchinleck made his own feelings plain: "Great allowances must be made for a Government with a majority of one playing politics with a bitter

175

Opposition, part of whom at least are isolationist in sentiment. Whatever your and our personal feelings may be, it is our duty at all costs to prevent an open dispute with the Australian Government. Any public controversy would injure foundations of Empire and be disastrous to our general position in the war."

"I would feel inclined to suggest informal message should be made to Australian Government suggesting the replacement of Blamey whose conduct I regard as weak and disingenuous," Lyttelton counselled from Cairo, advice which the Premier felt it prudent to ignore. On 30 September, he once more appealed to Fadden to modify his decision, leaving two Australian brigades still in Tobruk – a request Fadden refused on the day that his Government, too, was overthrown.

The new Australian Premier, Labour's bespectacled John Curtin, gave Churchill more cause for hope. On assuming office he had made two top-level requests: an increase in Australia's petrol supplies and the dispatch of a first-class battleship to the Pacific.

Although Churchill bore more than his fair share of the blame for the decision that followed, this request for a battleship did originate with Curtin – who might still be prevailed on to retain those brigades in Tobruk. Accordingly – "in spite of protests from the Commander-in-Chief, Home Fleet" – Churchill reluctantly agreed to humour the Australians – "we are sending forthwith our newest battleship, *Prince of Wales*, to join *Repulse* in Indian Ocean."

If he had hoped for a benign turn-about in Canberra as a result, he had hoped in vain. On 15 October, Curtin proved as adamant as his predecessor: the brigades were to be withdrawn from Tobruk. Now Churchill's sense of black frustration was complete. "We are at war with almost every country," he was to rage bitterly to Beaverbrook, "including Australia!"

*

On the eastern front, *Fähnrich* Peter Neumann knew a constant turmoil of emotions. One day he would be fully convinced that the S.S. mission was just. On the next, agonising doubts would assail him all over again.

At Lvov, in the Ukraine, on 3 July, despite the pall of filth and decay hanging over the city, Neumann felt better. In their pell-mell retreat, the Red Army had spared nothing and nobody. Bodies of Russian and Polish "political" prisoners – often men and women jailed for being late for work – lay where they had been gunned down all over the courtyard of the N.K.V.D. prison. Fleeing in trucks and carts, the soldiers had opened fire on every building indiscriminately. In the silent streets, relatives were rummaging among the dead, and blue-black clouds of flies rose from the piled corpses.

No longer would he feel such remorse in liquidating Russians, Neumann told himself confidently.

But at Zhitomir, on 28 July, he again had cause to wonder. By degrees, as the Viking Division adapted to its executioner's role, the screw was tightening: now not only Commissars but all Jewish functionaries, civil or military, were to be shot without trial. Shocked, Neumann watched his fellow ensign Karl von Reckner, empty his Mauser without compunction into a group of labour camp officials. Was this the same Karl he had once watched as a schoolboy, playing softball on the sands by the *Aussen-Alster*, Hamburg? His finger had not even wavered on the trigger.

As the division forged deeper into the Ukraine the war of nerves was stepped up. In some ruined villages, every object remaining was a potential booby-trap – the interior of a samovar, a vodka bottle, a bucket suspended in a well. Neumann and the others learned to toss a handful of grenades into any building before entering it, triggering off the explosions.

Always they were conscious of the partisan presence, whole battalions of eyes noting their passage, yet always they were invisible. In the forest of Krasnaja, their TCVs, jolting over ruts and potholes, covered every road for a radius of twenty miles and found no one. But the partisans were there. On 23 September, the bodies of three S.S. sentries were recovered from the woods. One man's face was no more than an obscene wound; after beating him to death and bayoneting him the partisans had rammed a tree branch into his mouth.

In the hamlet of Krasnaja, *Untersturmführer* (Second-Lieutenant) van Kolden, a thick-set Dutchman of the Nordland Regiment, had assembled the entire population in the market square. In front of them, screened by grey blankets, lay the German dead. One of the S.S. men was sobbing quietly.

Van Kolden was holding himself in check, but not for long. "Walk them past it," he ordered two of his men, "let them taste and smell it, so that they can see what might happen to them." Then anger, like a haemorrhage, flooded his mind, and he seized a machine pistol from a non-com. "What *is* going to happen to them," he screamed, opening fire.

Chaos descended. The Russians in the front rank slumped and fell like straw men. The dusty expanse of the market square was suddenly a sea of shabbily-clad peasants, fighting to get away. Almost every S.S. man present had lost control. The hammering of machine-pistols was unbearably loud, drowning out the terrified screams of women and children. Great splashes of blood stained the ochre-coloured ground; a suffocating cloud of black smoke was rising from the thatched roofs.

Neumann realised that all semblance of discipline had gone: they were beasts and nothing could check them. Nonetheless he must try. He saw *Rottenführer* Libesis, propped stupefied against a wall, swaying from side to side as if he was drunk, and he shouted urgently into the corporal's ear: "Libesis, you must help me to stop this horror" But above the shattering barrage of sound Libesis could barely hear him. "Nothing to be done," he mumbled stupidly.

Neumann expostulated, "But these people didn't kill the men on guard duty."

"Doesn't matter," Libesis answered, like a man in a trance, "They could have saved themselves by giving us information. They must pay."

Neumann could bear it no longer; the screams seemed to be exploding inside his head. Grabbing his Mauser, he hastened on to *Unterscharführer* Diekener of his own platoon. The Sergeant's whole face was scored with blood-red streaks: the scars left by women's fingernails.

"Diekener," he shouted, "call your men to order. This frightful butchery is unworthy of the uniform we wear!" Diekener's response was no more than an ugly grin. "You're an S.S. man now, *Fähnrich*. It's your pals that have been butchered."

Neumann was beside himself: "I shall have you sent to punishment camp for refusing to obey an order." The threat was like a cold douche, bringing Diekener to his senses. "*Entschuldigen, Herr Fähnrich, zu Befehl*" (I'm sorry, sir. As you say, sir!), he answered, with a sharp click of the heels. But no one heeded the long blast that Diekener blew on his whistle.

In a black rage, *Untersturmführer* von Kolden came striding up. For a moment he listened incredulously to Neumann's stammered protests then cut him brutally short: "Massacre? You haven't seen anything yet, you poor bloody little *Fähnrich*. If we don't teach these damned moujiks a few sharp lessons . . . listen, Neumann . . . in war a soldier kills and enjoys killing."

A sudden hush had fallen on the market square. All firing now ceased. Dazedly, like men deep in shock, the S.S. soldiers were staring at the piles of black-clad bodies, at the blood staining their hands, as if somehow striving to establish a connection. A woman kneeled beside a corpse, her arms raised to heaven, howling terribly like a dog.

Truck horns were sounding urgently and whistles shrilled: it was time to be gone.

Neumann slumped at the wayside, his head in his hands. Kill or be killed, he thought desperately, but where did the true justice lie? Assuming, of course, that such a thing even existed.

*

Not all were so squeamish. In the wake of the advancing armies, 3,000 black-clad S.S. men, travelling in trucks that bore the sign of the swastika, were embarking on a holocaust. For the first time in history murder

178

was being planned on an assembly line basis: they were hunting five million Jews spread over a million square kilometres of territory, a sword of genocide sweeping from east to west.

As far back as January, twelve top S.S. leaders had answered a summons from *Reichsführer* Heinrich Himmler, the mild-mannered ex-chicken farmer heading the Gestapo and S.S., to convene at Wewelsburg, an unique replica of a medieval castle near Paderborn, Westphalia. Among those present were Reinhard Heydrich, chief of the Reich Security Main Office (R.S.H.A.), S.S. General Karl Wolff, and *Obergruppenführer* (Lieutenant-General) Erich von dem Bach-Zelewski, an expert on partisan warfare.

As yet there had been no official announcement regarding Barbarossa, until Himmler revealed bluntly that the Führer had decided to strike a mortal blow against Russia. "The purpose of the campaign", he told them, as Zelewski was to recall it, "is to reduce the Slav populations by thirty millions." His precedent, according to Wolff, was the Spanish Inquisition – "what the Jesuits did for Rome, the S.S. must do for the Nazi Party!"

In the weeks that followed, Heydrich and Zelewski were busy men, but in the meantime Himmler had succeeded in his quest for someone who, in his own words, was "superhuman-inhuman" – a man devoid of every humane reflex. Located at 116, Kurfürstenstrasse, Berlin, as head of Department B4, the Section for Jewish Affairs, this was Adolf Eichmann, a man who so hated Jews that as a teenager he had learned Yiddish and Hebrew, the better to wage war against them. It was Eichmann who now took charge of Aktion 14 F 13, the "final solution" of the Jewish question.

This most secret objective of Hitler's career was never committed to paper by the Führer himself. Only on 3 March, weeks before his notorious "Commissar" directive to his generals, did he dictate to Jodl: "The Bolshevist-Jewish intelligentsia must be eliminated, as having been the 'oppressor' up to now." No hint was given that the life of every Jew would be forfeit – although by 16 July, conferring with Göring and others, Hitler was plainly aware that mass executions were under way. These were necessary, he maintained, to pacify the vast terrain – "shoot everyone who shows a wry face".

By April, the leaders of the four *Einsatzgruppe* (Action Groups) had been briefed as to the targets they sought: all male Jews, Communist functionaries, "second-class Asiatics" and "gypsies". No group must operate within 200 kilometres of an Army headquarters, in case the fighting men got wind of it, but their territories were clearly defined. On 15 July, when they went into action, Group A, under *Brigadeführer* (Brigadier) Walter Stahlecker spread a reign of terror through Latvia, Lithuania and Estonia, Group B, under Arthur Nebe, operated between the Baltic states and the Ukraine: Dr Otto Rasch's Group C had the Ukraine as their killing-ground, while Otto Ohlendorf's Group D worked between Bessarabia and the Crimea.

The tally of their dead beggared description. By April, 1942, Stahlecker's group had eliminated 249,420 victims, three-quarters of them by gassing. In this grisly numbers game, the other groups, by comparison, lagged far behind – 95,000 destroyed by Rasch's men, 90,000 by Ohlendorf's, some 45,000 by Nebe's – but of six million Jews for whom a "final solution" was found, two million were to meet their fate at the hands of the *Einsatzgruppen*.

They did not die in dignity. "S.S. drove the people along the road at a running pace," testified one eye-witness to the massacre of 5,000 Jews at Rovno, Poland, "hitting them until they reached the waiting freight train. Coach after coach was filled as the screaming of women and children and the cracking of whips and rifle shots resounded unceasingly. Since families or groups had barricaded themselves in strong buildings, where the doors could not be forced, they were blown open with handgrenades. . . . Younger people tried to get across the railway tracks and over a small river to get away. Part of the area was illuminated by rockets. . . . All through the night these beaten, hounded and wounded people moved along. . . . Women carried their dead children in their arms, children pulled and dragged their dead parents by their arms and legs down the road towards the train. . . . Again and again the cries 'Open the door, open the door' echoed through the ghetto."

No one was immune. "I saw dozens of corpses of all ages and both sexes," the same witness recalled. "Pieces of clothing, shoes, stockings, jackets, hats, coats, were lying in the streets. At the corner of a house lay a baby less than a year old with its skull crushed. Blood and brains were scattered over the house wall. The child was dressed only in a little shirt. The S.S. commander, Pütz, was walking up and down a row of about eighty to a hundred male Jews, who were crouching on the ground. He had a heavy dog-whip in his hand."

All over Russia, as September wore on, the same nightmare was re-enacted. Now 1941 saw the true nadir of World War Two, a world unknown to Afrika Korps men and Luftwaffe fighter pilots, a world in which ideological aims constituted an absolute. One unwilling witness, Major Rösler, commanding the 528th Infantry Regiment, always recalled how a fierce fusillade of rifle fire aroused him in his billet at Zhitomir. Hastening to investigate, he chanced on a pit brimming with Jewish bodies of all ages and both sexes – among them an old white-bearded man clutching a cane in his left hand. Horrified to see he was still breathing, Rösler ordered a policeman to shoot him. Smiling, the man shook his head: "I have already shot him seven times in the stomach. He can die on his own now".

It was no lone example. In their fearful zeal, the *Einsatzgruppen* seemed to vie with one another for mindless bestiality. Russian Jews were tortured with red-hot iron bars; eyes were gouged out, stomachs ripped open, feet, hands, fingers, ears and noses hacked off. One Russian battalion commander and his Commissar were nailed to stakes by the arms and legs before five-point stars were carved in their bodies with knives.

In this catalogue of horrors, one of the worst of all the massacres was perpetrated by *Standartenführer* Paul Blobel, a tall bearded one-time architect attached to Action Group C. On 29 September, after Kiev, the beautiful capital of the Ukraine had fallen, almost 34,000 Jews were herded into a sandy gorge called Babyi-Yar, the Ravine of the Women, on the outskirts of the city. An old woman guarding a cemetery, M. S. Loutsenko, remembered that day: "Right there they were laying them down . . . and they were screaming . . . Mother of God, how they were screaming . . . and they were smashing their skulls with shovels".

Unknown to most Germans, mass genocide was already a fact of life inside the Third Reich. Every householder knew – many of them with shame – that the Jews had long been targets for discrimination: special ration cards, freckled with tiny "Js" denied them the purchase of fresh vegetables, meat and chocolate. From September on, they were further distinguished by a yellow Star of David, the size of a side-plate, sewn on their clothing; from October, all family allowances and sickness benefits were revoked. The first stage had been deprivation; the next was deportation.

It began, on a gigantic scale, in mid-October. From all the main-line city stations, Berlin and Hamburg, Munich and Frankfurt-am-Main, goods trains loaded with human freight, 1,000 strong, began heading north; 20,000 souls were to leave on 15 October alone. Their destination was the ghetto at Lodz, but soon more trains still were leaving for other ghettos: Warsaw, Kovno, Minsk and Riga. Two years earlier, Eichmann had even toyed with the concept of a mighty ghetto for 4 million Jews under an S.S. police government on the island of Madagascar, but that time was long past. The ghettos had replaced that fancy, but these, too, were no more than a transitional phase before the real slaughter began. "The faster we get rid of them the better," exulted Eichmann's aid, Rolf Günther.

In the contemporary documentation, euphemisms abounded, a strange example of high-level military schizophrenia. On 31 July, Göring, as chairman of the Ministerial Defence Council, sent a jargon-clogged memo to Heydrich, ordering him to "prepare a master plan for the measures – organisational, concrete and material – preparatory to the implementation of the sought-for final solution". "Special treatment" or "emigration" stood in for evacuation and deportation; "disposition" was, in truth, "extermination". And the means for this had long been at hand.

All through 1940 and 1941, the concentration camps had been growing in number, replacing the onetime labour and detention camps until they were thirty in all: names that would live in infamy, like Auschwitz, housing up to 100,000 victims over fifteen square miles, Bergen-Belsen, Chelmno, Neuengamme, Birkenau and Treblinka. The pattern for all of them had been set in the summer of 1941, when Eichmann called on Auschwitz' commandant, Rudolf Höss, to discuss practicable ways and means of eliminating not only every German Jew but suspect Poles, "idlers", gypsies, psychopaths with criminal records and many dissident clergymen. That could only be achieved by gassing, Höss ventured. Given suitable gas-proofed premises, he thought it possible to dispose of 800 people at a time.

The gas in question was Cyclon B, a prussic acid preparation used to destroy vermin, and, mercifully, few of those who succumbed to its fumes had any inkling as to their fate. At Auschwitz and other camps, a polite fiction was maintained; all new arrivals must shower and undergo a delousing process. Even close at hand, the gas chambers, labelled BATHS, looked altogether innocuous; the manicured lawns and trim flower-borders that masked their roofs also hid the mushroom vents which housed the gas crystals. Only sprightly music, selections from *The Merry Widow* and *The Tales of Hoffmann,* soothed them on their way, played by an orchestra of pretty young girls in white blouses and navy-blue skirts.

Only when they had undressed and the massive doors of the bath chamber slid shut did the more perceptive note that the floor had no drains, that no water spouted from the overhead showers. Then, as the gas came hissing from the vents, mass panic set in, but by now it was too late. Thirty minutes later it was all over. The bodies had ceased to writhe, the gold teeth and the women's hair, which Himmler had specified as "strategic material", had been removed by special commando teams, the last journey to the crematoria had begun.

"I began to hate the Jews," one Hebrew teenager wrote feelingly about this time, "Not only the Orthodox, but all of them. I hated their names, their faces, their manner of speech, their humour and their nervous diligence . . .

"I hated the Jews because I hated the sight of death."

*

A golden opportunity had been lost, and every soldier serving on the eastern front knew it. The chance of dealing Russian Communism a mortal blow and toppling Josef Stalin's regime had gone irretrievably.

From the first, Hitler's fatal error had been to look on Russia as one nation – a homogeneous race of despised *untermenschen*. The truth was that 187 million Russians were made up of 170 different races speaking 140 different tongues – among them embittered ethnic minorities like the Balts, the Ukrainians and the Cossacks, who remembered that 20 million had died in the purges since the October Revolution.

The first German troops to cross the border were overwhelmed by their reception. In Kiev, which fell on 19 September – ten days before the enormity of Babyi-Yar – Reinhold Pabel, who entered with the 6th Division, watched with astonishment as an old white-bearded patriarch draped a huge roll of unused street-car tickets round a sergeant's neck, in the style of a Hawaiian garland. Another approached the first car-load of German officers bearing a tray with a loaf of bread and a salt-shaker – the traditional Slavic symbol of welcome. Families vied with one another to bear the conquering soldiers home for a bath and a meal; huge posters proclaiming HITLER THE LIBERATOR loomed everywhere.

"The people look on us as liberators," Guderian wrote home to his wife, Gretel. "It is to be hoped they will not be disappointed."

Many top commanders shared this hope. Von Rundstedt's first action in the Ukraine was to restore the churches to the people; soon ikons and chalices which had been hidden from the Commissars gleamed once again on the altars, and in the eighteenth-century church at Poltava, when von Rundstedt attended Divine Service, *Te Deums* resounded again from the old walls. At Borisov, north-east of Minsk, when the *Wehrmacht* refurbished the Orthodox Church, until then a Bolshevik store, thousands crowded the square and streets for the opening service; von Bock, arriving from Army Group Centre, passed over a carpet of clean white sand into a nave decked out with green branches.

On his own initiative, von Bock had already taken steps to harness this chain of good-will. Attached to his headquarters with the rank of Captain was a 45-year-old Riga businessman, Wilfred Strik-Strikfeldt who had served in the Tsarist Army. What Bock proposed, using Strikfeldt as his liaison officer, was a scheme that had the full approval of Göbbels, for one: the creation of a Russian Liberation Army aligned with a puppet government modelled on Vichy lines.

Plainly, when 11,000 Red Army men deserted overnight from one assault group alone, this was fertile ground. In the space of months, Strikfeldt had enlisted 800,000 Red Army personnel – "our Ivans" – in a war against Josef Stalin.

Another visionary with high hopes for the future was Alfred Rosenberg, a leading Nazi thinker, who had been appointed Commissioner for the East European Region; he was looking, he told his staff on 20 June, to the "voluntary co-operation" of 40 million men. But this dream, like von Bock's, was to remain an illusion. On 4 August, visiting Bock's headquarters, Hitler significantly refused to receive Stikfeldt and hear his report on progress to date.

No reply was later forthcoming from the *Wolfsschanze* when von Bock passed on an offer from the city fathers of Smolensk to raise a liberation army of one million men – but a curt order was passed to the Ministry of Propaganda, forbidding Göbbels to visit the front for discussions with von Bock.

In a Russia dominated by the Third Reich such citizens as survived would serve no other function than as slave-labour for the conquerors. To elevate them to combatant status, even to educate them, would be fatal, in Hitler's view – "the people should know just enough to recognise the signs on the roads".

Thus, by perverse irony, Nazi ideology ultimately brought about the very results that it was pledged to destroy. In time the ravages of the *Einsatzgruppen* would unite the Russian people against the invader as never before. Within four years the Communist floodtide would engulf all Eastern Europe – the Baltic States, Poland, Hungary, Rumania, Bulgaria, East Germany, Czechoslovakia were all to become Soviet vassals.

A victory over Bolshevism had been thrown away.

*

It was not the only mistake to cost Hitler dear that autumn. Already, despite the doubts of many advisers, he had insisted that Russia must be invaded. He had delayed stubbornly in ordering an advance on Moscow. Now, with the collapse of the Ukraine to the south and Leningrad invested to the north, he once more switched priorities. On 26 September, he ordered a vast new offensive – Operation Typhoon, timed for 2 October – to concentrate on Moscow itself.

Only the sixty divisions required for the army of occupation in a defeated Russia had thus far been issued with winter clothing – but the new edict decreed that the *Wehrmacht* must "break the enemy on the threshold of winter".

Hitler had no plans for a winter campaign at all.

9

"Let No One Forget, Let Nothing Be Forgotten"

1 October–5 November, 1941

THE HUSHED ENCLAVE of the British Embassy in Moscow was suddenly alive with bustling urgency and rumours. Harold Elvin, now back on night duty, should long ago have retired to bed. But somehow he could not resist inventing minor chores as an excuse for lingering on all morning in the main hallway – "the world buzzed so; and was so alive".

On 28 September, a full-scale Anglo-American mission, more than forty strong, led by Lord Beaverbrook and Averell Harriman, had arrived in Moscow for talks with Stalin and Molotov. In the next three days of conferences, much that was crucial to the outcome of World War Two would be decided – and Elvin had the heady sense of living through history.

It was a delegation which the Military Mission, after kicking its heels with black frustration since 26 June, viewed with mixed feelings. From the first the Russian attitude had been one of surly suspicion – coupled with a greedy readiness to take while yielding nothing in return. "The Russian motto", Lieutenant General Mason-MacFarlane reported angrily to the War Office, "is 'give nothing at all – as slowly as possible' "; his Mission had degenerated into "an inglorious battle of wits between two powers supposedly in the position of allies". His colleagues fared no better. Laurence Cadbury, heading the Economic Mission with two oil experts to advise him, was told bluntly: "What is there to confer about? All we need from you is a supply of arms and a Second Front." Air Vice Marshal Conrad Collier, of the Air Supply Committee, had to do all his business with the Foreign Affairs Liaison Department; no one would even tell him where the Air Ministry building was located.

What were the medium frequency bands used by Russian fighters? The Russians refused to say. How did they set about tackling tanks from the air? The answer was a sullen silence. How many anti-tank guns were allotted to a division? That would depend on the type of division. For example an infantry division? That would depend on where it had to fight.

When Sir Stafford Cripps protested spiritedly to Stalin, the dictator replied sarcastically, "Is it proposed to exchange all State secrets in future?"

The Americans on the spot knew an identical problem. Ambassador Laurence Steinhardt reported to the State Department that in the course of 1940 fully 300 letters had gone unanswered by Molotov and things were little better now. American military observers had been forbidden all access to the war zone – yet a blatant request had been routed to the War Department for Soviet engineers to tour U.S. military plants. "The list of the military secrets requested itself shows very efficient espionage," commented Assistant Secretary of State Adolf A. Berle.

Into this bleak climate of mutual distrust, Beaverbrook, the go-getting Canadian newspaper proprietor, arrived like a buoyant wind from the steppes. The new Minister of Supply saw it as a hurry-up operation from the first. "If one goes to do a job like this and stays in a place more than six days you lose your authority," he told Under Secretary of State for Air Harold Balfour. To this end Beaverbrook had long decided that his mission was to be "a Christmas tree party . . . there must be no excuse for the Russians thinking they were not getting a fair share of the gifts on the tree".

"They want the moon and we haven't got it," Ismay, who made one of the party, wrote to Brooke-Popham, but all along Beaverbrook acted as if the British had. Harriman, for one, saw danger in this: "Beaverbrook was disposed to hand over every conceivable American weapon or material to the Russians without counting the cost to Britain". But Beaverbrook, far-sightedly, sensed that for the foreseeable future Britain's war-role would be mainly peripheral. In the months to come the entire war would hinge on the success or failure of Russian resistance.

If the first meeting with Stalin – at 9 p.m. on 28 September, in a second-floor office littered with brimming ashtrays, overlooking the Moscow River – was cordial enough, the second, at 7 p.m. on 29 May, reduced Beaverbrook and Harriman to "an indigo blue mood". "Unmannerly and disinterested," the dictator tossed aside letters of introduction from Roosevelt and Churchill without even glancing at them. "The paucity of your offers clearly shows that you want to see the Soviet Union defeated," he told Harriman rudely.

Not until a third meeting, on the evening of 30 September, did Stalin's mood change mercurially. "It is up to the three of us to prove Göbbels a liar," he remarked expansively, doodling red wolves on the scratch-pad before him, and it was now with some dismay that Harriman time and again heard Beaverbrook yield to the Russian front Great Britain's share of American supplies: 25,000 tons of electrolytic copper, 1,800 fighter aircraft, 2,250 tanks, 500 anti-tank guns, 23,000 tommy-guns, 27,000 tons of rubber, 250,000 greatcoats. It was small wonder that their interpreter, the former diplomat Maxim Litvinov, forgetting his humble role, bounded from his chair, crying, "Now we have won the war!"

At 6 p.m. on 1 October, the bulk of the Beaverbrook-Harriman entourage glimpsed Stalin for the first time in a strangely sybaritic setting: a pillared French-style dining room in the Kremlin, lined with banked arum lilies, its sixteen-foot high double doors inlaid with gold-leaf carving and the arms of Catherine the Great surmounted by golden cherubs. As the dictator entered, clad in a pepper-and-salt gabardine tunic buttoned to the neck, an eerie hush descended on the room. "He moved stealthily like a wild animal in search of prey," Ismay noted, but Harold Balfour was less impressed. "At first glance he looks like a typical jobbing gardener, until you look at his eyes . . . (they) bear out his name – The Man of Steel – although they twinkle kindly."

In the three and a half hour banquet which followed, a Tsarist feast in which caviar gave place to sucking pig, soup, fish and two varieties of game, those eyes rarely ceased their twinkling: Stalin was geniality itself. In the course of drinking thirty-two toasts he downed an entire bottle of champagne – an evening only marred, in Cripps' view, by Stalin's sneering reference to Roosevelt's policy of keeping out of the war "in order to be able to impose peace terms when the right moment arrived". Balfour preserved a warmer memory: at the moment he proposed a toast to the Soviet Air Force, the dictator, whose son Vasily was a pilot at Stalingrad, rose from his seat and walked heavily down the table to clink glasses with Balfour.

On the final day, 2 October, Beaverbrook, too, was in euphoric mood as the leaders gathered to sign a trade agreement in Molotov's office. Here, he wisecracked, were the seeds of a profitable business: to buy hundreds of ordinary two shilling pens and sell them at vast profit as "the genuine pen that signed the Moscow Conference Agreement". Although Litvinov achieved a passable translation, Molotov's face remained frozen: such capitalist levity was lost on him.

"Everything now depends on getting the pig to market," Beaverbrook wrote to Hopkins next day, and he was as good as his word. Back in London, where the Cabinet was dismayed to realise that Britain had been stripped to the bone, Beaverbrook now engulfed his colleagues with a flood-tide of pro-Soviet memoranda. "Surely Americans will be willing to go a bit short for Russians who are actually fighting," ran one of the more scathing, urging U.S. planes for Archangel. "We must give the Russians their daily bread," ran another, "we must take a pull at own own belts so that our friends may sit at our dinner table". He urged the Colonial Office – vainly – to strip Malaya of locomotives, the better to ship Russian supplies along the trans-Iranian railway. "You are expected to respect the production lines always and treat them as the Ark of the Covenant," he berated the Secretary of State for War, David Margesson, when delivery of 500 trucks to Russia fell behind schedule.

"The public are at last unanimous in accepting the wicked ogre of last year as the loyal friend of today," he enthused to his old friend Sir Samuel Hoare.

British manufacturers, too, were taken severely to task. Enraged to learn that a U.S. Office of Production Management team had found British machine tool factories so inefficient they were cancelling all Lend-Lease supplies until further notice, Beaverbrook summoned 200 factory chiefs to a secret session in Essex Hall, off the Strand. "This is not the easy war we had last time," he tongue-lashed them. "It is harsh and cruel and everyone of us is bound to be hurt, you, me and everybody." The time had come, he told them flatly, for British industry to put its house in order, so that America might once again ship them machine tools – for the benefit of Russia.

It was none too soon. At this same moment, on a 150-mile front defended only by 15 half-trained Soviet "armies", the Germans, like Napoleon before them, were lancing towards Moscow.

*

In those first golden days of autumn, success seemed assured. In one short day, Guderian's Panzer Group Two forged 85 miles towards Moscow; on the fourth day, Orel, 256 miles south of the capital, crumbled before the *Wehrmacht*. From 8 October, in one of the most perfect battles of encirclement in military history, the double battle of Vyazma and Bryansk, the Russians were to lose 663,000 prisoners, 12,412 tanks, and 5,412 guns. The road to Moscow had been cleared.

The advance would be a near-run thing, even so. On 6 October, as *Feldmarschall* Fedor von Bock left his command train at Smolensk, he noted that the Russian sky was now leaden grey; a chill and ominous wind was blowing from the north. By afternoon, a cold rain was falling on the northern sectors of Army Group Centre's front. Towards evening, the temperature dropped still further; the rain was turning to snow.

Following an agitated telephone call from Guderian, Bock teletyped the Army High Command: where were his long-promised winter supplies? The reply was ambivalent at best: if Bock attended to his responsibilities, the supply officers would attend to theirs.

In the lower echelons, a certain unease prevailed. In the 3rd Battalion of Infantry Regiment 18, *Assistenzart* Henrich Haape noted with dismay the absence of winter clothing – and that as his unit thrust on for Sychevka, the trucks were churning the snow ever deeper into the moist rich earth. Soon men were struggling in black mud up to their knees.

"The mud seemed bottomless," Haape noted; there was good reason for the soldiers to christen it "buna" – synthetic rubber – for often it sucked the calf boots from their legs. Now the pace was slowed again, from eight miles a day to three. Supply columns could no longer reach the front; petrol for the stranded panzers was brought by huge cargo-carrying gliders towed by Heinkels, crash-landing near the lines. The thirty daily train loads of supplies on which Bock depended were no longer forthcoming; hot food was now the exception, not the rule. Awarded the Iron Cross First Class for devotion to duty, Haape celebrated with a hot meal he would long remember: potatoes French-fried in castor oil.

Despite this snail's pace, the mood in Moscow was now frantic. On 7 October, Marshal Semeon Timoshenko and his deputy, General Eremenko, were relieved of their commands; with the realisation that the road to Moscow was virtually undefended, Stalin flung the bitingly-sarcastic General Georgi Zhukov into the breach as commander of Western Army Group.

All through the night of 7 October, Zhukov toured the Western Army front – intently studying a map with the aid of a flashlight, fighting off fatigue by stopping the car for 300-yard jogging sessions. The situation was desperate; to cover the 135-mile Moscow front Zhukov had a total of 45 battalions against the 150 he needed. But Zhukov would contenance no strategic withdrawal. "He ordered us to stand to the death," General Konstantin Rokossovsky, commanding the 16th Army, recalled, "without retreating a step."

A thousand miles away, in Tokyo, one man now contrived to swing the balance: the master-spy Richard Sorge, whose earlier warnings concerning Barbarossa had gone for nothing. Now, as if by way of atonement, Stalin belatedly gave credence to the tenor of Sorge's recent reports: Japan had no plans to attack Siberia, as Hitler had urged, but instead was contemplating an attack on Britain and the United States. Thus near Borodino, 62 miles from Moscow, where Napoleon had fought another battle as bloody, the *Wehrmacht*, on 14 October, met the first of 30 Siberian divisions – the 32nd Rifle – that Stalin was transferring from the Far East. They died where they stood, but they, and the vast sea of black mud, bought time for Moscow.

It was as well, for a wave of defeatism had swept the city – heightened by the funeral pyre of black smoke from the Kremlin's chimneys as secret papers were burned, the news that Lenin's coffin had been removed to safety from the mausoleum in Red Square. "The maddened Fascist beast is threatening Moscow", *Pravda* trumpeted, on 16 October, but three days later the Stavka, the State Defence Committee, in declaring a state of siege, nipped the panic in the bud. More than 200,000 Muscovites were called to the colours, given twenty days field training, then shipped to the front. More than half a million old men, women and teenagers were mobilised to build a second line of defence: 1,400 pill-boxes, 60 miles of anti-tank ditches, more than 5,000 miles of infantry trenches.

By mid-October, Moscow was a city on the move: almost 500 factory complexes and their 200,000 workers were moving house in 71,000 freight cars, to the safety of the Urals and Siberia. Mile after mile of boxcars with little smokestacks, housing the workers, and flat cars transporting lathes, generators and stamping mills were hammering east over the trans-Siberian railway, to the floodlit factory towns beyond the range of the German bombers: Chelyabinsk, in the southern Urals, Sverdlovsk, where Tsar Nicholas and his family had met their death. Almost two million people were leaving the capital – among them Harold Elvin.

It was on 15 October that the young night watchman got his marching orders: all foreign embassies were to transfer to Kuibyshev, once Samara, the terminus of the ancient caravan route from India and China, 525 miles to the east. It was one of the most hectic days that Elvin could ever remember; before even packing his bags he had to cart sack after sack of documents to the Embassy's incinerator, working against time.

At 9 p.m., picking his way through the teeming chaos of Moscow's Kazan Railway Station, Elvin was thoughtful. Under the soaring arches of the waiting hall, every inch of floor space was choked with women, children, soldiers and militia. The air was thick with mingled odours: woollen shawls and poverty, damp sheepskin, human breath rank with herring and chopped onion. But it was the contrast between the refugees' lot and his own that came home to him now.

At his feet were three suitcases crammed with clothes and books, but Elvin had left much more behind: two armchairs, a second-hand piano. But the armchairs and pianos of these people were already piled in the streets as barricades. The shabby kaftans and the rag coats were all the clothes they had. Back in London, Elvin had a home to call his own, but this station floor was their only home, the bundles they carried the sole furnishings: the woman with her one electric kettle, the old man with his iron bedstead.

Tonight, he would be out of it, Elvin thought, moving 500 miles nearer to safety, but where would these people be? Perhaps crammed with dozens of others into an open truck meant for two horses, blanketed by drifting snow, with no lavatories, only the loaves they had brought for sustenance. So did they resent him, warm in his eight-guinea overcoat, favoured as less than 500 people in this territory of 187 millions were favoured?

They would be justified, surely, in tearing him asunder – and didn't he, in his heart of hearts, know that they would?

Of course, once in Kuibyshev he would feel differently, Elvin knew. In Kuibyshev, the painful multitude would have faded from his vision. There would come a way – given time – to square it all with his conscience.

*

190

By October, four Russian cities – all of them under siege – loomed large in the world's headlines. How steadfastly they held out was a yardstick for the future, a token of the collective will to resist.

Inevitably, most attention focussed on Moscow, where Stalin and the Politburo were staying put, but other cities knew greater hardship. Sevastopol, on the Black Sea, early adapted to siege conditions: from 30 October onwards, thousands moved underground, to the onetime champagne cellars of Tsarist days, to set up munitions workshops and tailors' co-operatives off the narrow warren of passages christened "Trade Union Lane" and "Internationale Street". Here they held out for eight months, sustained by a communal kitchen, a first-aid post, a crèche, a nursery, a school, a cinema and a lecture and games room.

Two hundred and fifty miles north, in the port of Odessa, the citizens displayed an almost Anglo-Saxon phlegm; already 86,000 troops had left the city but despite a nightly bombardment of 2,000-lb parachute mines life by day went on much as usual. Housewives in summer dresses, armed with string bags, still went shopping for cabbages in the open air market; later, sitting comfortably on their porches, they converted old caviar tins into land-mines before strolling with their husbands to the defence posts at the city limits. Outside the telegraph office a placard set the placid keynote: "We deliver cables to all parts of the Soviet Union but for the moment we cannot absolutely guarantee punctual delivery". The stoicism was in vain; by 16 October, in a daring Dunkirk-style operation executed by night, the last 35,000 troops were shipped out to reinforce Sevastopol.

No Russian city faced a greater endurance test than Leningrad. The white city of Peter the Great – once known as Petrograd, once as St Petersburg – had always been an unique metropolis: the city of Pavlov and Njinsky, Dostoevsky and Pushkin. Here in the network of canals and castles – "a stone labyrinth", Trotsky had called it – offset by the glory of the Winter Palace and the Hermitage Museum, great art and architecture had flowered but so, too, nourished by poverty and oppression, had the Russian Revolution.

For this reason alone, Hitler had decreed that the "Venice of the North", which was equally the cradle of Bolshevism, must be obliterated from the earth.

From 8 September on, Leningrad had effectively been isolated from the world behind 5,000 pill boxes, 480 miles of anti-tank batteries, 17,874 miles of trenches, besieged by Von Leeb's 700,000-strong Army Group North. As early as 21 August, the alarm had been sounded, "The enemy is at the gates!"; the defensive Luga Line, which followed the Luga River, as close as forty miles southwest of the city was crumbling. Now the biggest guns in all Europe were trained on the city from six great artillery investments: cannon from Skoda, Krupp and Schneider, railway guns of

191

calibres as high as 420 mm, firing 900-kilo shells over distances of up to 31,000 yards. At least 100,000 of these shells were to destroy 3,174 buildings.

Ahead of the citizens stretched 900 days of a like ordeal.

On 9 September, when Dmitri Pavlov, a dark vigorous 36-year-old supply official despatched by Moscow, reached Leningrad airport in his DC-3, he found the city's reserves in sorry shape. To support more than three million inhabitants and 200,000 Red Army defenders, Leningrad had just 33 days supply of meat, 35 days of grain and flour, 30 days of cereals. The only supply route open lay across Lake Ladoga, the huge body of water to the north-east – but there were no boats, piers, road and rail facilities or warehouses to accumulate substantial supplies.

Worse, on the very day that Pavlov arrived, German incendiaries fired the vast Badaev warehouse, Leningrad's four-acre larder, which had housed almost all of the city's flour, butter and sugar. The time was not far distant when men and women would unashamedly grub at the charred earth to salvage grains of melted sugar and chocolate.

But there was no thought of surrender. For almost two and a half centuries Leningrad had been a proud city, its cultural heritage derived from Paris and Rome, disdainful of uncouth, provincial Moscow. Time and again in the months that followed Pavlov was forced to reduce the rations, until by 20 November no heavy worker could expect more than five ounces of bread a day. But they would not yield. Rather than surrender their city to Hitler, Admiral Vladimir Tributs, commander of the Baltic Fleet, had orders to blow it up – with thousands of buildings mined to explode at the touch of a plunger.

Hunger became a preoccupation ousting all others. Dogs and cats went early to the pot; by November, pet-owners were as extinct a species as their pets. The guinea pigs and rabbits vanished from their cages at the Erisman Hospital. Some scavenged in the Botanical Gardens, rooting up valuable flower bulbs to eat. Others were reduced to eating leather, tree-bark, carpenter's glue, even lipstick and face powder. Hunger allowed no choice.

To appease their craving, Pavlov showed rare ingenuity. To combat scurvy, fruiterers were instructed to extract Vitamin C from pine needles, thirty tons of infusion per day. A nauseating if nutritious jelly was compounded from 2,000 tons of sheep guts, spiked with cloves to disguise the smell. Edible cellulose and chaff helped stretch the bread ration still further.

In November, the deaths began: 11,085 deaths from dystrophy were recorded for this month alone. Of Leningrad's three million inhabitants, at least a million would die before this siege had ended. "Today it is so simple to die", a housewife, Yelena Skryabina, recorded in her diary, "you just begin to lose interest, then you lie on the bed and you never again get up."

192

Whatever the cost to their souls, some were determined to survive. In the Sennaya (Haymarket), the infamous slum haunted by pimps and peddlers, where Dostoevsky had written *Crime and Punishment*, men and women with fine rosy faces were known to feast covertly on meat patties made from human flesh.

Soon the bright red and yellow sleds of the children began to appear, narrow sleds, their runners squeaking everywhere on the broad boulevards. There were no more automobiles in the city; the sleds had been brought into use to transport the dead.

The bodies lay everywhere – not only in their beds but in the streets and the yards, inside trolley buses that had frozen in their tracks in the heart of the city. Often they lay there for days at a time. When the snow came to carpet the streets many disappeared altogether – only to re-emerge from their shrouds of ice when the sun brought a sharp spring thaw.

It was the coldest winter that Leningrad had ever known. Even in the hospital wards, which lacked both electricity and heating, the temperature never rose above 35 degrees Fahrenheit. In apartment houses, where bombardment had broken eighty per cent of all windows, it was worse. Water pipes froze, then burst. At least 10,000 wooden houses were torn down for firewood. Most citizens went to bed wearing both topcoats and gloves. "Even the tears froze within the people of Leningrad," one survivor recalled.

Yet life of a sort went on among the ruins. On the night of 19 September, the composer Dmitri Shostakovich, invited three friends to his fifth-floor apartment on Skorokhod Ulitsa to hear the opening movements of his uncompleted Seventh Symphony, the "Leningrad" Symphony. As he launched into the Second Movement, the air-raid siren sounded, but defiantly, to the crashing counterpoint of bombs and anti-aircraft fire, Shostakovich played on.

Only years later did he reveal that the anger and anguish exploding from every chord was prompted as much by his revulsion against the Kremlin's reign of terror as by Hitler's onslaught – "it's not about Leningrad under siege, it's about the Leningrad that Stalin destroyed and Hitler merely finished off".

Most theatres were still packed out, though to beat the nightly air-raid siren all performances were timed for 4 p.m.: *La Dame Aux Camellias* enjoyed as long a run as Tchaikovsky's *Eugene Onegin*. At one theatre, where the last act of Shakespeare's *Othello* was cut short by the siren, first-timers crowded backstage after the all-clear to ask the cast: "Did Desdemona get killed – and was Iago found out?"

On 18 November, a frail hope dawned for the first time since the blockade began. A small reconnaissance party organised by Andrei Zhdanov, the Leningrad party chief, set off on foot across ice-bound Lake Ladoga, followed cautiously by a man on horseback. What they

193

found excited them profoundly: the ice was now five inches thick, strong enough to bear horse-drawn sleds with light loads. But four days later, a truck column was to make it, returning with 33 tons of supplies. What all Leningrad came to know as "The Road of Life" was achieving a tenuous reality.

It was 237 miles long and in places 80 miles wide and it terminated at the railheads of Podborove and Zabore. Only much later, in January, did the ice freeze to a depth of three feet, enough to bear the weight of fully-loaded trucks. For the most part, until the city was relieved in January, 1944, it was a team of 350 horsemen who made the trip, sharing their bread with their horses as they rode. At best they could bring in 361 tons a day against the 2,000 needed, but what mattered to Leningrad was that they tried.

Long after, the courage of those who held out was to be enshrined in a tribute from the poet, Olga Berggolts, etched on a wall in the city's Piskarevsky Cemetery:

> We cannot number the noble
> Ones who lie beneath the eternal granite,
> But of those honoured by this stone
> Let no one forget, let nothing be
> forgotten

*

The stubbornness of the Russian resistance was not lost on the world – particularly on the German home front.

Ironically, it was Hitler himself who drew attention to their valour – by a stunt which Göbbels was to describe as "the worst mistake he had ever come across in propaganda". On 9 October, the Reich Press Chief, Dr Otto Dietrich, called a special noonday Press conference in the red plush theatre hall of the Ministry of Propaganda. To the baffled foreign correspondents who attended, Dietrich announced that as of this moment the Russians were finished, locked in two German steel pockets before Moscow – "on that, gentlemen, I stake my whole journalistic experience!"

A tidal wave of euphoria followed. All over Germany the huge red headlines of the Nazi party's official newspaper *Der Völkischer Beobachter* proclaimed: THE GREAT HOUR HAS COME! THE EASTERN CAMPAIGN HAS ENDED! In Berlin, an excited butcher hailed every bystander into his shop to dole out free gifts of sausages. In Baarz's beer-hall, behind Unter den Linden, weeping customers rose to sing *Deutschland über Alles*. Wreaths of roses were hung on every tank in sight. Bookshops broke out with a rash of Russian grammars.

In fact, Hitler's sole purpose in ordering the announcement had been to apply pressure on an indecisive Japan: if they wanted to acquire Siberian territory, now was the time to join in the war. Hence Dietrich's briefing: to signal a victory-that-never-was in the east.

The result was a bitter backlash of disillusion. A cynical public noted that the *Sondermeldung* special High Command victory broadcasts – were now invoked even for one-horse Russian villages absent from any map. Newspaper sales slumped by 40 per cent; now the people listened more attentively to the ticking clock featured by the B.B.C.'s Foreign Service, the German voice that murmured after every seventh tick, "Every seven seconds a German dies in Russia. Is it your husband? Is it your son? Is it your brother?". For Leningrad and Sebastopol were still holding out, and each week the letters returned from the front stamped in red ink GEFALLEN were increasing.

The lesson was being taken boldly to heart: Hitler was no longer the invincible force of 1940. Even Turkey, which in June had signed a treaty with Germany, despite an already existing Anglo-Turkish alliance, was drawing apart. Although under relentless pressure from Hitler's economic negotiator in the Balkans, Dr Karl Clodius, to ship valuable chrome to Germany, Numan Menemencioglu, of the Turkish Foreign Office, was stalling adeptly. The previous trade agreement with Britain, he explained blandly, was the stumbling block; it was valid until 1943.

Thus the final German-Turkish dinner, at Karpiç's restaurant in Ankara, where champagne was priced at £35 a bottle, was a glum affair. Ambassador Franz von Papen and Clodius were visibly smarting at that day's final rebuff. Plainly German stock was reaching a low ebb; the stalemate on the eastern front was making its mark.

The evening came to an end finally, and now Karpiç's dance musicians seized their cue. As the German delegation, headed by von Papen, filed dourly from the restaurant, the orchestra swung of one accord into a time-honoured favourite, "I Can't Give You Anything But Love, Baby".

*

In the North Atlantic, the long cold war was suddenly hotting up. The camouflage of U.S. neutrality was wearing paper-thin; "all measures short of war" had become a shooting war.

Thursday 4 September marked a turning-point in U.S. naval history. At 8.40 a.m. on that day, the warship U.S.S. *Greer* was proceeding at a steady $17\frac{1}{2}$ knots on the Iceland mail run, when a British naval plane, patrolling overhead, signalled the captain, Lieutenant-Commander Laurence H. Frost, that a U-Boat was lurking in her vicinity. Promptly *Greer* began an erratic zig-zag, increased speed and went to general quarters, maintaining sound contact with the submarine for three hours. The pilot asked whether *Greer* planned to attack, but Frost's reply was negative. After dropping depth charges at random the British plane retired.

The "incident" the U.S. Navy had so long awaited was suddenly established fact. Stung, the U-Boat lashed out indiscriminately; the white wake of a torpedo streaked towards the little destroyer. Miraculously dodging first one, then two torpedoes, the *Greer* let fly with depth charges. At latitude 62° 45'N, longitude 27° 37'W, the sea was suddenly boiling like a vortex as America entered World War Two.

Five days later, after *Greer* had safely reached Iceland, Roosevelt gave Hitler due warning. In a Fireside Chat that became known as the "shoot-on-sight" speech, he declared resolutely, "We have sought no shooting war with Hitler. We do not seek it now. But . . . when you see a rattlesnake poised to strike, you do not wait until he has struck before you crush him. . . . From now on, if German or Italian vessels enter the waters, the protection of which is necessary for American defence, they do so at their own peril."

It was a speech which bitterly disappointed both allies and interventionists alike. From Pretoria, Field Marshal Jan Smuts demanded of Eden: "One wonders what stronger situation he is looking forward to. If he is determined to leave the initiative of entering the war to Germany, he may be disappointed". Roosevelt was unperturbed. "He said that if he asked for a declaration of war, he wouldn't get it and opinion would swing against him," Halifax reported to Churchill, "declarations of war were . . . out of fashion." But "provided he put the right label on the bottle, it might not be too difficult to get acceptance of anything he wanted".

When David (later Lord) Eccles, of the Ministry of Economic Warfare, urged a more belligerent course on the President, Roosevelt was less circumspect: "You might as well ask me to piss into the wind".

For Roosevelt saw the dichotomy clearly: while 70 per cent of Americans wished to break Hitler, 70 per cent equally wanted to stay clear of war at all costs. Theirs was still a land of peace and plenty: an August move by Secretary of the Interior Harold Ickes to conserve gasoline by locking all filling-station pumps twelve hours a day provoked savage hostility. Returning from vacation, Ickes found his entire backyard piled with spoiled cabbages and dead cats.

"If Hitler makes a peace offer," Ickes noted in his diary, "it is going to make a very difficult domestic situation. Americans want war so little . . . we are in an age when we are more interested in movies and the radio and baseball and automobiles than in the fundamental verities of life."

Even so, some of Roosevelt's Cabinet were standing up to be counted and voice the President's unspoken thoughts – none more stridently than his doughty Republican Secretary of the Navy, Frank Knox. "The time to use our Navy to clear the Atlantic of the German menace is at hand," he told one Boston audience, prompting a delighted reaction from Supreme

Court Justice Felix Frankfurter: "When you're impeached, can I leave the Bench and become one of your Counsel?" In October, Knox was to tell the American Bar Association at Indianapolis, "When we have defeated Hitler and destroyed this Nazi bid for world dominion, we must set up conditions which will prevent the rise of new Hitlers." It brought a spontaneous tribute from the columnist Walter Lippmann: "It is the speech that Woodrow Wilson should have delivered in 1917 . . . you said it magnificently, as men do when they speak the whole truth."

Other incidents, following hard on the *Greer*, helped temper public opinion. 17 October saw the first U.S. casualty list of World War Two: on this dark and icy night a torpedo striking on the starboard side of U.S.S. *Kearny*, one of a division of five destroyers escorting a convoy of fifty merchantmen, took the lives of eleven men, the first of 292,000 Americans to die in the battles of World War Two. On 31 October, 600 miles west of Ireland, the destroyer *Reuben James* took a torpedo in her port side; of that ship's company of 160 men, only 45 – no officers among them – were saved.

But by then America had taken one more step – this time a giant one – towards total war. On 27 October, in a properly apposite setting – the annual Navy League dinner in the vast Gold Ballroom of Washington's Mayflower Hotel – Roosevelt came out with a fighting speech reporting his readiness to the American people: "We have wished to avoid shooting. But the shooting has started. And history has recorded who fired the first shot."

On 13 November, though by the chillingly narrow margin of 212 to 194, Congress duly amended the Neutrality Act – thus permitting the future arming of all U.S. merchantmen and granting them free passage to the war zones.

It seemed a qualified endorsement of Roosevelt's own words: "In the long run, however, all that matters is who will fire the last shot."

*

Roosevelt was sighting on the wrong target; as yet all Hitler's preoccupations were centred on the east. One group of men, by contrast, were already on the brink of an all-out war against the United States.

The story went back at least as far as 31 July – five days after Roosevelt had frozen all Japanese assets and cut off her oil supplies. Then Admiral Osami Nagano, the Naval Chief of Staff, sought an audience at the Imperial Palace with the Emperor Hirohito. Warning of an imminent oil famine, he suggested a desperate attack.

"Will you win a great victory?" asked the 40-year-old Emperor directly, "Like the battle of Tsushima?" – the occasion when Japan had worsted the Russian Fleet in May, 1905.

197

"I am sorry but that will not be possible," Nagano answered ruefully. "Then," the Emperor predicted, "this war will be a desperate one."

By the morning of 6 September, Hirohito had reached a decision. Summoning the Marquis Koichi Kido, the Lord Keeper of the Privy Seal, to his presence, the Emperor announced a break with precedent. When the Imperial Conference began at 10 a.m. that day, he would make his own views known. Both his ministers and service chiefs would receive due warning that so long as prospects for peace remained he would not sanction war.

This decision was in keeping with the sentiments of his Prime Minister, Prince Fumimaro Konoye, an effete hypochondriac who likewise opposed war but lacked both drive and resolution. To date Konoye's most telling blow for peace had been struck in July when he submitted the resignation of himself and his Cabinet. Promptly the Emperor had invited him to head up a new one, and Konoye complied – but this time the pro-Axis Yosuke Matsuoka, who had conferred with Hitler in March, was dropped as Foreign Minister.

As always, according to precedent, the conference of 6 September was held in Room One, East, of the Imperial Palace, the Emperor seated before a golden screen, the delegates, in their stockinged feet, sitting at attention on hard chairs, their fingers, in deference to the imperial power, rigid along the seams of their trousers. But as the conference got under way, Hirohito saw plainly that all talk of further negotiations with the United States was so much verbiage. Bereft of the strategic materials they needed to support a population increasing by millions annually, the delegates' minds were already geared to war.

Abruptly, "very flushed in the face", Hirohito rose. The delegates were nonplussed; except to formally open and close a conference, the Emperor never spoke.

Had not the chiefs of his armed forces, he asked, no opinion as to which should prevail – war or diplomacy? If so, why had they not stated it? "As for myself," Hirohito ventured, "I have no doubt of the answer. I would like to read you a poem which was written by my grandfather, the great Emperor Meiji." Then, drawing a piece of paper from the pocket of his formal suit, he recited in a plaintive high-pitched voice:

> *The seas surround all quarters of the globe,*
> *And my heart cries out to the nations of the world*
> *Why then do the winds and waves of strife*
> *Disrupt the peace between us?*

The Emperor sat down and the company bowed their obeisance. No man present had any doubt as to his meaning. It was a tacit invitation, in Kido's phrase, to "wipe the slate clean", to "go back to blank paper".

But when the discussions began, on 23 October, a new factor had emerged: one week earlier, Prince Konoye had resigned and the former Minister for War, 57-year-old Hideki Tojo, took his place. An incisive quick-thinking *samurai*, whose Army nickname was "The Razor", Tojo, who fretted his way through fifty cigarettes and twelve cups of coffee a day, was not irrevocably war-oriented. Still, he was determined to break the deadlock of indecision.

Ten days of deliberations followed – at times desultory, at others tense and ill-humoured. But over every meeting one spectre hovered like a thunderhead: the oil of which Roosevelt had deprived them. If Japan went to war, she had one year's oil supply at best – and the Navy alone used 400 tons per hour. To switch to synthetic oil would involve a three-year conversion programme costing two billion yen.

By 30 October, the delegates saw just three alternatives. A policy of caution would mean at least ten years of hardship, or *gashin-shotan* – literally "to sleep on kindling and lick gall" – for the people. Or Japan could declare war now, with all the risk that this entailed. Thirdly, she could pursue the policy favoured by Foreign Minister Shigenori Togo – "to undertake both diplomacy and military operations simultaneously".

On 1 November, a decision on deadlines dragged on into an angry seventeen-hour meeting. General Ko Tsukada, the Army Vice Chief of Staff, saw a deadline no later than 13 November as imperative – a proposal denounced by Togo as "outrageous". The Navy were prepared to defer their deadline until 20 November – although Admiral Nagano warned with great emphasis: "The time for war will not come later". In the end, Prime Minister Tojo himself swung the balance: midnight on 30 November.

At the fourteen-man Imperial Conference of 5 November, these decisions were finalised. Preparations for war would go ahead, while striving to settle matters by diplomacy. In silence, the Emperor heard that an experienced career diplomat, Saburo Kurusu, who one year earlier had signed the Tripartite Pact with Germany and Italy, was en route to Washington to bolster the flagging morale of old Admiral Nomura.

Their task would be no easy one. Under Plan "B", which the diplomats were authorised to discuss with Cordell Hull, Japan would agree to move her troops from southern to northern Indo-China – but in return the United States must supply her with one million tons of aviation fuel a year, help ensure a supply of raw materials from the Dutch East Indies, and cease all aid to Chiang Kai-shek's China.

No man doubted that the gulf could be bridged. But it was up to the United States to do the bridging.

10

"Just Read This – And The War Is Won"

6 November–6 December, 1941

THE BRITISH SAW the Japanese threat as still little more than hypothetical. As far back as 12 August, aboard H.M.S. *Prince of Wales*, Churchill had told his ministers that he did not think the Japanese would go to war with Britain. As late as 1 December, his attitude before the Cabinet was unwontedly passive – "we should not resist or attempt to forestall a Japanese attack on the Kra Isthmus (in the Gulf of Siam) unless we had satisfactory assurance from the United States that they would join us."

Thailand (formerly Siam) would, like every Balkan State before her, be urged to resist aggression, although no arms or aircraft could be spared to help out – prompting a spirited protest from the Minister in Bangkok, Sir Josiah Crosby. "The men now in power in Thailand (Siam) are nearly all of them little more than children. This is especially true of the Prime Minister . . . would it not be franker for us to advise Thailand to put up no physical resistance . . . to play the role of Denmark and content herself with a verbal protest against invasion? . . . I find our attitude towards Thailand disconcertingly ambiguous."

It was the Middle East, not the Far East, that was still absorbing Britain – a preoccupation wholeheartedly shared by their old adversary Rommel.

In Rome on 15 November, "The Desert Fox" was celebrating his fiftieth birthday along with General Hans von Ravenstein, commanding 21st Panzer Division, and their respective wives. But over lunch at the smart Hotel Eden, Ravenstein sensed that despite his chief's presence in the Eternal City, his heart and mind were rooted in the desert. For a time Rommel listened abstractedly as Lucie Rommel and Frau von Ravenstein extolled the wonders of St Peter's. Suddenly he broke in: "You know, von Ravenstein, I've been thinking again about what we ought to do with those infantry battalions . . ."

Rommel had cause for preoccupation; once again he had won a victory over his own top brass. Told off by the High Command to concentrate on an imminent British attack and leave Tobruk alone, Rommel was beside himself. With von Ravenstein he flew to Rome for a bitter wrangle with the Military Attaché, General Enno von Rintelen, whose advice, Rommel suspected, had prompted the ukase. Reviling von Rintelen as "a coward and a friend of the Italians", Rommel promptly seized the phone and called Jodl, in Berlin.

"I hear that you wish me to give up the attack on Tobruk," Rommel stormed. "I am completely disgusted." The 21st Panzer Division, he insisted, whose commander was there beside him, could counter any British advance whilst Tobruk was invested. "Can you guarantee," Jodl asked cautiously "that there is no danger?" When Rommel shouted that they had his personal guarantee, Jodl gave in. The attack was timed for 23 November.

For two months now, Rommel had postponed this offensive – bedevilled by a system of priorities which had sped 154 divisions to the Russian front yet grudged more than two for North Africa, hampered by non-stop British harassment of his Mediterranean supply convoys. From Naples, *Oberst* Gerhart Müller, of the 5th Panzer Regiment, reported more than 1,000 Afrika Korps men bogged down in the port, vainly awaiting transportation – while on the African shores, a shortage of trucks decreed that only three-quarters of the stores arriving ever reached the front. For the first time Rommel was forced to acknowledge the truth of von Ravenstein's sour dictum; "The desert is a tactician's paradise and a quartermaster's hell."

As yet, Rommel had no suspicion of the magnitude of a British thrust, code-named Crusader, nor of its grandiloquent objective: to engage and destroy all Axis armour at one stroke and reoccupy Cyrenaica. Simultaneously, on the code-word "Pop", the besieged garrison of Tobruk – 32,000 men, including those of Major-General Stanislaw Kopanski's Polish Brigade, who had been shipped in on moonless autumn nights following Curtin's ultimatum to replace the original Anzac defenders – would stage a breakout. Their target was the tiny fort of El Duda, 8 miles south; here they would link up with the forces advancing to relieve Tobruk.

This was Britain's threefold chance to redeem the shame of Operation Battleaxe: a second front to help the Russians, with the hope of knocking Mussolini's troops out of the war for good and all and of convincing Washington's sceptics that the Middle East campaign rated more than a number four priority.

But as Wavell's successor, General Sir Claude Auchinleck had two serious failings: a poor judgement of the man for the job, a bigoted loyalty to the man thus picked. Moreover – like Wavell but unlike Rommel – Auchinleck had opted to conduct his war from G.H.Q., almost 600 miles from the front line. Standing in for him at Advanced H.Q., Fort Maddalena, as Commander of the newly-formed Eighth Imperial Army was his personal choice for the post, General Sir Alan Gordon Cunningham, 54, the younger brother of the Admiral. Cunningham, who had never commanded armour nor seen service in the desert, had been given just two months to form and train the major fighting arm that replaced Western Desert Force.

At 9 p.m. on 16 November, deep in his underground dugout, Cunningham, flanked by war correspondents sipping whisky-and-sodas round a plain trestle table, had appeared confident enough. "A hoarse-voiced cherub of a man", as one recalled him, he promised them: "I am going to seek old Rommel out and destroy him and his armour."

Unknown to the war correspondents was the uncompromising verdict which Major-General Bernard Freyberg had delivered to Cunningham two days back. In one sentence Freyberg had charted the woeful misfortunes of Eighth Army for the next seven months.

"You are attacking five Italian divisions and more than a German division with two brigades of South Africans," he warned Cunningham. "You will fail and we shall be ordered in the end to march upon Tobruk."

Along with Major-General William "Strafer" Gott, of the 7th Armoured Division, and Lieutenant-General Sir Willoughby Norrie, commanding 30 Corps, Freyberg had urged a powerful force of three armoured brigades striking as one. Now, to his dismay, Cunningham planned not only to split armour from armour but tanks from infantry – leaving every unit wide open to be engulfed by Rommel.

Even so, hopes were high. At first light on 18 November, under a sullen downpour split by forked white lightning, the men of the Eighth Army heard the burst of machine-gun fire that signalled the "off" as the force moved out across the desert – "like a regiment of monstrous snails", as one man saw them, heading for The Wire, the rust-corroded barrier, 6 feet high and 9 feet wide, that Mussolini had erected in 1932 to stop the Bedouins leaving Libya.

For the first time since Beda Fomm, most men felt a warm glow of confidence. At last there was an abundance of everything – more than 375,000 fighting men, 700-plus gun-armed tanks, among them 200 Chrysler M-3s, known as Honeys, the first U.S. Tanks ever to taste war. Unit after unit thrilled to the thunder of 700 R.A.F. planes criss-crossing the lowering skies – snub-nosed Hurricanes, big twin-engined Beaufighters, even high Flying Fortresses. The Chief Engineer of 30 Corps, Brigadier George Clifton, was so sure of victory he had taken along 24 cans of Rheingold beer to celebrate. Even the dubious Freyberg had at last overcome his reservations. He assured Brigadier John Harding of 13 Corps: "Good God! We are frothing to go. We are not frightened of a few tanks."

Auchinleck was less confident. Goaded to action by Churchill's constant nagging – "there are always excellent reasons in favour of retreats. Victory rewards those whose willpower overcomes these reasons" – he confided his doubts in letters to Ismay. "This is not really a very flexible army," he wrote. "One can not just pick up a division and hurl it across the map as one did at staff college," and later, "All these months of labour and thought can be set at nought in one afternoon."

At Ain El Gazala Rommel was taken entirely by surprise. *Leutnant* Heinz Werner Schmidt was always to recall that when he handed Rommel the first report of the frontier crossing from Reconnaissance Unit 33, "The Desert Fox" commented only, "Unbelievable!" Still obsessed with the capture of Tobruk, he had always been unwilling to accept Crusader as more than a cautious British probe. When von Ravenstein sought permission to move an armoured troop towards the frontier, Rommel cautioned: "We mustn't lose our nerve."

Now, Cunningham, too, erred fatally. Puzzled by Rommel's failure to react to his first thrust, he spread his armour on a seek-and-find mission across the face of the desert. One brigade, the 22nd Armoured, was sped to Bir El Gubi, south of Tobruk, to tangle with the Italian Ariete Division. The 7th Armoured made for Sidi Rezegh, a key airfield off the main Axis highway. The 4th stayed put at Gabrh Saleh, 50 miles inside the wire.

Already those close to Cunningham felt he was fast losing his grip. To ten weeks of overwork and emotional strain was added now the uncertainty of a battle he was ill-equipped to control. Moreover, a heavy pipe-smoker, he had been forced, on the eve of battle, to quit smoking by his oculist on account of eye-strain. Haggard with nervous fatigue, he confided in Air Marshal Sir Arthur Tedder, Air Commander of the Middle East: "I wish I knew what Rommel meant to do."

What Rommel, now alerted, meant to do was what he had done so often before: to profit by the British misuse of their own armour. From the first luck was with him. On the night of Saturday, 22 November, *Oberstleutnant* Hans Cramer's 8th Panzer Division by chance overran the H.Q. of Brigadier Alec Gatehouse's 4th Armoured Brigade – capturing 35 tanks and all their guns and armoured cars. The most substantial armoured force in 8th Army had ceased to be a fighting entity.

On 23 November, the aptly named *Totensonntag* (The Sunday of the Dead), the date marked in the Lutheran calendar for the Germans to recall the fallen of World War One, Rommel closed in for the kill at Sidi Rezegh.

What followed was stark slaughter – a battle as pitifully uncoordinated as any that Eighth Army was to wage. Achieving little more than "a cavalry charge on tracks", the remnants of 4th Armoured Brigade and the 22nd Brigade hit the battlefield 75 minutes apart – with no more coherent purpose than to shoot it out with any German tank in sight. Swinging away and back across five miles of desert, in whirlwinds of yellow dust, "tanks duelled with tanks", as one man pictured it, "in running almost hand-to-hand fights, firing nearly point-blank, twisting,

203

dodging, sprinting, with screaming tracks and whining engines that rose to a shriek as they changed gear".

For every man who fought at Sidi Rezegh there were painful often indelible memories. For Private Reginald Crimp, an infantryman, it was the crash of mortar bombs "like train doors slamming at Clapham Junction, South London, in the rush hour". For Reuter correspondent Alaric Jacob it was a knocked out tank burning with a red lambent flame "like a roasted chestnut". Few men bore from this battlefield as strange a souvenir as Gunner Andy Graham, from Christchurch, New Zealand: the armour-piercing shell that had torn off his left foot.

No man more exemplified this suicidal derring-do than Brigadier "Jock" Campbell, of Cunningham's Command Support Group. Determined that his tanks should carry out a cavalry charge against an enemy now outnumbering them by two to one, the stalwart 48-year-old Campbell, attired in a brown leather golf jacket and corduroy trousers, wheeled among the tanks standing bolt upright in an open staff car, waving alternate red and blue flags for Stop and Go. At times manning a machine-gun on a disabled Stuka, at others, a 25-pounder, Campbell harried the British tanks as relentlessly as he did the Germans – hurling both rocks and abuse at any commander who dared reverse from the action.

When one officer protested that a frontal charge was plain suicide, Campbell – awarded the Victoria Cross for this day's action – blazed at him: "That's what you're soldiers for – to die". If any tank withdrew one yard, Campbell threatened, his artillery would open fire on it.

It was small wonder that Rommel, meeting up with a captured brigadier, harangued him like a war college lecturer: "What difference does it make if you have two tanks to my one when you spread them out and let me smash them in detail? You presented me with three armoured brigades in succession."

Twenty miles due north of Sidi Rezegh, at Tobruk, the break-out was under way but with fearsome losses. Shuffling through darkness along a corridor of white marker tape, the 2nd Battalion of The Black Watch, the kilted Highland regiment, moved out into no-man's-land to "press against a solid wall of lead" – rallied by Pipe-Major Roy's bagpipes skirling the regimental march *Highland Laddie*. Soon a forest of rifles embedded in the sand by their bayonets – the signal for stretcher-bearers – told of the break-out's grim toll. Hit three times, Pipe-Major Roy was carried to the Regimental Aid Post – playing on, swathed in bandages, to the astonishment of wounded German P.O.W.s, who tried to peer beneath his kilt.

But almost three-quarters of the Highlanders had fallen before they had won a sally-port 400 yards broad and deep – and four more blood-stained days would elapse before a British Tommy and a New Zealand infantryman clasped hands at El Duda.

Incredibly, Cunningham as yet had no inkling that the battle was almost lost; due to delays and inaccurate situation reports, no up-to-date intelligence had reached Fort Maddalena. Not until the evening of *Totensonntag* was the paralysing truth revealed to him: 7th Armoured Brigade, which had joined battle with 129 tanks, had lost every one. The 22nd Armoured, starting with 158, had lost all but 30. Of the 4th Armoured Brigade, nothing was known.

Then, at 10.30 a.m. on 24 November, Rommel embarked on the one manoeuvre Cunningham had dreaded. Leaving *Oberst* Siegfried Westphal, his Chief of Intelligence, in charge of H.Q., Rommel and the Afrika Korps set off on a wild dash for The Wire, a 40-mile-long column bent on spreading chaos among the British rear echelons like wolves stampeding a flock of sheep.

Over 1,000 square miles of desert, confusion spread like fire under a leaning wind. At H.Q. Corps, Cunningham was mulling over his course of action with General Sir Willoughby Norrie when the first dull *crump* of shells was heard from the west. Hard on their heels came Rommel himself, upright in his staff car, sunglasses pushed up on his forehead, urging his escort of twenty despatch riders "General Cunningham! Go and take him!" Barely in time, Cunningham was bundled into a staff car, driven, accelerator to floorboards, to the nearest desert strip and hustled aboard a departing Blenheim. As it took off it cleared a three-ton truck by inches.

Now the retreat became total. Columns of inky smoke pockmarked the desert as clerks fired secret records. Signallers fumbled frantically to coil up the miles of wire which made up the telephone networks. But not only the British were confused. So headlong was Rommel's dash for The Wire that he entirely overlooked the two crucial storage dumps, each 6 miles square, on which Cunningham's forces were depending: Field Supply Dump 63, 15 miles south-east of Bir El Gubi and Dump 65, 15 miles south-east of Gabrh Saleh. "If we had known about those dumps," von Ravenstein was later to mourn, "we could have won the battle."

The omission was not surprising. Entire units – British, German and Italian – were now hopelessly intertwined. "Libya was a madhouse," one man recorded. "Operational maps now looked like surrealistic masterpieces." One British military policeman spent several hours on point duty patiently directing German transport and everywhere there were strange encounters. One officer, seeking refuge in an apparently deserted truck, found its Italian driver fast asleep in the cabin. Calling on his faulty Italian, he jammed a pistol in the man's stomach, whispering "*Alto in mano*". Swift to comply, the Italian corrected him politely, "*Mani in alto*" (Hands up). Few men were more off course than the truck driver whom Captain the Earl of Onslow met heading for Msus – once more in Rommel's hands. Doggedly insistent that a rest and recreation area had been set up there, the driver was carrying a grand piano to deliver to its canteen.

Above all, on the night of 24 November, Rommel himself was lost. Shortly after storming through the gap in The Wire that Eighth Army had breached, along with his Chief of Staff, *Generalmajor* Alfred Gause, Rommel's staff car broke down. By chance, General Ludwig Crüwell, Afrika Corps Commander, with his Chief of Staff, *Oberst* Fritz Bayerlein, hove in sight driving a captured British vehicle – to offer the lonely shivering figures a ride.

Impatient as ever, once the driver could not locate the gap, Rommel grabbed the wheel himself – "barging fruitlessly up and down The Wire like a bewildered bee on a window-pane." Finally even Rommel gave up. Only when dawn broke did they realise they had passed a restless night among the scattered positions of the 4th Indian Division. Unchallenged they slipped away.

With the realisation that in four days Crusader had cost Eighth Army 530 tanks, disillusion stretched to the topmost levels. Among those most embittered was Freyberg, now convinced like many Commonwealth commanders that British tactics, profligate of lives, would see the end of his Kiwis. Standing on his right he demanded – and got – his forces transferred to Syria.

Auchinleck was swift to act. Arriving from Cairo, following a secret summons from Cunningham's Chief Staff Officer, Brigadier Sandy Galloway, he told Cunningham curtly, "It is not your business to consider Egypt's safety but to get on with the battle". But by 25 November, Tedder, the R.A.F. commander, had gone further still. Returning to Cairo from the front, Tedder reported to Captain Oliver Lyttelton, Churchill's Minister of State for the Middle East.

"You mean that Cunningham is not confident of winning the battle?" Lyttelton asked. When Tedder assented, Lyttelton decided, "Then he must be relieved tonight. I shall urge this course on Auchinleck." On 26 November, a new commander took over: Lieutenant-General Neil Ritchie.

*

More than 2,000 miles west of Hawaii, on Wake Island, in the North Pacific, one man had an unique opportunity to ponder Japan's intentions at first hand: Major James Patrick Sinnott Devereux, commander of the 378-strong Detachment of the 1st U.S. Marine Battalion on Wake Island. As the island's senior officer, Devereux's duties included the welcoming of all dignitaries passing through on the Pan-American Clipper – and thus, on 12 November, he found himself in the lobby of Wake's Pan-American Hotel, sipping highballs with Saburo Kurusu, Japan's newest envoy to Washington.

Plump and suave, in a pin-striped business suit, Kurusu seemed cordial enough, although confessing to one anxiety. "Please", he begged, "I don't want to be bothered by the Press." Devereux was reassuring. Few pressmen had ever set foot on Wake Island, a desolate two-square mile atoll of sand and coral discovered by the British in 1796 and claimed as a U.S. possession in 1899. Until Pan-American had set up a Clipper refuelling station in 1935, Wake had been notable only as a designated bird sanctuary. Even now Devereux's Marines and 1,200 civilian contractors engaged in converting the island base into a $20 million naval air station made up the sole population.

Twice, in their hour-long talk, Devereux noted, Kurusu mentioned his American wife, the former Alice Little of Chicago, as if to establish kinship. "If people could travel more," he said, "and come to know each other in their home countries perhaps these things would not come up."

Devereux was genuinely puzzled. What was the real purpose behind this man's mission? Was it a smokescreen, with Japan already bent on war? Or was Kurusu in earnest when he said, "I am just going to Washington to see what I can do. I hope I can straighten out affairs and avoid trouble?"

In his heart, Devereux believed that Kurusu meant it – but when the time came for the envoy to board the Clipper for San Francisco the Major could still not be sure.

Kurusu's intentions were not the only problem to confront Devereux since assuming command of Wake's Marines on 15 October. A dapper wiry 38-year-old with a pencil-line moustache, 5 feet 5 inches in height, Devereux in no way resembled the archetypal U.S. Marine but in eighteen years service he had known his share of trouble-spots: China, Nicaragua, Cuba. But now, in mid-November, the biggest problem was posed by Wake itself.

In the event of war, Wake Island would form a vital link in the chain of widely separated American islands stretching from Dutch Harbor in the Aleutians almost to the Equator. These outposts would become the U.S. first line of defence, of which the core was the Hawaiian island of Oahu, the base of the U.S. Pacific Fleet at Pearl Harbor. The nearest American bases were Midway, 1,000 miles east, and Guam, 1,000 miles west – but of all these island outposts it was Wake, with its trim white buildings and green woods, where the ocean swell on the reef boomed incessantly night and day, that lay nearest to Japan.

Yet if war threatened, the U.S. had thus far taken few precautions. Even now, Devereux was woefully understrength; his establishment was set at 43 officers, 939 men, but when the 6th Marine Battalion would arrive to backstop him, and bring him up to strength, nobody knew. No briefing had been given him on taking up command – and until an emergency arose, he lacked authority to set the contractor's men to work on gun emplacements. Much of the time his Marines had to suspend their training to act as refuelling crews for the new B-17s bound for the Philippines – leaving too little time to work up their skills as artillerymen.

Sometime in November, a message arrived from Naval Headquarters at Pearl Harbor to give Devereux further food for thought. It read:

INTERNATIONAL SITUATION INDICATES
YOU SHOULD BE ON THE ALERT

Promptly Devereux queried:

DOES INTERNATIONAL SITUATION INDICATE
EMPLOYMENT OF THE CONTRACTOR'S MEN ON
DEFENSE INSTALLATIONS WHICH ARE FAR
FROM COMPLETE?

It was two days before the reply arrived: negative. But Devereux at once felt easier. The situation must be less explosive than he had thought.

Even so, he worried: Wake Island's radar equipment had gone missing. Searching enquiries established that it had long been crated but was still sitting on the dockside at Pearl Harbor awaiting shipment – a long way down the list of assigned priorities. Understandably, Devereux chafed, for at the moment he was totally dependent on the look-outs atop Wake's two 50-ft steel water towers. Their eyes and ears were the sole detection devices he had.

Devereux looked back wryly to January, 1941, when he had arrived in Washington on leave to see his family. No sooner had he reached the capital than he was under orders to depart: a posting to Pearl Harbor had come up. His brother Ashton, driving him to the railroad station, had wondered what the sudden orders signified.

Devereux laughed. "Oh," he hazarded, "I'll probably wind up on some little spit-kit of an island."

And if war came?, his brother wondered.

Devereux was to prove all too accurate a prophet. "Your guess is as good as mine – but I'll probably end up eating fish and rice."

*

In Washington, D.C., Cordell Hull was angry. In the last week of November, he saw the British and the Chinese as greater threats to the fragile balance of peace than Japan itself.

On 20 November, Thanksgiving Day, Nomura and the newly-arrived Kurusu had handed the Secretary of State the current set of proposals which the Imperial Conference had finalised on 5 November in Tokyo. "It was an ultimatum," Hull was to recall, ". . . the commitments we should have to make were virtually a surrender."

Even so, Hull persevered. For two days he and his staff worked hard on

208

a counter-proposal, a three-month *modus vivendi* which would tide both parties over while future talks continued. Japan, Hull posited, should withdraw from southern Indo-China – and reduce her forces in northern Indo-China to 25,000. In return, the U.S. would agree to a limited resumption of trade: petroleum, though for civilian use only, food and medical supplies, raw cotton. Meanwhile all U.S. restrictions on Japanese imports would be lifted.

At the same time, the State Department would urge Britain, Australia and the Dutch East Indies to take similar measures.

Whether Japan would have entertained any such proposition is open to doubt – but in the event they had no chance. In Chungking, Chiang Kai-shek, outraged by the proposal, fired off a cable to Churchill, who, in turn cautioned Roosevelt, "Of course it is for you to handle this business, and we certainly do not want an additional war. There is only one point that disquiets us. What about Chiang Kai-shek? Is he not having a very thin diet?" The Cabinet, too, were uneasy: "a Munich in the Far East?", queried Dalton in his diary. In Washington, Chiang's brother-in-law, T.V. Soong, along with the Chinese Ambassador, Professor Hu Shih, reacted so violently in a meeting with Roosevelt that the President, alarmed, soothed Soong: "Don't take your shirt off."

Simultaneously, on the morning of 26 November, came an intelligence report of Japanese troop movements heading south of Formosa. The truce formula was dead from that moment on. Hull was instructed on 26 November to draw up a ten-point proposal reiterating all Washington's most imperative demands.

Roosevelt was not, perhaps, displeased. At a Cabinet meeting on 7 November, as Attorney General Francis Biddle noted, the President was hopeful that an "incident" in the Pacific – not the Atlantic – would force the issue of war – "everyone would think of this as naval warfare, excluding the possibility of an (American) expeditionary force". The dark shadow of "foreign wars" was never far from the conference table.

Hull, though, was incensed beyond measure: because of Churchill and Chiang, his efforts for a Far Eastern concordat had gone for nothing. "It would have been better," he wrote Halifax angrily, "if Churchill had sent a strong cable back to Chiang Kai-shek telling him to brace up and fight with the same zeal as the Germans and Japanese are displaying."

For the weary old Secretary of State, it was the end of the line. "I have washed my hands of it," he told Secretary for War Stimson, "and now it is in the hands of you and Knox – the Army and the Navy."

*

Hull's faith, if touching, was unfounded. From the South China Sea to the Pacific, America's outposts lay naked to attack.

Of all these bases, none was more vulnerable than Pearl Harbor itself. Sited eight miles from the Hawaiian capital of Honolulu and the bars and clip-joints of downtown Waikiki, Pearl had long spelt home to the officers and ratings manning the 96 ships which made up the U.S. Pacific Fleet.

Yet for ten years its nakedness had been a byword. From 1931 on, every member of each graduating class in Japan's naval academy had faced one $64,000 question: How would you launch a surprise assault on Pearl Harbor? Back in 1936, the U.S. war games and drills in the Hawaiian Islands had all been planned on the basis of a surprise attack on Pearl – in which Japan had been code-named "Orange". In 1938, the defenses had cropped up again in a War Department survey – "there can be little doubt the Hawaiian Islands will be the initial scene of action".

The problem was that the Islands lacked any unified command. On paper, the Army, under Lieutenant-General Walter C. Short, commanding general of the Hawaiian Department, was responsible for defence, including the naval base and its military installations. In practice, though, Short kept a respectful distance from Admiral Husband E. Kimmel, the caustic Kentuckian C-in-C of the Pacific Fleet, and Kimmel maintained the same distance from Short. Cordial companions on the golf course, they were still chary of trading inter-service intelligence.

Not that there was much to trade. Neither Kimmel nor Short – any more than Vice-Admiral William F. Halsey, commanding the carriers of Task Force 8 from his flagship *Enterprise* – were aware that back in August 1940, Colonel William Friedman, the chief cryptoanalyst of the War Department, had cracked the Japanese diplomatic cipher system, code-named "Purple". The next step, emulating the British success with "Enigma", had been to build a replica of the "Purple" Machine. Between 1 July, 1941, and 7 December, 294 Japanese messages were to be intercepted, deciphered, translated into English and given the code-name "Magic".

But the men in command at Pearl Harbor – "America's billion-dollar fist in the Pacific", to the propagandists – were never privy to these messages. So tight was naval security that no "Purple" Machine even existed at Pearl; while four were retained in Washington, a fifth was held by the naval base at Cavite, in the Philippines. Even in Washington, the distribution methods had a cloak-and-dagger ring. Digests – but never verbatim transcripts – of up to 130 intercepts a day were rushed in locked brief-cases by special messengers to Roosevelt and his chief advisers who scanned them without taking notes while the messenger stood by. All copies but one were then burned.

Not until around 1 December did Kimmel, for the first time, light on a chance reference to "Purple" in a dispatch from the Chief of Naval Operations, Admiral Harold Stark. "What," he asked his Fleet Intelligence Officer, Lieutenant-Commander Edwin T. Layton, in bafflement, "is a purple machine?" Layton, equally in the dark, promised to try and find out.

Kimmel, who had been promoted over thirty-two Admirals to his present post, was far from complacent. To counter a surprise attack by fast carrier based aircraft he had time and again pressed for a pool of 250 reconnaissance planes – but the Navy Department, seeing a more pressing need elsewhere, refused to supply them. Thus, when Halsey's carriers were absent on a mission, Kimmel was forced to keep his battleships anchored in Pearl for lack of air cover.

Back in January, 1941, his predecessor, Admiral James O. Richardson had pressed both Roosevelt and Knox to recall the Fleet to the West Coast; Pearl Harbor was accessible only through a single entrance channel which all ships, coming and going, had to use. The interview concluded, Roosevelt asked Knox in disgust. "What's the matter with Jo? Has he become yellow?" Shortly after, Richardson was relegated to the General Board – "the boneyard".

Six months later, in June, Kimmel, who saw Pearl Harbor as "a damned mouse trap", told Roosevelt the same unpalatable truth. "If they sink one ship in the entrance of the harbor they have the whole Fleet bottled up and it can't get out," he emphasised, "The only place for the Fleet to be if the Japanese should attack is at sea, and not in port."

This simple equation had even been perceived by 22-year-old Margaret Spruance, daughter of the newly-appointed commander of Cruiser Division 5. On a sightseeing tour around Honolulu, the ships lined up on "Battleship Row", alongside the palm-fringed naval air station at Ford Island, struck her as appallingly at risk. "Dad," she asked, "what is there to stop the Japs from bombing our ships in the harbor?" His voice pregnant with sarcasm, Admiral Raymond A. Spruance replied, "They are not supposed to do it that way."

In justice to the service chiefs, the very volume of "Magic" intercepts was self-defeating. As often as danger threatened Hawaii, alarums were reported from the Panama Canal, from San Diego, Vladivostok, the Philippines, the Caribbean. Thus, on 27 November, when Stark routed a signal to Kimmel which began, "This is to be considered a war warning", the C-in-C's first reaction was, Where? The Kra Peninsula? Borneo? Siberia?

Lacking salient facts, men now jumped to false conclusions. Kimmel, fearing a submarine attack, warned the Fleet accordingly. General Short, similarly alerted by Army intelligence, saw danger from one source only: sabotage by Hawaii's 157,905 Japanese civilians. As a precaution he ordered that all planes at Hickam and Wheeler Fields should line up on their ramps wingtip to wingtip, as neatly as at an air review. Then he reported on his action – but no adverse comment was forthcoming from the War Department.

211

Nor was Short ever warned that a vital code-phrase, *Higashi No Kaze Ame* (East Wind Rain) was on the point of being transmitted. Its purport was "Please destroy all code papers": relations between Japan and the United States were about to be severed.

At this time another factor was troubling Kimmel – though he did not see fit to confide his worry to Short. On 1 December, his combat intelligence Division, under Lieutenant-Commander Joseph J. Rochefort, had reported that the Japanese Navy had changed its call signs; since 16 November they had had no contact with the carriers of the First and Second Japanese Fleets, still believed to be in their home waters in the Kure-Sasebo area.

On 1 December, Kimmel asked Commander Layton to check with Cavite as to the carriers' whereabouts – but next day Layton reported that he had drawn a blank.

"What, you don't know where the carriers are?" Kimmel said incredulously, "Do you mean they could be rounding Diamond Head (the extinct volcanic crater dominating Waikiki) and you wouldn't know it?"

Layton was optimistic. He hoped the carriers would be sighted long before that.

*

In a six-roomed air-conditioned penthouse on the fifth floor of the Manila Hotel, a man was pacing. At this time of day, the "blue hour", as the cocktail hour was known, it had become his evening routine, pacing as the setting sun dipped in splendour behind the Bataan Peninsula, pacing as the clangour of bells drove swooping battalions of bats from belfries all over the city; as rhythmically as a metronome, back and forth without cessation, while a cooling breeze from the balcony brought the scent of the white ginger flowers that he loved. At 60, Lieutenant-General Douglas MacArthur, recently-appointed chief of the U.S. Army Forces in the Far East, had good reason to pace and much to ponder.

"By God, it was Destiny that brought me here! It was Destiny," was MacArthur's reaction to his appointment, and the hyperbole was typical of the man. In fact, MacArthur had been a fixture in the Manila Hotel on Dewey Boulevard since 1936, serving as Military Adviser to the new Commonwealth Government of the Philippines under President Manuel Quezon. But when Roosevelt imposed his Japanese oil embargo on 26 July and created a new Army command in the Philippines – calling the forces of the Philippine Department and the Philippine Army into U.S. service for the duration of the emergency – MacArthur, five years on the spot, had seemed the logical choice for C-in-C.

Flamboyant, mercurial, a showman to his fingertips, MacArthur had no doubt he would succeed. Success was as much a part of him as his public persona: the long ebony cigarette holder, the crisply starched

212

uniforms he changed three times daily, his habit of punctuating every monologue with, "Get me? Understand? Follow me?" Some people found his presence overwhelming – "a tendency to deliver a speech to a hundred instead of answering a simple question in a few words", noted his counterpart in Singapore, Brooke-Popham – yet his staff gave him the same devoted loyalty as his wife of four years, Jean, to whom the General, after a character in Mark Twain's *A Connecticut Yankee at the Court of King Arthur*, was always "Sir Boss".

"I don't *think* that the Philippines can defend themselves," MacArthur had told Quezon, as long ago as 1934, "I *know* they can," and this unswerving optimism was to bring about a drastic last-minute policy reversal in the Far East. Fired by MacArthur's belief that enemy troops could be met at the waterline and driven back into the sea – and the promise of 100 B-17 heavy bombers, the Flying Fortress, by December – the idea had gained currency in Washington that the main island, Luzon, perhaps other islands as well, could be held against a Japanese attack.

This was in marked contrast to the earlier view that while Hawaii must be held at all costs, the Philippines, when it came to the crunch, were virtually indefensible. But just as Stalin had looked to the postponement of war until the Red Army called the shots, Roosevelt, too, was anticipating a war which, conveniently for America, would not erupt until 1 April, 1942.

"Dick", MacArthur hailed his Chief of Staff, Major-General Richard K. Sutherland, on 4 November, when an "Eyes Only" letter from General George Marshall arrived from Washington, "They are going to give us everything we have asked for." But again his infectious enthusiasm was outpacing events. Although the letter approved his fight-them-on-the-beaches strategy, promising tanks, guns and infantrymen, these promises, too, were predicated on an April, 1942 completion date.

At best, by mid-December, MacArthur would have 137,000 men under arms against the 200,000 he had anticipated – at least 80,000 of them Filipino trainees outfitted with cheap pith helmets, rubber tennis shoes and ancient Lee-Enfield rifles. The planes, too, would be forthcoming – but work on the airfields to house them had only now begun.

In the final outcome the Philippines were as helpless against attack as Pearl Harbor, but to the end, even if he suspected this, nothing of it showed in MacArthur's mien.

Clark Lee, Manila's Associated Press correspondent, who glimpsed him about this time, could only marvel at the confidence of the man as he strode towards his office at No 1, Calle Victoria: the rigidly-braced shoulders, the jaunty tilt of his gold-braided cap, the cigarette smouldering in the long holder.

"He looked completely sure of himself," Lee recalled, "He looked like a man who couldn't lose."

Fifteen hundred miles south-west of Manila, in a one-story wooden frame building inside the Singapore Naval Base, Air Chief Marshal Sir Robert Brooke-Popham, the British C-in-C, Far East, faced problems of a different order. Unlike MacArthur he knew the terrible vulnerability of his command structure. His difficulty was to drive this home to Churchill and the Chiefs of Staff.

For sixteen years, the "impregnable fortress" of Singapore had been a myth in the making. Only a select few on the spot knew the painful reality: Singapore was a £60 million floating dockyard whose sole defence was six 15-inch naval guns pointing mutely out to sea. From the landward side, "Singraltar", as the embittered Secretary of Defence for Malaya, C. A. Vlieland, dubbed it, was guarded only by a skein of barbed wire.

As far back as 1923, the Chief of Air Staff, Air Chief Marshal Sir Hugh Trenchard, had protested vigorously at this antediluvian system of defence, urging that air power must play its part – a theory totally rejected by the First Sea Lord, Admiral of the Fleet Earl Beatty. At that time Trenchard had pressed for three squadrons of torpedo bombers, a squadron of fighters, two of bombers and a reconnaissance flight. But the Navy had won the day. In 1926 – in what he later acknowledged as "the worst blunder of my career" – Trenchard had backed down.

The basic concept was that a frontal assault on the naval base by a hostile fleet could be held off for ninety days – after which the Eastern Fleet would arrive. But in November, 1941, the Eastern Fleet was a reality only on paper. Just as with MacArthur's Philippine task force, the Admiralty was looking to March, 1942, as the earliest possible assembly date.

A year earlier, on assuming command, Brooke-Popham had been fatally acquiescent. "Our job in the Far East is not to press for facilities that cannot be given," he wrote virtuously to Ismay, "but to utilise every resource that we have got or can acquire locally." Too late he was to realise that only a tactic of unrelenting pressure could ever galvanise the Chiefs of Staff. While agreeing in principle that "582 aircraft is an ideal" they felt that "336 should give very fair degree of security" – but even these were never to arrive.

Unlike the Philippines, which had planes in plenty but few airfields to accommodate them, Brooke-Popham had fully thirty airfields, all of them garrisoned by combat troops, but only 141 operational planes. Of these most were obsolescent Lockheed-Hudsons, Brewster Buffalo fighters and Wildebeeste torpedo-bombers – for the Chiefs of Staff held that "the Buffalo appears to be eminently satisfactory and would probably prove more than a match for any Japanese aircraft".

Behind this myopia lay a crucial fallacy: that Singapore Island and its naval base could be held without defending the three million acres of rubber plantations that made up the Malayan Peninsula. In 1937, the Chief of Staff to the G.O.C., Malaya Command, Colonel Arthur Percival – who by 1941 was himself G.O.C. – had pointed out that an attack from Thailand or Northern Malaya was both feasible and probable, but the War Office had turned down all requests for tanks. The north-east monsoon would make an east coast landing impossible; the jungle, in any case was "impenetrable" to troops. It was a belief that died hard. The one man who disagreed, Lieutenant Colonel Ian Stewart, commanding the 2nd Battalion, Argyll and Sutherland Highlanders, who led his troops on a 90-mile jungle route march, found no favour with Percival's staff officers – "Stewart's ideas on jungle training are those of a crank".

A disturbing lack of urgency was everywhere apparent. Brigadier Ivan Simson, Malaya's Chief Engineer, was shocked to find up-country troops totally ignorant of neutralising enemy tanks – yet he knew that official War Office pamphlets on the subject had arrived from London months ago. Investigating, he found them still lying, neatly tied in bundles, in a cupboard at Military Headquarters in Fort Canning. No one had ever seen fit to distribute them.

The R.A.F. were as bad. At Seletar airfield, on Malaya's east coast, Pilot Officer Roy Bulcock, an Australian, was staggered to see the Transit Store piled almost to the roof with 3,000 cases of material. All of them were destined for up-country airfields – but had lain there undistributed for more than eighteen months.

All over the Far East, the "fortress" mentality prevailed with British and Americans alike. "No place is indefensible . . .," MacArthur was to assert. "To say the Philippines are indefensible is merely to say that they are inadequately defended." A similar myth was then current regarding Pearl Harbor; "the island of Oahu, due to its fortifications, its garrison, and its physical characteristics is believed to be the strongest fortress in the world", General Marshall maintained in a minute to Roosevelt, and later he added, "Presence of Fleet reduces threat of major attack". "Singapore was not a fortress, though this was a thing few were allowed to know," one of Percival's staff officers revealed, "or, if they knew, to admit, for this would have been imperial heresy."

Though separated by thousands of miles of ocean, life in Manila and Honolulu still had much in common with life in Singapore and in the British Crown Colony of Hong Kong. All were polyglot commercial entrepôts, where money talked loudest, and in a babel of tongues; in Malaya, the nine largest tin mining companies had shown an average profit increase of 321 percent in 1940. In a climate as warm and steamy as a Turkish bath, the siesta was everywhere a way of life; rarely did the temperature drop below 80 degrees Fahrenheit. All were communities where, even in 1941, with half the world in arms, life for the expatriates was still ordered and secure, soothed by a minimum of three Chinese or Filipino servants.

There were still certain niceties and social gradations observed; in Hong Kong status was determined by how far up the Peak, 1,823 feet above sea level, a householder lived. At the Peninsula Hotel, just as at Honolulu's Royal Hawaiian, white dinner jackets were *de rigueur* and ten-page menus commonplace; the "in" drink was the gimlet, gin, lime juice and ice, the only hard liquor that General MacArthur touched. There was still time for pleasures that much of the world had forgotten; the weekly racing at Hong Kong's Happy Valley and tournaments on Honolulu's Mainalua Golf Course, sea-bathing parties, midnight movie matinees and charity balls. At Singapore's Seaview Hotel, one Sunday ritual had lately been established: before luncheon was served, the drinkers on the pillared terrace seized up the small rectangular song-sheets placed on each table and launched into a lusty chorus of *There'll Always Be An England*.

Whether American or British, these communities had another factor in common: an abiding contempt for the Japanese. They saw them, without exception, as a race of comical little men with thick spectacles, bow legs and buck teeth. Because they rode on their mothers' backs as babies they were known to suffer from vertigo; they were so near-sighted that only one in 5,000 of their rifle shots would ever register. They read and wrote backwards, and turned a key to the left to open a door. Their assembly lines could turn out 200 planes a month at most. (The true figure was 426.) Their pilots were a byword for ineptitude. (In fact, cadets had a minimum 300 flying hours against a U.S. cadet's 200; carrier pilots averaged 800 hours). Above all, the notion that they could worst red-blooded Americans or true-blue Britons in battle was farcical, so say the least.

It was an attitude perfectly summed up by the distasteful query of an Australian battalion commander when Brooke-Popham inspected his troops. "Don't you think, sir," he asked, "that they are worthy of some better enemy than the Japanese?"

*

On Monday, 1 December, Hull made one last attempt to stem the Japanese tide. In his large gloomy State Department Office, which most closely resembled a railway station waiting room, dominated by an 11-ft high rubber plant, Kurusu and Nomura sat as they had done so many times before, slumped awkwardly in deep black leather armchairs. "Japan does not have to use a sword to gain for herself a seat at the head of the table," Hull emphasised yet again, unimpressed by Kurusu's assertions that Japan's purposes were different from Hitler's and that Premier Tojo could keep the military in check. "I put them wholly on the defensive," Hull later reported by phone to Halifax, ". . . I let them understand that I couldn't take care of things any longer as long as they kept inching on and on . . . I made it just as clear as I could."

No doubt he succeeded – but both Nomura and Kurusu were well aware that in Tokyo a different clock was ticking. Since the fateful Imperial Conference of 5 November, Japan had been pressing urgently for guarantees that in event of war Germany would honour the Tripartite Pact – even should Japan prove the aggressor. That would be automatic, Ribbentrop had assured them. On 30 November, the Japanese Ambassador in Berlin, General Hiroshi Oshima, warned both Hitler and Ribbentrop: "This war may come quicker than anyone dreams".

None knew this better than Kurusu. Soon after the meeting with Hull, he had discussed the darkening diplomatic horizon with Hidenari Terasaki, a young Foreign Service official. "Mr Ambassador," Terasaki asked him boldly, "why don't you become a national traitor? Why don't you go ahead and say to the Americans: 'We *will* get out of China?' . . . The war party knows . . . they will have to leave China, but they all prefer war with the United States . . . to admitting they have made such a mistake."

But time was running out, and both men knew it. On 3 December, in the Embassy's backyard on Massachusetts Avenue, clerks were already at work burning bales of secret papers.

Events now moved swiftly. On this same day, using Raoul Desvernine, a Washington attorney for the Japanese Mitsui interests as an intermediary, Kurusu met up at the Mayflower Hotel with a man who had once enjoyed a close relationship with Roosevelt: the 71-year-old financier and economist, Bernard Baruch. Urgently, Kurusu hammered home his message: the Japanese people and the Emperor wanted peace, but the war lords "were sitting with a loaded gun in each hand". The one solution, as Kurusu saw it, was to immobilise the military – with the President making a direct personal appeal to the Emperor.

Baruch was non-committal. The proposal, he wrote in a memo, "did not seem to be anything into which anybody could put their teeth". But at this eleventh hour anything was worth a try. He would, he promised Kurusu, convey his message to the White House.

*

It was already too late. On Thursday, 4 December, a squat (5ft 3in) muscular man awkwardly clad in a blue civilian suit was shouldering his way through the rush hour crowds at Yokohama Central Station. Like almost all his fellow passengers, he carried a large *furoshiki* – a square of coloured cloth tied at the corners – the accepted Japanese way of carrying parcels. But this was a parcel with a difference. Inside it, glinting with gold braid, was the uniform of a full admiral of the Imperial Japanese Navy.

Admiral Isoroku Yamamoto, C-in-C of the Japanese Combined Fleet, was en route to Hiroshima, where his flagship *Nagato* lay at anchor, surrounded by seven of the world's largest battleships.

It was to be his last day ashore for some time; the Admiral had been making his farewells. He took time out to visit his geisha, Kikuji, whom he had loved for six years, and sprawl on the straw-matting floor to play a game of *hana fuda* – flower cards – for a small wager. Then, having won seven yen, he dropped in on a small private party at Naval Headquarters. Many toasts were drunk to the success of Yamamoto's mission, though the Admiral, a teetotaller, took only token sips of *sake*.

As his train steamed southwards from Yokohama, through the frost-speckled rice fields, Yamamoto's mind went back over the angry arguments of the last months – arguments which had only been clinched, on 20 October, by his threat to resign his commission and retire to civil life. Only then had Admiral Nagano, as Chief of Naval Staff, given Yamamoto his reluctant blessing: "If he has that much confidence he must be allowed to carry on".

A onetime Naval Attaché in Washington, Yamamoto was bitterly opposed to war; he had seen the nation's industrial might from close quarters. Yet if war was inevitable, he remained convinced, the one way to remove a danger to Japan's southern flank was to wipe out the U.S. Pacific Fleet at Pearl Harbor, Hawaii – much as Hermann Göring had sought to knock out the R.A.F. as a prelude to the invasion of Britain.

His fellow admirals, seeing too many risks attached, had tried to argue him out of it. It was in vain. No sooner were objections raised than Yamamoto and his staff came up with solutions that worked. His plan for aerial torpedo attacks faced two prime obstacles: Pearl Harbor was both narrow (only 500 yards at some points) and shallow (thirty-eight feet) and was probably equipped with torpedo nets. To solve this problem, Yamamoto ordered the naval ordnance factories to supply him with 1,000-lb torpedos on the British model – but to equip them with special wooden stabiliser fins, ensuring they ran straight when hitting the water.

Such an operation called for well-trained pilots, daring enough to launch their torpedos from as low as 25 feet, but Yamamoto had these, too. At Kagoshima Bay, south of Kyushu, he had found a harbour that was a replica of Pearl, accessible only through a single entrance channel – and from then on the three-man crews had the time of their lives. In line of duty, their instructions were to buzz civilians and buildings impartially – dodging between telephone posts and chimneys, terrifying every fishing boat skipper across the bay. After fifty practice runs, low-altitude flights became second nature; bombing results showed an eighty per cent success rate.

Nothing was left to chance. Aboard *Akagi*, the flagship of Vice-Admiral Chuichi Nagumo commanding the six carrier task force, Commander Minoru Genda, in charge of planning, and Commander Mitsuo Fuchida, commanding all groups of the First Air Fleet, worked for days on a seven-foot square mock-up of the island of Oahu. At length they had memorised every hangar and drydock, the lay-out of the Navy Yard, the alignment of the battleships along the two-mile stretch of Ford Island.

Yet Yamamoto still remembered it as all too close for comfort. Had it not been for his threat of resignation – staking everything on his belief – "Operation Z", as it was code-named, would already be no more than a bulky folder gathering dust in a drawer at Naval Headquarters.

In Hiroshima, the wide waters of the bay seemed curiously empty when he arrived to board his flagship, Yamamoto knew why. At 5.30 p.m. on 2 December, with the diplomatic deadline long past, a coded signal had gone from Naval Headquarters in Tokyo to the powerful Pearl Harbor Striking Force, thirty-two ships strong. Already they were far away, pitching in the sullen waters of the North Pacific, bound for Pearl Harbor.

The message was one they had long awaited: CLIMB MOUNT NIITAKA. It meant: Begin The War.

*

At 7 a.m. on 4 December, before Yamamoto had even boarded his train in Yokohama, a convoy of twenty troop transports, all of them under 10,000 tons, had steamed at a laborious nine knots out of Samah Harbour, on Hainan Island, in the South China Sea. In a tiny airless cabin aboard the armoured headquarter's ship, *Ryujo Maru*, General Tomoyuki Yamashita, newly-appointed commander of the 25th Japanese Army, was in reflective mood.

His briefing was to invade north-eastern Malaya without warning and ultimately to capture the naval base at Singapore – tasks which seemed to call for tactics well-known to Hitler's *Wehrmacht* but alien to the Japanese until now.

It was an undertaking that the stocky imperturbable Yamashita had viewed soberly from the first. Following a brief parting from his wife, Hisako, in a cold bare room in the Japanese Officer's Club, Tokyo, he had flown to Hainan via Formosa and Saigon, making only one modest purchase along the way: a straw mat to sleep on in the tropical heat. At Samah, where the hotel proprietress had offered him her own daughter as a compliment, Yamashita had ordered a staff officer: "Take this girl away. She is a victim. When I am going to fight the enemy so soon how can I take a virgin tonight?"

Just as at Pearl Harbor, the Malayan attack called for speed and surprise, and Yamashita's formations had been pared down accordingly.

219

Streamlined for speedy landings and for moving fast through jungle, each division numbered only 12,000 men. Thus he would hit the Malayan coastline with barely 24,000 men – reinforced by 12,000 more from Indo-China and a submissive Thailand when the time came for the assault on Singapore.

The plan had called for much re-thinking. The men of the 5th and 18th Cavalry Divisions, mostly tough ex-coal miners from northern Kyushu, had been forced to undergo remount training, abandoning their horses in favour of bicycles; more than 6,000 cheap Japanese bicycles were now packed into the holds of the troop transports. As Yamashita envisaged it, the bicycle brigades would streak ahead of tanks and infantry as Hitler's Panzers had carved through France in 1940: 6,000 cyclists armed with rifles and grenades, pedalling as one, often for twenty hours a day, carrying only two days supply of rice, with the supply trucks often 100 miles behind. Two mechanics, attached to each battalion, would service up to twenty bicycles a day.

Since most had only seen service in Manchuria, Colonel Masanobu Tsuji, the Director of Military Operations, had come up with an ingenious concept: 40,000 copies of a pamphlet crammed with all the tropical expertise that a staff of thirty had gleaned from talks with sea captains, merchants and University professors. Covering everything from weapon care – "Make sure damp weapons do not rust" – to bivouacs – "the wood of mangrove trees burns well in its native state" – its title was buoyantly optimistic: "JUST READ THIS – AND THE WAR IS WON".

And Tsuji had made another decisive contribution to the campaign. On 22 October, after a five-hour reconnaissance flight in an unarmed plane, he noted that the airfields of Kota Bharu and Alor Star must be the prime objectives of the invasion. Failing this, British torpedo-bombers would certainly wreak havoc with the convoy's escort – two cruisers, ten destroyers and five submarines, which, for security reasons, were travelling 200 miles distant until the appointed Malayan rendezvous.

Yamashita, in approving these targets, still had minor reservations. Headquarters had been able to provide only small-scale maps of Malaya, and none of Singapore at all; thus far the man slated to topple the Singapore bastion had done all his planning from a high school atlas. And there was one other drawback, though doubtless he would overcome it: all his Army service had been in Europe or Manchuria.

Until the week he had paused in Saigon. the occasion of his fifty-sixth birthday, Yamashita had never seen a jungle in his life.

*

Saturday, 6 December, dawned crisp and cloudless in Washington, D.C. In Rock Creek Park, at the northern end of Connecticut Avenue, early morning horseback riders noted a hint of frost in the air, but a high bright sun was rising to the east, gilding the dome of the Capitol Building.

At 9.30 a.m., Stephen T. Early, the Presidential Press Secretary, was holding his usual morning conference with Washington's newsmen in the White House's west wing – but, he stressed, he could not "see any need for pads and pencils or even minds" that morning. The President had given them a day off to do their Christmas shopping.

"I suppose he is over at the White House writing a declaration of war personally," one reporter hazarded, but Early had to disappoint him. "He is over at the White House but he is not writing at the present time. He is shaving . . . no appointments for today and none for tomorrow and I don't assume there will be."

In the low rambling Navy Department building on Constitution Avenue, Secretary Frank Knox was winding up his daily top-level naval meeting. "Gentlemen," he asked, as if seeking reassurance, "Are they going to hit us?"

Rear Admiral Richmond Kelly Turner, Chief of the Naval Operations War Plans Division, spoke for all those present. "No, Mr Secretary. They are going to hit the British. They are not ready for us yet."

All over the capital there was the same relaxed air, as if war and declarations of war were the last things on the public mind; this was a week-end for picnics in the Blue Ridge Mountains or the Sunday afternoon football game at Griffith Stadium. Only a few men, in a position to know or suspect, sensed that every tick of the clock was bringing the United States closer to war.

At 11 a.m. Saburo Kurusu was receiving a courtesy call from an old friend, Ferdinand L. Mayer, a 54-year-old retired career diplomat whom he had known when both had been assigned to Lima, Peru. "Fred," he had confided, after making sure that none of the Embassy Staff was within earshot, "we are in an awful mess."

Mayer was puzzled. All through their hour-long talk, he had an intuition that Kurusu was trying to convey "something of the most shocking import" – words that he could not bring himself to utter. More than once he reaffirmed that "the show was up" in China, that Tojo was only trying to save face; the stumbling block, as Kurusu saw it, was Hull and the State Department, who distrusted him profoundly. "We believe that President Roosevelt as arbiter between ourselves and the Chinese is the best move from our point of view," he told Mayer seriously.

As a longstanding friend, Mayer placed more faith in Kurusu's intentions than Baruch had done. He begged the Ambassador to dine at 8 p.m. at the Georgetown mansion of his friend, Ferdinand Lamot Belin, multi-millionaire industrialist and former Ambassador to Poland. There they might discuss some way of establishing a more personal link with the President.

221

But Roosevelt, after three leisurely days digesting Baruch's report, had at last decided to act. For much of this Saturday afternoon he was labouring on an appeal to Emperor Hirohito, to be conveyed by the Ambassador, Joseph C. Grew, urging a Japanese withdrawal from Indo-China. The people of the Philippines, the East Indies, Malaya and Thailand, he stressed "were sitting on a keg of dynamite – it is clear that a continuance of such a situation is unthinkable".

"I address myself to Your Majesty at this moment in the fervent hope that Your Majesty may, as I am doing, give thought in this definite emergency to ways of dispelling the dark clouds. . . ."

As his secretary, Grace Tully, withdrew to type it up, the President's wife, Eleanor, looked in with an old friend, Justine Polier, a children's court judge from New York. "Well, Justine", Roosevelt greeted her, "this son of man has just sent his final message to the Son of God".

It was again too late. A bureaucratic bottleneck in the Tokyo military censorship department was to hold up the coded cable for ten and a half hours – too late for the Emperor to even consider intercession.

Meanwhile, in the Navy's Cryptographic Department, where most of the staff were preparing to leave at noon, one translator, Mrs Dorothy Edgers, had grown curious. With time to kill, she had begun leafing through low-priority "Magic" intercepts: those dealing with Hawaii had been piling up for days. Now she was electrified by a message from Tokyo to Consul-General Kita in Honolulu, dated 2 December. From this time on he was to report daily concerning all movements of ships, berthing positions and torpedo netting at Pearl Harbor. There were other later messages in the same vein.

Intrigued, Mrs Edgers elected to stay on duty and work overtime. By 3 p.m. she had brought the intercepts up to date – in time to present her evidence to Lieutenant Commander Alvin Kramer, Chief of the Translation Department, who had just checked in for duty. Incredibly, Kramer was more intent on criticising her translation – until finally he laid the intercepts aside. "We'll get back to this on Monday," he dismissed the indignant Mrs Edgers.

All over Washington on this day there was the same resolute refusal to believe the worst – as if the one thing to be feared was the over-dramatic gesture or reaction. In the Navy Department building, by 4.30 p.m., thirteen parts of a wordy Fourteen-Part "Magic" message from Tokyo to the Washington Embassy had now reached the decoders' desks – but Commander Laurence E. Safford, Chief of Security Intelligence Communications, saw no reason to set aside his evening engagement. He left his best man, Lieutenant George W. Lynn, to sort out the tangle.

Elsewhere in the building, the same unbelief prevailed. In his office, Rear Admiral Richmond Kelly Turner was about to switch off his desk lamp when he looked up. The Chief of the Intelligence Division, Rear

Admiral Theodore Stark Wilkinson, was standing before his desk. "You are mistaken, Kelly," he said quietly.

Turner was nonplussed. "Mistaken in what?"

"Mistaken that Japan would attack the United States."

Turner only shrugged. Back in July he had named Pearl Harbor as a "probable" target – but not, as he had told Knox that morning, in the forseeable future. In silence, the two men walked side by side down the long corridor.

Even at the Japanese Embassy there was no overriding sense of urgency. Just as on Constitution Avenue, the first thirteen parts of the message had arrived and been sent to the decoding room, but after deciphering the first nine parts, the staff adjourned. Since a colleague was being posted to a new station, a farewell party was in order.

It was 10 p.m. before they returned to the job – by now muzzy with *sake* and with less heart for the task ahead. Nonetheless, by midnight, four more parts had been completed. But the vital fourteenth part had still not arrived.

On Constitution Avenue, the Navy Department had worked faster; the first thirteen parts of the message had been decoded by 8.30 p.m. It was now that Commander Kramer saw a probability that Japan was breaking off negotiations. He began placing a series of urgent calls.

Soon after 9 p.m. Kramer drove to the White House, handing a sealed pouch to the officer on duty, Lieutenant Lester Schulz. In the second-floor Oval Office, Schulz found Roosevelt working on his stamp collection, chatting with Hopkins, who was reclining on the sofa.

It took Roosevelt a good ten minutes to digest Japan's explanation of why they could not accept Hull's peremptory note of 26 November as a basis for negotiations. Then, passing the sheaf of papers to Hopkins, he said tersely, "This means war". Hopkins was disgruntled. "Since war is undoubtedly going to come at the convenience of the Japanese, it's too bad we can't strike the first blow."

"No, we can't do that," Roosevelt argued, "We are a democracy and a peaceful people." Then, raising his voice a trifle, "But we have a good record". Abruptly, he lifted the phone; he wanted an immediate connection with the Chief of Naval Operations. But the operator explained that Admiral Stark was not in his quarters; he was with a party at the National Theatre, watching *The Student Prince*.

Roosevelt hung up; he would call later. "I don't want to cause public alarm by having him paged in a theatre," he told Hopkins. He, too, was wary of the dramatic gesture.

On Massachusetts Avenue, the hour was late; midnight had come and gone, but the Embassy was still awaiting the fourteenth part from Tokyo.

Finally, the staff gave up and went home; war or no war, a man needed his sleep. And Sunday might be quite a long day.

223

11

"What Was That Place? Could You Spell It?"

7–13 December, 1941

NEVER HAD HAWAII seen a dawn like this. In the early morning light, the Pacific Ocean, 230 miles north of Oahu, teemed with shipping, their battle ensigns snapping in the wind: the giant aircraft carriers *Akagi*, *Kaga* and *Soryu*, the vast new flattop *Zuikaku*, the light carriers *Hiryu* and *Shokaku*, two brand-new cruisers, the *Tone* and the *Chikuma*, nine destroyers and two old battleships, all of them pitching in heavy grey swells that rolled them from 12 to 15 degrees. Normally, when a swell exceeded 5 degrees, all manoeuvres were cancelled. But today there could be no turning back.

Aboard the command ship, *Akagi*, Admiral Chuichi Nagumo, knew exactly what his planes had to do. At 5.30 a.m. this morning, Sunday, 7 December, two Zero float-planes from *Chikuma* and *Tone* would carry out a last pre-attack reconnaissance – checking that the U.S. Pacific Fleet, following long-standing custom, had returned to Oahu for the week-end. Then, if all was reported in order, two mighty waves, 353 planes in all, would hit Pearl Harbor: the first wave to be launched at 6 a.m., the second at 7.15 a.m. Mitsubishi high-level medium bombers, Aichi Type 99 dive bombers, Nakajima Type 97 torpedo bombers – all had their roles to play.

Below decks, pilots and crews had been chafing for hours; by 3.30 a.m., Hawaiian Time, all of them had been rousted from their bunks. Each man had pulled on clean *mawashi* (loincloths), good-luck bellybands and freshly-pressed red shirts – to indicate a warrior's disdain for blood. Breakfast brought an extra treat – *sekihan*, rice with red beans, and tai, a red snapper fish, both of them dishes reserved for ceremonial occasions. To mark the solemnity of this day, many men now donned traditional *hashamaki* headbands. Then it was time for final instructions; in the dimly-lit briefing room of the *Akagi*, Commander Mitsuo Fuchida noted, it was so crowded that many pilots were huddled in the passage-way. As Fuchida left to board the commander's plane, singled out by its red and yellow striped tail, Commander Minoru Genda, who had planned this entire attack, quietly placed a hand on his shoulder. No words passed between them; there was no need.

Now, slowly, the six carriers swung into the east wind. Already, the planes were lined up on the flight decks, ready for take off, engines roaring and sputtering in the final warmup. Green lamps waved in a slow solemn arc, and one by one the fighters, led by Lieutenant Yoshio Shiga, raced down the runways, the torpedo planes and the dive bombers following, 183 planes streaking for Pearl Harbor.

On Oahu, at 6.30 a.m., one man had already written a small and intriguing footnote to history: Lieutenant William Woodward Outerbridge, U.S. Navy, who two days earlier had taken over his first command, the obsolescent destroyer U.S.S. *Ward*. At this hour, the harbour's torpedo net had been raised for an approaching vessel, the target ship *Antares*, and Outerbridge, roused from his bunk in the charthouse, was peering off the port bow at what he took to be a submarine's conning tower. Although Outerbridge could not know it, twenty Japanese submarines – including five midgets – were scheduled to wreak such havoc as they could once the main attack had started.

As Outerbridge shouted, "Go to general quarters", *Ward*, churning at 25 knots, closed to 100 yards; as her No 3 gun blasted the conning tower, the midget began to sink. "Drop depth charges," Outerbridge yelled, and four times the destroyer's whistle blasted, and four charges rolled from her stern.

But if Outerbridge was alerted to wage war, most men clung doggedly to peacetime. Because of a delay in decoding, *Ward*'s notification of the attack did not reach Captain John B. Earle, Admiral Kimmel's Chief of Staff, until 7.12 a.m. and even then Earle was doubtful. "We get so many of these false sightings," he told Admiral Claude C. Bloch, commander of the Fourteenth Naval District, and the Admiral agreed. "Ask for this to be verified," was his first reaction.

Forty miles north of Pearl Harbor, at Kahuku Point, Oahu's northernmost tip, two men briefly scented danger. Private George Elliott, Jnr., of the 515th Aircraft Signal Warning Service, had just spotted a large blip on his radar unit and called on his senior, Private Joseph Lockard, for clarification. Lockard was first convinced that the machine was acting up; no group so large had ever been registered on the oscilloscope. By now Elliott had traced the blip on the plotting board: 137 miles to the north and three degrees east. Excitedly, he urged the reluctant Lockard to call Fort Shafter, the Army's administrative headquarters.

Finally Elliott himself made the call – only to draw a blank. On this sleepy sun-drenched Sunday, the Information Centre could trace no one in authority save for Lieutenant Kermit Tyler, who was just finishing a four-hour shift at the Army's new interceptor centre. Though Tyler took the call and spoke to Lockard, he saw no occasion for urgency: planes were due in from the carrier *Enterprise* and Flying Fortresses were constantly passing through. But the blips were getting bigger by the minute, Lockard told him, now only 90 miles from Oahu. "Well," Tyler reassured him, before hanging up, "don't worry about it."

Aboard the 96 vessels – including eight battleships, eight cruisers and twenty-nine destroyers – in harbour this morning, many men faced pressing problems – or so it seemed to them at this moment. Yeoman Durrell Conner had chosen the seclusion of the flag communications office in the battleship *California* to finish wrapping his Christmas presents on time. In the galley of the aircraft tender *Curtiss*, the cooks were praying that the turkey they had just committed to the oven would be done in time for lunch. Perhaps the most worried man in the U.S. Pacific Fleet this morning was Ensign Joe Taussig, aboard the battleship *Nevada*. He had never stood watch for morning colours before – so what size American flag should he order to be flown?

On this bright Sunday morning, with a light north east trade wind caressing the green cane fields, the white puffs of cumulus cloaking the peaks of the Koolau Range, it seemed the least probable place on earth for an all-out war to begin. This thought came vividly home to Fleet Chaplain William A. Maguire, aboard *Arizona*, as he marvelled at the dazzle of the sun on the blue-grey water. "Joe," he told his assistant, Seaman Joseph Workman, "this is one for the tourist!"

High above Kahuku, Commander Fuchida, now circling the west coast of Oahu, had much the same feeling: fringed by blue-green cane fields, the waters of Pearl glimmered blue and brilliant in the sun, recalling the huge mock-up he had studied for so long. At exactly 7.49 a.m., he radioed the code-phrase, "To . . . to . . . to", back to *Akagi*; it meant, "First wave attacking", and that at any moment the Americans would be fighting back. Yet now, as he neared the target, Fuchida was riveted with surprise. Of the 231 Army planes on Oahu, all were lined up wingtip to wingtip on Hickam, Bellows and Wheeler Fields, like the Marine planes at Ewa – secure against the sabotage that General Short had feared. Not even a puff of ack-ack stained the crystal sky.

It was now 7.53 a.m. and Fuchida radioed Nagumo again, "Tora, Tora, Tora!", firing a blue flare to alert the nearest fighter squadron as he did so. Translated, this meant "Tiger, tiger, tiger", or "Surprise Attack Achieved"; without a hint of opposition, the torpedo planes could head straight for "Battleship Row".

Now confusion arose. When the fighter leader failed to waggle his wings in acknowledgement, Fuchida fired a second blue flare; promptly Lieutenant Shiga took this as a warning that surprise had not been achieved. Then, following the pre-arranged plan, he headed for Hickam Field to clear the sky of U.S. fighters. Lieutenant Commander Kakuichi Takahashi, leading fifty-one dive bombers, misread the signal, too; he veered off to knock out Pearl Harbor's ack-ack. Only the forty torpedo planes under Lieutenant Commander Shigeharu Murata read the signals

226

correctly, streaking for the forest of masts that was "Battleship Row". On the southern side of Ford Island they let fall the first torpedoes "like dragonflies dropping their eggs".

At 7.55 a.m., in the signal tower atop the Navy Yard water tank, seamen were just then hoisting the flag known as Prep, a white square in a solid field of blue, indicating that morning colours would rise in five minutes. It was at this moment that Pharmacist's Mate William Lynch, aboard *California*, heard a shipmate call: "The Russians must have a carrier visiting us. Here come some planes with the red balls showing clearly".

Within seconds he knew his error. As the first planes hurtled for Ford Island, the urgent voice of Commander Logan Ramsey, the Navy patrol plane operations officer, crackled from loudspeakers all over the harbour complex: "Air Raid Pearl Harbor! This is no Drill!"

The enormity of the attack was hard for any man to grasp. Few had even remotely suspected that hostilities were at hand. In the destroyer *Monaghan*, a seaman complained to Boatswain's Mate Thomas Donahue, "Hell, I didn't even know they were sore at us". Amid the shattering roar of the explosions, the geysering columns of water, the instinct of most was still to do what they had always done at this time. Aboard *Nevada*, Leader Oden McMillan and his 23-man band were already in position to play morning colours when Fuchida's 49 Kate bombers began their run-in. As the flight leader lay prone on his belly, watching through a peephole until his hurtling bombs "became small as poppy-seeds", McMillan's musicians crashed into "The Star-Spangled Banner" – and kept playing. Once they had started the National Anthem it never once occurred to them that they could stop – though they broke frantically for cover once the final note died.

Now, just after 8 a.m., the attack had barely started. Aboard *California*, the First Lieutenant, Lieutenant Commander M. N. Little, saw a high-flying plane bank steeply, followed by the bubble track of a torpedo; as it exploded a vast column of water mushroomed to port. Seaman W. W. Parker, on *Arizona*'s blister top, thought he was watching a dive-bombing practice; next instant a bomb had hit the forward turret, knifing downwards into the bowels of the ship. Then the battleship's boilers and forward magazines blew up, and with a violence few men have witnessed a column of blood-red smoke spewed thousands of feet skywards.

In one searing flash, 1,000 men had been wiped out. Even far above the target, Commander Fuchida felt his plane bouncing in the shock-wave like a ping-pong ball on a jet of water.

Radioman Glenn Lane, blown clean off the quarterdeck, was only one of many; from the cruiser *New Orleans*, 500 yards distant, Chaplain Howell Forgy saw the waters round *Arizona* as one vast "mass of bobbing oil-covered heads". And soon the fires were spreading; eighty feet to windward, *Arizona's* flames caught the stern and port quarter of the battleship *Tennessee*. Seaman S. F. Bowen, seeing a melting ball of fire shaped like a basketball descending, ran for dear life, noting that even his shoe laces were burning.

Now a wall of oily flame was advancing on the *West Virginia*; bomb splinters ripped at her bridge, cutting down Captain Mervyn Bennion with a fatal stomach wound. Soon she was listing so heavily that men crawled like flies along her decks; at once Lieutenant Claude Ricketts made for the counterflood valves, a brave but vain attempt. Although the after magazine was successfully flooded, to flood the forward magazine proved impossible; the water was now almost up to the main deck.

By 8.40 a.m., the second Japanese wave reached the target, 170 air-craft under Lieutenant Commander Shigekazu Shimazaki, but now the skies were so crowded they had to circle for fifteen minutes, like jet liners stacked by an airport. Chief Flight Petty Officer Juzo Mori's ambition – to die for a battleship rather than a cruiser – now seemed a vain one. Almost every battleship was already in mortal distress.

Midway along "Battleship Row", five torpedoes had struck the *Okla-homa* in as many minutes, cutting out her power, gouging open all that was left of her port side. As she wallowed into a 90-degree list, Comman-der Jesse Kenworthy ordered; "Abandon ship!"; *Oklahoma* was fast capsizing. Eight minutes later, she was bottom-up in the harbour mud, men scrambling as if on a giant treadmill along her rolling sides.

Aboard her, fully 125 men were still trapped, fighting for breath in a topsy-turvy world of random air-pockets, often no more than six inches square. Some never realised this until time had elapsed; Seaman George Murphy, splashing through the operating room of the ship's dispensary, wondered what section of *Oklahoma* could have rated a tiled ceiling. It never occurred to him that he was looking at the floor.

It would be thirty-six hours before rescue crews, working all night with oxy-acetylene torches, cut the surviving 32 men free from her hull.

Away from the harbour area, few citizens even realised a war had started; the tendency was to seek for natural causes. Nurse Freda Conine, awoken from off-duty sleep in the Navy Yard Hospital, imagined that technicians were blasting in the yard nearby. In the hillside suburb of Makalapa, Mrs Hall Mayfield, wife of Admiral Bloch's intelligence officer, also dismissed the explosions; she thought workmen were dyna-miting a hole for her new mail-box post. Lieutenant Clarence Dickinson, heading inland from the carrier *Enterprise* with a squadron of Dauntless dive bombers, put the black drifting smoke down to farmers burning their cane fields – until swooping Zeros holed his gasoline tank and killed his radioman. Numb with shock, Dickinson bailed out.

Some found the news impossible to take in. Soon after landing on a dirt road west of Ewa Field, Dickinson hitched a lift from an elderly couple

228

driving a blue sedan. The back seat was piled with a wicker basket and a Thermos bottle; the couple were bound for a picnic with friends at Fort Weaver. But although Dickinson begged them, "I must have a lift to Pearl Harbor. I've just been shot down!" his urgency escaped them. Time and again, as if explaining to a moron, the woman repeated, "But our friends are waiting for us. We are bringing the potato salad and they have the chicken".

It took a long time before it sank in: as of this moment the United States was at war.

Some were phlegmatic. Tai Sing Loe, the Navy's unofficial photographer, who specialised in souvenir portraits, stood amid all the holocaust, calmly snapping pictures of the burning fleet to adorn that year's Christmas card. Hubert Coryell, a senior citizen, watched the attack judicially from his hillside home, then, remarking, "Well, that was quite a show", drove off with his bow and arrows for archery practice at Kapiolani Park.

One man was consumed by bitter self-disgust. In his office at the submarine base, Admiral Husband E. Kimmel was standing with a group of officers, watching in ominous silence as the raid fanned across the harbor. Suddenly, with a slight "ping", a spent 50-calibre bullet broke through the window glass, striking Kimmel on the left breast before dropping to the floor. For a moment Kimmel just looked at it, then said quietly, "To bad it didn't kill me".

Most, once the realisation struck home, took thought mainly for others. In the Navy Yard Hospital, a shattered plaster cast beside a vacant bed was mute testimony that an officer with an injured leg had somehow contrived to hobble back to his ship. Lieutenant Harry Walker, junior medical officer of the *New Orleans*, who had undergone an appendectomy four days earlier, taped himself up and was on his feet for six hours at the Navy Hospital – operating, amputating, ingeniously using sterilised Flit guns to spray first-degree burns.

Inevitably, a few hewed resolutely to the rule book. At Wheeler Field, Second Lieutenant Robert Overstreet, of the 69th Aviation Ordnance Company, was arguing with a stubborn ordnance sergeant: Overstreet wanted both rifles and pistols, but the sergeant, shouting above the noise of the bombs, doubted he could supply them without written authorisation. When Overstreet exploded, "Hell, man, this is war", the non-com reluctantly gave in.

Even Ed Sheehan, a young shipyard worker employed at Drydock One, felt the need to go through the motions: arriving at the Shipfitter's Shop, in response to an urgent radio summons, his first instinct was to punch the time clock. But Foreman Dave Melville cut him short: "Never mind that, Eddie, for Christ's sake. Get on to Ten-Ten Dock and do what you can to help".

Obediently, Sheehan hastened on to Ten-Ten, the long quay facing Ford Island, on the harbour's eastern side, then he stopped dead. What he saw in that moment would live with him for ever.

The battleships were broken, crippled wrecks, seeming to writhe in an inferno of "orange flame and obscene black smoke". Only the cage-like top sections of the *West Virginia* and the *Tennessee* emerged dimly across the roiling waters. The *California* was listing heavily, licked by snapping fires. The *Arizona* was now almost completely hidden, her superstructure tilting crazily, among oily clouds rolling skywards in black cauliflower shapes.

Heads were bobbing in the black water; small white figures spilled from the sides of ships. Muffled explosions rumbled. Sudden gouts of flame stabbed the smoke, as fires ignited fuel or ammunition stores, illuminating the mass grave where 2,113 had died.

Rarely had men or ships taken such a beating – yet perversely they refused to acknowledge defeat. Once the first trauma of the attack had passed, seamen on ship after ship began fighting back with everything they had.

In the cruiser *New Orleans*, the lights had gone out and the ammunition hoists were out of action, but in the darkness men now formed human chains to move shells and powder from the magazines to the guns. All the time Chaplain Howell Forgy – himself forbidden to take any material part in this battle – slapped their grimy sweating backs, exhorting them, "Praise the Lord and pass the ammunition". It was no lone example. In *California*, before the order to abandon ship came at 10.20 a.m., Chief Radioman Thomas Reeves hung on alone in a burning passageway, manhandling ammunition until at last he fell unconscious and died. Water was surging into her forward air compressor station, but Machinist's Mate Robert Scott was still labouring to feed air to the five-inch guns. Though others, evacuating the station, begged Scott to follow them, he refused – "I'll stay here and give them air as long as the guns are going." The watertight doors closed behind him for the last time.

All rank and precedence were forgotten today. On the Flag Bridge of *Maryland*, Captain W. R. Carter, the Chief of Staff, told Commander W. F. Fitzgerald, the Staff Duty Officer, "We can't do much good up here. Let's go down to the guns and give them a hand". Promptly each man weighed in among the gun crews of the five-inch ack-ack batteries. Ensign Bill Ingram, who had swum from *Oklahoma* to man one of them, did receive a rebuke from the bridge – "on *Maryland* an officer is expected to wear his cap when he fights" – but others fought their first World War Two battle in less formal dress: *aloha* shirts, even bathing trunks. In the old cruiser *Raleigh*, Captain Bentham Simons directed the gun crews still dressed in the blue pyjamas he had worn when the attack began. Ensign Thomas Lombardi, helping the wounded on *West*

Virginia, cut a more bizarre figure still; arriving back from shore leave, he was still wearing a tropical dinner jacket and black tie.

Not only the warships were in fighting mood. Henry R. Danner, a Navy Yard machinist, noticed that gunners were needed on the battleship *Pennsylvania*, at present immobilised in Drydock One; without hesitation he doubled up the gangplank to become perhaps the first civilian in Navy history to form part of a combat gun crew. Aboard the YG-17, a 110-foot yard garbage scow, Chief Boatswain's Mate L. M. Jansen paused from collecting refuse to fight his old "honey barge" like a flagship, ordering his men to train their single fire hose on the burning *West Virginia* as strafing planes screamed low across the water.

Some ships tried to make a run for it – with only partial success. At 8.30 a.m. *Monaghan* was the first destroyer under way; en route down the channel she rammed the second midget sub to fall foul of the U.S. Navy, drove ashore, then righted herself, steaming out to sea while all the ships nearby rang with cheers. At 8.50 a.m., it was *Nevada*'s turn; already, for forty-five minutes, her guns had blazed defiance, downing at least one torpedo plane. Now she, too, made a break for it, steaming south-west down the channel – to many men the most inspiring sight they saw that day. But soon urgent signals were fluttering from the Naval District water tower: Stay clear of the channel. Reluctantly, the senior officer aboard, Lieutenant Commander Francis Thomas, saw the logic of it: if the Japanese sank *Nevada* in the entrance channel, the entire Pacific Fleet would be bottled up. Cutting his engines, Thomas nosed the battleship into Hospital Point, on the harbour's south shore. Again the dive bombers found her, wiping out the boat deck and most of its personnel.

At 1 p.m. back on *Akagi*, a heated discussion was at its height. Commander Fuchida felt he had arrived back just in time; refuelled and rearmed planes were being lined up on the flight deck, in readiness for a third attack, but Commander Genda, for one, was bitterly opposed to it. Hoping to sway the balance, Fuchida hastened to the bridge to report to Admiral Nagumo and his chief of staff, Rear Admiral Ryunosuke Kusaka.

"Four battleships definitely sunk," Fuchida reported succinctly, "One sank instantly, another capsized, two settled to the bottom of the bay and may have capsized."

Nagumo, he noted, looked pleased. "We may then conclude," he observed weightily, "that anticipated results have been achieved."

Fuchida was less certain. How much damage, he wondered, had been inflicted at Hickam and Wheeler Fields? (In fact, 188 planes had been destroyed and 159 damaged.) "We have achieved a great amount of destruction", he argued, "but it would be unwise to assume that we have destroyed everything. There are still many targets remaining that should be hit." In conclusion he stressed, "Therefore I recommend that another attack should be launched."

Genda disagreed. He was not in favour of risking planes and carriers any further. They had achieved all they could hope to do. By now the surprise factor had been lost. Fuchida saw it differently: a third attack might be vital to the outcome of the war. There were virtually no defences left – and a third raid might draw in carriers like the *Enterprise.*

Back in the home port of Kure, Admiral Yamamoto had already anticipated the final decision. Nagumo, like the Chief of Naval Staff, Nagano, and the other admirals had all fought bitterly against the attack on Pearl. Overruled, Nagumo, in the best traditions of the Imperial Japanese Navy, had given of his best to the operation and achieved everything that had been asked of him. But he was not a man to press his luck further.

Almost to himself, in the operations room of his flagship, *Nagato*, Yamamoto whispered: "Admiral Nagumo is going to withdraw".

Minutes later, just as he had anticipated, the news came through. On *Akagi*'s bridge, Admiral Kusaka had advised, "We should withdraw", and Nagumo had nodded his assent. "Please do."

The signal flags ran up on the yardarm then, ordering the change of course. By 1.30 p.m., the great fleet had swung about, heading for home across the Pacific.

*

All that Sunday morning, official Washington had been on edge. Everybody was expecting something big to break – not knowing what. As early as 7.30 a.m. Colonel Rufus S. Bratton, heading the Far Eastern Section of the Army's Intelligence Branch (G2) was relieved to find that a "Magic" intercept of the long-awaited fourteenth part of the Tokyo-Washington telegram had at length reached his desk.

Just as he had surmised, its conclusion was quite final: "The Japanese government regrets to have to notify hereby the American government that in view of the attitude of the American government it cannot but consider that it is impossible to reach an agreement through further negotiations".

Before 9 a.m., yet another intercept reached Bratton: "Will the ambassador please submit to the United States government (if possible to the Secretary of State) our reply to the United States at 1 p.m. on the 7th, your time".

By 11.30 a.m., men were sure of at least one thing: Something significant was timed for 1 p.m. this day. To Rear Admiral Theodore Stark Wilkinson, at the Navy Department, the fourteenth part constituted "fighting words". General George C. Marshall, as Chief of Staff, felt that a warning to Hawaii, Panama and the Philippines was called for – yet he hesitated to use the "scrambler" on his telephone in case of a wiretap.

In the end he decided to send a coded telegram through commercial channels, Western Union and R.C.A. Assigned no priority, it finally reached General Short via a messenger boy on a bicycle just as the attack was ending.

Admiral Stark had also noted the 1 p.m. deadline, but was fearful that a further alert, following his 27 November "war warning", might be crying wolf. Accordingly he made no further attempt to contact Kimmel.

At the State Department, Cordell Hull, who had also studied Togo's telegram, heard towards noon that Nomura and Kurusu had sought an appointment at 1 p.m. But at 1 p.m., Nomura phoned again: could Hull defer the meeting until 1.45?

Although Hull ascribed these delaying tactics to Japanese duplicity, the reverse was the case: the Embassy on Massachusetts Avenue was hopelessly ill-organised. Not until 10 a.m. this Sunday was the decoding office fully staffed – yet no regular secretary could be entrusted with typing up a top-secret message. The one man with security clearance, Katsuzo Okumura, a junior diplomat, was a two-finger typist at best. By 11 a.m., when he completed the first thirteen parts, Nomura was still unaware of what message he was to deliver at 1 p.m.

At this point, Okumura compounded confusion. Convinced that his amateurish typing would lose him face, he began typing the thirteen parts all over again.

In the large Oval Office at the White House, it was just another peaceful Sunday afternoon. Roosevelt, after finishing a leisurely tray lunch, was paring an apple; Hopkins, in a V-necked sweater and slacks, was lounging on the sofa, while Fala, Roosevelt's Scottie, begged for scraps. The brass ship's clock on the President's desk showed 1.47 p.m.

At that moment, the phone jangled, and Roosevelt, answering, heard the curiously calm voice of Frank Knox, calling from the Navy Department: "Mr President, it looks like the Japanese have attacked Pearl Harbor . . ."

"NO!" was Roosevelt's first shocked reaction, before calling Hull to break the news, though he added a caution, "We haven't confirmed it yet."

It was already 1.50 p.m., but Nomura and Kurusu had not yet reached the State Department; both men were still fretting in the Embassy foyer, waiting for the laggard Okumura to peck his way through the fourteenth part. It was 2.05 p.m. before an usher finally showed them into the State Department's waiting room.

Had the note been delivered at 1 p.m., Japan would have abided – albeit strictly – by the rules of war: at 7.50 a.m., Hawaiian Time, the time of the attack, it was 1.20 p.m. in Washington. The delivery of the note would have preceded the strike by perhaps twenty minutes – twenty-five at most. At 2.20 p.m., when Hull, having given the envoys fifteen minutes to cool their heels, agreed to receive them, Pearl Harbor had been under attack for more than an hour.

When Nomura apologised for the delay in decoding, Hull asked pointedly, "Why one o'clock?". But the Ambassador genuinely did not know. His black-ribboned prince-nez adjusted, Hull began to read the message all over again. Kurusu and Nomura remained awkwardly, standing; no one had invited them to sit down.

At last, with cold measured anger, Hull let fly. "In all my fifty years of public service," he told them, "I have never seen a document that was more crowded with infamous falsehoods and distortions; infamous falsehoods and distortions on a scale so huge that I never imagined until today that any government on this planet was capable of uttering them."

Nomura made to speak, then, but Hull, his right arm raised, cut him short. "Good day," he said with icy finality, but as the envoys departed, he reverted to the log-cabin language of his native Tennessee; an angry explosion of "scoundrels and piss-ants" burst from him.

At 5 p.m. secretary Grace Tully was called to Roosevelt's study. "I'm going before Congress tomorrow," the President told her, "I'd like to dictate my message. It will be short."

Then, inhaling deeply, he began – the same calm tone in which he always dictated his mail, Grace Tully noted, only today there was one difference. As he spoke each word, slowly and incisively, the President was specifying every punctuation mark and paragraph.

"Yesterday comma December 7 comma 1941 dash a date which will live in infamy dash . . ."

*

It was equally a date which would live in history. At long last, and irrevocably, the two-ocean war had come to America. A nation which had awoken dubious and divided on the morning of 7 December was now, by early afternoon, united by a common enemy, a common hurt.

For many, the news came with bewildering suddenness. In Washington, listeners to a sponsored radio programme heard an abrupt: "Flash! The Japanese have attacked the United States Fleet in Pearl Harbor! End of Flash – use Sweetheart Soap!" In New York, a disgruntled taxi-driver told Lieutenant-Commander Ewan Montagu, on a mission from the Admiralty in London, "They're putting out some radio programme like that one about the Martians invading the earth . . . something about the little yellow-bellies bombing Pearl Harbor." Only as he entered the Oyster Bar at Grand Central Station did the truth dawn on Montagu: a blind drunk naval rating, jamming a cigar into the officer's mouth, sobbed, "Thank God we're buddies again!" Thus Montagu learned that England had a new ally.

There were early flashes of panic. Henry Morgenthau, who as Secretary of the Treasury controlled White House security, called for the entire guard to be quadrupled and issued with machine-guns – until Roosevelt, with his habitual calm, defused the tension. One helmeted bayoneted sentry for every 100 feet of fencing was all he would permit – nor would he shelter in the Treasury vault, he said, unless he could play poker with Morgenthau's hoard of gold.

All over the United States, the mood in these first hours, was uneasy. An incensed patriot chopped down four Japanese cherry trees in Washington's Tidal Basin. Soldiers at Santa Cruz, Monterey and Carmel evacuated 1,000 householders along a 40-mile stretch of coastline, speeding them inland for safety. Bellboys on the roof of Boston's Hotel Statler poured gallons of paint to mask the arrow indicating the airport. In Scarsale, New York, mothers began a vigil in parked cars outside the High School, ready to spirit their children home if bombers appeared.

In downtown Honolulu, nerves were at snapping point. Now, just as in London and Paris, in Berlin and Moscow, the street lamps had gone out. The few military cars in evidence crawled with blue-painted headlights. Silent frightened groups of people huddled in the lobbies of hotels and boarding-houses, listening for the first cry of the siren that would herald the Japanese return. "This town is sitting right on the edge of its chair," one observer noted, "all ready to get up and run somewhere."

Slowly the mood changed – to one of sober restraint and resolution. "Pull yourself together, young man," Hull told the lamenting Thai Minister, "we're going to lick the Hell out of them." Long lines piled up outside the recruiting offices; one New Yorker, finding the Army line too long, switched to the Navy line. The year's end would see 28,349 men newly enlisted. Tin Pan Alley weighed in with two eminently forgettable pop tunes, *Goodbye, Mama, I'm Off to Yokohama* and *I'm Gonna Slap a Dirty Little Jap*. In Honolulu, the sale of defense bonds increased tenfold. Under a misty ragged moon, crowds five deep pressed against the White House railings for hours on end. There was nothing they could usefully do there, but it seemed the place to be.

"That day ended isolation for any realist," that most xenophobic of Senators, Arthur Vandenberg, noted in his diary, and he spoke for hundreds of thousands like him. On 8 December – the day that Roosevelt, in a long blue Navy cloak, asked Congress for a declaration of war and got it within six-and-a-half minutes – the America First Committee disbanded, calling on all its members to support the war effort.

Now, like every American dwelling, the White House was dark at night; although the housekeeper, Mrs Henrietta Nesbitt had gone shopping for blackout material, she had secured only three bolts of cloth.

Black sateen shades and windows painted black proved the final solution. Under the portico of the driveway leading from the Pennsylvania Avenue entrance, the great white light that had burned for as long as anyone could remember was now dark.

Late on 8 December, it was Samuel I. Rosenman, Roosevelt's speech-writer, who pointed out this phenomenon to his collaborator, Robert E. Sherwood. "I wonder how long it will be before that light gets turned on again," he pondered.

Sherwood's reply voiced the sober truth. "I don't know – but until it does, the lights will stay turned off all over the world."

*

Elsewhere, reactions were mixed. Few were so uncompromising as Ramón Serrano Sŭner, Franco's pro-Axis brother-in-law and Minister of Foreign Affairs; on his instructions, his entire staff left their visiting cards at the Japanese Legation as a mark of esteem. More were fearful of what this portended, like old Marshal Pétain in Vichy. "Never before has the whole world been at war," he quavered to Admiral Leahy, ". . . I don't know what will come of it."

In the *Wolfsschanze*, East Prussia, Hitler's first reaction was to slap his thighs in delight, announcing "The turning point!" then he raced from his bunker through the icy darkness to break the news to Keitel and Jodl. Then a sobering thought struck him: "How strange that with Japan's aid we are destroying the positions of the white race in the Far East – and that Britain is fighting against Europe with those swine the Bolsheviks!" Nonetheless the Tripartite Pact must be honoured. On 11 December, Ribbentrop, summoning the hapless U.S. Chargé, Leland Morris, to the Foreign Office, screamed at him, *"Ihr Präsident hat diesen Krieg gewollt; jetzt hat er ihn."* (Your President has wanted this war; now he has it.) On the same day Mussolini followed suit.

In England, the news was like a sudden reprieve. At 3 p.m. Washington time – 9 p.m. in London – the First Secretary, William Hayter, calling on behalf of Lord Halifax, broke the news of Pearl Harbor to a sleepy sounding Resident Clerk at the Foreign Office. The news, Hayter stressed, should be passed to the Prime Minister, but the clerk seemed doubtful of Churchill's interest. "What was that place?" he asked languidly, "could you spell it?"

In fact, Churchill's first intimation of the attack came, like most Britons, when the B.B.C.'s Alvar Lidell read the 9 p.m. news bulletin. Week-ending at Chequers, along with Ambassador Winant and Harriman, Churchill had spent much of dinner lost in thought, his head buried in his hands. Only when his butler-valet Sawyers carried in a small flip-top radio, a present from Hopkins, and the news came through, was

236

Churchill galvanised. Starting for the door, he announced resolutely, "We shall declare war on Japan." Winant, too, was swift to leave the table. "Good God," he expostulated, "you can't declare war on a radio announcement."

Not without difficulty, he coaxed the Premier into waiting until a call had been put through to the White House. "Mr President, what's this about Japan?" Churchill demanded peremptorily, once the connection was made, and Roosevelt told him, "It's quite true. . . . We are all in the same boat now."

"So we had won after all!" was the first thought that flashed through Churchill's mind.

Yet the mass of Britons knew no such euphoria. After twenty-seven weary months of war, the capacity to feel and react was almost dead. Not one American flag, Harold Nicolson noted, flew in the streets of London. In many regions Mass Observations reported "a feeling sometimes verging on sadistic pleasure that at last America is to know fully what war means". "All they have to do is send out . . . Errol Flynn and everything will be all right," was a typical sarcastic comment.

Even so, Britain now needed all the allies she could command. At 2 a.m. on 8 December, following three soaring red flares from the head-quarters ship *Ryujo Maru*, 100 motor boats breasting nine-foot waves were bringing 24,000 men of the 25th Japanese Army ashore at Kota Bharu, Malaya. At 7 a.m. thirty-six Japanese fighters wiped out the entire island air force – seven planes – at Hong Kong's Kai Tak airport.

Now the battle was as wide as the world.

*

Port by port, fort by fort, the Far East was invested. Thailand capitulated without a shot after five-and-a-half hours. Guam Island, 1,000 miles west of Wake, fell on 10 December within the space of a morning, despite bitter resistance by blue-jackets and Marines; a Japanese naval captain, entering the nurses' quarters, told Ensign Leona Jackson: "So sorry to tell you – all your fleet sunk. All your ships on bottom. No more." Only one blue-jacket, Radioman 1st Class George Ray Tweed, relying on skills learned on hunting trips in Oregon, escaped the dragnet; taking to the underbrush armed only with a handsaw, a machete and a pocket-knife he survived for two-and-a-half years like a latter-day Robinson Crusoe, amassing $6,000 in back-pay.

It was not only at Pearl Harbor that the Americans were caught unawares. At noon on 10 December, eighty Japanese bombers winged their way unopposed to Cavite, eight miles south-west of Manila, the only American naval base in the Far East beyond Pearl Harbor, pounding it to rubble – a blow so crippling that Admiral Thomas C. Hart, commanding the United States Asiatic Fleet, reported Manila as no longer tenable. For three days earlier, in a disaster as great as Pearl Harbor itself, the Japanese had hit Clark Field, 65 miles north of Manila, destroying all but three out of 35 Flying Fortresses.

That it happened is undisputed; why will always be open to doubt. As Major-General Lewis Brereton, commanding the Far East Air Force, told it, five-and-a-half hours after the attack on Pearl – 7.30 a.m., 7 December, Manila time – he sought permission to bomb Formosa, known to be a Japanese stronghold, 600 miles north. But MacArthur's chief of staff, Major-General Richard K. Sutherland, after consulting with his chief, refused: "The General says . . . don't make the first overt act."

At 9.25 a.m., Brereton phoned Sutherland again – and again permission was refused. But some time after 10 a.m., Brereton was to claim, he discussed with MacArthur a photographic reconnaissance of Formosa by three Flying Fortresses, a prelude to a subsequent bombing attack. Later MacArthur hotly denied any knowledge of a Formosan sortie, although a radiogram bearing his name, perhaps sent by Sutherland, went to General Marshall on this day, mentioning a Formosa attack on 9 December. And at 11 a.m., following another call from Sutherland, Brereton was able to tell his staff that a bombing mission had been authorised – once photographs revealed the nature of the targets.

At this hour, the Fortresses were cruising over Mount Aryat, to avoid being caught on the ground; coded recall signals now instructed them to return to Clark. Three were equipped with cameras; 100-lb and 300-lb bombs were hoisted into the others. Now, inexplicably, Brereton called in all his fighters, fifty-plus P-40s, for refuelling. At noon, not one fighter was circling Clark Field.

Around this time, Luzon Island's one radar set, at Iba, on the west coast, picked up the first blips of a vast armada: 108 Mitsubishi bombers and 84 Zeros were heading for Clark. The warning never reached the field; the teletype operator, along with both pilots and crewmen, was then at lunch. All of them were off guard, since few of them even credited the news of Pearl Harbor; they dismissed it as a ruse by the top brass to keep them on their toes.

Some time after 12.10 and before 12.40 – such were the discrepancies in timing – pilots and crewmen, lolling on the parched grass, were smoking and passing the time of day, watching the three Fortresses of the reconnaissance unit taxi into position. Just then, a mile east of Clark, at Fort Stotensberg, taxi-driver George Setzer saw a great huddle of silver planes arriving from the northwest. "It's about time they came to help us," he said gleefully. At Clark Field the reaction was the same. As someone shouted, "Here comes the navy," a sergeant carefully focused his Kodak on the first V of planes – dropping now to 22,000 feet.

Lieutenant Edgar D. Whitcomb, a navigator with Colonel Eugene Eubank's 19th Bombardment Group, was heading for the colonel's headquarters seeking news of the mission. At the door he ran into his pilot, Lieutenant Ed Green. "Are we going to bomb?" he asked.

"Still no orders to bomb," Green replied, "but we may get some photos."

They never did. Abruptly Whitcomb heard "a loud crackling sound like that of dry boards being broken"; near at hand a pilot asked bemusedly, "Why are they dropping tinfoil?" In anguished reply, another man yelled, "That's not tinfoil, those are goddamned Japs." Already the P-40 pilots were racing for their cockpits – but only three of them even left the ground.

An inferno of flame swept the airfield. The reconnaissance Fortresses were the first to take fire, burning with a white lambent flame; flash fires sprang up in the long cogon grass, "roaring and crackling like an evil beast". Men ran frantically for slit trenches, finding all too few of them; in this sudden unforeseen attack, 55 were to die and more than 100 were wounded. Waves of planes – heavy bombers, dive bombers, fighters – swept the field for almost an hour until it was all but unrecognisable. A corona of dust and black oily smoke towered above the charred aircraft, visible as far as Manila, 65 miles away.

The sum total of American striking power in the western Pacific had been wiped out – and the war had barely started.

*

The British were faring as badly. Five days before Pearl Harbor, on 2 December, the battleship *Prince of Wales* – which ever since Placentia Bay had been known jovially as "Churchill's Yacht" – arrived in Singapore as an integral part of Force Z: the battleship herself, the old cruiser *Repulse* and the destroyers *Electra*, *Express*, *Vampire* and *Tenedos*. "A rumour was whispered," noted Gunner Russell Braddon, of the 2/15th Field Regiment, 8th Australian Division, "that they came to Malayan waters because the Australian Government had (using the possible withdrawal of its troops in the Middle East as a weapon) blackmailed the British Government into sending two capital ships out to Singapore."

Braddon and his mates had also noticed one strange omission: *Prince of Wales* and her sister ships had no air cover at all. The explanation was a last-minute mishap; the crack new aircraft carrier H.M.S. *Indomitable*, with a squadron of nine Hurricanes, which was to have watched over Force Z had run aground in the West Indies. Repairs would not be completed for twenty-five days – and with the situation in the Far East worsening daily, the two capital ships had been sent ahead in the hope of stabilising events.

Nor could the newly-appointed C-in-C of the British Eastern Fleet, Admiral Sir Tom Phillips, who had made *Prince of Wales* his flagship, rely on local reinforcements: Brooke-Popham's paucity of aircraft was now all too apparent. Following on his decision to sail north, intercept the Japanese convoys and sink their transports, Phillips thought he could wreak havoc among the invasion fleet given a modicum of fighter cover. Before sailing on 8 December, he made three requests of the air commander, Air Vice-Marshal Charles Pulford: reconnaissance 100 miles north of Force Z during daylight on 9 December, 100 miles reconnaissance, pivoting on Singora, 120 miles north of Kota Bharu, starting at first light on 10 December, and fighter protection in the area during this same day. Fulford's final reply, though unhelpful in tone – "Regret fighter protection impossible" – was nonetheless ambiguous.

Later, experts were to speculate that Phillips took this signal to mean that no fighter cover would be available anywhere in the Gulf of Siam – whereas the air chief was specifying the Singora area alone.

At mid-day on 8 December, Phillips had, in any case, made his decision plain at a meeting of his staff. There was the option, he said, of sailing "away to the East – Australia. Or we can go out and fight. Gentlemen, we sail at five o'clock."

At 53, Phillips, whose 5 ft 1 in. had earned him the nickname of "Tom Thumb" was not a man easily gainsaid. Moreover, like many naval officers, he had long believed that a properly-armed well-fought ship had nothing to fear from air power. This conviction had even led his old friend, Air Vice Marshal Arthur "Bomber" Harris, to tease him, "One day, Tom . . . your ship will be smashed to pieces by bombers and torpedo aircraft; as she sinks your last words will be, 'That was a ------- great mine!'"

This light-hearted prophecy was unknown to the officers and ratings of *Prince of Wales*, but at twilight on Monday, 8 December, as the ships drew out into the Straits of Johore, the palm trees ashore etched against a blood-red sunset, some men had a curious intuition of disaster. Midshipman Kenneth Townsend-Green, transferred at the last minute to the Oerlikon guns, recalled telling the Gunnery Officer Lieutenant Commander Colin McMullen, that he felt he needed more practice – and how McMullen had replied, "Yes, well, I think you will tomorrow – and you'll be lucky if you live it out there." Back in Singapore, aboard H.M.S. *Mauritius*, Midshipman Henry Leach thought of his father's worried mien during their farewell dinner the night before. "Let 'em come," young Leach had said vaingloriously, "Let's have a go at them," and was startled when Captain Leach replied, "I don't think you have any idea of the enormity of the odds we are up against."

By 1.45 p.m. on 9 December, *Prince of Wales* and her escort were deep into the Gulf of Siam, steaming at 14 knots beneath lowering clouds, swept by dense squalls of tropical rain. Sighting nothing, they were unaware that they themselves had been sighted: on the Japanese submarine I–56 a radioman was at this moment tapping out an urgent message to the Navy's 22nd Air Flotilla in Saigon. But static made receipt of his message well-nigh impossible; not until 3 p.m. did Rear Admiral Sadaichi Matsunaga get word of the sighting. At once he ordered planes to prepare for an attack at sea.

Now a strange confusion arose. In *Prince of Wales'* "A" turret, soon after 9 p.m., a gunnery rating spotted a small flicker on his radar screen. Excitedly, he told Sub-Lieutenant Michael Buxton, "Do you know, sir, I think I saw something." For an instant Buxton saw it too – what appeared to be a small biplane 3,000 yards away – and rang the bridge. Phillips reached a logical conclusion: they had been spotted by Japanese planes and the surprise element was lost. Shortly, the disgruntled officers and men of Force Z heard a change of plan: they were returning to Singapore.

In fact, the planes which had forced Phillips to turn back had been Allied planes and had never even seen the British Fleet, but as the ships turned southward, Phillips received a sudden message from Singapore's Naval Base: ENEMY REPORTED LANDING AT KUANTAN – on Malaya's east coast, midway between Singapore and Kota Bharu. Soon after midnight, Phillips changed course, once more heading north for Kuantan.

Off Kuantan, fully an hour had passed before a heliograph from H.M.S. *Electra*, which had sped inshore to investigate, blinked across the water: PERFECT PEACE. Sub-Lieutenant Buxton was only one of many who cursed angrily: what on earth was the force doing, hanging about like this? By this time he and many like him had lost all confidence in Phillips.

As the morning wore on, it was the heat more than the Japanese that occupied men's minds. In the Cypher Office, five decks below, Paymaster Sub-Lieutenant Alec Compton noted a temperature of 110 degrees Fahrenheit; each man worked with a towel round his neck, to mop the perspiration, sipping constantly at fresh lime juice. In the boiler rooms, conditions were worse; the temperature by the gauge board showed 135 degrees Fahrenheit.

By 9 a.m. three Japanese groups – 96 high-level torpedo bombers, 10 search planes – had almost abandoned their quest for the British; banked clouds obscured their view. Then, at 10.15 a.m., as they turned for home, one plane sighted them; two battleships and three destroyers, 70 miles south-east of Kuantan. The fourth destroyer, *Tenedos*, was already returning to Singapore to refuel.

At 10.30 a.m. the search planes in turn made radio contact with the twenty-seven torpedo planes of Kanoya Air Group. The group's three squadrons now altered course.

In *Prince of Wales'* look-out station, Ordinary Seaman Daniel Stowell

241

saw them first: a wave of high-level bombers glinting against the sun. Small black spheres were spilling from their hatches; to Sub-Lieutenant Alan Franklin they seemed to fall in diamond patterns. On all five ships bugles blared; from the loudspeakers came the urgent command, "Enemy aircraft approaching! Action Stations!" Within six minutes, battle was joined.

The noise was deafening. Aboard *Repulse*, C.B.S. correspondent Cecil Brown noted that even the chatter of the pom-poms, the "Chicago pianos" was obscured by the hard sharp crack of the 4-inch high altitude guns; red-blue flames burst from the muzzles, and empty cordite cases tumbled from their scuttles like a berserk jackpot machine. On the funnel-shaped muzzles the black paint began rising in blisters as big as a fist.

Yet few hits were scored. Once again, as in the *Bismarck* action, the pom-poms were jamming, one gun suffering twelve failures, another eight. Midshipman Townsend-Green noted disgustedly, "We might just as well have been firing blanks." At 11.41 a.m. the Japanese readied for the coup-de-grace: nine torpedo planes under Lieutenant Sadao Takai, dived for *Prince*'s port side. From her bridge, Midshipman Michael Pruett saw them clearly: pale blue torpedoes with silver fins.

On *Prince of Wales*' compass platform, Lieutenant Commander R. F. Harland, the torpedo specialist officer, had just remarked, "I think they're going to do a torpedo attack." But Phillips, he was almost certain, replied, "No they're not. There are no torpedo aircraft about."

At 11.44 a.m. they knew their error. At least one torpedo – possibly two – struck on the port side, aft of her bridge: in the Cypher Office Alec Compton was conscious of "a strange vibration like a boy running a stick along a stretch of corrugated iron". The projectile had found the 240-foot port after propellor shaft, but still it rotated like a giant flail, churning at 204 revolutions per minute, slicing through the water-tight comparments. In the S 4 turret, Boy Seaman Edward Grindley heard a vast booming sound as they burst one by one; more than twenty in the space of four minutes. The power supply had gone, and in the stifling darkness below decks the lights were going out.

At 12.10 p.m. the two black balls which told the other ships of Force Z that *Prince of Wales* was no longer under control were hoisted from her yardarm.

All over the doomed ship men had their private yardsticks of how serious things were. Leading Telegraphist Eric Shawyer, of Phillips' staff, was in the Wireless Office when he chanced to peer down the voice-pipe; in the Coding Office below he saw water racing and frothing, then blackness. The water had reached the top of the pipe. In the Bakery Flat, Petty Officer Charles Firbank was shaken to see a kettle of lime-juice tilt gently into a horizontal position. Leading Seaman Douglas

Spinks, in the Radar Office, realised that the ship had slowed to three knots.

At 12.33 p.m. *Repulse*, struck by five torpedoes, was seen capsizing two miles astern, along with 513 members of her crew still aboard. Still, some could barely take it in. Outside *Prince*'s Central Receiving Office, a stoker pelting down a ladder yelled, "The *Repulse* has gone!" prompting a vague query, "Where to? Singapore?" The reply was withering: "No, you bloody fool – to the bottom."

Within three days of Pearl Harbor, the myth of the impregnable battleship had ended for ever – but still the legend died hard. At 12.04 Captain William Tennant, aboard *Repulse*, had taken it on himself to signal Singapore: ENEMY AIRCRAFT BOMBING, and eleven old Brewster Buffalo fighters lumbered off to the rescue. Phillips, though, was stubborn to the last, seeking a naval solution. His one signal – at 12.50 p.m. – besought only destroyers and tugs.

There was little that either ships or aircraft could have done now. At 12.40 p.m. ten of Lieutenant Takeda's 2nd Squadron, Minoro Attack Group, flying wingtip to wingtip, loosed a salvo of seven bombs from directly overhead; one, bursting through an armoured deck, exploded in the Cinema Flat, where patients of an overflow casualty clearing station were clustered. In this narrow space, hundreds now died screaming, skinned alive by scalding steam.

From this nightmare of rushing water and red-hot steam, men bore brief indelible impressions. Leading Stoker Alfred Llewellyn saw a turret whip out of control to cut a boy seaman clean in half. Others recalled those who tried to fight their way through portholes but never made it. Marine Douglas Hall felt a depression so deep that even after swimming for safety he was swallowing great gulps of water and fumbling for the knot on his lifebelt, hoping to die.

Some were taking elaborate final precautions: Sub-Lieutenant Joseph Blackburn, scenting the pungent whiff of cordite, promptly put on his gas-mask. Sick Berth Attendant Walter Bridgewater safeguarded his stock of pound notes in the approved Navy way – inside a contraceptive. Others felt urgent last-minute regrets. Sub-Lieutenant Franklin recalls thinking, "I wish I'd studied harder at school". Midshipman Townsend-Green felt a sudden desperate need to live – "I can't die before I'm married".

Six minutes earlier Captain Leach, seeing the position as hopeless, had ordered all hands to abandon ship: *Express*, *Electra* and *Vampire* were already moving in to pick up survivors across a sea packed with bobbing heads "like a football field". Soon hundreds were lying prostrate on their red-hot decks, retching up black oil and sea-water. Even now, with the ship listing 40 degrees to port, there was no panic, only a strange decorum. Ordinary Seaman Douglas Marshall noted little groups carefully taking off their shoes, lining them up tidily by the taffrail as if outside a hotel bedroom door. Then men jumped, slid or dived into a black velvety carpet of oil two feet deep. At 1.20 p.m., with Admiral Phillips, Captain Leach and 327 officers and ratings still aboard, *Prince of Wales* wallowed from sight – creating a suction so great that Leading Telegraphist Bernard Campion, plunging far below the water, surfaced stripped of all his clothing save for one sock.

It was Lieutenant Haruki Iki, who had led the 3rd Squadron of the Kanoya Air Group, who paid a final tribute to the *bushido* with which the British had fought. Next day, at dawn, flying low over the sunken ships, he dropped bunches of wild flowers.

*

No Japanese bouquets were forthcoming for the defenders of Malaya, Hong Kong or the Philippines. In all three theatres, the Japanese re-action was unanimous: initial bewilderment gave place to scathing contempt.

As their troops thrust ever further from the Malayan frontier General Yamashita and his Director of Operations, Colonel Tsuji, at first were puzzled men. In thirty-six hours, they had met no enemy resistance worthy of the name. Abandoning the frontier the British had fallen back – blowing a trench 30 yards deep and 100 yards long across the road down which they retreated. "Is it the enemy we must fear?" one officer asked Tsuji. The Colonel was sceptical. "What we have to worry about is the quantity of gunpowder he has available for use."

On the rainy pitch-dark night of 11 December, Tsuji had proof of this. Thirty miles south of the frontier, the much-vaunted Jitra Line, six months under construction and intended as a divisional strongpoint for three months, was breached in fifteen hours by barely 500 men – at a cost of 27 killed, 83 wounded. More than 3,000 British and Indian troops surrendered. Behind them those who fled left 50 field-guns, 50 heavy machine guns, 300 trucks and armoured cars, plus three months provisions and ammunition.

Already fear was abroad – the fear expressed by one senior staff officer of 3 Indian Corps: "The little men will go through everything. Swamp, jungle, rivers, crocodiles – nothing seems to stop them." As early as 12 December, General Murray-Lyon, the commander of 11th Division, remarked uneasily of his troops, "I have not seen that look in men's eyes since March, 1918." Afterwards, Lieutenant-General Percival, as G.O.C., commented sourly that Lieutenant-General Sir Lewis Heath, 3 Corps Commander, had developed "a withdrawal complex", while Major-General Gordon Bennet, the Australian G.O.C., was jittery from the first – "the question of his own escape . . . I believe became an obsession with him". Yet Percival's own dispositions were equally to blame. Hewing strictly to the concept of "Fortress Singapore", he had retained five crack battalions to defend the island, leaving the rest of Malaya to his weakest divisions.

Air-cover was now non-existent – as the men of Force Z had discovered to their cost. At Kuantan, a new coastal airfield, the pilots of one Australian Hudson squadron had decamped for Singapore on the day of the invasion, leaving all their bombs and spare equipment on the field. "For the first and last time in my life I felt ashamed of being an Australian," confessed Pilot Officer Roy Bulcock, the transport officer, but many airfields witnessed the same scene. "There have been instances where aerodromes appear to have been abandoned in a state approaching panic," Brooke-Popham charged angrily. "Stores that will assist the enemy in his further advance have been left behind, material that is urgently required has been abandoned, and a general state of chaos has been evident."

To Alfred Duff Cooper, Churchill's resident Adviser for Far Eastern Affairs since September, that chaos had been evident for months. "Brooke-Popham", he wrote frankly to the Premier, "is a very much older man than his years warrant . . . sometimes seems on the verge of nervous collapse", nor was he much impressed by the Governor of the Straits Settlements, Sir Shenton Thomas – "the mouthpiece of the last person he speaks to". Percival came in for more damning comment still – "a nice, good man who began life as a schoolmaster. I am sometimes tempted to wish he had remained one . . . it is all a field-day at Aldershot to him. He . . . is always waiting for the umpire's whistle to signal cease fire and hopes that when that moment comes his military dispositions will be such as to receive approval."

For there was no brooking the facts: the commanders in Malaya were never remotely a match for the Japanese. "Carrying on even if reduced to a meagre diet of rice and rats and finally after firing one's last round dying sword in hand in the innermost keep may be romantic," Brooke-Popham had written truthfully, "but of little practical value." Yet in the long run his troops would have no other choice. Although he had been baffled, in December, 1940, to find that the War Committee had no agenda and kept no minutes, in one year as C-in-C he had wrought no change.

Percival, too, seemed unperturbed that there was barely enough artillery ammunition to fire twelve rounds a day and that all over Malaya 1918 Rolls Royce Armoured cars stood in for tanks. Cornered late in December by Brigadier Ivan Simson as to why he would permit no anti-tank defences, underwater obstacles, fire traps or mines to stall the Japanese advance, Percival, a tall negative man with buck teeth, gave the astonishing reply: "Defences are bad for morale – for both troops and civilians."

245

It was then that Simson realised that barring a miracle Singapore was as good as lost.

As the retreat continued the civil administration set no shining example. To the fury of Sir Shenton Thomas, all white civilians secretly evacuated Penang, the chief seaport of northern Malaya, abandoning their Asiatic servants in a town plastered with slogans, "Thanks to the Royal Air Force Your Homes Are Safe". Streaming in their wake, to the capital of Kuala Lumpur and beyond, came long lines of military lorries packed with carpets, rattan chairs, golf clubs, tennis rackets, even canaries in cages.

Thus abandoned, it was not surprising that many Asiatics, recalling their exclusion from the Atlantic Charter, made common cause with the invader. At Alor Star, on 13 December, Major Mohan Singh, a handsome Sikh prisoner from the 1/14 Punjab Regiment, met up for the first time with Major Iwaichi Fujiwara, of the 8th Section, 2nd Bureau, Imperial General Staff. Coining such slogans as "Asia for the Asiatics", it was the section's job to coax dissident Indians, Burmese and Thais to throw in their lot with Japan. Before the year was out, Mohan Singh had agreed to lead an Indian National Army, 10,000 strong, to fight against the British.

Behind the strangely craven conduct of troops and civilians lay a stark realisation: for the first they were facing up to Japan's true mettle. "Well," Sir Shenton had commented when Percival phoned him with news of the landings, "I suppose you'll shove the little men off." But by mid-December, he was writing ruefully to a friend: "The Jap is good. In the air and on land he has already done things which we didn't expect . . . we have underestimated (his) skill." Overnight, British and Americans alike were recognising the Japanese for what they were: hardy, fearless warriors, whose sharpshooting was accurate up to 1,000 yards, equipped with slit-toed rubber shoes that helped them climb swiftly and silently, men able to survive for five days on minimal rations of fish and rice, who were even equipped with medicine kits to treat themselves for malaria.

All over the Far East, it was the same melancholy story of too little and too late. In Hong Kong, the G.O.C., Major-General Christopher Maltby, had adopted the ambitious plan of defending the island from the mainland along an eleven-mile redoubt of pill-boxes called the Gin Drinker's Line – in happier days the scene of alcoholic picnics. Here two infantry brigades – six battalions – were to hold for at least a week while dockyards and oil installations were destroyed. Fate decreed otherwise. On the left of the line, covering the southern slopes of Tai Mo Shan mountain and the Shingmun Redoubt, was the 2nd Battalion, Royal Scots – now, racked with malaria, only 600 strong. On the night of 9 December, an all-out attack by Major-General Sano's crack 38th Division, took them by surprise. In disorder and confusion they fell back.

By mid-day on 11 December, a retreat across the harbour to the 32 square miles of Hong Kong island was the one way out.

That evening, the harbour in the dockside area of Kowloon was a scene of ugly chaos. All the time the little green Star ferries shuttled back and forth across the water, but hordes of angry cursing Chinese roamed the waterfront, looting and pillaging; swirling smoke from the dockyards, the mainland power station and the cement works, all destroyed on Maltby's orders, blanketed the wharves. To Ellen Field, wife of a ship's engineer, making the crossing with her three small daughters, "it was as though a great stone had been overturned and all sorts of creepy-crawly things were coming out".

There were flashes of initiative, even so. At G.H.Q., Admiral Chan Chak, a one-legged sea dog on loan from Chiang Kai-shek, no sooner heard the problem than he cried, "I fix. I go!" Stumping from the room to make his base on the waterfront he organised a fleet of motor sampans, the flat-bottomed riverboats used by all the Hong Kong Chinese. Soon they had joined the Star ferries, scurrying backwards and forwards with stores, ammunition and refugees.

As the troops fell blindly back, many were cut off from their units, but one man saw the need to regain his regiment without delay: 52-year-old Sweeper Bhokar, of the 2/14 Punjabis, who for thirty-three years had daily tended and scoured the "thunderboxes" – portable wooden commodes – of the Officer's Mess. Finding himself alone on the quayside, with the Japanese closing in, Sweeper Bhokar found an abandoned lifebelt and paddled his way across 500 yards of channel – once more attendant on the bowel movements of his *sahibs*.

The voyage across the harbour was to be the last journey for many. Gwen Dew, a free-lance American journalist, never forgot her ferry trip with a company of wounded men – watched over by a nurse who was herself bleeding profusely. "You are wounded, you must stop," one man espostulated. "I must go on," the nurse replied, "and I am dying." She was dead before the ferry reached the island's capital, Victoria.

That night, from balconies all over the city, the watchers saw no Christmas lights, only the rich red flames of the blazing oil-tanks, lapping the heavy skies above Kowloon. Zigzag flares of red and green leapt across the harbour. Smoke swirled in weird coils, forming fantastic designs of jet and sable. Outlandish rumours multiplied: incredibly, the Japanese had landed a cavalry troop on the island itself. From G.H.Q., Captain Freddie Guest, General Maltby's G 3 (Operations) investigated hastily – to find that racehorses had wormed loose from their stables and were cantering round Happy Valley Racecourse.

Manila, too, wore a cloak of darkness, a town beset by tensions. Trigger-happy sentries fired at any light that moved – often through open lounge windows. Offshore, the aircraft tender *Langley*, along with the light cruiser *Boise*, opened non-stop fire on a silver object someone had glimpsed through a telescope. Half an hour later they gave up sheepishly: they had opened fire on Venus.

On 10 December, at Aparri, 250 miles from Manila, on Luzon's north coast the Japanese had landed troops, and again at Vigon, on the north-east coast, 200 miles from the capital. Three days later, on 13 December, they struck in force at Legaspi, south-west of Manila. Each time, through no fault of their own, MacArthur's green troops suffered an ignominious mauling. Few men in his North Luzon Force, Major-General Jonathan M. Wainwright revealed, had steel helmets, entrenching tools, blankets, raincoats or even modern arms.

What little equipment they had reached them too late. If their mortars were twenty-five years old, 70 per cent of their shells were defective. And just as in Malaya what Lieutenant Colonel Ernest B. Miller, of the 194th Tank Battalion (National Guard) called "the poison of apathy" prevailed. Although Miller's M-3 tanks were equipped with 37-mm guns, oil, ammunition – and even permission to fire the guns – were withheld until the last. Only when the Japanese were looming in their sights did Miller's tanks first open fire.

All perspective vanished. From a nation of comic-strip warriors the Japanese had overnight become a race of supermen. At Aparri, an Air Force company under Lieutenant Alvin C. Hadley, was ordered to engage the enemy – but Hadley and his men, reporting 10,000 Japanese advancing, retreated without firing a shot. (The total Japanese involved: 400.) On this same day, Captain Colin P. Kelly, a B-17 pilot over Aparri, attacked what he thought was a battleship – then, winging back to his base, was fatally strafed by two Zeros. Soon the Press in Manila were exulting that Kelly had sunk the battleship *Haruna* – then 1,500 miles away in the Gulf of Siam. No battleship had been sunk at all – but Kelly, the war's first "hero", won a posthumous Congressional Medal of Honor.

But slowly, just as in the United States, the mood in the Far East was hardening. In the proud tradition of Leningrad and Tobruk, people were coming to terms with siege conditions, and a Hong Kong nurse, Day Sage, wrote for all the threatened strongholds: "Days were just people and their exposed nerves and their courage and sometimes their craven fear." Swiftly they learned to adapt. In Manila, the gleaming white Residence of the High Commissioner Francis B. Sayre, with its ground-floor fernery and semi-circular ballroom, now spelt home to 120 hard-pressed officials and their families – all of them sleeping in their clothes on mattresses, on floors buff-coloured from leaking sandbags, harassed by the constant wail of the air-raid siren.

In Hong Kong, the glossy Peninsula Hotel was equally stripped for action; a chequerboard of sticky paper festooned the plate-glass windows, as a precaution against blast; carpets and curtains had been piled at the ballroom's far end. At the Jockey Club Relief Hospital, the betting booths stood in as hospital cubicles, and Nurse Mabel Redwood found herself sharing, with four others, a huge blackwood bed once used by Chinese opium smokers. "Good job my husband shot himself," a room mate remarked conversationally. "He couldn't have stood this."

All were now aware of the new skills needed in a world engulfed by war: how to cook in brackish well water, how to sleep as and where they lay down each night. At Singapore General Hospital, Elfrieda (Freddy) Retz, a comely New York widow, signed on as an auxiliary nurse; each night she steeled herself to make her rounds among wounded men, armed with torch, forceps and kidney basin, extracting writhing maggots from their wounds – maggots laid by omnipresent tropical flies. In Manila, Father Forbes Monaghan, a Jesuit priest attached to the university, always remembered the student he found one night in the Ateneo de Manila's patio, catching sleep on a stone bench before sentry-go. When Monaghan suggested a cushion for his head and a mosquito net, the quiet reply came back: "No, Father. I don't want any of those things. I want to harden myself for the battlefield."

But wry humour, Monaghan noted, would be another potent weapon. American ineptitude had been so shocking that two Filipino Scholastics felt it was time to take precautionary measures, a large sign painted on the Ateneo roof: DON'T BOMB – WE ARE STUDYING JAPANESE.

*

On Wake Island, it was all as Major James Devereux had feared. No reinforcements would now be forthcoming from the 6th Marine Battalion, stranded in Honolulu. He and his 378 Marines must soldier on alone.

Although no longer the island's senior officer – a post which had been filled late in November by Commander Winfield Scott Cunningham, U.S. Navy – Devereux' Marines still constituted the island's fighting force; none of the 75 officers and blue-jackets who had arrived with Cunningham to man the naval air station was even armed. True, four days before war began, the twelve Grumman Wildcat fighters that made up Marine Fighter Squadron 211, under Major Paul Putnam, had flown into Wake – but on this new type of plane none of the pilots had more than 30 hours flying time.

By 11.30 a.m. on Monday, 8 December – still the morning of 7 December in Hawaii – the wiry little major had been working against the clock for four hours. He had still been shaving in his tent when news of Pearl Harbor reached him – so plainly it would soon be Wake's turn. Meanwhile there were endless details to finalise. What about bomb shelters and caches for supplies? How would he keep his strongpoints,

249

thinly scattered across the four mile long island, supplied with food and water? As a priority, extra ammunition must be rushed to all positions.

Work was already proceeding apace on protective bunkers for the first six of Putnam's planes – and though none was available for immediate occupancy, all would be completed by 2 p.m. At seven strategic points, Devereux had 5-inch and 3-inch batteries in readiness – seventeen guns in all – but he was conscious of scraping the barrel. His "mobile reserve" would consist of four machine guns on a truck, manned by twelve Marines – ready to race to any point where the Japanese attempted a landing.

At 11.57 a.m., eight of Putnam's planes were parked on the strip, while four more patrolled uneasily – too high above the cloud ceiling to sight the bomber force skimming low above the water. At 11.58 a.m., it became an all too-familiar story.

In his office, sited at Camp One, Devereux was passing routine instructions by phone to Lieutenant Wally Lewis, commanding the guns at Peacock Point, the island's most easterly tip. Suddenly Lewis broke in urgently: "Major, there's a squadron of planes coming in from the south. Are they friendly?"

Next instant twenty-seven gently gliding bombers broke at barely 2,000 feet from a gusting squall of rain. Atop the 50-feet water towers the look-outs had seen and heard nothing; the booming surf on the reef blotted out all sound and for this last silent dive the Japanese had cut their motors. "Look! Their wheels are falling off!" a contractor's man shouted. Simultaneously, Devereux heard the first bombs exploding.

Just as at Pearl and at Clark Field, Putnam's planes were caught like sitting ducks. In one searing whoosh of flame, 25,000 gallons of aviation gasoline in the airfield's main tank soared upwards like a gusher, trembling above the coral like a heat-haze. Now the planes came lower still, making their bomb runs from 1,500 feet, too low for effective 3-inch fire to deter them. Four of Putnam's fliers fell, cut to pieces by bullets, in the act of racing for their planes. Unhampered, the bombers strafed Wake Island at will, plastering the Pan American station, riddling the Clipper at its dock like a colander.

The raid lasted only ten minutes – but thirty-four men lay dead or wounded, seven planes had been destroyed outright and the auxiliary engine of an eighth had been damaged beyond repair. Minutes later, as the four-plane patrol touched down, a ninth, bouncing over the pitted coral, broke its airscrew.

Three-quarters of Wake's air power had been knocked out with one punch – and hardly one blow that registered had been struck in return.

Calm and phlegmatic, Devereux did the best he could. If the Japanese were seeking a siege, Wake's Marines would do their best to oblige. The runway, mined with dynamite, was now connected with three generators, covered by machine-gun posts round the airfield. Beach patrols were organised to stand night watch along the shore. Devereux arranged with burly Dan Teters, the contractor's general superintendent, to take charge of all feeding arrangements – releasing more men for duty, though all would be restricted to two meals a day. It was now that Teters' men, though civilians, showed their fighting spirit – weighing in as look-outs and gun crews, hauling ammunition, repairing bomb damage.

Sixteen days of eternal vigilance was all that lay ahead of them now.

It was Private First Class Verne L. Wallace who unwittingly provided Wake's one diversion in that first twenty-four hours. At his look-out point on Peale Island, a coral spit to the west of Wake, he at last received a letter from his girl friend in Haverford, Pennsylvania. It had arrived with the Clipper that morning, but Wallace had been heeding the call to arms; by the time he received it from a friend that night, it was too dark to read. But just before manning his guns for the dawn alert he slit it open.

By mid-morning, his girl's words of comfort had passed all over the island, even reaching Devereux in the underground command post he had set up – "As long as you have to be away, darling, I'm so very, very happy you are in the Pacific where you won't be in any danger if war comes."

12

"Some Chicken! Some Neck!"

14 December, 1941–1 January, 1942

LATE ON THE afternoon of 5 December, St Nicholas' Eve, *Assistenzart* Heinrich Haape of Infantry Regiment 18, had stood with his friend *Oberleutnant* Graf von Kageneck in a whirling world of white, surveying the small and nondescript town of Klin. In the deathly silence the two men had eyes only for an unusual symbol: a small stone shed crammed with benches, an old wooden bin clamped to one wall. On the litter of tickets inside the bin, the two men could distinguish the cyrillic letters which by now they knew spelled MOSKVA.

This was the Klin tramway station, only ten miles from the capital's centre, and in this moment both men divined that no member of Hitler's *Wehrmacht* would ever advance farther than they towards the city.

For Haape and the men of the 3rd Battalion, these had been weeks of bitter frustration. As the cold tightened its grip, von Bock's Army Group Centre had ground to a halt almost within sight of Moscow. In this period of acute stalemate, Haape had battled against diseases unknown in Germany yet endemic all along the front: typhus and Kramer's hepatitis, Weil's disease, a spirochete caused by rat-polluted water, tularaemia, a sickness spread by the meat of infected animals.

"Moscow *must* fall," Kageneck had mused on that silent afternoon, "yet . . . I wonder."

But in the days that followed Haape had become ever more convinced that Moscow would remain inviolate. On 5 December, he had looked forward to nothing more than the seven weeks leave that was due to him; back in Duisburg, he and his fiancée Martha Arazym had planned to celebrate the New Year by formally announcing their engagement. Then, early on 17 December, an officer in an armoured car arrived with bleak news from 6th Divisional Headquarters: "A short directive has just been received from the Führer's headquarters cancelling all leave."

Haape soon knew why. In the small hours of 5 December, sensing that the Germans had reached the peak of their effort, Marshal Georgi Zhukov, combining three armies – the First Assault, the Tenth and the Twentieth – in one giant counter-offensive, struck back. Now, all along the front, 51 German divisions were in retreat.

For Haape each day became a nightmare. Swiftly the temperature was dropping – once to minus forty-eight degrees, four times colder than a deep-freezer. As the rough little pony ambulances struggled back towards Gorki, men's toes and feet froze into solid blocks inside their boots. All day his orderlies were at work, massaging the frozen limbs with snow or icy water until they became soft and pliable, before packing them in cotton wool and bandaging them heavily. Wounds froze as if in a tourniquet of ice. Even to urinate was agony.

By mid-December the Volga front seemed stunned into glacial silence. Often it took fifteen hours to start a vehicle, by dint of lighting small fires below the gear-box. Bread had to be hacked apart with an axe, then thawed out piece by piece. At night in the forests eerie cracks resounded as sharply as rifle shots: the sap was freezing in the trees.

In one division Guderian lost 1,200 men to frostbite in one day. On 9 December, one corps reported 1,500 cases – of which 350 warranted amputation. Eleven hundred army horses perished daily. The bitter blizzards were decimating Germans and Russians alike. Near Ozarovo, a rearguard of the 3rd Rifle Regiment chanced on a Russian cavalry troop motionless in the flickering light – the men huddled against horses which stood like equestrian statues, heads held high, eyes closed, tails caught by the wind. All of them were standing waist deep in snow and all of them were dead.

The German High Command's blind incomprehension of their needs enraged both generals and privates. In mid-November, Panzer Group Three had received their first sparse consignment of winter clothing – one greatcoat to each gun crew. At Fourth Army headquarters, the men received no warm clothing or ammunition at all: merely two goods trains of red wine frozen solid. On 30 November, von Bock had protested angrily to von Brauchitsch from a forward command post within sight of Moscow, emphasising that no winter supplies had arrived – "the army group no longer commands the strength to force a decision". Still von Brauchitsch repeated woodenly: "The Führer wants to know when Moscow will fall."

Too subservient to Hitler to speak his mind openly, von Brauchitsch now tossed and turned night after night, arguing with the Führer in his sleep.

Some were now openly in revolt. On 28 November, von Kleist's Panzer Group One had been driven from the great industrial city of Rostov, on the Don. Forbidden to dig in on the line of the Mius River, von Rundstedt resigned his command of Army Group South. Hitler was unrepentant. In a mood of black misanthropy, he told Erik Scavenius, the Danish Foreign Minister, who was visiting the *Wolfsschanze*, "If the German people are no longer so strong and ready for sacrifice that they will stake their own blood on their existence, they deserve to pass away and be annihilated by

253

another, stronger power." On the same day he told a Croatian diplomat, Mladen Lorković, "If that is the case I would not shed a tear for the German people."

In his own view, Hitler had valid reason for bitterness. Plainly victory in 1941 was now impossible – and with this realisation would come a reorientation of the entire German economy. Mindful always of the lessons of World War One, Hitler had long sought to avoid a repetition of 1918, with its collapse of home front morale. Until now his blitzkrieg economy, with its quick easy victories, had always cushioned the public from the impact of total war: more consumer goods had been produced in the Third Reich in 1941 than in all of 1940. By contrast, fighter production had only risen from 183 to 244 planes a month, bombers from 217 to 336. Machine guns came off the assembly line at half the 1918 level. But from now on, of necessity, the people must tighten their belts. They would come to know the years of pinching shortage long familiar to the British and the French.

But one commander as yet had no intention of resigning: *Generaloberst* Heinz Guderian. On 20 December, just as in August, he flew to East Prussia, intent on changing the Führer's mind by reasoned argument. Once again, it proved fruitless; indeed the gesture was to cost him his command. In his gloomy bunker at the *Wolfsschanze*, dominated by its oval portrait of Frederick the Great, Hitler argued passionately: "Once I've authorised a retreat there won't be any holding them. The troops will just run . . . (they) must dig their nails into the ground; they must dig in, and not yield an inch."

"My Führer," Guderian interposed, "the ground in Russia at present is frozen solid to a depth of four feet. No one can dig in there."

Hitler was patronising. "Then you must get the mortars to fire at the ground to make shell craters. That's what we did in Flanders in the first war."

"In Flanders," Guderian explained patiently, "the ground was soft. But in Russia the shells now produce holes no more than four inches deep and the size of a wash-basin – the soil is as hard as iron."

Five hours of inconclusive argument followed, before Guderian, leaving the situation room, heard Hitler remark to Keitel, "There goes a man I have not been able to convince."

But now all three German armies received a categorical order which revealed Hitler's ruthless aptitude to command: whatever the cost, they must stand fast. If overtly inhuman, it was still logical: though the toll was appalling and some positions were yielded, the Russians did not break through and there was no panic retreat. When the spring thaws came the *Wehrmacht* would still stand on a line deep inside "the endless land".

The cost was high. Reputations were tarnished; ranks were stripped away overnight. At least thirty-five divisional and corps commanders were relieved. Life was cheap; of the 800 men of the 3rd Battalion, Infantry Regiment 18, only twenty-eight came back, although one of them was Heinrich Haape. He was to soldier on for two more years on the Russian front, once tending 521 wounded in one day, before returning to marry his Martha, seeing out the rest of the war as Medical Officer for Strasbourg. But he long remembered how the news of impending change reached the battalion on the bitter Christmas Day of 1941.

It was in a small hamlet near Kosnarovo that his friend Kageneck broke the news to Haape and *Oberleutnant* Stolze, commanding the 10th Company. "Nearly all of our generals have been relieved of their posts," he told them, plainly shocked.

"Brauchitsch?" asked Stolze.

"Yes."

"Guderian?"

"Yes."

"Von Bock?"

"Yes."

"Kluge?"

It was the one count on which Kageneck could reassure them. Kluge was still in the field, having taken over Army Group Centre from von Bock. But *Generaloberst* Adolf Strauss had lost Ninth Army, *Generaloberst* Hermann Hoth had left Panzer Group Three, Leeb had been stripped of Army Group North. "We have a Christmas present, gentlemen," Kageneck told them, relishing their mystification, "a new commander."

Then, seeing the urgency in their faces, he broke it to them: "*Gefreiter* Adolf Hitler has assumed complete command of the entire German *Wehrmacht*."

*

As the armies reeled under the weight of Zhukov's counterthrust, Churchill was once again on the high seas.

Ever since the news of Pearl Harbor reached him, the Premier had nourished but one ambition: before the year was out, he and Roosevelt must renew the dialogue which had begun with such promise at Placentia Bay. Not a moment must be lost. By noon on Friday, 12 December, Churchill and his party, still stunned by the appalling news of *Prince of Wales*, had already reached Greenock and been piped aboard the battleship *Duke of York*.

Although Churchill was to describe the eight-day voyage as "like being in prison with the extra chance of being drowned", all who travelled with him – Harriman, Beaverbrook, Pound, Portal, Dill – observed something

255

more than a sea-change. His personal physician, Sir Charles Wilson, noted in wonder: "A younger man has taken his place . . . the tired dull look has gone from his eye; his face lights up as you enter his cabin". Yet Churchill, he knew, was not lacking in preoccupations. Foremost in his mind was the thought he expressed to Wilson: "They may concentrate upon Japan and leave us to deal with Germany. They have already stopped the stream of supplies that we were getting."

By 22 December, his impatience had reached fever-pitch; it was now as if every second counted. No sooner had the *Duke of York* berthed at Hampton Roads, Virginia, than Churchill, attired in the double-breasted knee-length coat and fore-and-aft cap of an Elder Brother of Trinity House, a British life-saving association, reached a snap decision: he must fly to meet the President. Harriman, Beaverbrook, Portal and Wilson should travel with him; the rest could follow by train. At precisely 6.58 p.m., following a forty-five minute flight, his Lockheed was screaming down the long necklace of light marking the runway at Washington's National Airport. A little way off, Roosevelt was already waiting, propped beside a black bulletproof limousine that had once belonged to Al Capone.

"I clasped his strong hand with comfort and pleasure," Churchill recalled later.

Already his arrival had caused a stir in the White House. Always as intent on impressing Churchill as the Premier was on impressing him, Roosevelt had insisted that a lion-skin rug presented to him years earlier by Emperor Haile Selassie of Abyssinia, must be unearthed at once and installed in the Oval Office. After hours of searching, housekeeper Henrietta Nesbitt ran it to earth in a nearby warehouse, but the White House guards set up for Churchill's visit refused her readmission; she had forgotten her pass. The lion – reeking strongly of mothballs – reached Roosevelt's study with only minutes to spare.

The President's chiefs of staff were equally concerned. Ensconced in the North-East Suite, with its tasteful Victorian prints, Churchill was located on the same corridor as Roosevelt and Hopkins – free to confer with them at hours when no service men were present. Though Roosevelt was wont to retire early, often the Premier's cavalier disregard of the clock prolonged the sessions until the small hours. Both leaders now slept late, with "Do Not Disturb" signs prominently displayed.

Refreshed by sleep, Churchill would then monopolise Roosevelt's every waking minute, bursting in at all hours in his dressing gown; when Senator Alben Barkley asked if he could "borrow" the Premier for a luncheon on Capitol Hill, Roosevelt whooped with joy. "For Heaven's sake, do! Give him a glass of Scotch and a good lunch and . . . I will get on with some desk work."

Thus Marshall, Stark and Arnold all had cause to wonder: how many commitments of American manpower to say nothing of hardware would Churchill cajole from the President?

On the surface, all was harmony. At twilight on Christmas Eve, a crowd 20,000 strong gathered outside the Executive Mansion, with Premier and President watching from a balcony, as the great Christmas tree was lighted in the White House grounds. Next day, falling in with the President's suggestion – "It is good for Winston to sing hymns with the Methodies" – he accompanied Roosevelt to the Foundry Methodist Church, standing side by side to sing "O Little Town of Bethlehem". Next day, facing Congress at his most eupeptic, Churchill confided, "I cannot help reflecting that if my father had been American and my mother British, instead of the other way round, I might have got here on my own." A shock wave of laughter rippled beneath the great dome, then as Churchill, in a slighting reference to the Japanese, demanded passionately, "What sort of people do they think we are?" they rose as one man, cheering him to the echo.

Behind the bonhomie, Churchill was urgently seeking the answers to three questions. Would Roosevelt stick to his former Atlantic First policy, with Germany as the Number One enemy? If so, how could Japan be slowed down in the Pacific during the interim? And how could an Allied command be coordinated through the vast theatres of the Atlantic and the Pacific?

On the first score, Roosevelt left him in no doubt. Germany was still the primary foe; the first objective must be victory in Europe. Meanwhile, the Western Hemisphere presented fewer problems than anticipated. The twenty-one republics of Latin America – which the State Department had warned could prove the springboard for any German attack on the United States – had shown a heartening degree of solidarity with their neighbour.

Cuba, Panama, the Dominican Republic, El Salvador, and Guatemala had all declared war on the Axis. Costa Rica, after discovering that she had already been at war with Germany for twenty-four years – a revolutionary government which took power in 1917 had not been recognised at Versailles – had affirmed her stance afresh. Nicaragua's General Anastasio Somoza, virtually a U.S. puppet, had promptly interned all aliens regardless of their sympathies. Brazil, Mexico and seven other republics, while neutral, were pro-U.S. Even Argentina, where pro-Axis newspapers like *El Pampero* employed five editors to serve jail sentences for subversion alternately, was standing by the Havana Convention of 1940.

Thus reassured, Churchill pressed ahead with his plans for Europe. If Germany was held in Russia, they might yet attack through Spain or Portugal into North Africa. To counter this he proposed a plan codenamed "Gymnast" – an American invasion of northwest Africa in the Casablanca area, to link up with an Eighth Army drive from the east into

Tunisia.* But to this suggestion Roosevelt and his chiefs of staff remained cool. An African adventure – drawing on United States manpower and weapons as from a common pool – smacked to them of the "peripheralism" for which Churchill had been criticised. Their thinking inclined to a long slow build-up, followed by a massive and lethal thrust into the heart of Germany

As the meetings wore on, tempers flared repeatedly – so hotly, Mrs Nesbitt noted in alarm, that during working repasts men angrily stubbed out their cigarette ends on the damask table cloths. Urged to remonstrate, Eleanor Roosevelt professed herself powerless – but later, one servant noted, the President was seen guiltily covering the latest burn under a salt cellar.

It was on Christmas Day, inappropriately, that the warmest dispute arose. On the previous evening, Marshall learned, Roosevelt and Churchill had discussed diverting to the British in Malaya reinforcements scheduled for the Philippines – should it prove impossible to get them to MacArthur. At once Marshall, Arnold, and a new War Department aide, Brigadier-General Dwight D. Eisenhower, called on Stimson to protest. Stimson, as angry as the chiefs, promptly rang Hopkins, threatening resignation if Roosevelt went ahead. Hopkins, equally concerned, taxed the two leaders with Stimson's bombshell – although both promptly denied the charge.

Yet the suggestion had been in the air. As early as 22 December, Portal and Air Vice Marshal Arthur "Bomber" Harris, heading the R.A.F. Mission in Washington, had met up for preliminary discussions with General "Hap" Arnold. Portal, Arnold noted at the time, was perfectly clear as to where the priorities lay. "The British," he stated complacently, "cannot afford to see Singapore pass by the board."

Unabashed, Arnold stared right back at him. "*We*," he said unequivocally, "cannot afford to see the Philippines pass by the board."

The argument was academic. Even as they spoke the Pacific and the entire Far East were already passing by the board.

*

Soon it would be dawn. In his command post, an underground ammunition magazine lying east of the airfield, Major James Devereux felt suddenly as helpless as "a blindfolded man in a prize fight". All communication with most of Wake Island's forward positions had been cut off.

At 1 a.m. on 23 December, Devereux had still had the situation in hand. At this hour a Japanese landing had been reported at Toki Point, the westernmost tip of the coral spit known as Peale. Twenty minutes later, machine-guns had opened fire on the southerly spit called Wilkes.

* As Operation Torch it was finally launched on 8 November, 1942.

Movements were reported off the southern beach of Wake; simultaneously, in four places, the Japanese were coming ashore. All along the reef red flares were bursting. Then the lines began to go dead, and the old "walkie-talkie" hand-sets proved useless as a stand-by.

Just as in Crete, the last hours on Wake were to become a series of small private battles, men feinting and lunging through darkness, uncertain as to who was friend or foe.

For Devereux it was a tragic outcome. Until this moment his Marines had inflicted on their aggressor what Commander Masatake Okuniya was later to call "one of the most humiliating defeats the Japanese Navy had ever suffered". Now the end was near.

After that first devastating air-raid on 8 December, the pattern of the assault had been clear. On 9 December and again next day, Japanese bombers had blasted the island until it was plain that the 24th Air Flotilla planned a piecemeal destruction of both ack-ack and seacoast batteries. Then, following the third strike, in the black pre-dawn silence of 11 December, a force 450 strong attempted a landing near Peacock Point.

Obstinately, Devereux had held his fire to the last: since the Japanese could outgun him, why reveal the strength and location of his sea-coast batteries before he needed to? "What does that little bastard want us to do?" one aggrieved gunner muttered, "Let 'em run over us without even spitting back?" But not until 6.10 a.m., when the eleven ships of the task force were within 4,500 yards of Peacock Point, did Devereux give the word.

His precaution paid off. On Wilkes, the two five-inch guns of Lieutenant John McAlister three times opened fire on the destroyer *Hayate*; enveloped in a black cloud of smoke the ship slid from sight. Now the gunners cheered so lustily that the outraged Sergeant Henry Bedell yelled at them, "Knock it off, you bastards. What d'ya think this is, a ball game?"

Other salvoes straddled the flagship, the light cruiser *Yubari*; the destroyer *Kisaragi* sank in a flaming orange ball. Then Major Paul Putnam's four remaining Wildcats swooped low over the task force, machine guns raking *Yubari*'s bridge. At once Rear Admiral Sadamichi Kajioka ordered the force to withdraw. Devereux's Marines had notched up their first victory.

It was the onset of a courageous stand which became a legend in its lifetime. In one day, Major Walter Bayler, a qualified recruiting officer, had to turn down 186 would-be Marines from Dan Teters' construction staff; without uniforms to distinguish them the Japanese might classify them as armed guerillas, fodder for a firing squad. A willingness of heart was everywhere apparent. As late as 17 December, a team under Lieutenant John Kinney was performing miracles keeping Putnam's planes aloft

– trading engines from plane to plane, even building new engines from spare parts and scrap.

"If they want this island," Corporal Hershal L. Miller avowed stubbornly, "they gotta pay for it."

The situation could hardly have been grimmer but men still found time to laugh – often, in classic banana-skin tradition, at the misfortunes of others. Food was short, but 17-year-old Private Roger Bamford, Wake's youngest Marine, who had lied about his age to enlist, foraged until he located a real meal: a can of chili con carne intended for thirteen men. Thereafter Bamford's frantic dives for the latrine produced howls of mirth. Sergeant Raymon Gragg, a Marine Corps veteran and a stickler for hygiene, found what he thought was a supply of foot powder and liberally doused his feet. He awoke to find his darkened foxhole alive with rats; by mistake he had used powdered cheese.

What little they heard of the outside world moved Wake's defenders to anger. One Stateside commentator's claim that Devereux had vaingloriously radioed, "SEND US MORE JAPS" provoked a bitter outcry. Devereux himself was irked by a non-stop barrage of banal instructions from Pearl Harbor: all personnel must keep their sleeves rolled down as a protection against bomb blast. Or, if they lacked glass to put in their barrack windows, use seismograph paper. For days now the men of Wake, grimy and sweating, reeking like polecats, had lived in foxholes, dizzy from lack of sleep, and the incessant pounding of the bombers – yet nobody at Pearl Harbor seemed to grasp the desperation of their plight.

Now, towards dawn on 23 December, Devereux knew that plight to be more desperate yet.

At least they would go down fighting. Lieutenant Robert Hanna, commanding the .50 machine guns at the airstrip, streaked for the beach to man the one gun that could immediately be brought to bear on the invaders: a three-inch ack-ack gun that lacked a crew. Blasting at the offshore destroyers he fired until the crowded decks were like a slaughter-pen; by the light of burning ships he could see Japanese soldiers tumbling from their sides, struggling to reach the shallows. All along the shoreline the Marines advanced to meet them, machine pistols chattering, grenades hurtling, until the inshore surf was churned to bloody froth.

At 5 a.m. Commander Winfield Cunningham, as the island's senior officer, sent a terse message to Pearl Harbor: "ENEMY ON ISLAND ISSUE IN DOUBT". But in truth there was little doubt left.

Though every step was contested, Devereux could spare only 85 Marines to guard the southern shoreline; there were all too many vulnerable landing places elsewhere. On the beach, Major Putnam's little band of aviators and crewmen fought their way back to Hanna's ack-ack gun then stopped dead – "This is as far as we go." Waves of Japanese burst against the tight little rock of twenty men, who could be killed or maimed but who would not retreat.

Devereux knew nothing of this. Was Putnam holding out? Were they ready to blow the airstrip as instructed? Again he had no means of knowing. Suddenly a wild-eyed civilian, near to collapse, clattered down the rocky steps into the dug-out. He had been cut off when the Japanese overran a strongpoint manned by Lieutenant Arthur Poindexter near Camp One. "They're killing 'em all," he mouthed, too overwrought to say more.

Suddenly Corporal Robert Brown, Devereux's linesman, stiffened. He was listening in on the warning network, and someone was whispering. The same words, repeated over and over like a litany: "There are Japanese in the bushes . . . there are definitely Japanese in the bushes. . . ."

"Who's there? Where are you?" Brown asked urgently, but the whispering just went on, carefully, monotonously, an unknown man, murmuring into a telephone, somewhere in the dark, trying to warn them before he died.

"There are Japanese in the bushes . . . there are definitely Japanese. . . ."

Then there was a burst of sound and what might have been a scream and no more whispering at all.

"I guess they got him," Brown said bleakly.

Dawn was breaking.

*

Crawling from his dug-out, Devereux could see the Japanese Fleet. The sight was breathtaking. The ships lay in a vast circle, girdling the entire island, far out of range of any gun he possessed. Their number seemed endless – some men counted twenty-seven of all types – although only thirteen were in sight of the island at this time.

It was 7 a.m., time to return to his command post and report to Commander Cunningham. But, Devereux stressed over the phone, any report must be based on guesswork and probabilities. No explosion had been heard from the airstrip, which suggested that the Japanese had now forged past that position. In which case, all forward positions had been overrun or were isolated in small "last stand" pockets. "That's the best I can judge the picture on the dope I've got," he concluded.

After a long pause, Cunningham replied, "Well, I guess we'd better give it to them."

Devereux could not believe his ears. Never in sixteen days had the thought of surrender occurred to him. All along he had thought only of buying time until a task force came to their rescue.* A Marine never surrendered. Then, by degrees, he saw the logic of Cunningham's decision. The lives of 1,200 unarmed civilians were at stake. And the Japanese had the island surrounded. As Marine commander he could go on spending lives – but there was nothing he could now buy with them. "I'll pass the word," he said finally.

Hanging up, he ordered Sergeant John Hamas, a veteran of twenty years standing, "Fix up a white flag and pass the word to cease firing."

For a moment Hamas was thunderstruck. "Yes, sir," was all he said before leaving the dugout. Outside Devereux could hear him shouting; the sound was like a child, fighting back tears: "Major's orders! We're surrendering . . . Major's orders. . . ."

Close to tears himself, Devereux yelled from the dug-out entrance, "It's not my order, God damn it!"

These were memories he would carry with him through almost four years captivity in China and Japan: the tired dirt-streaked faces of the men as they threw away their machine pistols, Old Glory fluttering down from the flagpole, the last painful trek down the rocky road to meet the Japanese advance party, just a white rag tied to a swab handle hoisted above his head.

*

By Christmas Eve, the drums were sounding retreat. From Manila Bay to the South China Sea, men, dazed, dishevelled and uncomprehending, were falling back. It was a fitting climax to 1941, a year which had seen more ignominious withdrawals than any in history.

In blacked-out Manila, civilians behind closed shutters listened uneasily to the sound of mass withdrawal: the muffled drone of truck motors moving out of Fort McKinley's gates, tyres crunching over a brittle carpet of glass, the harsh cries of unseen sentries, pious Filipino troops responding with their password, *Adios Ko* (God be with you). As everywhere in 1941, their path was marked by destruction: the sickly-sweet stench of burning sugar cane on Highway 3, near San Fernando, a drizzling black rain of fuel showering down on the oil dumps at Pandacan. Enough petroleum to operate the Asiatic Fleet for two years was burning like a vision of hell.

Belatedly, MacArthur had shrugged off his first irresolution to attempt what the Japanese were to hail as "a great strategic move" – a sideslip into Bataan, twenty miles west, a rugged peninsula 25 miles long and 20 miles wide, its jungle-clad mountain spines rising to 4,700 feet. Here, if need

* The carrier *Saratoga*, with the men of Task Force 14, was 424 miles west of Wake on 23 December when Vice-Admiral William S. Pye, who had replaced Kimmel, recalled her to Pearl Harbor, two-and-a-half hours before the surrender. Pye was convinced that the timing was too fine, that the carrier would be lost along with Wake.

be, a last-ditch stand could be made for six months – provided the Navy could furnish supplies and reinforcements.

Yet until 23 December, MacArthur had stubbornly resisted any such move. Charging defeatism, he had refused all suggestions from his operations officers to stock Bataan with provisions as "a safety measure". Thus all supplies had been concentrated in the beach areas, where the Philippine Army of which he spoke so proudly would smash the Japanese at the waterline.

On 22 December, at Lingayen Gulf on Luzon's west coast, this proud vain dream fell apart.

Fighting with rifles and ancient water-cooled machine guns, the two green divisions of Philippine troops were in no shape to contest 43,000 men of General Masaharu Homma's 14th Army armed with tanks, pouring ashore from eighty-five transports. To MacArthur's chagrin they broke and ran.

Now a dearth of ships to run the Japanese blockade, a lack of planes to dominate the skies, made a retreat to Bataan inevitable.

It was no easy manoeuvre. To succeed, MacArthur had to coordinate two armies 160 miles apart, the North Luzon Force, 28,000 strong, under Major-General Jonathan "Skinny" Wainwright, and the 15,000 men of the South Luzon Force under Brigadier-General Albert M. Jones. In this masterpiece of split-second timing, MacArthur had to leapfrog his divisions as they fell back on a series of five delaying lines, holding, then blowing, 184 vital bridges in succession.

The retreat was a quartermaster's nightmare. Only 1,300 Q.M. troops existed to shift supplies for the 80,000 men who would ultimately reach Bataan, and everywhere the supply system broke down. Lieutenant-Colonel Ernest P. Miller, of the 194th Tank Battalion, never forgot the sight he and his men saw at Calumpit, twenty-five miles northwest of Manila, the penultimate bridge to be blown. As they watched a convoy of 150 supply trucks moved past them into the peninsula – and every one of them was empty.

It was the same story all over the island. At Cabanatuan, 50 million bushels of rice was left behind for the Japanese; almost all Fort Stotensberg's stores, near Clark Field, stayed on the warehouse shelves. In Manila's Port Area everything from sacks of wheat flour to canned cherries was abandoned to the mercy of looters. Nurse Juanita Redmond, arriving at Bataan with the staff of Base Hospital No 1, was horrified to see one soldier chewing on worm-infested wild rice. Still chewing calmly, the G.I. told her, "Listen, sister, you'll be eating worse than this . . . and be damn glad to get it." The soldier was right; by the first week of January, MacArthur was to place all personnel on half rations.

Yet despite the overtones of muddle, the retreat was a triumph of its kind. By 29 December, Wainwright had reached the last of the delaying lines, ten miles northeast of Calumpit. Here his three divisions and a cavalry regiment would have to stall the Japanese until field guns and the men of the South Luzon Force had passed into the peninsula. By a minor miracle they achieved it. For two days and nights, Calumpit became a ten-mile log-jam of naval guns, Long Toms (155-mm cannon), broken-down taxis, horse-drawn *calesas*, Packard limousines and ox-carts, shuttling back and forth with men and supplies. At first light on 31 December, the South Luzon Force began their crossing. At 6.15 a.m. on New Year's Day, following Wainwright's terse command, "Blow it", Calumpit Bridge disintegrated in a Niagara of molten fragments. Here, until 9 April, 1942, the defenders of Bataan held out.

MacArthur, too, was pulling out. At 9 a.m. on 24 December he knew it was time to bid farewell to his sumptuous penthouse on Dewey Boulevard. To save the civil population from the horrors of bombardment, Manila was to be declared an open city. Now MacArthur and his staff, along with the ailing President Manuel Quezon, Commissioner Francis B. Sayre, and a coterie of Philippine officials, would transfer their headquarters to the one installation that could truly be called a fortress: the island of Corregidor, three miles long and a third of a mile wide, called "the Gibraltar of the Pacific", thirty miles away across the bay, its mighty 100-foot long Malinta Tunnel protected by 300 feet of solid rock and soil.

It was a time for last-minute decisions: permitted only one suitcase, what did one pack when facing an uncertain future? As Christmas approached, MacArthur had sent his aide, Lieutenant-Colonel Sid Huff, to shop for lingerie and size-twelve dresses for Jean, his wife, but somehow Jean MacArthur didn't feel that such costly gifts would fit in with fortress life. "Sir Boss," she said, "they are beautiful," then tucked them away in a closet, as if knowing she would never see them again. Instead she packed her husband's gold field marshal's baton* and a white fuzzy stuffed rabbit called "Old Friend", the cherished toy of their three-year-old son Arthur.

Sid Huff, priding himself on his enterprise, found room in his suitcase for a fifth of whisky. He reached the island to find every man in the party had had the same idea. MacArthur himself packed a small pistol which had belonged to his father, himself a general, when serving in the Philippines. Typically, he went on record for history: "They'll never take *me* alive, Sid."

At dusk on Christmas Eve, MacArthur was the last man to step aboard the inter-island steamer *Don Esteban*. Soon they were gliding across the moonlit water towards the massive outline of the fortress, everyone lost in thought. "Mummy," young Arthur announced at frequent intervals, "I'm tired of Corregidor. Let's go home."

* MacArthur had been appointed a Field Marshal on becoming Quezon's Military Adviser in August 1936.

264

It was a sentiment that all would soon come to echo. For more than two months – when the island was abandoned and MacArthur ordered to Australia – 12,000 men and women were to live like moles in a temperature that rarely dropped below 95 degrees, in quarters so cramped that even bedside lockers were a physical impossibility. All night the tubercular Quezon's coughing fits racked the damp subterranean air. There was no laundry and no hot water; even cold water was limited and, at times, not to be had. "What shall I do with this?" one of Commissioner Sayre's aides asked him perplexedly one morning, holding out a half glass of water, "I drank a little of it, I shaved with some, I washed my face and brushed my teeth, and there's a whole half glass left over."

After midnight mass, Quezon noted, somehow nobody could find it in their hearts to wish each other "Merry Christmas".

*

Nurse Mabel Redwood was perplexed. It was the early afternoon of Christmas Day, and as she made her round of the wards in Hong Kong's Jockey Club Relief Hospital, thunder was rolling from the hills. Yet this was a day of crisp bright sunlight; not a thundercloud was in sight.

It was too early for her to realise that this was the ever-present sound of destruction. The guns of Hong Kong, which had fired almost non-stop for seventeen days, were being blown apart prior to surrender.

For hours the din of battle had been unremitting. In the sampan town of Aberdeen, Sub-Lieutenant Lewis Bush, R.N.V.R., of the 2nd Motor Torpedo Boat Flotilla, was deafened by the screech of mountain guns as the Japanese closed in from three directions, the rattle of machine gun fire, the steady crump of bombs. Incongruously, between lulls in the firing, a voice from a small cargo boat stranded in the harbour boomed over the water as a psychological warrior sought to soften up morale: "Go home, British soldiers, go home . . . think of the Cup Final and the Boat Race . . . Fish and chips. Roast beef and Yorkshire pudding. Piccadilly Circus. Leicester Square."

It had been a melancholy festival for all the island's defenders. Captain Charles Pope, of the Royal Engineers, toasted Captain Bill Price, of the Royal Rifles of Canada – one of two Canadian battalions sent to boost the morale of Chiang Kai-shek – in tinned beer, then settled to bully beef and biscuits. Bandsmen Johnny Hymus and Charlie Dickens dined in the open air on pickled onions and cognac. In his underground "battle box" headquarters, Major-General Christopher Maltby and his A.D.C., Second-Lieutenant Iain MacGregor sat on upturned ammunition boxes for a Christmas dinner of tinned asparagus and half a bottle of lukewarm Liebfraumilch.

Maltby knew full well that surrender was imminent. Seven days earlier, the Japanese had gained a foothold on the island; by noon on 20 December, half of Hong Kong was in their hands, and several strongpoints were already under siege. At the luxurious Repulse Bay Hotel, on the southern side, guests like the millionaire industrialist Jan Hendrik Marsman, who paid £10 a day for their suites, were queuing up for a drinking water ration surrounded by 500 Japanese; an attempt to seize the West Wing had only been foiled by a party of gunners and Canadians under Major Robert Templer, an artilleryman, hurtling grenades along a pile-carpeted corridor "for all the world as if we'd been in a bowling alley."

Yet only one days' water supply remained intact, fires were raging everywhere and ammunition was running low.

There had been many acts of spontaneous gallantry. At the Power Station of the Hong Kong Electric Company, *taipans* of the hitherto-derided Hong Kong Volunteer Defence Corps, most of them close to sixty, fought to the bitter end – men like the Hon. J. J. Paterson, chairman of Jardine, Matheson and Co, and Captain Jacques Egal, a Shanghai wine merchant, famed for his impeccable tussore suits and flowing cravats. Between them they held the station for a day and a night against a tidal wave of Japanese. That was on 19 December – the same day that Brigadier John Lawson, commanding the Canadian contingent, the Royal Rifles of Canada and the Winnipeg Grenadiers, had phoned Maltby from his Brigade Headquarters to announce matter-of-factly, "They're all round us. I'm going outside to shoot it out." On Christmas Day, when his body was found, eight Japanese lay dead in a semi-circle beside Lawson.

Twice – on 13 December and again on the 17th – the Japanese had sent a three-man peace mission to the Governor, Sir Mark Young, to be rebuffed on each occasion. "Cameraman?" one of them hailed the journalist, Gwen Dew, as they stepped from their launch, "Don't you want to take pictures?" As she snapped away Gwen Dew guessed that surrender was imminent; in the Hong Kong and Shanghai Bank building, American consular officials were burning bales of papers. But she could not then know that Sir Mark's hands were tied. On 21 December he was to beseech Whitehall: "Only remaining resistance open to us will be to hold for short time only a small pocket in centre of city, leaving bulk of mixed population to be over-run. I feel it will be my duty to ask terms before this position is reached. If H.M. Government feel able to give assent, please cable single word "Ability".

To this Churchill, in a spirit reminiscent of Omdurman but which took no account of the civil population, replied in part: "Every part of the island must be fought and the enemy resisted with the utmost stubbornness. . . . There must be vigorous fighting in the inner defences and, if the need be, from house to house. . . ."

At 3 p.m. on 25 December Maltby made a determined pilgrimage to Sir

Mark Young in Government House, emphasising that no further useful military resistance was possible. Fifteen minutes later, orders went out to all commanding officers to break off the fighting.

Now, fearing reprisals from drunken Japanese soldiers whose officers had lost all control of them, guests at the Repulse Bay and other hotels began dumping all available liquor down the bathroom drains. But soon these grew clogged, and a heady river of champagne, bourbon, Scotch and gin was coursing down the marble stairs.

It was just in time. At the St Stephen's College Emergency Hospital, on the narrow Stanley Peninsula, and at the Jockey Club Relief Hospital, fighting-drunk Japanese privates rampaged through the wards, bayoneting patients and raping nurses impartially; seventy were killed at St Stephen's alone. Soon the tiled floors were running red; mattresses and cushions saturated with blood lay everywhere. One by one the bodies, some with their ears cut off, were lugged to the courtyard, piled on top of mattresses and ignited, a pyre that was still blazing when darkness fell.

That was Christmas Day on Hong Kong Island in the year of Our Lord, 1941.

*

One woman was observing Christmas in the true spirit of the festival – risking her life that others might go free. In the frontier farmhouse at Urrugne, France, Andrée de Jongh, who on Christmas Eve was preparing to deliver four more "parcels" to the British, now loomed large on the Gestapo's "wanted" list.

The alarm had been sounded late in August, at the time when Andrée had impatiently awaited clearance by the Consulate in Bilbao. In that same period, a grey Opel car had drawn to a halt outside her parents' home at No 73, Avenue Emile Verhaeren, Brussels, and two tall blond civilians descended to ring the doorbell.

"Where is your daughter Andrée?" they asked Frédéric de Jongh without ceremony.

De Jongh shrugged resignedly, a father sadly disillusioned by the younger generation. "She left home months ago," he told them, "Young girls – you understand." Both his wife, Alice, and Andrée's married sister, Suzanne, lent credence to the charade. Who could have restrained a girl so headstrong? "Nowadays one cannot keep track of what young people will do," Frédéric de Jongh complained fretfully.

After an hour of inconclusive questioning, the Gestapo left. But it was plain that in some way they had obtained a complete description of Andrée.

Andrée's first intimation of this had come in the nick of time. On the way back to Brussels she had stopped off for the night at the house of

Elvire de Greef, near Anglet, the first place of refuge for the "parcels" after their journey from Bayonne. Here one of the network's couriers, a young ex-airman, Charles Morelle, had arrived with alarming news. Their colleague, Arnold de Pé, Andrée's earliest collaborator, had been arrested with all his party in the railway station at Lille – and under pressure someone had talked.

"Dédée, the Gestapo is looking for you," Morelle had warned, "You cannot go back to Belgium."

Andrée had accepted that truth stoically – but she was far from defeated. Now she would stay on in France and work from there. Her father would take over her role in Brussels and Morelle would act as go-between. She had made three trips over the Pyrenees since that time, delivering nine "parcels" in all. It was fitting that tonight, Christmas Eve, should mark the fifth.

In the farmhouse kitchen, a new guide, who had replaced Tomas, the smuggler, Florentino Goicoechea, a mighty Basque, sat in silence, swigging contentedly at his *bota*, a goatskin bottle of mountain wine, as Andrée outlined the route for the benefit of her "parcels". The four men – Tom Cox, Jack Hutton and Len Warburton, all R.A.F. aircrew non-coms, and Albert Daye, a Canadian – listened with frowning attention. Sometimes, Andrée warned them, a man could lose contact with his party in the darkness, risking internment in the Spanish concentration camp at Miranda del Ebro. Thus it was prudent to memorise landmarks from the map in advance: the wheeling beams of the lighthouse at Fuenterrabia and the lights of the frontier seaport of Irun; the foaming torrent of the Bidassoa River and the three peaks of the Trois Couronnes, marking the climax of the journey.

At 10 p.m. it was time to go. In the orange glow of the lamplight, Florentino now finished packing a bulky rucksack. Then, taking a giant draught of cognac, he inspected each man in turn, checking the fit of their rope-soled *espadrilles*. A man lagging behind with blistered feet could endanger the whole party. Finally he armed each with a stout stick.

The night was dry, yet the wind had a sickle-edge. With short quick steps like an Indian, Florentino took the lead; Andrée, following close behind, had perfected the same gait, to make the going easier. The airmen followed as best they could, toiling ever upward over rock and shale towards a sky hobnailed with stars. Halfway along the coast from St Jean de Luz, they glimpsed briefly, through howling blackness, the dark swooping shadows that the Fuenterrabia light cast across the valley. A long way off were pinpoints of light: the dockside and wharves of Irun.

Abruptly the weather changed. A stinging sleet swept the mountains and the path grew slippery. In this alien element, the airmen began to stumble and fall. But they scrambled on, bruised and breathless, clinging for dear life to shrubs and gnarled roots. Andrée, burdened only by a small pack, began to worry about Albert Daye. The Canadian had confided that his skull was fractured, held in place by gold clamps, a fact he had concealed from his Air Force medical board. "Don't worry if I black out," he had told her, "It often happens when I'm flying, but never for long."

But on a night like this, in mountain passes rising more than 4,000 feet? More than once Andrée cast an anxious glance to her rear.

Now began the tortuous descent to the Bidassoa valley. Mercifully the sleet died away. Tonight's escape would hinge on the weather, for a heavy snowfall or rain would render the Bidassoa impassable on foot. Then the only feasible crossing was inland, over a bridge which though floodlit was unguarded by sentries – but a further sixteen hours march for weary men.

Far away a roadway gleamed, leaden under the stars, marking the Spanish side of the river. Momentarily a car's headlights flickered, gilding a cascade of white water: the Bidassoa in spate. It was quiet there in the valley, on the eve of the nativity, with only the iron music of church bells borne on the cold air.

By degrees, a deep rhythmic pulsing became audible. Soon it filled the air until speech became impossible: the thunder of the Bidassoa tumbling towards the sea at Irun. "*Couchez-vous*", Florentino mouthed. Not far off, a brightly-lit frontier post glittered in the night, and armed men were patrolling. Squatting by the boiling water, the Basque stripped off his trousers, knotting them round his neck, before testing the water for depth. Andrée, who was wearing fisherman's trousers, did the same, bidding the airmen follow suit. Then one by one they stumbled out into the torrent until they were waist deep, the cold invading their loins like the chill of imminent death.

Once across the river came the riskiest part of all. With Florentino still in the lead, they scaled a rocky embankment to reach a railway line. In the distance they could see the red glow of an engine against the night. Scrabbling and cursing through a tangle of bushes, they reached the frontier road: the moment of truth.

Florentino had fallen flat, couched as still as a hare. From a thorn bush he saw the sentry at the frontier post, 100 yards away, wheel and turn. In a strange sprinting run the Basque flashed noiselessly across the roadway, then again fell flat. Doubling at intervals in his wake, came the airmen, now nearing the end of their tether; the last man across, Albert Daye, fell backwards with a clatter. It was Andrée, watchfully bringing up the rear, who hauled him to safety.

Now the way ahead, skirting the road which circled the Trois Couronnes, seemed endless. Still Florentino climbed, as effortlessly as a shepherd, rallying them at intervals with a cry of "*Dos cien metros*". Briefly, cresting the peak of a slope, they rested, wolfing bread and cheese. Generously Florentino passed round his *bota*, but Andrée, concerned, permitted them only one swig apiece. Already they were light-headed with fatigue, and several hours of marching lay ahead.

As the saffron dawn of Christmas Day suffused the sky, the four were lagging badly. Then, like a small determined terrier, Andrée brought up the rear, now cajoling, now rebuking. The heavy morning dew soaking their clothes, they moved blindly on. Now a sweet tintinnabulation of bells came through the morning mist; all at once they were blundering among a flock of sheep. They were nearing the village of Oyarzun.

Now Florentino moved ahead towards a small isolated farmhouse, eyes wary for the green uniforms and cocked hats of *carabineros*. Stooping to pick up a pebble, he tossed it at an upper window. Seconds later, a door swung open; a stout peasant woman, bustling them into her kitchen, set to work preparing *tortillas* and coffee.

But Andrée's Christmas Day was only now beginning. Even as the weary airmen were collapsing onto goosefeather beds, Andrée, after changing into the blouse and skirt she had brought in her pack, was setting off on a five-kilometre walk across the fields to Rentiera. From here, a tram ride took her to the flat of Señor Aracama, the garage proprietor, where she rested up for the day. That night, Aracama's car bore her back to the farmhouse to collect her "parcels" then on to a lonely rendezvous on the San Sebastian road. There a Sunbeam Talbot with CD plates, driven by Michael Creswell's chauffeur, Antonio, bore them on the next step of their journey to freedom.

She would make thirty-one more Pyreneean journeys, escorting 118 servicemen to the Allies, before the misty afternoon of 15 January, 1943, when Gestapo agents swooped on the farmhouse at Urrugne. Thereafter she fought her own private war: to survive the misery of two years in Ravensbrück and Mauthausen concentration camps.

But an ambition conceived as 1941 dawned – an escape line which brought 770 men to safety by June 1944 – had been realised. Andrée de Jongh had kept faith.

*

In his office in the West Wing of the White House, Press Secretary Stephen T. Early was belatedly catching up on his Christmas mail. It was with feeling that he wrote to his old friend Samuel I. Rosenman: "A week ago tonight a certain Naval person arrived. He left yesterday for Ottawa, I am sorry he has gone. Contrarily I am sorry that he is coming back. Pearl Harbor wasn't enough. We had to have Churchill too. Either one was enough. Both have been too much."

The man whose teams of secretaries and advisers had done so much to galvanise the staid small-town atmosphere of the White House was on this day, 29 December, engaged in goading and stimulating the Canadian Parliament – conjuring up a visionary future in which the separate elements of nation-states were annealed in the fires of war. He looked back to that time in 1940 when he had warned the French that whatever happened Britain would fight on alone – and how the generals had told Premier Reynaud and his Cabinet, "In three weeks England will have her neck wrung like a chicken."

Glowering across the lectern and the embattled months since he and Hopkins dined in Glasgow, Churchill's jaw was out-thrust, his voice a bulldog's growl. "Some chicken!" he rejoined defiantly, "Some neck!"

The cheering seemed to ring over the whole city of Ottawa.

It had been a year which marked the turning point of World War Two. Despite the bleak tenor of events, the seeds of victory had been sown in defeat; all that ensued in the next three years had already been foreshadowed. The era of battleship power had ended – as the Japanese would discover in June 1942 off Midway Island. The myth of the impregnable fortress had been severely dented, if not dispelled: Singapore would fall in February, yet Leningrad held out until January, 1944. Neutrality was now a luxury few could afford; in all Europe, only Sweden, Switzerland and Turkey remained uneasily on the sidelines until the end. Even the ultimate holocaust had been foreseen. On 17 December, at a top-secret meeting of twenty physicists in Tokyo's Naval Club, Captain Itoh of the Imperial Navy broached the possibility that some among them might develop an atomic weapon for Japan. But the doyen of the scientists, Dr Asada, was gloomy: "In my opinion only the United States has the potential to develop an atomic weapon."

The shadow of the Manhattan Project hung even then over the thirty-seven nations who were now at war. From a localised conflict which many had hoped to evade – or see ended by a fragile truce – the whole world had drifted towards Armageddon, "the battle of the great day of God Almighty".

The shifting of the war to the Far East was to end the white domination which had marked the last two hundred years. Britain, about to lose an empire, was to fight on for almost four years to regain it – "all, all shall be restored", Churchill said. America, by contrast, hoped to replace British dominion in the east with her own predominance. Both sides were doomed to disappointment, notably in Korea and Vietnam; already "Asia for the Asiatics" had won a moral victory, ending the age of imperialism.

So, too, with "Operation Barbarossa". The stubborn resistance of the Russian defensive, prompted in part by the *Einsatzgruppen*, would become a ferocious counteroffensive; the tidal wave of Russian "liberation", which few save Churchill would foresee, rang down an iron curtain "from Stettin, in the Baltic, to Trieste, in the Adriatic". This same

271

relentless repression prompted the vast exodus of Jews to the modern state of Israel – fomenting a Jewish–Arab conflict which has never been resolved.

Strangely, as 1941 ended, so many of the participants seemed like actors trapped in a gigantic frieze – condemned to mime the same gestures which had typified them all along. In Moscow, Stalin was still badgering Eden and Cadogan, who had arrived on a mission, for two prize concessions: a British Second Front and recognition of the new frontiers carved out by his 1940 annexation of the Baltic States. In Chungking, Chiang Kai-shek's demands for American money and supplies grew daily more clamant. Between Tito and Mihailović, in Yugoslavia, it was still war to the knife. De Gaulle, ever more intent on creating a rift between Roosevelt and Churchill, had on Christmas Eve enraged the State Department by seizing the Vichy-held island colony of St Pierre and Miquelon off the south coast of Newfoundland.

Only Rommel – for the time being at least – conceded that events had moved on and left him standing. By 9 December, having lost 33,000 killed, wounded and imprisoned and 300 tanks, he decided to temporarily abandon Tobruk – beating a fighting retreat through Gazala back to Agedabia. Six red flares arching into the winter sky marked the relief of Tobruk by its own garrison, and a corps commander despatched a signal that became a classic in Eighth Army circles: "Tobruk is relieved, but not as relieved as I am."

Thus, feinting and skirmishing like fighting cocks, the Germans fell back, with Eighth Army in spirited pursuit. "We chased them until 20 December," one tanker sergeant noted in his diary, "until they were right back behind the Agheila salt flats. We ran round them, over them and underneath them."

On New Year's Eve – when both sides saluted each other with a mammoth firework display of green, red, yellow and white flares – it was all as if it had never been. Once again Rommel's forces stood almost where they had when he assumed command eleven months back – in the great Sirte bend between Agedabia and Tripoli. And again Eighth Army held the airfields in the "bulge" of Cyrenaica.

Propped on the mantelpiece of a flat in the old port of Benghazi, the Germans had left the advancing British a point to ponder. Written in English, the message read: "We'll be back in three months, but in the meantime – A Merry Christmas!"

*

Early on New Year's Day, 1942, Roosevelt had a brainwave. For days, both during Churchill's visit and his sojourn in Ottawa, the two men had been pondering a fitting label for the league of twenty-six co-belligerents

272

that now made common cause against the Axis. "Allied and Associated Powers" seemed a ponderous terminology, with a faint smack of Woodrow Wilson, though neither man could come up with anything better. But now time was pressing: Churchill had returned the previous night and the first signatures on the joint declaration were to be affixed that day.

Now Roosevelt saw the light. Pressing a bell he asked to be wheeled to the North-East Suite – to find Churchill still wallowing happily in his bath, at intervals ducking beneath the water, then surfacing again, blowing like a grampus. At first Roosevelt made to withdraw – until Sergeant Patrick Kinna, Churchill's shorthand writer, heard the Premier, naked and unashamed, extend a greeting often considered apocryphal: "Come in – I have nothing to conceal from the President of the United States!"

"How about United Nations?" Roosevelt called, as Churchill lifted a soapy head from the water.

Churchill paused to consider. Then, ducking again to rinse the last of the soap from his eyes, he re-surfaced, to turn a dripping gaze on the President.

"That," he said, "should do it."

There was a true climate of optimism then, four years before the Iron Curtain rang down. So perhaps their innocence could be forgiven.

ACKNOWLEDGEMENTS

This book, like its companion volume, *1940: The World in Flames*, derives in part from the recollections of several hundred eye-witnesses and in part from records and archive repositories in the United States and Great Britain. Those participants whose testimonies I have used are hereby gratefully acknowledged; the details of their individual contributions are listed in the appropriate section of the source apparatus.

I have to thank Dr Daniel J. Boorstin, Librarian of Congress, Washington, D.C., for the facilities he so kindly granted me during my visit, and especially Paul T. Heffron, Acting Chief of the Manuscript Division and his assistant, Marianne Roos. I am equally indebted to Dr William R. Emerson, Director, Franklin D. Roosevelt Memorial Library, Hyde Park, New York, for similar facilities, and to Mark Renovitch, Susan Bosanko, and John Ferris who generously directed my attention to a number of recent acquisitions. In Washington's National Archives, Edward J. Reese, Modern Military Branch, Military Archives Division, proved equally helpful.

British archives for this period have been growing apace annually, and for permission to study, and in many cases to quote from, the records in their keeping, I am grateful to the following: A. J. Nicholls, St Antony's College, Oxford; Corelli Barnett, Keeper of the Archives, Churchill College, Cambridge, and his most able assistants, Marion Stewart and Clare Stephens; Dr B. S. Benedikz, Head of Special Collections, University Library Birmingham; Dr Maurice Bond, Clerk of the Records, House of Lords and Dr A. J. P. Taylor; Patricia Methven, Military Archivist, and her assistant, Bridget Evans, of the Liddell Hart Centre for Military Archives, University of London, King's College; Catherine Pickett, of the India Office Library and Records (Foreign and Commonwealth Office); Professor David Pocock and Dorothy Wainwright, University of Sussex (The Mass-Observation Archive); Angela Raspin, British Library of Political and Economic Science (London School of Economics); Robert Shackleton, The Bodleian Library, Oxford, and Dr Peter Thwaites, Department of Documents, and his deputy, Philip Reed, at the Imperial War Museum, London.

As in the past I have been singularly lucky in the loyal band of researchers and translators who have continued to work at my side. Hildegard Anderson, as always, scrupulously covered many phases of my American research. Pamela Colman delved in many university libraries, and conducted a number of telling interviews. Joan St George Saunders solved many last-minute queries. Alexandra Lawrence pioneered the forbidding mass of documentation at the Public Record Office, later nobly reinforced by Margaret Duff, who also travelled hundreds of miles to interview scores of survivors. A special note of thanks, too, to Kim Marabella, who saw to all my travel arrangements from Pearl Harbor on.

My English and American publishers, Christopher Sinclair-Stevenson and Alfred A. Knopf Jr waited with exemplary patience for a manuscript long overdue, and I must acknowledge once again the matchless editorial counsel of Roger Machell. My agents in London and New York, Graham Watson and James Oliver Brown, offered the usual sterling moral support. Jill Beck oversaw a typescript which arrived at protracted intervals with her old aplomb. In addition I must thank the staffs of the Library of Congress, Printed Books Division, the New York Public Library, the Public Record Office, the British Library, the London Library and the Wiener Library for the help and courtesy that they at all times afforded.

My deepest debt, though, is to my wife, to whom this book is dedicated. Apart from typing the first draft she travelled with me many thousands of miles on our joint research project. The support she offered every inch of the way made all of it seem worthwhile.

274

SOURCE APPARATUS

Chapter One: "Thy People Shall Be My People"
The Hopkins' dinner is related by Moran. Hotel details of that time were kindly furnished by Judy Lask and Deborah Dudley, of British Transport Hotels Information Services, and P. K. Masser, General Manager, North British Hotel. For that day's weather I am grateful to J. G. Allardice, Senior Meteorological Officer, Glasgow Weather Centre.

For shipping losses and the Home Front, see Balfour, Calder, Costello and Hughes, Longmate, McLaine and Marwick. Woolton's statement is from the Woolton MSS., folio 12, Churchill to Woolton, January 2. Morale is dealt with by Mass Observation Files 568, *Morale in 1941.* and 925, *Absenteeism from Industrial Work.* Aspects of Hopkins are from Birkenhead, *Halifax*, Childs, William Crozier, Kenneth Davis and Harriman. Hopkins' own impression of his mission – including his talk with King George VI – are found in FDR, PSF, Safe File, Box 4, *Harry Hopkins* folder, and the Sherwood/Hopkins' papers, Box 304, Folder A, *Hopkins in London.*

General background to Lend-Lease is furnished by Acheson, Burns, Davis and Lindley, Kenneth Davis, Ickes, Jonas, Langer and Gleason, and Lash, *Roosevelt.* For isolationism and interventionism, see Chadwin, Dawson, Frye and Wheeler-Bennett, *Special.* Roosevelt's inauguration is based on items in Early's Papers, Scrapbook 1, Wickard's diary entry for 6 January, and Leonard Baker. Isolationist cartoons feature in *Time's* issue of 24 February. For Willkie in London, see Nicolson's MSS. diary entry for 1 February; for Dublin, see Beaverbrook Papers, File D 417, Beaverbrook to Churchill, 6 June. Barkley is in FDR, PPF, 5160, memo of 17 February.

General background on Greece (and in Chapters III and IV) is furnished by Buckley, *Greece*, Cadogan, Cervi, Eden and Parkinson. For the Balkans, especially Bulgaria, see PRO AIR 40/2023 and Foreign Relations of the United States (hereafter FRUS), Vol I, 273; also Dalton's diary entries of 3 February and 18 November. Prince Paul is from F.O. 954/33, fol. 241, Campbell to F.O., and Channon. For Greek intelligence, see Davidson Papers, File K, *Episodes Concerning Winston Churchill.*

Doubts on Greece are in Dalton's diary entry for 19 February, CAB 65 (WM) 19, and Edwards' diary for 7 March. Palairet's reaction is from F.O. 954/11, fol. 40, 7 March; Wavell's is fol. 26, 27 January. For Prince Paul to Eden, see F.O. 954/33, fol. 269, 19 March. Discussions with the Dominions are in CAB 65 (WM), 20, 21 and 26. Admiral Turner's views are in Hopkins' Papers, Box 154, Folder *Great Britain*, memo of 12 April. For MacVeagh to Roosevelt, see FDR, PSF, Box 54, *Greece* folder, letter of 8 March.

Material on Rommel (and in Chapters II, III, V, X and XIII) derives from the German monographs listed in the MSS bibliography, and from works by Carell, *Foxes*, Irving, *Fox*, Esebeck, Mellenthin, Heinz-Werner Schmidt and Desmond Young.

Hitler's strategy throughout is based on studies by Bullock, Friedlander, Hinsley, *Strategy*, Irving, *War*, and Rich. The story of Harold Elvin (and in Chapters V, VI, VIII and IX) is based on an interview he kindly granted the author to supplement his book. Mlle Andrée de Jongh, Sir Michael Creswell, and Lieutenant-Colonel J. M. Langley most helpfully furnished escape line material (and in Chapters VII and XII). Marcel-Gerard Comeau's story (continued in Chapters II, III and V) is adapted from his book, supplemented by an interview. Ruth Mitchell's story is as she told it, with supporting information from Mrs Ruth Van Breda Yahn, Mrs Lewis Pillsbury, and Robert G. Carroon, Curator of Research Collections, Milwaukee Country Historical Society. Anglo-American financial tensions are mirrored in CAB 65/(WM) 19 and 29, Wickard's diary entry for 16 January, and works by Blum, Ickes and Thorne. Churchill to Nicolson is the latter's MSS.

diary entry for 21 March. For the salmon run, see Hopkins' Papers, Box 155, Folder *Great Britain, Food*, Hopkins to Winant, 22 June.

Chapter Two: "Convoys Mean Shooting and Shooting Means War"
The American mission to London is derived from Bellush and Harriman; F.O. reactions to Winant are in F.O. 954/29, fol. 233, n.d. Roosevelt's unneutral neutrality is charted by Burns and by Matloff and Snell. U.S. – Yugoslav relations are in FRUS II, 944, 962 and Fotić; promises to Greece are in FRUS II, 670–712. For Roosevelt on Abyssinia, see FDR, PSF, Box 93, folder *Cordell Hull*, letter of 20 February. For the pact and subsequent coup in Yugoslavia, see Dalton's diary entries of 21, 27, 30 March and 17 April, and accounts by Elisabeth Barker, Brock, Hoptner, Kapetanović, King Peter II, Maitland, St John, Stowe and Leigh White. Subotić's encounters with Butler are found in F.O. 954/33, fols. 252 (21 March) and 273 (7 April). For Matsuoka, see Bullock, Davis and Lindley, Paul Schmidt, and Toland, *Sun*. Foreign Office apprehensions are in CAB 65 (WM), 14, plus Cadogan, Eden and Sir John Kennedy. For U.S. policy in China, see, principally Divine and Shaller; Morgenthau's argument with Roosevelt is his MSS diary entry for 21 April. Accounts of Tobruk from the Allied viewpoint are from Heckstall-Smith, Gavin Long, Wilmot and Yindrich.

Chapter Three: "Do Not Succumb to Provocation"
Churchill and the Poles is Nicolson's MSS diary entry for 26 March; the "frog" is from Maisky. The conference at Tatoi Palace is as described by Heckstall-Smith and Baillie-Grohman. Smuts' counsel on aircraft is from CAB 65 (WM), 27. The first concept of the Atlantic Charter is from Pickersgill.
Overall accounts of Iraq appear in Buckley, *Ventures*, Hirsowicz, Mockler and Stark. Secret intelligence on Rashid Ali is in F.O. 954/12, fol. 393 (7 April); Lampson's reactions are fols. 395 (3 May) and 396 (6 May). Auchinleck's warnings are from the Alanbrooke Papers, File 6/D/4bE, 12 April. For Attlee on Wavell, see Dalton's diary entry for 30 May. General Clark's report and the dilemma regarding the U.S. Minister are F.O. 954/12, fols. 401 (3 July) and 403 (17 July).
For Tito, see Auty, Clissold, *Whirlwind*, Dedijer and Djilas. Warnings to Stalin are featured by Bialer, Deakin, *Sorge*, Höhne, *Direktor*, Trepper and Weth, *War*; appeasement of Hitler is dealt with by Laqueur and Weinberg. For Cripps in Moscow, see Dalton's diary entry for 29 January. The American military attachés' reports are in the Hopkins' Papers, Box 188, *Military Intelligence Division Reports*, passim.
The best overall account of Hess' mission is in Douglas-Hamilton, supplemented by accounts from Colville, Ilse Hess, Kirkpatrick and Leasor. Fighter Command reactions were gleaned from the author's interviews with the late Duke of Hamilton, Marshal of the R.A.F. Lord Douglas of Kirtleside, C. H. Leman, "Dickie" Richardson and Sadie Younger. For Whitehead's view, see F.O. 954/29, fol. 209, 10 June.

Chapter Four: "He'll Never Beat Men Like These"
The exploits of Starheim's network are described in varying degrees by Cookridge, *SOE*, Hansson, and Kennedy, *Pursuit* – which also deals with initial preparations at Scapa Flow and the subsequent *Bismarck* battle. For my own account of the battle I have drawn on ADM 199/357, ADM 199/1187 (*Pursuit and Destruction of Bismarck*), ADM 1/11726 (*Loss of H.M.S. Hood*), supplemented by eye-witness accounts from the following: Derek Aylwin, Michael Buxton, Surgeon Vice-Admiral Sir Dick Caldwell, Bernard Campion, Peter Dunstan, Rear-Admiral John Dyer-Smith, Basil Elsmore, Charles Firbank, Lieutenant-Commander Alan Franklin, Edward Grindley, Douglas Hall, David Hunter, Leonard Jackson, Thomas Jenkins, William Johns, Frederick Kenshole, Jack Knight, Alfred Llewellyn, Herbert Minnett, Ronald Mullins, Norman Portlock, Michael Pruett, Commander Arthur Skipwith, Douglas Spinks, Lieutenant-Commander Richard Thomas-Ferrand, Kenneth Townsend-Green and Charles Wright. The majority of these also contributed material to Chapters VIII and XI. Published accounts of the battle are by Apps, Ash, Bekker, *Naval*, Broome, Busch, Cain, Franklin, Jameson, Sopocko and Thompson. For A. V. Alexander, see Dalton's diary entry for 26 May; the Ministry of Information reaction is from the Monckton Papers. File *B.B.C. Home News Criticism*, 31 May.

Operations in Crete are based on the file PREM 3/109, in particular fols. 31/34, Churchill's trenchant criticism of 14 June, and on published accounts by Bartz, Belchem, Buckley, *Greece*, Alan Clark, Davin, Heydte, Hill-Rennie, Jacobsen, Kippenberger, Lewin, Gavin Long, Mrazek, Sandford, Singleton-Gates, Spencer, Stephanides, Stewart and Whiting. Caccia's report, transmitted by Lampson to Eden, is F.O. 954/11, fol. 64, 27 May. Goltz' story is a typescript kindly loaned to the author by Marcel-Gerard Comeau.

Roosevelt's "State of Emergency" derives from published accounts by Davis and Lindley, Manchester, *Glory*, Rosenman and Sherwood. His "gradualness" is from Wood's papers (A 410.4), Halifax to Churchill, 13 June; his rebuke from Bullitt is from FDR, PPF, 1124, *William Bullitt*, 21 May; the floodtide of Lend-Lease is from FDR, PSF, Box 16, Folder *Lend-Lease*, items of 16 April, 7 May. Dunn's report is from Beaverbrook Papers, File D 417, Beaverbrook to Churchill, 5 June.

Chapter Five: "No Peace, No Rest, No Halting Place, No Parley"
Published sources on Crete are as listed for Chapter IV. For Wavell's despair, see F.O. 954/5, fol. 77, Lampson to Eden, 30 May; for Tedder to Portal, see PREM 3/109, fol. 73, 30 May. Churchill at Church House is Nicolson's MSS diary entry for 10 June. British morale is from Mass Observation Weekly Report No 1, dated 9 June.

The bitter Dominions reaction is denoted by F.O. 954/4, fol. 305 (New Zealand) and fols. 318–22 (Australia). Lampson's contribution is F.O. 954/11, fol. 65, Lampson to Eden, 28 May. Cunningham's report is from the Cunningham Papers, RKCN 1/9, Cunningham to Admiral Sir Algernon Willis, 12 June. For Portal to Royce, see Arnold's Papers, Box 39, 31 July. Churchill to Cranborne is from Garner; Blamey's comment from Thorne. For Menzies to Wilson, see Brooke-Popham Papers, V/1/13, Ismay to Brooke-Popham, 15 June. American disillusion is noted by Dalton in his diary entry for 2 June; his record of Cabinet dissensions is likewise from diary entries of 29 October, 1940, 26 February, 1941, 22 May, 11 and 27 June, 8 August, 17 September and 19 November, supplemented by Hollis and Leasor, Reith, and Roskill, *Hankey*.

Vichy material is based on studies by Cole, Crawley, Langer, *Gamble*, Lukacs, and Paxton. Darlan's "superman" concept is Leahy's MSS diary entry for 1 August. Hull to Henri-Haye is from Hull's Papers, Box 58, Folder 28, *Vichy France*, 18 January; to Halifax, from Folder 214, *Great Britain*, 7 March. Eden's pipeline to Weygand is in CAB 65 (WM) 8 and F.O. 954/8, fols. 141–44, 17 January. Aspects of de Gaulle are discussed by Elisabeth Barker, Boothby, Crawley and Schoenbrunn. For Pétain on de Gaulle, see FDR, PSF, Box 41, Folder *France*, Leahy to Roosevelt, 19 March. Dalton on de Gaulle is his diary entry for 7 October.

Parr's report is from F.O. 954/8, fol. 165, 14 May; Hoare's advice is from Beaverbrook's Papers, File C 308, *Sir Samuel Hoare*, 14 May. Wavell's reluctance is from F.O. 954/15, fol. 33, Lampson to F.O., 29 May. The Churchill – de Gaulle phone call was related to the author by Air Commodore James Coward, a luncheon guest.

The Syrian campaign is amply covered in works by Cecil Brown, Buckley, *Ventures*, Fergusson, *Trumpet*, Hirsowicz, and Mockler. For Spears to Bracken, see Churchill College Papers, ref. Sprs 1/50, 25 May; for Lampson's confirmation, see F.O. 954/5, fols. 130–33, Lampson to Eden, 25 October. The "Robin Moor" episode is from Metzler. Hitler's unique view of the U.S. is from Compton, Friedlander, and Weinberg, *Image*.

The Iceland take-over is in Hull's Papers, Box 49, Folder 145, Churchill to Roosevelt, 14 June, and Morgenthau's MSS. diary entry for 10 July. Stark's apprehension is from FDR, PSF, Box 55, *Iceland* Folder, Stark to Hopkins, 17 June. Portuguese aspirations feature in FDR, PSF, Box 93, Folder *Cordell Hull*, State Department report of 26 March. Neumann's story follows his own account. For the "Commissar Order", see Irving, *War*, Keitel, Krausnick, Macksey, *Guderian*, Manstein, Toland, *Hitler*, and Wheeler-Bennett, *Nemesis*.

Eve-of-Barbarossa Soviet impressions are from Bialer and Erickson; German reactions from Carell, *Hitler*, Malaparte, Pabel and Schutz.

Chapter Six: "We Have Only To Kick In The Door"
Barbarossa battle material is from Bialer, Blumentritt, Carell, *Hitler*, Erickson, Freiden, Macksey, *Guderian*, Malaparte, Manstein, Pabel, Pabst, Salisbury and Seaton. For Hitler's peace offer via Turkey, see F.O. 954/28, fol. 128, Knatchbull-Hugessen to F.O., 22 June,

and Nicolson's MSS diary entry for 23 June. World-wide Barbarossa reactions are from Chadwin, Ciano, Eden, Murphy, Sherwood, and Toland, *Hitler*.

Hilda Neal's reaction is from her diary entry of 23 June, likewise Kathleen Phipps' diary notations of 27 July and 7 August. Alba's dispatch is from Crozier, *Franco*. For Cripps, see F.O. 954/24, fol. 331, 2 July. Pownall is Nicolson's MSS. diary entry for 9 July. American reactions are noted by Burns, Davis and Lindley, Dawson and Fehrenbach. For Hopkins on Stalin, see Ismay Papers, ISMAY/IV/HOP, Hopkins to Ismay, 7 August. Cox and Berle are in the Sherwood/Hopkins' Papers, Box 305, Folder *Russia Attacked – Early Political Decisions*, Cox to Hopkins, 23 June, Berle to Hopkins, 30 July.

For Hungary, see Fenyo and Horthy. Mussolini at Verona was related to the author by General Enno von Rintelen. Bomber Command operations are covered by Barker, *Strike*, Frankland, Hastings, Richards and Wykeham. British complacency concerning the Russian campaign features in Mass Observation Weekly Report No 3, dated 23 June. For a Balkan report on the British attitude, see FDR, PSF, Box 54, Pell to Roosevelt, 21 October. For Sinclair to Hopkins, see the Arnold Papers, Box 38, Folder *Aircraft Allocations*, 27 July. Churchill's meeting with the airman is Dalton's diary entry for 12 December.

Chapter Seven: "At Last – We've Gotten Together"
Facets of European resistance and the V for Victory campaign are covered by Archer, Michael Balfour, Ehrlich, Kraus, Michel, Petrow, Viorst and *Time*'s issues of 10 March, 17 March, 28 July, 4 August, 11 August and 29 September. For Tito's partisans see Auty, Clissold, *Whirlwind*, Colaković and Djilas. The principal sources for the Atlantic Charter are Franklin, H. V. Morton, Pawle, Reilly, Spring and Theodore Wilson. Darlan's reaction on Indo-China is from FDR, PSF, Box 4, Safe File *France*, Leahy to the State Department, 1 August. Churchill's estimation of Barbarossa is from the Sherwood/Hopkins Papers, Box 306, Folder *Atlantic Conference*, as is Freeman's letter to Hopkins of 11 August. For Roosevelt's determination not to declare war and Churchill's response, see F.O. 954/4, fol. 340, Churchill to Smuts, 9 November. For Arnold and Freeman, see the Arnold Papers, Box 39, *Strategy* Folder, memo of 10 August. Auchinleck's press conference crops up in F.O. 954/15, fol. 78, Churchill to Auchinleck, 11 July.

Chapter Eight: "Shoot Everyone Who Shows A Wry Face"
Guderian's journey to the *Wolfsschanze* is described by Carell, *Hitler*. For the German presence in Tehran, see *Documents on German Foreign Policy*, Vol XIII, P 103/4, and Kahn, *Spies*. War Cabinet pressure on Iran is from CAB 65 (WM) 79 and 82 and F.O. 954/19 fols. 129, 131, 8 and 11 August. Accounts of the campaign and the Shah's eccentricities are drawn from Brock, Buckley, *Ventures*, Dimbleby and Michie. The Shah's appeal to Roosevelt is from FDR, PSF, Box 55, *Iran* Folder, 26 August; Roosevelt replied on 2 September. Churchill's rebuke to Bullard and orders to seize the Shah are CAB 65 (WM) 89 and 93. Nicolson's flirtation with kingmaking form his MSS. diary entries for 13, 19 and 23 September. Dreyfus and the young Shah are in FRUS III, 470. For Beaverbrook's meeting with Hess, see Beaverbrook Papers, File D 443, *Rudolf Hess*. Moscow background is from Bourke-White, Caldwell, Cassidy and LeSueur.

British enthusiasm for Russia is explored in the following Mass Observation holdings: File No 848, *Public Opinion About Russia*, 27 August; File 915, *Second Front*, 16 October, and Weekly Reports No 12 of 11 August and No 21 of 22 September. The topic also features in the Sherwood/Hopkins' Papers, Box 397, Folder 1, *Postal Censorship Reports*, 25 July, and in works by Addison, Calder and Maisky. Pro-Communist posters are in the Bevin Papers, ref. BVN 2/2.

For the Atlantic Charter ferment see Collis, Louis and Thorne. U Saw's appeal to Roosevelt is FDR, PSF, Box 34, *Diplomatic, Burma*, letter of 26 November. For Calcutta, see Brooke-Popham Papers, BP V/1/2, Brooke-Popham to Ismay, 15 November, 1940.

Laski's letter, dated 13 August, is in the Frankfurter Papers, Container 75. For de Gaulle in Syria, see Elisabeth Barker, *Churchill*, Chandos and Mockler. Churchill's fury and M.I.5's surveillance of de Gaulle is from Spears Papers, St Antony's College, ref IIA/2, H. Somerville-Smith to Spears, 29 August and 6 September. For Dominions disputes see Channon, Hasluck, and CAB 65 (WM) 94 and 106, recording the demand for the *Prince of Wales*.

Genocide in Russia is fully dealt with by Bracher, Fest, Frischauer, Höhne, *Death's Head*, Musmanno, Reynolds, Russell and St George. The Jews are the subject of detailed studies by Davidowicz, Hilberg, Krausnick, Poliakov and Reitlinger, *Solution*. The teenager quoted is Lind. For the lost opportunity in Russia see Blumentritt, Cecil, Pabel, St George, Seaton and Strik-Strikfeldt.

Chapter Nine: "Let No One Forget, Let Nothing Be Forgotten"
Beaverbrook's Moscow mission is drawn principally from a typescript account by Harold Balfour and from the Beaverbrook files, D 90, *Cripps Controversy* and D 100, *Aid to Russia and the Russian Narrative*, plus published accounts by Harriman, Standley, A. J. P. Taylor, and Kenneth Young. Cadbury's dilemma is noted by Dalton on 19 September. Steinhardt to the State Department is FRUS I, 866. The Sherwood/Hopkins' Papers, Box 305, Folder *Russia Attacked*, contain Berle to Welles, 30 July and Beaverbrook to Hopkins, 4 October. Ismay to Brooke-Popham is BP V/1/17 of 16 September. Other Beaverbrook references are as follows: on the Americans, File D 71, *Balfour Visit to USA*, letter of 4 November; on inefficient British production, File D 78, *Meetings with Manufacturers*, conference transcripts of 28 October and 11 November; File D 359, Beaverbrook to Margesson, 1 September; File D 332, Beaverbrook to the Colonial Office, 3 September; File C 308, Beaverbrook to Hoare, 28 August.

For Leningrad I have drawn on works by Goure, Inber, Pavlov, Salisbury, Shostakovich, Skomorovsky, and Werth, *War*. Disillusion in Germany is noted by Michael Balfour, Fredborg, Howard Smith and Turney. The Ankara scene is reported by Brock.

The North Atlantic scene is covered by Morison. Smuts to Eden is F.O. 954/4, fol. 331, 13 September. For Halifax to Churchill, see Wood's Papers (A 410.4), letter of 11 October. Roosevelt to Eccles is Dalton's diary entry for 25 August. Knox's Papers, Container 4, *General Correspondence*, include Frankfurter's letter of 2 July and Lippmann's of 2 October. Events in Japan follow accounts by Butow, Ike, Mosley, *Hirohito*, Toland, *Shame* and Toland *Sun*.

Chapter Ten: "Just Read This – And The War Is Won"
Churchill's passivity is shown by CAB 65 (WM) 122. Thailand features in F.O. 954/6, fol. 485, Crosby to the F.O., 1 December. For British participation in the Middle East, see Agar-Hamilton, Barnett, Clifford, Connell, *Auchinleck*, Crimp, Fielding, Jacob, Maule, Onslow, and Tedder. Churchill's prodding of Auchinleck is from the Alanbrooke Papers, 6/d/4/C, 20 July. Auchinleck's letters are in Ismay/IV/CON/1A and IV/CON/1/IC, dated 29 September and 6 November.

Wake Island material (and in Chapters XI and XII) is based on an interview kindly granted by Brigadier-General James P. S. Devereux, as a supplement to his book, and on accounts by Bayler, Cunningham, Hough and Karig. Burns, Hull and Leith-Ross describe the attempted compromise with Japan; Dalton's diary entry is for 26 November. Roosevelt's hoped-for Pacific "incident" is from Biddle's Papers, Cabinet Meetings Folder, 7 November. Hull's anger with Halifax is shown by his letter of 29 November, Box 58, Folder 214, *Great Britain*.

Pearl Harbor's unpreparedness is based on the hearings of the Pearl Harbor Committee, and on analyses by Barnes, Brownlow, Buell, Burtness and Oder, Lombard, Lord, Pogue, Theobald, Trefousse, Waller and Wohlstetter. MacArthur material abounds in Brereton, Hersey, Huff, Clayton James, Kenney, Clark Lee, Manchester, *Caesar*, Matloff and Snell, Muggah and Charles Willoughby. Brooke-Popham's comment on MacArthur is from BP V/1/18, dated 10 October; his reluctance to press for equipment is BP V/11, dated 26 October, 1940. Malaya's ineffective defences follow Vlieland's MSS account; for Buffalo aircraft see F.O. 954/6, fols. 422–433, 11 April. The overplus of aerodromes is from Percival's Papers, File P 21, Item 49, *Personal Observations of Lt. Col. Ashmore*. Stewart's jungle training is from ADM 199/234, *Escapes from Hong Kong and Malaya*. General accounts appear in works by Louis Allen, Barber, Boyle, Bulcock and Simson; for Hong Kong social life see Carew and Lindsay. The Australian battalion commander is from BP V/1/8, letter to Ismay of 26 March.

Last-ditch negotiations in Washington are fully covered by Baruch, Butow, Davis and Lindley, Feis, Hoehling, Hull, Mosley, *Hirohito*, and Toland, *Sun*. Hull's telecon with

Halifax is in Hull's Papers, Box 66, Folder 289, *Great Britain, General*, memo of 1 January, 1942. Yamamoto and Yamashita derive from biographies by Potter. Malayan intelligence is from Tsuji. For Early's press conference, see the Early Scrapbook, Vol. II.

Chapter Eleven: "What Was That Place? Could You Spell It?"
    The following accounts of Pearl Harbor, from the viewpoints of both participants, have been used for this reconstruction: Brownlow, Blake Clark, Page Cooper, Dickinson, Forgy, Barry Fox, Fuchida, Hough, Karig, Lord, Millis, *Pearl Harbor* (The Army Times) Sheehan, Toland and Wallin. Reactions in Washington and elsewhere are recorded by Acheson, Davis and Lindley, Fergusson, *Maze*, Hayter, Hoehling, Hull, Manchester, *Glory*, Montagu, Mosley, Reilly, Rosenman, Tully, Winant, and *Time's* issues of 15 and 22 December. For the White House blackout dilemma, see the Nesbitt Papers, Box 2, 7 December diary entry. The Honolulu mood is caught by Robert Casey.
    For British apathy, see Mass Observation File No 1004, *Anti-American Sentiment*, report of 21 December, and Nicolson's MSS diary entry for 12 December.
    The fall of Guam is described by Karig and Tweed; for Cavite, see Agoncillo, Toland, *Shame*, and William L. White. The riddle of Clark Field is treated at length by Brereton, Edmonds, Manchester, *Caesar*, Ernest P. Miller, Louis B. Morton, and Whitcomb. The loss of the *Prince of Wales* and *Repulse* is based primarily on the files ADM 199/1149, PREM 3/163/2, ADM 1/12181 (Reports of Survivors), ADM 1/11043 (Parliamentary Report) and ADM 116/4554 (Bucknill Committee Report), supplemented by reports by all those credited in Chapter IV, plus the following additional testimonials: Admiral Sir Henry Leach, the First Sea Lord; Joseph Blackburn, Alec Compton, Gerald Cooper, Anthony Gibbons, Graham Kipling, Geoffrey Marshall, Lieutenant-Commander Ronald Matheson, Eric Peal, Ronald Peal, J. E. Richardson; Eric Shawyer and Daniel Stowell. Published accounts from the British viewpoint are in Cecil Brown, Gallagher and Middlebrook and Mahoney; the Japanese viewpoint is given by Toland, *Sun*.
    For the Japanese in Malaya, see Tsuji. The growing fear among the Allied contingent is from Percival's Papers, File P 24, item 75, typescript narrative by Lt. Col. F. R. N. Cobley. Percival's comments on Heath and Bennett are from File P 21, Percival's notes on the *Official History*. Brooke-Popham's anger is from BP V/5/49, dated 24 December. Duff-Cooper's verdict on the commanders is from PREM 3/161/2, dated 18 December. "Rats and rice" is from BP V/11 letter to Ismay, 26 October, 1940. The civilian retreat in Malaya is in PREM 3/168/7A, typescript account by G. Morgan of 23 July, 1942. Mohan Singh is based on Lebra, Sivaram and an interview granted to the author by Mohan Singh at Bidadari Camp, Singapore, in September, 1945.
    Shenton Thomas' reassessment of the Japanese is from PREM 3/161/2, letter to Sir C. Parkinson, 17 December. For Hong Kong (and in Chapter XII) I have drawn on the files PREM 3/157/1 and 2, and CO 129/588/12, on diaries by Barbara Anslow, Day Sage Joyce, Dr Isaac Newton and Mabel Redwood, and on published works by Bertram, Wenzell Brown, Bush, Carew, Dew, Field, Guest, Harrop, Lindsay, Marsman and Priestwood. Events in Manila and the Philippines (and in chapter XII) derive from studies by Agoncillo, Coville, Friend, Hatchitt, Huff, James, Long, Manchester, *Caesar*, Monoghan, Claire Phillips, Prising, Quezon, Redmond, Sayre, Van Landingham and Amea Willoughby.

Chapter Twelve: "Some Chicken! Some Neck!"
    December on the Volga front is taken from accounts by Carell, *Hitler*, Haape, Irving, *War*, Kern and Turney. Hitler's blitzkrieg economy is analysed by Cecil, Milward and Noakes.
    Churchill's visit to Washington is noted in the Nesbitt Papers, Box 12, diary entry for 22 December. Strategic disagreements are recorded by Burns and Pogue. The situation in Latin America is from the Hopkins' Papers, Boxes 141, 142 and 143, FBI reports on "*The Fifth Column in Latin America*"; for Argentina in particular, see also Bradford. The Malaya-Philippines argument is from the Arnold Papers, Box 180, *Conference File*, notes for 22 December. For Early to Rosenman, see Early Papers, Box 26, letter of 29 December. Other aspects of Churchill's trip are noted by Barkley, Harriman and Moran.
    The bathroom conference is from Davis and Lindley, and Pawle.

BIBLIOGRAPHY
PRINTED SOURCES

Acheson, Dean, *Present At The Creation*, London: Hamish Hamilton, 1970.

Addison, Paul, *The Road to 1945*, London: Jonathan Cape, 1975.

Agar-Hamilton, J. A., *The Sidi Rezegh Battles*, London: Oxford University Press, 1957.

Agoncillo, Teodoro, *The Fateful Years*, Vol. 1, Quezon City, Philippines: R. P. Garcia, 1945.

Allan, James, *No Citation*, London: Angus and Robertson, 1955.

Allen, Gwenfread, *Hawaii's War Years*, Honolulu: University of Hawaii Press, 1945.

Allen, Louis, *Singapore, 1941–42*, London: Davis-Poynter, 1977.

Andersson, Ingvar, *A History of Sweden* (trans. Carolyn Hannay), London: Weidenfeld & Nicolson, 1956.

Andreas-Friedrich, Ruth, *Berlin Underground* (trans. Barrows Mussey), London: Latimer House, 1948.

Apps, Lieut-Cdr. Michael, *Send Her Victorious*, London: William Kimber, 1971.

Archer, Laird, *Balkan Journal*, New York: W. W. Norton, 1944.

Armstrong, H. F., *Tito and Goliath*, London: Victor Gollancz, 1951.

Arnold, Gen. H. H., *Global Mission*, London: Hutchinson, 1951.

Ash, Bernard, *Someone Had Blundered*, London: Michael Joseph, 1960.

Attiwill, Kenneth, *The Singapore Story*, London: Frederick Muller, 1959.

Auty, Phyllis, *Tito*, London: Longman, 1970.

Auty, Phyllis & Clogg, Richard (eds), *British Policy Towards Wartime Resistance in Yugoslavia and Greece*, London: Macmillan, 1975.

Bahnemann, Gunther, *I Deserted Rommel*, London: Jarrolds, 1961.

Bailey, Douglas, *We Built and Destroyed*, London: Hurst & Blackett, 1944.

Baker, Leonard, *Roosevelt and Pearl Harbor*, New York: Macmillan, 1970.

Baldwin, Hanson W., *The Crucial Years*, London: Weidenfeld & Nicolson, 1976.

Balfour, Michael, *Propaganda in War, 1939–45*, London: Routledge & Kegan Paul, 1979.

Balfour, Neil and Mackay, Sally, *Paul of Yugoslavia*, London: Hamish Hamilton, 1980.

Barber, Noel, *Sinister Twilight: the Fall and Rise Again of Singapore*, London: William Collins, 1968.

Barker, Elisabeth, *Churchill and Eden at War*, London: Macmillan, 1978; *British Policy in South-East Europe in the Second World War*, London: Macmillan, 1976.

Barker, Ralph, *Strike Hard, Strike Sure*, London: Chatto & Windus, 1963.

Barkley, Alben W., *That Reminds Me*, Garden City, N.Y.: Doubleday, 1954.

Barnes, Harry Elmer, *Pearl Harbor After a Quarter of a Century*. New York: Arno Press and the New York Times, 1962.

Barnett, Corelli, *The Desert Generals*, London: William Kimber, 1960.

Bartz, Karl, *Swastika In The Air*, London: William Kimber, 1956.

Baruch, Bernard, *The Public Years*, London: Odhams Press, 1960.

Bayler, Lt.-Col. Walter L. J. (with Cecil Carnes), *Last Man Off Wake Island*, Indianapolis: Bobbs Merrill, 1943.

Beard, Charles A., *President Roosevelt and the Coming of War*, New Haven: Yale University Press, 1948.

Beesly, Patrick, *Very Special Admiral*, London: Hamish Hamilton, 1980; *Very Special Intelligence*, London: Hamish Hamilton, 1977.

Bekker, Cajus, *The Luftwaffe War Diaries* (trans. Frank Ziegler), London: Macdonald, 1966; *Hitler's Naval War* (trans. Frank Ziegler), London: Macdonald, 1974.

Belchem, Maj.-Gen. David, *All In the Day's March*, London: William Collins, 1978.

Bellush, Bernard, *He Walked Alone*, The Hague: Mouton, 1968.

Belote, James, *Corregidor*, New York: Harper & Row, 1967.

Bennett, Lt.-Gen. H. Gordon. *Why Singapore Fell*. Bombay: Thacker, 1945.

Bennett, Geoffrey. *The Loss of the Prince of Wales and the Repulse*, London: Ian Allen, 1973.

Bergot, Erwan, *The Afrika Korps* (trans. Richard Barry), London: Allan Wingate, 1976.

Berle, Adolf, *Navigating the Rapids* (ed. Beatrice Bishop Berle and Travis Beale Jacobs), New York: Harcourt Brace Jovanovich, 1973.

Berthold, Will, *The Sinking of the Bismarck* (trans. Michael Bullock), London: Longman Green, 1958.

Bertram, James M., *The Shadow of a War*, London: Victor Gollancz, 1947.

Bess, Demaree, *Our Frontier on the Danube*, in the Saturday Evening Post, Philadelphia, 24 May, 1941.

Bethell, Nicholas, *The Palestine Triangle*, London: André Deutsch, 1979.

Bialer, Seweryn (ed.), *Stalin and His Generals*, London: Souvenir Press, 1970.

Bird, Lt.-Col. Eugene, *The Loneliest Man In The World*, London: Secker & Warburg, 1974.

Birkenhead, Earl of, *Halifax: The Life of Lord Halifax*, London: Hamish Hamilton, 1965.

Bloom, Sol, *The Autobiography of Sol Bloom*, New York: Putnams, 1948.

Blum, John Morton, *From the Morgenthau Diaries: Years of Urgency, 1938–41*, Boston: Houghton Mifflin, 1965.

Blumentritt, General Gunther, *Rundstedt, The Soldier and the Man* (trans. Cuthbert Reaveley), London: Odhams Press, 1952.

Bohlen, Charles, *Witness to History*, London: Weidenfeld & Nicolson, 1973.

Bokun, Branko, *Spy in the Vatican*, London: Tom Stacey, 1973.

Bölcke, Willi A. (ed.), *The Secret Conferences of Dr Goebbels*, 1939–43 (trans. Ewald Osers), London: Weidenfeld & Nicolson, 1970.

Bolitho, Hector, *A Penguin in the Eyrie*, London: Hutchinson, 1955.

Bond, Brian (ed.), *Chief of Staff: The Diaries of Lieutenant-General Sir Henry Pownall*, Vol. II, London: Leo Cooper, 1974.

Boothby, Lord, *Recollections of a Rebel*, London: Hutchinson, 1978.

Borg, Dorothy & Okamoto, Shumpei (with Dale, K. A. Finlayson), *Pearl Harbor as History*, New York: Columbia University Press, 1973.

Borodin, George, *Red Surgeon*, London: Museum Press, 1944.

Borrie, John, *Despite Captivity*, London: William Kimber, 1975.

Bourke-White, Margaret, *Shooting the Russian War*, New York: Simon & Schuster, 1943.

Bourne, Geoffrey H., *Starvation in Europe*, London: George Allen & Unwin, 1943.

Boyle, Andrew, *Trenchard*, London: Collins, 1962.

Bracher, Karl Dietrich, *The German Dictatorship* (trans. Jean Steinberg), London: Weidenfeld & Nicolson, 1971.

Braddon, Russell, *The Naked Island*, London: Werner Laurie, 1951.

Bradford, Ernle, *The Mighty Hood*, London: Hodder & Stoughton, 1959.

Brereton, Lt.-Gen. Lewis H., *The Brereton Diaries:* New York: William Morrow, 1946.

Brock, Ray, *Nor Any Victory*, New York: Reynal & Hitchcock, 1942.

Broome, Capt Jack, R. N., *Make a Signal!* London: Putman, 1955.

Brown, Cecil B., *Suez to Singapore*, New York: Random House, 1942.

Brown, Wenzell, *Hong Kong Aftermath*, New York: Smith & Durrell, 1943.

Brownlow, Donald G., *The Accused: The Ordeal of Admiral Kimmel*, New York: Vantage Press, 1968.

Bryant, Sir Arthur, *The Turn of the Tide: The Alanbrooke Diaries*, London: William Collins, 1957.

Buchanan, A. Russell, *The United States and World War Two*, Vol. I, New York: Harper & Row, 1964.

Buckley, Christopher, *Five Ventures*, London: H.M.S.O., 1954; *Greece and Crete*, London: H.M.S.O., 1952.

Buell, Thomas, *The Quiet Warrior*, Boston: Little Brown, 1974.

Bulcock, Roy, *Of Death But Once*, Melbourne: F. W. Cheshire Pty Ltd., 1947.

Bullock, Alan, *The Life and Times of Ernest Bevin*, Vol. II, London: Heinemann, 1967; *Hitler*, London: Odhams Press, edn. of 1965.

Burns, Eugene, *Then There was One*, New York: Harcourt Brace, 1944.

Burns, James McGregor, *Roosevelt, The Soldier of Freedom*, London: Weidenfeld & Nicolson, 1971.

Burridge, Trevor, *British Labour and Hitler's war*, London: André Deutsch, 1976.

Burtness, Paoul S. (& Oder, Warren W.), *The Puzzle of Pearl Harbor*, Evanston, Ill.: Row, Peterson, 1962.

Busch, Fritz-Otto, *The Story of the Prinz Eugen* (trans. Eleanor Brockett), London: Robert Hale, 1960.

Bush, Lewis, *The Road to Inamura*, London: Robert Hale, 1961.

Butow, Robert J. C., *Tojo and the Coming of the War*, Princeton, N.J.: Princeton University Press, 1961.

Cadogan, Sir Alexander. *The Diaries* (ed. David Dilks), London: Cassell, 1971.

Caffrey, Kate, *Out in the Mid-Day Sun*, London: André Deutsch, 1974.

Cain, Lt.-Cdr. T. J. and Sellwood, A. V., *H.M.S. Electra*, London: Frederick Muller, 1959.

Calder, Angus, *The People's War*, London: Jonathan Cape, 1969.

Caldwell, Erskine, *Moscow Under Fire*, London: Hutchinson, 1942.

Cameron, Ian, *Red Duster, White Ensign*, London: Frederick Muller, 1959.

Carell, Paul, *Hitler's War on Russia* (trans. Ewald Osers), London: George Harrap, 1964; *The Foxes of the Desert* (trans. Mervyn Savill), New York: E. P. Dutton, 1961.

Carew, Tim, *The Fall of Hong Kong*, London: Anthony Blond, 1960.

Carlgren, W. M., *Swedish Foreign Policy During the Second World War* (trans. Arthur Spencer), London: Ernest Benn, 1977.

Carroll, Joseph T., *Ireland in the War Years*, New York: Crane Russak, 1975.

Casey, Lord, *Personal Experience*, London: Constable, 1962.

Casey, Robert J., *Torpedo Junction*, London: Jarrolds, 1944.

Cassidy, Henry C., *Moscow Dateline, 1941–3*, London: Cassell, 1943.

Cazalet, Victor, *With Sikorski to Russia*, London: The Curwen Press, 1942.

Cecil, Robert, *Hitler's Decision to Invade Russia*, London: Davis Poynter, 1975.

Cervi, Mario, *The Hollow Legions* (trans. Eric Mosbacher), London: Chatto & Windus, 1972.

Chadwin, Mark, *The Hawks of World War Two*, Chapel Hill, N.C.: University of North Carolina Press, 1968.

Chandos, Lord, *Memoirs*, London: The Bodley Head, 1962.

Channon, Sir Henry, *Chips, the Diaries of Sir Henry Channon* (ed. Robert Rhodes James), London: Weidenfeld & Nicolson, 1967.

Childs, Marquis W., *The President's Best Friend*, in The Saturday Evening Post, Philadelphia, April 19–26, 1941.

Churchill, Sir Winston S., *The Second World War*, Vol. III, *The Grand Alliance*, London: Cassell, 1950.

Ciano, Count Galeazzo, *The Ciano Diaries, 1939–43* (ed. Hugh Gibson), New York: Doubleday, 1946.

Ciano's Diplomatic Papers (ed. Malcolm Muggeridge, trans. Stuart Hood), London: Odham's Press, 1948.

Ciechanowski, Jan, *Defeat in Victory*, London: Victor Gollancz, 1947.

Clark, Alan, *The Fall of Crete*, London: Anthony Blond, 1962.

Clark, Blake, Remember Pearl Harbor, New York: Harper, 1942.

Clark, Ronald, *The Man Who Broke Purple*, London: Weidenfeld & Nicolson, 1977.

Clifford, Alexander, *Three Against Rommel*, London: George Harrap, 1943; *Crusader*, London: George Harrap, 1942.

Clissold, Stephen, *Whirlwind: An Account of Marshal Tito's Rise to Power*, London: The Cresset Press, 1949; (ed.), *Yugoslavia and the Soviet Union, 1939–73*, London: Oxford University Press, 1975.

Coffey, Thomas M., *Imperial Tragedy*, New York: Pinnacle Books, 1970.

Coit, Margaret L., *Mr. Baruch*, London: Victor Gollancz, 1958.

Colaković, Rodoljub, *Winning Freedom* (trans. Alec Brown), London: Lincolns-Prager, 1962
Collier, Richard, *The City That Wouldn't Die*, London: William Collins, 1960; *Duce!* London: William Collins, 1971; *The War in the Desert*, Alexandria, Va; Time-Life Books, 1977.
Collis, Maurice, *Last and First in Burma*, London: Faber & Faber, 1956.
Colville, Sir John, *Footprints in Time*, London: William Collins, 1976.
Comeau, Marcel, *Operation Mercury*, London: William Kimber, 1961.
Compton, James V., *The Swastika and the Eagle*, London: The Bodley Head, 1968.
Connell, John, *Wavell: Scholar and Soldier*, London: William Collins, 1964; (with Michael Roberts), *Wavell: Supreme Commander*: London: William Collins, 1969; *Auchinleck*, London: Cassell, 1959.
Cooke, Colin, *The Life of Richard Stafford Cripps*, London: Hodder & Stoughton, 1957.
Cookridge, E. H., *Gehlen, Spy of the Century*, London: Hodder & Stoughton, 1971; *Inside S.O.E.*, London: Arthur Barker, 1966.
Cooper, Diana, *Trumpets from The Steep*, London: Rupert Hart-Davis, 1969.
Cooper, Page, *Navy Nurse*, New York: McGraw-Hill, 1946.
Costello, John and Hughes, Terry, *The Battle of the Atlantic*, London: William Collins, 1977.
Craigie, Sir Robert, *Behind the Japanese Mask*, London: Hutchinson, 1946.
Crawley, Aidan, *De Gaulle*, London: William Collins, 1969.
Crimp, R. L., *The Diary of a Desert Rat* (ed. Alex Bowlby), London: Leo Cooper, 1971.
Crisp, Robert, *Brazen Chariots*, London: Frederick Muller, 1959; *The Gods were Neutral*, London: Frederick Muller, 1960.
Crozier, Brian, *Franco*, London: Eyre & Spottiswoode, 1967; *The Man Who Lost China*, London: Angus & Robertson, 1977.
Crozier, William, *Off the Record* (ed. A. J. P. Taylor), London: Hutchinson, 1973.
Cruikshank, Charles, *Deception in World War Two*, Oxford: Oxford University Press, 1979.
Cunningham of Hyndhope, Admiral of the Fleet, Lord, *A Sailor's Odyssey*, London: Hutchinson, 1951.
Cunningham, W. Scott (with Lydel Sims), *Wake Island Command*, Boston: Little Brown, 1961.
Current, Richard, *Secretary Stimson*, New Brunswick, N.J.: Rutgers University Press, 1954.
Czapski, Joseph, *The Inhuman Land* (trans. Gerard Hopkins), New York: Sheed & Ward, 1962.
D'Albas, Andrieu, *Death of a Navy* (trans. Anthony Rippon), London: Robert Hale, 1957.
Dallin, Alexander, *German Rule In Russia*, 1941–4, London: Macmillan, 1957.
Dallin, David J., *Soviet Russia's Foreign Policy, 1939–1942*, New Haven, Conn.: Yale University Press, 1943.
Dangerfield, Elma, *Beyond the Urals*, London: British League for European Freedom, 1946.
Darling, Donald, *Secret Sunday*, London: William Kimber, 1975.
Dawidowicz, Lucy S., *The War Against the Jews, 1939–45*, London: Weidenfeld & Nicolson, 1975.
Davies, Joseph E., *Mission to Moscow*, London: Victor Gollancz, 1942.
Davin, D. M., *Crete*, Wellington, N.Z.: Departmental of Internal Affairs, War History Branch, 1953.
Davis, Forrest and Lindley, Ernest K., *How War Came to America*, London: George Allen & Unwin, 1943.
Davis, Kenneth S., *The American Experience of War*, London: Secker & Warburg, 1967.
Dawson, Raymond H., *The Decision to aid Russia*, Chapel Hill, N.C., University of North Carolina Press, 1959.
Deakin, F. W. (with G. W. Storry), *The Case of Richard Sorge*, London: Chatto & Windus, 1966.
Dedijer, Vladimir, *With Tito Through the War*, London: Alexander Hamilton, 1951; *Tito Speaks*, London: Weidenfeld & Nicolson, 1953.

De Guingand, Maj.-Gen. Sir Francis, *Generals At War*, London: Hodder & Stoughton, 1964.

Demianova, Genia, *Comrade Genia*, London: Nicolson & Watson, 1941.

Devereux, Brig.-Gen. James P.S., *Wake Island* (revised edn), Canoga Park, Calif.: Major Books, 1978.

DeVilliers, Catherine, *Lieutenant Katia* (trans. Charlotte Haldane), London: Constable, 1964.

Devins, Joseph H. Jr., *The Vaagso Raid*, London: Robert Hale, 1967.

Dew, Gwen, *Prisoner of the Japs*, London: Hutchinson, 1944.

Dickinson, Clarence, *The Flying Guns*, New York: Charles Scribner, 1943.

Dimbleby, Richard, *The Frontiers are Green*, London: Hodder & Stoughton, 1943.

Divine, Robert A., *The Reluctant Belligerent: American Entry into World War Two*, New York: John Wiley, 1965.

Dixon, Cecil and Helibrunn, Otto, *Communist Guerilla Warfare*, London: George Allen & Unwin, 1954.

Dixon, Pierson J., *Double Diploma*, London: Hutchinson, 1968.

Djilas, Milovan, *Wartime* (trans. Michael B. Petrovich), London: Secker & Warburg, 1977.

Documents on British Foreign Policy, London: H.M.S.O., 1946 –

Documents on German Foreign Policy, London: H.M.S.O., 1948 –

I Documenti Diplomatici Italiani, Rome: Ministero degli Esteri, 1952.

Dönitz, Admiral Karl, *Memoirs: Ten Years and Twenty Days* (trans. R. H. Stevens and David Woodward), London: Weidenfeld & Nicolson, 1951.

Douglas-Hamilton, James, *Motive for a Mission*, Edinburgh: Mainstream Books, 1979.

Douglas of Kirtleside, Lord Marshal of the R.A.F. (with Robert Wright), *Combat and Command*, New York: Simon & Schuster, 1966.

Dulles, John W. F., *Vargas of Brazil*, Austin, Texas: University of Texas Press, 1967.

Durnford-Slater, Brigadier John, *Commando*, London: William Kimber, 1953.

Eden, Rt. Hon. Anthony (Lord Avon), *Memoirs, Vol II; The Reckoning*, London: Cassell, 1965.

Edmonds, Walter D., *What Happened at Clark Field*, in The Atlantic Monthly, Boston, July, 1951.

Ehrlich, Blake, *The French Resistance*, London: Chapman & Hall, 1966.

Elvin, Harold, *A Cockney in Moscow*, London: The Cresset Press, 1958.

Engel, Gerhard, *Heeresadjutant bei Hitler, 1938–43*, Stuttgart: Deutsche Verlags-Anstalt, 1974.

Ericson, John, *The Road to Stalingrad*, London: Weidenfeld & Nicolson, 1975.

Esebeck, Hans Gertt von, *Afrikanische Schicksaljahre, 1941–43*, Wiesbaden: Limes Verlag, 1949.

Falk, Stanley, *Seventy Days to Singapore*, London: Robert Hale, 1975.

Farago, Ladislas, *The Broken Seal*, London: Arthur Barker, 1967; *The Game of the Foxes*, London: Hodder & Stoughton, 1972.

Farran, Roy, *Winged Dagger*, London: William Collins, 1948.

Fearnside, G. H., *Sojourn in Tobruk*, Sydney: Rue Smith Pty Ltd., 1944.

Fehrenbach, T. R., *F.D.R.'s Undeclared War*, New York: David McKay, 1967.

Feis, Herbert, *The China Tangle*, Princeton, N.J.: Princeton University Press, 1953; *Churchill-Roosevelt-Stalin*, Princeton, N.J.: Princeton University Press, 1957; *The Road to Pearl Harbor*, Princeton, N.J.: Princeton University Press, 1950.

Fenyo, Mario D., *Hitler, Horthy and Hungary*, New Haven, Conn.: Yale University Press, 1972.

Fergusson, Bernard, *The Watery Maze*, London: William Collins, 1961; *The Black Watch and the King's Enemies*, London, William Collins, 1950; *The Trumpet in the Hall*, London: William Collins, 1970.

Fest, Joachim, *Hitler* (trans. Richard and Clara Winston), London: Weidenfeld & Nicolson, 1974.

Field, Ellen, *Twilight in Hong Kong*, London: Frederick Muller, 1960.

Fielding, Sean, *They Sought Rommel*, London: H.M.S.O., 1942.

Foot, M. R. D., *Resistance*, London: Eyre Methuen, 1976; and Langley, J. M. *M19*, London: The Bodley Head, 1979.

Ford, Corey, *Donovan of O.S.S.*, London: Robert Hale, 1971.
Foreign Relations of the United States (7 vols), Washington, D.C.: U.S. Government Printing Office, 1956–62.
Forgy, Howell, M., *And Pass the Ammunition*, New York: D. Appleton-Century Co., 1944.
Fotitch, Constantin, *The War We Lost*, New York: Viking Press, 1948.
Fox, Barry, *That Day of Pearl Harbor*, in Harper's Magazine, New York, January, 1943.
Frank, Wolfgang, *The Sea Wolves* (trans. Lt.-Cdr. R. O. B. Long, RNVR), London: Weidenfeld & Nicolson, 1958.
Frankland, Noble, *The Bombing Offensive Against Germany*, London: Faber & Faber, 1965.
Franklin, Alan and Gordon, *One Year of Life: The Story of H.M.S. Prince of Wales*, Edinburgh: William Blackwood, 1944.
Fredborg, Arvid, *Behind the Steel Wall*, London: George Harrap, 1944.
Freedman, Max (ed.), *Roosevelt and Frankfurter*, London: The Bodley Head, 1968.
Freiden, Seymour and Richardson, William (ed.), *The Fatal Decisions*, New York: William Sloane, 1956.
Friedlander, Saul, *Prelude to Downfall: Germany and the United States, 1939–41*, New York: Alfred Knopf, 1967.
Friend, Theodore, *Between Two Empires: Ordeal of the Philippines, 1929–46*, New Haven, Conn.: Yale University Press, 1965.
Frischauer, Willi, *Himmler*, London: Odhams Press, 1953.
Frye, Alton, *Nazi Germany and the American Hemisphere, 1933–41*, New Haven, Conn.: Yale University Press, 1967.
Fuchida Mitsuo, *I led the Air Attack on Pearl Harbor*, in United States Naval Institute Proceedings, Annapolis, Md., September, 1952.
Gafencu, Grigore, *Prelude to the Russian Campaign* (trans. E. Fletcher-Allen), London: Frederick Muller, 1945.
Gallagher, O. D., *Retreat in the East*, London: Harrap, 1942.
Garner, Joe, *The Commonwealth Office*, London: William Heinemann, 1978.
Gaulle, Gen. Charles de, *The Call to Honour, 1940–42* (trans. Jonathan Griffin), London: William Collins, 1955.
Gellhorn, Martha, *Travels with Myself and Another*, London: Allen Lane, 1978.
Geve, Thomas, *Youth in Chains*, Jerusalem: Rubin Mass., 1958.
Gilbert, Martin, *Final Journey*, London: Allen & Unwin, 1979.
Gilmour, O. W., *Singapore to Freedom*, London: E. J. Burrows, 1943.
Glover, Edwin, *In Seventy Days*, London: Frederick Muller, 1946.
Goldstein, Bernard, *The Stars Bear Witness* (trans. & ed. Leonard Shatzkin), London: Victor Gollancz, 1950.
Görlitz, Walter, *Paulus and Stalingrad* (trans. R. H. Stevens), London: Methuen, 1963.
Goure, Leon, *The Siege of Leningrad*, Stanford, Calif.: Stanford University Press, 1963.
Grenfell, Russell, *Main Fleet to Singapore*, London: Faber & Faber, 1951; *The Bismarck Episode*, London: Faber & Faber, 1948.
Grew, Joseph C., *Turbulent Era, Vol. II*, London: Hammond & Hammond, 1953.
Guderian, Gen. Heinz, *Panzer Leader* (trans. Constantine Fitzgibbon), London: Michael Joseph, 1952.
Guest, Freddie, *Escape From the Bloodied Sun*, London: Jarrolds, 1956.
Haape, Heinrich (with Dennis Hinshaw), *Moscow Tram Stop*, London: William Collins, 1957.
Hahn, Emily, *China To Me*, Garden City, N.Y. Doubleday, Doran, 1945.
Haldane, Charlotte, *Russian Newsreel*, London: Secker & Warburg, 1942.
Halder, Gen. Franz, *War Diaries*, Vols V–VII, Washington, D.C.: Infantry Journal Press, 1950.
Hamilton, Thomas, *Soldier Surgeon in Malaya*, Sydney: Angus & Robertson, 1958.
Hancock, Sir William K., *Smuts: The Fields of Force, 1919–50*, Cambridge: The University Press, 1968.
Hansson, Per., *The Greatest Gamble* (trans. Martin Michael), London: George Allen & Unwin, 1967.

286

Harriman, W., Averell and Abel, Elie, *Special Envoy to Churchill and Stalin, 1941–46*, London: Hutchinson, 1976.

Harrisson, Tom, *Living Through the Blitz*, London: William Collins, 1976.

Harrop, Phyllis, *Hong Kong Incident*, London: Eyre & Spottiswoode, 1943.

Hart, Capt. B. H. Liddell, *The Tanks*, Vol. II, London: Cassell, 1959.

Harvey, Oliver, *The War Diaries* (ed. John Harvey), London: William Collins, 1978.

Hasluck, Paul, *The Government and the People, Vol I*, Canberra: Australian War Memorial, 1952.

Hassell, Ulrich von, *The Von Hassell Diaries, 1938–44*, London: Hamish Hamilton, 1948.

Hastings, Max, *Bomber Command*, London: Michael Joseph, 1979.

Hatchitt, Eunice C., *Bataan Nurse*, in Collier's, New York, 1 August, 1942.

Heckstall-Smith, Anthony, *Tobruk*, London: Anthony Blond, 1957; (with Vice-Admiral H. T. Baillie-Grohman), *Greek Tragedy*, London: Anthony Blond, 1961.

Hemingway, Ernest, *By-line* (ed. William White), New York: Charles Scribner, 1967.

Hersey, John, *Men on Bataan*, New York: Alfred A. Knopf, 1943.

Hess, Rudolf and Ilse, *Prisoner of Peace* (trans. Meyrick Booth, ed. George Piti.), London: Britons Publishing Co., 1954.

Hesse, Fritz, *Hitler and the English* (ed. & trans. F. A. Voigt), London: Allan Wingate, 1954.

Heydte, Baron Friedrich von der, *Daedalus Returned* (trans. W. Stanley Moss), London: Hutchinson, 1958.

Higgins, Trumbull, *Hitler and Russia*, New York: The Macmillan Co., 1966.

Hilberg, Raul, *The Destruction of the European Jews*, London: W. H. Allen, 1961.

Hilger, Gustav and Meyer, Alfred G., *The Incompatible Allies*, New York: Macmillan, 1953.

Hill, Russell, *Desert War, 1941–42*, London: Jarrolds, 1943.

Hill-Rennie, Melville C (with Allan A. Michie), *Parachutes Coming Down*, in Harper's Magazine, New York, January, 1942.

Hillgruber, Andreas, *Staatsmänner und Diplomaten bei Hitler* (2 vols), Frankfurt-am-Main: Bernard & Graefe, 1967–70.

Hinshaw, David, *The Home Front*, New York: Putnam, 1943.

Hinsley, F. H. (with Thomas, E. E., Ransom, C. F. G. & Knight, R. C.), *British Intelligence in the Second World War*, Vol. I, London: H.M.S.O., 1979; *Hitler's Strategy*, Cambridge: Cambridge University Press, 1951.

Hirszowicz, Lukasz, *The Third Reich and the Arab East*, London: Routledge & Kegan Paul, 1966.

Hitler, Adolf, *The Testament of Adolf Hitler* (trans. R. H. Stevens, ed. Francois Genoud), London: Cassell, 1961; *Table Talk* (trans. Norman Cameron & R. H. Stevens), London: Weidenfeld & Nicolson, 1953.

Hoare, Sir Samuel, *Ambassador on Special Mission*, London: William Collins, 1946.

Hoehling, A. A., *The Week Before Pearl Harbor*, London: Robert Hale, 1964.

Hoess, Rudolf, *Commandant of Auschwitz* (trans. Constantine Fitzgibbon), London: Weidenfeld & Nicolson, 1951.

Hoffman, Peter, *The History of the German Resistance*, 1933–45 (trans. Richard Barry), London: Macdonald & Janes, 1977.

Höhne, Heinz, *Codeword: Direktor* (trans. Richard Barry), London: Secker & Warburg, 1971; *The Order of the Death's Head* (trans. Richard Barry), London: Secker & Warburg. 1969.

Hollingworth, Clare, *There's a German just behind me*, London: The Right Book Club, 1943.

Hollis, Lt.-Gen. Sir Leslie and Leasor, James, *War At The Top*, London: Michael Joseph, 1959.

Hoptner, J. R., *Yugoslavia in Crisis, 1934–41*, New York: Columbia University Press, 1962.

Horthy, Admiral Nicolas, *Memoirs*, London: Hutchinson, 1956.

Hotz, Robert B., *With General Chennault: The Story of the Flying Tigers*, New York: Coward-McCann, 1943.

Hough, Frank O., Verde E. Ludwig and Henry I. Shaw, Jr., *Pearl Harbor to Guadalcanal*, Washington, D.C.: U.S. Marine Corps Historical Branch, 1958.

Hourmouzios, S. L., *Starvation in Greece*, London: Harrison, 1943.

Huff, Sidney L. (with Joe Alex Morris), *My Fifteen Years with General MacArthur*, Philadelphia: Curtis Publishing Co., 1964.

Hull, Cordell, *Memoirs, Vol. II*, London: Hodder & Stoughton, 1948.

Hunt, Frazier, *The Untold Story of Douglas MacArthur*, London: Robert Hale, 1954.

Huss, Pierre, *Heil! And Farewell*, London: Herbert Jenkins, 1943.

Hutton, G. Bernard, *Hess: The Man and His Mission*, London: David Bruce & Watson, 1970.

Ickes, Harold, *The Secret Diary of Harold Ickes, Vol. III: The Lowering Clouds*, London: Weidenfeld & Nicolson, 1955.

Idriess, Ion L., *Horrie The Wog-Dog*, Sydney, N.S.W.: Angus & Robertson, 1945.

Ike, Nobutaka (ed.), *Japan's Decision for War*, Stanford, Cal.: Stanford University Press, 1967.

Inber, Vera, *Leningrad Diary* (trans. Serge M. Wolff and Rachel Grive), London: Hutchinson, 1971.

Ind, Lt.-Col. Allison, *Bataan: The Judgement Seat*, New York: Macmillan, 1944.

Irving, David, *The Trail of the Fox*, London: Weidenfeld & Nicolson, 1977; *The Rise and Fall of the Luftwaffe*, London: Weidenfeld & Nicolson, 1974; *Hitler's War*, London: Hodder & Stoughton, 1977.

Ismay, Lord, *Memoirs*, London: William Heinemann, 1961.

Jacob, Alaric, *A Traveller's War*, London: William Collins, 1944.

Jacobsen, Dr Hans-Adolf and Rohwer, Dr Jürgen, *Decisive Battles of World War Two: The German View* (trans. Edward Fitzgerald), London: André Deutsch, 1965.

James, D. Clayton, *The Years of MacArthur*, Vols I & II, London: Leo Cooper, 1970.

Jameson, William, *Ark Royal, 1939–41*, London: Rupert Hart-Davis, 1957.

Johnen, Wilhelm, *Duel Under the Stars* (trans. Mervyn Savill), London: William Kimber, 1957.

Jonas, Manfred, *Isolationism in America*, Ithaca, N.Y.: Cornell Press, 1966.

Jones, Prof. R. V., *Most Secret War*, London: Hamish Hamilton, 1978.

Jordan, Philip, *Russian Glory*, London: Cresset Press, 1942.

Jovićić, Lena, *Within Closed Frontiers*, London: W & R Chambers, 1956.

Kahn, David, *Hitler's Spies*, London: Hodder & Stoughton, 1978; *The Code Breakers*, London: Weidenfeld & Nicolson, 1966.

Kallay, Nicholas, *Hungarian Premier*, New York: Columbia University Press, 1954.

Kamenetsky, Ihor, *Hitler's Occupation of the Ukraine*, Milwaukee, Wis.: The Marquette University Press, 1960.

Kapetanović, Nicola, *Tito and his Partisans*, Belgrade: Jugosolvenska Knijiga, 1953.

Karig, Walter and Kelley, Wellbourne, *Battle Report: Pearl Harbor to Coral Sea*, New York: Farrar & Rinehart, 1944.

Kase, Toshikazu, *Eclipse of the Rising Sun* (ed. David Nelson Rowe), London: Jonathan Cape, 1951.

Kato, Masuo, *The Lost War*, New York: Alfred Knopf, 1946.

Kedward, H. R., *The Resistance in Vichy France*, London: Oxford University Press, 1978.

Keitel, Field Marshal Wilhelm, *Memoirs* (trans. David Irving), London: William Kimber, 1965.

Kennan, George, *Memoirs, 1925–50*, London: Hutchinson, 1968.

Kennedy, Major-Gen. Sir John, *The Business of War*, London: Hutchinson, 1951.

Kennedy, Ludovic, *Sub-Lieutenant*, London: Batsford, 1942; *Pursuit: The Chase and Sinking of the Bismarck*, London: William Collins, 1974.

Kenney, Gen. George C., *The MacArthur I Know*, New York: Duell, Sloane & Pearce, 1951.

Kern, Erich, *Dance of Death* (trans. Paul Findlay), London: William Collins, 1951.

Kesselring, Field-Marshal Albert, *Memoirs* (trans. Lynton Hudson), London: William Kimber, 1953.

Killearn Diaries, The (ed. Trefor E. Evans), London: Sidgwick & Jackson, 1972.

Kimche, Jon, *Spying for Peace*, London: Weidenfeld & Nicolson, 1961.

Kimmel, Admiral Husband E., *Admiral Kimmel's Story*, Chicago: Henry Regnery, 1955.

King, Cecil, *With Malice Toward None* (ed. William Armstrong), London: Sidgwick & Jackson, 1970.

King, Ernest J., and Whitehill, Walter M., *Fleet Admiral King*, London: Eyre & Spottiswoode, 1953.

Kingscote, Flavia, *Balkan Exit*, London: Geoffrey Bles, 1942.

Kippenberger, Gen. Sir Howard, *Infantry Brigadier*, London: Oxford University Press, 1949.

Kirby, Stanley W., *Singapore: The Chain of Disaster*, London: Cassell, 1971.

Kirkbride, Sir Alec Sleath, *A Crackle of Thorns*, London: John Murray, 1956.

Kirkpatrick, Sir Ivone, *The Inner Circle*, London: Macmillan, 1959.

Knatchbull-Hugessen, Sir Hughe, *Diplomat in Peace and War*, London: John Murray, 1949.

Knight, Frida, *The French Resistance, 1940–44*, London: Lawrence and Wishart, 1975.

Kot, Stanislaw, *Conversations with the Kremlin and Dispatches from Russia* (trans. & arranged by H. C. Stevens), London: Oxford University Press, 1963.

Kraus René, *Europe in Revolt*, London: Jarrolds, 1943.

Krausnick, Helmut; Buckheim, Hans; Broszat, Martin and Jacobsen, Hans-Adolf, *Anatomy of the S.S. State* (trans. Richard Barry, Marian Jackson and Dorothy Long), London: William Collins, 1968.

Krock, Arthur, *Memoirs*, London: Cassell, 1970.

Kuzin, Ilya, *Notes of a Guerilla Fighter*, London: Hutchinson, 1943.

Langer, Lawrence, *Our Vichy Gamble*, New York: Alfred Knopf, 1947.

Langer, William L. and Gleason, S. E., *The Undeclared War*, London: Royal Institute of International Affairs, 1953.

Langley, J. M., *Fight Another Day*, London: William Collins, 1974.

Laqueur, Walter, *Russia and Germany: A Century of Conflict*, Boston: Little Brown, 1965.

Lash, Joseph P., *Eleanor and Franklin*, London: André Deutsch, 1972; *Roosevelt and Churchill*, 1939–41, London: André Deutsch, 1977.

Leach, Barry, *German Strategy Against Russia, 1939–41*, Oxford: Clarendon Press, 1973.

Leahy, Adm. William, *I Was There*, London: Victor Gollancz, 1950.

Leasor, James, *Rudolf Hess, the Uninvited Envoy*, London: Allen & Unwin, 1962.

Lebra, Joyce, *Jungle Alliance*, Singapore: Asia Pacific Press, 1971.

Lee, Clark, *They Call it Pacific*, London: John Long, 1943.

Lee, Gen. Raymond E., *The London Observer* (ed. James Leutze), London: Hutchinson, 1972.

Legg, Frank, *The Gordon Bennett Story*, Sydney: Angus & Robertson, 1965.

Leith-Ross, Sir Frederick, *Money Talks*, London: Hutchinson, 1968.

Lenczowski, George, *Russia and the West in Iran, 1918–48*, Ithaca, N.Y.: Cornell University Press, 1949.

Lesueur, Larry, *Twelve Months that Changed the World*, London: George Harrap, 1944.

Lewin, Ronald, *The Life and Death of the Afrika Korps*, London: Batsford, 1977; *Ultra Goes to War*, London: Hutchinson, 1978.

Lindsay, Oliver, *The Lasting Honour*, London: Hamish Hamilton, 1978.

Loewenheim, Francis L., Langley, Harold D., and Jonas, Manfred, *Roosevelt and Churchill: Their Secret Wartime Correspondence*, London: Barrie & Jenkins, 1975.

Lombard, Helen, *While They Fought*, New York: Charles Scribner, 1947.

Long, Gavin, *MacArthur as Military Commander*, London: B. T. Batsford, 1969; *To Benghazi*, Canberra: Australian War Memorial, 1952; *Greece, Crete and Syria*, Canberra: Australian War Memorial, 1953.

Long, Breckinridge, *The War Diary* (ed. Fred L. Israel), Lincoln, Neb: University of Nebraska Press, 1966.

Longmate, Norman, *How We Lived Then*, London: Hutchinson, 1971.

Lord, Walter, *Day of Infamy*, London: Longmans, 1957.

Louis, William Roger, *Imperialism At Bay: the United States and the Decolonisation of the British Empire, 1941–1945*, London: Oxford University Press, 1978.

Lu, David J., *From the Marco Polo Bridge to Pearl Harbor*, Washington, D.C.: Public Affairs Press, 1961.

Lucas, James, *Panzer Army Africa*, London: Macdonald & Jane's, 1977.

Luff, John, *The Hidden Years*, Hong Kong: South China Morning Post, 1967.

Lukacs, John, *The Last European War, September, 1939 – December, 1941*, London: Routledge & Kegan Paul, 1976.

Macdonald, Alexander, *Revolt in Paradise*, New York: Stephen Daye, 1944.

Macksey, Kenneth, *Kesselring: The Making of the Luftwaffe*, London: Batsford, 1978; *Afrika Korps*, London: Macdonald, 1968; *Guderian*, London: Macdonald & Jane's, 1975; *The Partisans of Europe in World War Two*, London: Hart-Davis, Macgibbon, 1975.

Maclean, Fitzroy, *Disputed Barricade*, London: Jonathan Cape, 1957.

MacMillan, Richard, *Mediterranean Assignment*, New York: Doubleday Doran, 1943.

Macmurtrie, F. E., *The Cruise of the Bismarck*, London: Hutchinson, 1942.

Maisky, Ivan, *Memoirs of a Soviet Ambassador, 1939–43*, London: Hutchinson, 1967.

Maitland, Patrick, *European Dateline*, London: The Quality Press, 1946.

Malaparte, Curzio, *The Volga Rises in Europe* (trans. David Moore), London: Alvin Redman, 1957.

Malay, Armando J., *Occupied Philippines*, Manila: Filipiniana Book Guild, 1967.

Manchester, William, *The Glory and the Dream*, London: Michael Joseph, 1975; *American Caesar*, Boston: Little Brown, 1978.

Manstein, Field-Marshal Erich von, *Lost Victories* (ed. & trans. Anthony G. Powell), London: Methuen, 1958.

Marchal, Léon, Vichy: *Two Years of Deception*, New York: Macmillan, 1943.

Marsman, Jan Hendrik, *I escaped from Hong Kong*, Sydney, N.S.W., Angus & Robertson, 1943.

Martin, David, *Ally Betrayed: The Uncensored Story of Tito and Mihailović*, London: W. H. Allen, 1946.

Masters, Anthony, *The Summer That Bled*, London: Michael Joseph, 1972.

Matloff, Maurice & Snell Edwin M., *Strategic Planning for Coalition Warfare, 1941–1947*, Washington, D.C.: Office of the Chief of Military History, 1953.

Maugham, Robin, *Come to Dust*, London: Chapman & Hall, 1945.

Maule, Henry, *Spearhead General*, London: Odham's Press, 1961.

McLachlan, Donald, *Room 39*, London: Weidenfeld & Nicolson, 1968.

McLaine, Ian, *Ministry of Morale*, London: George Allen & Unwin, 1979.

McNeill, W. H., *America, Britain and Russia*, London: Oxford University Press (for the Royal Institute of International Affairs), 1953.

Meissner, Hans-Otto, *The Man with Three Faces*, London: Evans Bros., 1955.

Mellenthin, Maj.-Gen. F. W. von, *Panzer Battles* (trans. H. Betzler), London: Cassell, 1955.

Meskill, Johanna, *Hitler and Japan*, New York: Atherton, 1966.

Metzler, Jost, *The Laughing Cow* (trans. Mervyn Savill), London: William Kimber, 1955.

Michel, Henri, *The Shadow War* (trans. Richard Barry), London: André Deutsch, 1972.

Michie, Allan, *Retreat to Victory*, London: Allen & Unwin, 1942.

Middlebrook, Martin and Mahoney, Patrick, *Battleship: The Loss of the Prince of Wales and the Repulse*, London: Allen Lane, 1977.

Milazzo, Matteo, *The Chetnik Movement and the Yugoslav Resistance*, Baltimore, Md: Johns Hopkins University Press, 1975.

Miller, Ernest, *Bataan Uncensored*, Long Prairie, Minn: The Hart Publications Inc., 1949.

Millis, Walter, *This is Pearl*, New York: William Morrow, 1947.

Milward, Alan S., *The Germany Economy at War*, London: Athlone Press, 1965.

Mitchell, Ruth, *The Serbs Choose War*, Garden City, N.Y.: Doubleday Doran, 1943.

Mockler, Anthony, *Our Enemies the French*, London: Leo Cooper, 1976.

Moffat, Jay Pierrepoint, *The Moffat Papers* (ed. Nancy Harvison Hooker), Cambridge, Mass: Harvard University Press, 1956.

Monaghan, Forbes, *Under the Red Sun*, New York: The Declan X, McMullen Co., 1946.

Montagu, Ewan, *Beyond Top Secret U*, London: Peter Davies, 1977.

Moorehead, Alan, *African Trilogy*, London: Hamish Hamilton, 1944.

Moran, Lord, *Winston Churchill: The Struggle for Survival, 1940–65*, London: Constable, 1966.

Morison, Elting E., *Turmoil and Tradition*, Boston: Houghton Mifflin, 1960.

Morison, Samuel Eliot, *The Rising Sun in the Pacific*, Boston: Little Brown, 1948; *The Battle of the Atlantic, 1939–43*, London: Oxford University Press, 1948.

Morrison, Ian, *Malayan Postscript*, London: Faber & Faber, 1942.

Morton, H. V., *Atlantic Meeting*, London: Methuen, 1943.

Morton, Louis, *The Fall of the Philippines*, Washington, D.C.: Office of the Chief of Military History, 1953.

Mosley, Leonard, *The Reich Marshal*, London: Weidenfeld & Nicolson, 1974; *Lindbergh*, London: Hodder & Stoughton, 1976; *Hirohito, Emperor of Japan*, Englewood Cliffs, N.J.: Prentice-Hall Inc., 1966.

Mrazek, James E., *The Glider War*, London: Robert Hale, 1975.

Muggah, Mary Gates and Railhiz, Paul H., *The MacArthur Story*, Chippewa Falls, Wis.: Chippewa Falls Book Agency, 1945.

Muir, Hugh, *European Junction*, London: Harrap, 1942.

Murphy, Robert, *Diplomat Among Warriors*, London: William Collins, 1964.

Musmanno, Michael, *The Eichmann Commandos*, London: Peter Davies, 1961.

Nazi-Soviet Relations (ed. Raymond James Sontag and James Stuart Beddie), Washington, D.C.: Department of State, 1948.

Neame, Lt.-Gen. Sir Philip, *Playing With Strife*, London: George Harrap, 1947.

Neave, Airey, *Little Cyclone*, London: Hodder & Stoughton, 1954.

Nepomuk, Jaroslav (with Owen John), *Hell's Mouth*, London: Peter Davies, 1974.

Neumann, Peter, *Other Men's Graves* (trans. Constantine Fitzgibbon), London: Weidenfeld & Nicolson, 1958.

Newlon, Clark, *The Fighting Douglas MacArthur*, New York: Dodd, Mead, 1965.

Nicolson, Harold, *Diaries and Letters, 1939–45* (ed. Nigel Nicolson), London: William Collins, 1967.

Nikitin, M. N. and Vagin, P. I., *The Crimes of the German Fascists in the Leningrad Region*, London: Hutchinson, 1946.

Noakes, Jeremy and Pridham, Geoffrey (ed.), *Documents on Nazism, 1941–45*, London: Jonathan Cape, 1974.

Okumiya, Masatake and Horikoshi, Jiro (with Martin Caidin), *Zero!*, New York: E. P. Dutton, 1956.

Onslow, The Earl of, *Men and Sand*, London: The Saint Catherine Press, 1961.

Orlow, Dietrich, *The History of the Nazi Party, Vol. II*, Newton Abbot: David & Charles, 1973.

Osgood, Robert E., *Ideals and Self-Interest in America's Foreign Relations*, Chicago: University of Chicago Press, 1953.

Pabel, Reinhold, *Enemies Are Human*, Philadelphia: John C. Winston Co., 1955.

Pabst, Helmut, *The Outermost Frontier* (trans. Andrew and Eva Wilson), London: William Kimber, 1957.

Padev, Michael, *Marshal Tito*, London: Frederick Muller, 1944.

Panter-Downes, Molly, *London War Notes*, London: Longman, 1972.

Parkinson, Roger, *Blood, Toil, Tears and Sweat*, London: Hart-Davis MacGibbon, 1973.

Pavillard, Stanley, *Bamboo Doctor*, London: Macmillan, 1960.

Pavlov, Dmitri, *Leningrad, 1941: The Blockade* (trans. John Clinton Adams), Chicago, Ill.: Chicago University Press, 1968.

Pavlović, K. St., *The Struggle of the Serbs*, London: Standard Art Book Co., 1943.

Pawle, Gerald, *The War and Colonel Warden*, London: George Harrap, 1963.

Paxton, Robert, *Vichy France*, London: Barrie & Jenkins, 1972.

Payne, Robert, *The Life and Death of Adolf Hitler*, London: Jonathan Cape, 1973.

Pearl Harbor and Hawaii: a Military History, by the Editors of The Army Times, New York: Walker & Co., 1971.

Pearl Harbor Attack: Hearing Before the Joint Committee on the Investigation of the Pearl Harbor Attack (39 vols). Washington, D.C.: Government Printing Office, 1946.

Pelz, Stephen E., *Race To Pearl Harbor*, Cambridge, Mass.: Harvard University Press, 1974.

Percival, Lt.-Gen. A. E., *The War in Malaya*, London: Eyre & Spottiswoode, 1949.

Perrault, Gilles, *The Red Orchestra* (trans. Peter Wiles and Len Ortzen), London: Arthur Barker, 1968.

Peter II, King of Yugoslavia, *A King's Heritage*, London: Cassell, 1955.

Petrow, Richard, *The Bitter Years*, London: Hodder & Stoughton, 1974.

Phillips, Claire (with Myron B. Goldsmith), *Manila Espionage*, Portland, Ore: Binfords & Mort, 1947.

Pickersgill, J. W., *The Mackenzie King Record*, Vol. I, Toronto: University of Toronto Press, 1960.

Pogue, Forrest, C., *George C Marshall*, Vol. II: Ordeal and Hope, 1939–42, New York: Viking, 1966.

Pokryshkin, Alexander, *Red Air Ace*, London: "Soviet War News", 1945.

Polevoi, Boris, *To the Last Breath*, London: Hutchinson, 1945.

Poliakov, Leon, *Harvest of Hate*, London: Elek Books, 1956.

Pollock, A. M., *Pienaar of Alamein*, Cape Town: Cape Times Ltd, 1943.

Poolman, Kenneth, *The Kelly*, London: William Kimber, 1954.

Popov, Dusko, *Spy/Counterspy*, London: Weidenfeld & Nicolson, 1974.

Posthumos, N. (ed.), *The Netherlands During German Occupation*, in the Annals of the American Academy of Political & Social Sciences, Vol. 245, Philadelphia, 1946.

Potter, John Deane, *Admiral of the Pacific*, London: Heinemann, 1965; *A Soldier Must Hang*, London: Frederick Muller, 1963.

Pratt, Julius W., *Cordell Hull* (2 vols), New York: Cooper Square, 1964.

Priestwood, Gwen, *Through Japanese Barbed Wire*, London: George Harrap, 1944.

Prising, Robin, *Manila, Goodbye*, London: William Heinemann, 1976.

Proudfoot, Malcolm, *European Refugees, 1939–52*, London: Faber & Faber, 1957.

Proulx, Benjamin A., *Underground from Hong Kong*, New York: E. P. Dutton, 1943.

Pyschoundakis, George, *The Cretan Runner* (trans. Patrick Leigh-Fermor), London: John Murray, 1955.

Quezon, Manuel, *The Good Fight*, New York: D. Appleton-Century, 1946.

Quirino, Eliseo, *A Day to Remember*, Manila: Benipayo Press, 1958.

Raczynski, Count Edward, *In Allied London*, London: Weidenfeld & Nicolson, 1962.

Raeder, Grand Admiral Erich, *Struggle for the Sea*, London: William Kimber, 1959.

Redmond, Juanita, *I Served on Bataan*, Philadelphia: J. B. Lippincott, 1943.

Reel, A. Frank, *The Case of General Yamashita*, Chicago: University of Chicago Press, 1949.

Rees, John (ed.), *The Case of Rudolf Hess*, London: William Heinemann, 1947.

Reilly, Michael F. (with William J. Slocum), *I Was Roosevelt's Shadow*, London: W. Foulsham, 1946.

Reiss, Johanna, *The Upstairs Room*, London: Oxford University Press, 1973.

Reith, Lord, *Diaries* (ed. Charles Stuart), London: Collins, 1975.

Reitlinger, Gerald, *The Final Solution*, London: Vallentine Mitchell, edn of 1968; *The House Built on Sand*, London: Weidenfeld & Nicolson, 1960; *The S.S.: Alibi of a Nation*, New York: Viking, 1957.

Reynolds, Quentin; Katz, Ephrain and Aldouby, Zwy., *Minister of Death*, London: Cassell, 1961.

Rich, Norman, *Hitler's War Aims* (2 vols), London: André Deutsch, 1973.

Richards, Denis, *Portal of Hungerford*, London: William Heinemann, 1978.

Ristić, D. N., *Yugoslavia's Revolution of 1941*, Stanford, Cal.: Hoover Institution Publication, 1966.

Ritchie, Charles, *The Siren Years*, London: Macmillan, 1974.

Roberts, Denis Russell, *Spotlight on Singapore*, London: Anthony Gibbs & Phillips, 1965.

Roberts, Michael and Trollip, A. E. G., *The South African Opposition*, London: Longman Green, 1947.

Rodger, George, *Desert Journey*, London: The Cresset Press, 1944.

The Rommel Papers (ed. B. H. Liddell Hart, trans. Paul Findlay), London: William Collins, 1953.

Romulo, Carlos P., *I Saw the Fall of the Philippines*, London: George Harrap, 1943.

Roosevelt, Elliott, *As He Saw It*, New York: Duell, Sloane & Pearce, 1946.

Roosevelt, James and Shalett, Sidney, *Affectionately F.D.R.*, New York: Harcourt Brace, 1959.

Rosenberg, Alfred, *Memoirs* (trans. Eric Posselt), Chicago: Ziff-Davis, 1949.

Rosenman, Samuel I., *Working with Roosevelt*, New York: Harper & Bos, 1952.

Roskill, Stephen, *Churchill and the Admirals*, London: William Collins, 1977; *Hankey, Man of Secrets*, Vol. III, London: William Collins, 1974.

Rossi, Angelo, *The Russo-German Alliance* (trans. John and Micheline Curren), London: Chapman & Hall, 1950.

Rozek, E. J., *Allied Wartime Diplomacy*, New York: John Wiley, 1958.

Rudel, Hans, *Stuka Pilot* (trans. Lynton Hudson), Dublin: Euphorion Books, 1952.

Ruge, Vice-Admiral Friedrich, *Sea Warfare* (trans. Cdr. M. G. Saunders, R.N.), London: Cassell, 1957.

Russell, Lord, *The Scourge of the Swastika*, London: Cassell, 1954.

Salisbury, Harrison, *The Siege of Leningrad*, London: Secker & Warburg, 1969.

Sandburg, Carl, *Home Front Memo*, New York: Harcourt Brace, 1943.

Sandford, Kenneth, *Mark of the Lion*, London: Hutchinson, 1962.

Sayre, Francis, *Glad Adventure*, New York: Macmillan, 1957.

Schellenberg, Walter, *The Schellenberg Memoirs* (ed. and trans. Louis Hagen), London: André Deutsch, 1956.

Schmidt, Heinz-Werner, *With Rommel In The Desert*, London: George Harrap, 1951.

Schmidt, Paul, *Hitler's Interpreter* (ed. R. H. C. Steed), London: William Heinemann, 1951.

Schoenbrun, David, *The Three Lives of Charles de Gaulle*, New York: Atheneum, 1966.

Schulze-Holthus, J. B., *Daybreak in Iran: A Story of the German Intelligence Service* (trans. Mervyn Savill), London: Staples Press, 1954.

Schütz, Dr W. W. and De Sevin, Dr B., *German Home Front*, London: Victor Gollancz, 1943.

Seaton, Albert, *The Russo-German War*, London: Arthur Barker, 1971.

Sevastopol, November 1941–July 1942, London: Hutchinson, 1943.

Shaller, Michael, *The U.S. Crusade in China, 1938–45*, New York: Columbia University Press, 1979.

Shaw, Stanford J. and Shaw, Ezal Kural, *History of the Ottoman Empire and Modern Turkey*, Vol. II. London: Cambridge University Press, 1971.

Sheehan, Ed., *One Sunday Morning*, Norfolk Island, Australia: Island Heritage Ltd., 1971.

Sherwood, Robert E., *The White House Papers of Harry Hopkins*, Vol. I, London: Eyre & Spottiswoode, 1948.

Shirer, William, *The Rise and Fall of the Third Reich*, New York: Simon & Schuster, 1959; *All About the Sinking of the Bismarck*, London: W. H. Allen, 1963.

Shostakovich, Dmitri, *Testimony* (as related to and edited by Solomon Volkov, trans. Antonina W. Bouis), London: Hamish Hamilton, 1979.

Simon, Rt Hon. Lord, *Retrospect*, London: Hutchinson, 1952.

Simons, Jessie, *While History Passed*, London: Heinemann, 1954.

Simson, Ivan, Singapore: *Too Little, Too Late*, London: Leo Cooper, 1970.

Sivaram, M., *The Road to Delhi*, Rutland, Vt: Charles E. Tuttle, 1966.

Skomorovsky, Boris and Morris, E. G., *The Siege of Leningrad*, New York: E. P. Dutton, 1944.

Smedley, Agnes, *The Battle Hymn of China*, New York: Knopf, 1943.

Smith, Gaddis, *American Diplomacy During World War Two, 1941–45*, New York: John Wiley, 1965.

Smith, Howard K., *Last Train from Berlin*, London: The Cresset Press, 1942.

Smuts, Field-Marshal Jan C., *Selections from the Smuts Papers*, Vol. VI (ed. Jean Van Der Poel), London: Cambridge University Press, 1973.

Smyth, Sir John, *Percival and the Tragedy of Singapore*, London: Macdonald, 1971.

Soames, Mary, *Clementine Churchill*, London: Cassell, 1979.

Sopocko, Eryk, *Gentlemen, the Bismarck Has Been Sunk*, London: Methuen, 1942.

Spears, Maj.-Gen. Sir Edward, *Fulfilment of a Mission*, London: Leo Cooper, 1977.

Speer, Albert, *Inside The Third Reich* (trans. Richard and Clara Winston), London: Weidenfeld & Nicolson, 1970.

Spencer, John Hall, *Battle for Crete*, London: Heinemann, 1962.

Spring, Howard, *In the Meantime*, London: Constable, 1942.

Stalin, Joseph, *Correspondence with Churchill, Attlee, Roosevelt and Truman*, Moscow: Foreign Languages Publishing House, 1957.

Standley, William H. and Ageton, Arthur A., *Admiral-Ambassador to Russia*, Chicago: Henry Regnery Co., 1955.

Stark, Freya, *East is West*, London: John Murray, 1945.

Stein, George H., *The Waffen S.S., 1939–45*, Ithaca, N.Y.: Cornell University Press, 1966.

Steinberg, Lucien, *Not as a Lamb: the Jews Against Hitler* (trans. Marion Hunter), Farnborough, Hants: Saxon House, 1974.

Stephanides, Theodore, *Climax in Crete*, London: Faber & Faber, 1956.

Stewart, I. McD. G., *The Struggle for Crete*, London: Oxford University Press, 1966.

St George, George, *The Road to Babyi-Yar*, London: Neville Spearman, 1967.

Stimson, Henry C. and Bundy, McGeorge, *On Active Service in Peace and War*, New York: Harper, 1948.

St-John, Robert, *Foreign Correspondent*, London: Hutchinson, 1960; *From the Land of Silent People*, London: George Harrap, 1942.

Stowe, Leland, *No Other Road To Freedom*, London: Faber & Faber, 1942.

Strik-Strikfeldt, Wilfred, *Against Stalin and Hitler: Memoir of the Liberation Movement, 1941–45* (trans. David Footman), London: Macmillan, 1970.

Sulzberger, C. L., *A Long Row of Candles*, London: Macdonald, 1969.

Syrkin, Marie, *Blessed is the Match*, London: Victor Gollancz, 1948.

Taylor, A. J. P., *Beaverbrook*, London: Hamish Hamilton, 1972; (ed.) *Churchill; Four Faces and the Man*, London: Allen Lane, 1969.

Tedder, Marshal of the R.A.F. Lord, *With Prejudice*, London: Cassell, 1966.

Theobald, Rear Admiral Robert A., *The Final Secret of Pearl Harbor*, New York: Devin-Adair, 1954.

Thomas, David, *Crete, 1941: the Battle At Sea*, London: André Deutsch, 1972.

Thompson, Kenneth, *H.M.S. Rodney At War*, London: Hollis & Carter, 1946.

Thompson, R. W., *Churchill and Morton*, London: Hodder & Stoughton, 1976.

Thomson, Richard Heywood, *Captive Kiwi*, Christchurch, N.Z.: Whitcombe & Tombs, 1964.

Thorne, Christopher, *Allies of a Kind: the United States, Britain, and the War Against Japan*, London: Hamish Hamilton, 1978.

Tiger Strikes, The, London: H.M.S.O., 1942.

Toland, John, *Adolf Hitler*, New York: Doubleday, 1976; *The Rising Sun*, London: Cassell, 1974; *But Not In Shame*, London: Anthony Gibbs & Phillips, 1961.

Trefousse, Hans L., *Failure of German Intelligence in the United States, in 1935–45*, in Mississippi Valley Historical Review, Nashville, Tenn., June 1955; *What Happened at Pearl Harbor*, New York: Twayne, 1958.

Trepper, Leopold, *The Great Game*, London: Michael Joseph, 1977.

Trial of the Major War Criminals before the International Military Tribunal, Nuremberg, 1947–49 (42 vols), Washington, D.C.: U.S. Government Printing Office, 1949/51.

Tsou, Tang, *America's Failure in China, 1941–50*, Chicago: The University of Chicago Press, 1963.

Tsuji, Col. Masanobu, *Singapore: the Japanese Version* (trans. Margaret E. Lake, ed. H. V. Howe), London: Constable, 1962.

Tuker, Lt-Gen. Sir Francis, *Approach to Battle*, London: Cassell, 1963.

Tully, Grace, *F.D.R. My Boss*, New York: Charles Scribner, 1949.

Turney, Alfred, *Disaster at Moscow*, London: Cassell, 1971.

Tweed, George R. (with Blake Clark), *Robinson Crusoe USN*, New York: McGraw Hill, 1945.

Umiatowski, Roman, *Poland, Russia and Great Britain, 1941–45*, London: Hollis & Carter, 1946.

Vali, Ferenc A., *Bridge Across the Bosphorous: the Foreign Policy of Turkey*, Baltimore, Md: Johns Hopkins University, 1971.

Van Creveld, Martin, *Hitler's Strategy, 1940–41: The Balkan Clue*, London: Cambridge University Press, 1973.

Vandenberg, A. H., *The Private Papers of Senator Vandenberg* (ed. Arthur H. Vandenberg, Jr, and Joe Alex Morris), London: Victor Gollancz, 1953.

Van Landingham, Charles, *I Saw Manila Die*, in The Saturday Evening Post, Philadelphia, 24 September, 1942.

Vian, Admiral of the Fleet Sir Philip, *Action This Day*, London: Frederick Muller, 1960.

Vintras, Roland, *The Portuguese Connection*, London: Bachman & Turner, 1974.

Viorst, Milton, *Hostile Allies: FDR and De Gaulle*, New York: Macmillan, 1965.

Virski, Fred, *My Life in the Red Army*, New York: Macmillan, 1949.

Vliensky, M., *War Behind Barbed Wire* (trans. O. Gorkachov), Moscow: Foreign Languages Publishing House, 1959.

Voyetekhov, Boris, *The Last Days of Sevastopol* (trans. Ralph Parker and V. M. Genne), London: Cassell, 1943.

Walker, David, *Death At My Heels*, London: Chapman & Hall, 1942.

Waller, George McGregor (ed.) *Pearl Harbor: FDR and the Coming of the War*, Boston: D. C. Heath, 1965.

Wallin, Vice-Admiral U.S.N., Homer, N., *Pearl Harbor: Why, How, Fleet Salvage and Final Appraisal*, Washington, D.C.: Office of Naval History, 1968.

Warlimont, Gen. Walter, *Inside Hitler's Headquarters* (trans. R. H. Barry), London: Weidenfeld & Nicolson, 1964.

Warmbrunn, Werner, *The Dutch Under German Occupation*, Stanford, Cal.: Stanford University Press, 1963.

Warner, Geoffrey, *Iraq and Syria, 1941*, London: Davis-Poynter, 1974.

Wason, Betty, *Miracle in Hellas*, London: Museum Press, 1943.

Wasserstein, Bernard, *Britain and the Jews of Europe, 1939–45*, Oxford: Clarendon Press, 1979.

Watson, Mark Skinner, *Chief of Staff: Pre-war Plans and Preparations*, Washington, D.C.: Office of the Chief of Military History, 1950.

Weinberg, Gerhard L., *Germany and the Soviet Union*, London: E. J. Brill, 1954; *Hitler's Image of the United States*, in The American Historical Review, Washington, D.C., July, 1964.

Weizsäcker, Ernst von, *Memoirs* (trans. John Andrews), London: Victor Gollancz, 1951.

Welles, Sumner, *The Time for Decision*, London: Hamish Hamilton, 1944.

Werth, Alexander, *Moscow '41*, London: Hamish Hamilton, 1942; *Russia at War*, 1941–45, London: Barrie & Rockcliff, 1964.

Westphal, Gen. Siegfried, *The German Army in the West*, London: Cassell, 1951.

Wettern, Desmond, *The Lonely Battle*, London: W. H. Allen, 1960.

Whaley, Barton, *Codeword Barbarossa*, Cambridge, Mass: M.I.T. Press, 1973.

Wheeler-Bennet, Sir John, *Special Relationships: America in Peace and War*, London: Macmillan, 1975; (ed.) *Action This Day*, London: Macmillan, 1968; *King George VI*, London: Macmillan, 1958; *The Nemesis of Power*, London: Macmillan, 1954.

Whelan, Russell, *The Flying Tigers*, London: MacDonald, 1943.

Whitcomb, Edgar, *Escape from Corregidor*, London: Allan Wingate, 1959.

White, Leigh, *The Long Balkan Night*, New York: Charles Scribner 1944.

White, Theodore, H. (with Annalee Jacoby), *Thunder Out of China*, London: Victor Gollancz, 1947.

White, W. L., *They Were Expendable*, London: Hamish Hamilton, 1942.

Whiting, Charles, *Hunters from the Sky*, London: Leo Cooper, 1975.

Wighton, Charles, *Eichmann: His Career and Crimes*, London: Odhams Press, 1951.

Wigmore, Lionel, *Australia in the War of 1939–45 (Army) The Japanese Thrust*, Adelaide: Griffin Press, 1957.

Williams, Francis, *A Prime Minister Remembers*, London: Heinemann, 1961.

Willoughby, Maj.-Gen. Charles A., *Sorge: Master Spy*, London: William Kimber, 1952; and Chamberlain, John, *MacArthur, 1941–51: Victory in the Pacific*, London: William Heinemann, 1956.

Wilmot, Chester, *Tobruk*, Sydney: Angus & Robertson, 1944.

Wiloughby, Amea, *I Was On Corregidor*, New York: Harper, 1943.

Wilson, Field Marshal Lord, *Eight Years Overseas*, London: Hutchinson, 1950.

Wilson, Theodore A., *The First Summit*, London: Macdonald, 1969.

Winant, John, *A Letter from Grosvenor Square*, London: Hodder & Stoughton, 1947.

Wingate, Sir Ronald, *Lord Ismay*, London: Hutchinson, 1970.

Wittner, Laurence (ed.), *MacArthur*, Englewood Cliffs, N.J.: Prentice-Hall, 1971.

Wohlstetter, Roberta, *Pearl Harbor: Warning and Decision*, Stanford, Cal.: Stanford University Press, 1962.

Wolff-Mönckeberg, Mathilde, *On The Other Side* (trans. and ed. Ruth Evans), London: Peter Owen, 1979.

Woodhouse, C. M., *The Struggle for Greece, 1941–9*, London: Hart-Davis, Macgibbon, 1976.

Woolton, Lord, *Memoirs*, London: Cassell, 1959.

Wright, Robert, *I Was a Hell Camp Prisoner*, London: Brown Watson, 1963.

Wykeham, Peter, *Fighter Command*, London, Putnam, 1960.

Young, Desmond, *Rommel,*, London: William Collins, 1950.

Young, Kenneth, *Churchill and Beaverbrook*, London: Eyre & Spottiswoode, 1966.

Young, Peter, *Storm from the Sea*, London: William Kimber.

Zhilin, Pavel, *They Sealed Their Own Doom*, Moscow: Progress Publishers, 1970.

Zieser, Benno, *In Their Shallow Graves* (trans. Alec Brown), London: Elek Books, 1956.

Zoller, Albert, *Douze ans auprès d'Hitler*, Paris: Juilliard, 1949.

MANUSCRIPT SOURCES

Aitken, Sir William Maxwell, 1st Bt., 1st Baron Beaverbrook, Ministry of Supply Papers and Personal Correspondence. (*House of Lords Record Office, London.*)

Alexander, Albert Victor, Earl Alexander of Hillsborough, First Lord of the Admiralty, Memos and Correspondence. (*Churchill College, Cambridge.*)

Anslow, Barbara Redwood, Hong Kong Diary, 1941–2. (*Imperial War Museum, Lambeth, South London.*)

Arnold, General Henry Harley, Chief of U.S. Army Air Force, Official Papers. (*Library of Congress MSS. Division, Washington, D.C.*)

Attlee, Clement Richard, 1st Earl Attlee, Lord Privy Seal, Miscellaneous Correspondence. (*Churchill College, Cambridge.*)

Balfour, Harold Harrington, 1st Baron Balfour of Inchrye, Under-Secretary of State for Air, Moscow Interlude: the Diary of a Mission. (*House of Lords Record Office, London.*)

Bevin, Ernest, Minister of Labour, 1940–5. Miscellaneous Correspondence. (*Churchill College, Cambridge.*)

Biddle, Francis B., U.S. Attorney-General, 1941–5. Records of Cabinet Meetings. (*Franklin D. Roosevelt Memorial Library, Hyde Park, New York.*)

Bötticher, Generalleutant Karl, The Occupation of Tobruk. (*MSS. D-062, Office of the Chief of Military History, National Archives. Washington D.C.*); The Role of Artillery in The Siege of Tobruk. (*MSS. D-045, repository as above.*)

Bollbrinker, Generalmajor Ernst. Surprise Attack on Tobruk. (*MSS. D-088, repository as above.*)

Brooke, Lieutenant-General Sir Alan Francis, 1st Baron Brookeborough, C-in-C, Home Forces, Chief of the Imperial General Staff, 1941–6. Diary and Miscellaneous Correspondence. (*Liddell Hart Centre for Military Archives, University of London, King's College.*)

Brooke-Popham, Air Chief Marshal Sir (Henry) Robert (Moore), C-in-C, Far East, 1940–1. Official Correspondence. (*Liddell Hart Centre for Military Archives, University of London, King's College.*)

Burgis, Lawrence Franklin. Assistant Secretary, War Cabinet, 1939–45. Memoirs. (*Churchill College, Cambridge.*)

Clapper, Raymond, author and political commentator. Miscellaneous Papers. (*Library of Congress MSS. Division, Washington, D.C.*)

Cox, Oscar D., legal adviser, U.S. Treasury; Division of Defense Aid, Office of Emergency Management. Diary, 1941. (*Franklin D. Roosevelt Memorial Library, Hyde Park, New York.*)

Coy, (Albert) Wayne, Special Assistant to the President; Office of Emergency Management. Official Correspondence. (*Franklin D. Roosevelt Memorial Library, Hyde Park, New York.*)

Cunningham, Admiral of the Fleet Andrew Browne, 2nd Viscount Cunningham of Hyndhope, C-in-C Mediterranean Fleet. Private Correspondence. (*Churchill College, Cambridge.*)

Dalton, (Edward) Hugh (John Neale), Minister of Economic Warfare, 1940–2. Diary, 1941. (*British Library of Political and Economic Science, London.*)

Davidson, Major-General Francis Henry Norman, Director of Military Intelligence, War Office, 1940–4. Miscellaneous Files. (*Liddell Hart Centre for Military Archives, University of London, King's College.*)

Dorman-Smith, Sir Reginald Hugh, Governor of Burma, 1941–6. Official Correspondence. (*India Office Library and Records, Foreign and Commonwealth Office, London.*)

Early, Stephen T., U.S. Presidential Press Secretary, 1933–45. Private correspondence and scrap-books. (*Franklin D. Roosevelt Memorial Library, Hyde Park, New York.*)

Eden, (Robert) Anthony, 1st Earl of Avon, Secretary of State for Foreign Affairs, 1940–5. Official correspondence and Memoranda. (*University of Birmingham, Warwickshire, Special Collections.*)

Edwards, Captain Ralph Alan Bevan, R.N., Director of Operations (Home). Private Diary. (*Churchill College, Cambridge.*)

Frankfurter, Justice Felix, Associate Justice of the U.S. Supreme Court, 1939–62. Private Correspondence. (*Library of Congress MSS. Division, Washington, D.C.*)

Hartmann, Oberst Hermann. Staff Libya, July–August, 1941. (*MSS. D-051, Office of the Chief of Military History, Washington, D.C.*)

Hodsoll, Wing-Commander Sir Eric John, Assistant Secretary. C.I.D. C.I.D. and Civil Defence Papers, 1941. (*Churchill College, Cambridge.*)

Hope, John Victor Alexander, 2nd Marquess of Linlithgow, Viceroy and Governor-General of India, 1936–43. Official Correspondence and Memoranda. (*India Office Library and Records, Foreign and Commonwealth Office, London.*)

Hopkins, Harry L. Special Adviser to the President, 1940–5. Official and Private Correspondence. (and Robert E. Sherwood). Official and Private Papers, Containers 304–8, forming the Robert E. Sherwood Collection). (*Franklin D. Roosevelt Memorial Library, Hyde Park, New York.*)

Holtzendorff, Generalmajor Hanshenning von. The Building of the Sidi Omar – Halfaya Pass Position. (*MSS. D-149, Office of the Chief of Military History, National Archives, Washington, D.C.*) The Build-up of the Gazala Position, May–June, 1941. (*MSS. D-212, repository as above.*) Reasons for Rommel's Successes. (*MSS. D-024, repository as above.*)

Hull, Cordell, U.S. Secretary of State, 1933–44. Official Correspondence and Memoranda. (*Library of Congress, MSS. Division, Washington, D.C.*)

Ismay, General Hastings Lionel, 1st Baron Ismay of Wormington, Deputy Secretary (Military) to War Cabinet, 1940–5. Private Correspondence and Memoranda. (*Liddell Hart Centre for Military Archives, University of London, King's College.*)

Joyce, Nurse Day Sage. Hong Kong Diary. (*Imperial War Museum, Lambeth, South London.*)

Kirchheim, Gen. Heinrich. Advance on Tobruk by the Italian Brescia Division, April, 1941. (*MSS. D-214.*) Withdrawal from Cyrenaica, April, 1941. (*MSS. D-349.*) Attack-Group Kirchheim, April–May, 1941. (*MSS. D-350, Office of the Chief of Military History, National Archives, Washington, D.C.*)

Knox, Franklin L. Secretary of the U.S. Navy, 1940–5. Diary; Official and Private Correspondence. (*Library of Congress, MSS. Division, Washington D.C.*)

Leahy, Admiral William D., Ambassador to Vichy France, 1941. Private Diary. (*Library of Congress, MSS. Division, Washington, D.C.*)

Marquis, Sir Frederick James, 1st Earl of Woolton, Minister of Food, 1940–3. Diary and Memoranda. (*Bodleian Library, Oxford.*)

Mass Observation Archive, The, Topic Files and Weekly Reports. (*University of Sussex.*)

Mellenthin, Generalmajor Friedrich Wilhelm. Supplement to Rommel's Successes in North Africa. (*MSS. D-084. Office of the Chief of Military History, National Archives, Washington, D.C.*)

Monckton, Sir Walter Turner, 1st Viscount Monckton of Brenchley, Director-General, Ministry of Information, 1940–1; Director-General of British Propaganda and Information Services, Cairo, 1941–2. Private Correspondence. (*Bodleian Library, Oxford.*)

Morgenthau, Henry, Jr, Secretary of the U.S. Treasury, 1934–45. Private Diary. (*Franklin D. Roosevelt Memorial Library, Hyde Park, New York.*)

Müller-Gebhard, Gen. Philip. Afrika Korps, 28-4-41–30-9-41). (*MSS. D-006, Office of the Chief of Military History, National Archives, Washington, D.C.*)

Neal, Hilda. London Diary. (*Imperial War Museum, Lambeth, South London.*)

Nehring, Gen. Walter et al. The African Campaign. (*Ref. T 3, Vols 1, 2, 3, 3a and 4, Office of the Chief of Military History, National Archives, Washington, D.C.*)

Nesbitt, Mrs Henrietta, housekeeper to the White House. Miscellaneous Papers. (*Library of Congress, MSS. Division, Washington, D.C.*)

Newton, Dr Isaac. Hong Kong Diary. (*Imperial War Museum, Lambeth, South London.*)

Nicolson, Harold George, Parliamentary Secretary to Ministry of Information, 1940–1. Private Diary. (*Balliol College, Oxford.*)

Penny, Henry. London Diary. (*Imperial War Museum, Lambeth, South London.*)

Percival, Lt.-Gen. Arthur, G.O.C. Malaya, Official and Private Papers. (*Imperial War Museum, Lambeth, South London.*)

Phipps, Nurse Kathleen, Private Diary. (*Imperial War Museum, Lambeth, South London.*)

Public Record Office, Kew, Surrey: Series ADM: Admiralty CAB: Cabinet Papers CO: Colonial Office Papers FO: Foreign Office Papers HO: Home Office Papers PREM: Prime Minister's Papers.

Rath, Generalmajor Hans-Joachim. 1st Stuka Wing, Feb.–May, 1941. (*MSS. D-004, Office of the Chief of Military History, National Archives, Washington, D.C.*)

Redwood, Mabel. Memoirs of World War Two. (*Imperial War Museum, Lambeth, South London.*)

Reissmann, Major Werner. Rommel's System of Fortifications in North Africa. (*MSS. D-082.*) Transportation of the 104th Armoured Infantry Regiment, April, 1941. (*MSS. D-047, Office of the Chief of Military History, National Archives, Washington, D.C.*)

Roosevelt, Franklin Delano. President of the United States, 1933–45. Papers As President, Official File (OF). Papers as President, President's Personal File. (PPF.) Papers As President, President's Secretary's File. (PSF.) (*Franklin D. Roosevelt Memorial Library, Hyde Park, New York.*)

Smith, Harold D., Director of the Budget, U.S. Treasury. Memoranda on Conferences with the President. (*Franklin D. Roosevelt Memorial Library, Hyde Park, New York.*)

Somerville, Admiral Sir James Fownes, R.N., C-in-C, Force "H". Personal and Naval Papers. (*Churchill College, Cambridge.*)

Spears, General Sir Edward Louis. Correspondence with Bracken, Churchill, Ismay etc. (*Ref Spears 1/50, Churchill College, Cambridge.*) Spears Mission Correspondence. (*Ref Spears 1/137. IIA 2–II/4, II/5, St Antony's College, Oxford.*)

Steinhardt, Laurence A., U.S. Ambassador in the Soviet Union. Private correspondence. (*Library of Congress, MSS. Division, Washington, D.C.*)

Strong, H. E., Miscellaneous Correspondence. (*Imperial War Museum, Lambeth, South London.*)

Vansittart, Sir Robert Gilbert, 1st Baron Vansittart, Chief Diplomatic Adviser to His Majesty's Government, 1938–41. Miscellaneous Cabinet Papers. (*Churchill College, Cambridge.*)

Vlieland, C. A., Secretary of Defence for Malaya, 1938–41. Disaster in the Far East, 1941–2: an unpublished monograph. (*Liddell Hart Centre for Military Archives, University of London, King's College.*)

Wickard, Claude, U.S. Secretary of Agriculture, 1940–5. Private Diary. (*Franklin D. Roosevelt Memorial Library, Hyde Park, New York.*)

Winant, John Gilbert, U.S. Ambassador to the Court of St James, 1941–6. Miscellaneous Papers. (*Franklin D. Roosevelt Memorial Library, Hyde Park, New York.*)

Wood, Edward Frederick Lindley, 1st Earl of Halifax. Selections from the Hickleton Papers. (*Ref.: A 410.4, 2 reels microfilm, Churchill College, Cambridge.*)

Wright, Leading Aircraftman Harry C., R.A.F.V.R. A Serviceman's Diary, 1941. (*Courtesy H. C. Wright, Whitehall, Hants.*)

Zeus, Major Franz. Defence of the Halfaya Pass, June 15–17, 1941. (*MSS. D 219, Office of the Chief of Military History, National Archives, Washington D.C.*)

Note: With the exception of the studies by Rath and Reissmann, listed above, all German monographs from the Office of the Chief of Military History were translated for the author by Hildegard Anderson.

INDEX

*Names, titles and posts are those held at the time
during the events described*

301

310